PENGUIN CANADA

MACLEAN'S PEOPLE

John Byrne Maclean published his first general-interest magazine in October, 1905, as *The Business Magazine*. It was renamed *The Busy Man's Magazine* before the year was out and in 1911 became known as *Maclean's Magazine*. Circulation has increased a hundredfold from five thousand in 1905 to half a million each week today.

Michael Benedict, *Maclean's* editorial director of New Ventures, has been with the newsmagazine in a variety of roles since 1986. Beginning his journalism career as a copy boy at the CBC newsroom in Montreal, he went on to reporting jobs with the St. John's *Evening Telegram* and in Ottawa's parliamentary press gallery for the *Toronto Star* and CTV. In 1980, he moved to Toronto and worked in communications for the government of Ontario and Canada Post before returning to his first love, journalism, with *Maclean's*. He is the editor of the bestselling *Canada at War* and of *Canada in the Fifties*, *In the Face of Disaster* and *On the Battlefields*, and co-editor of *Canada on Ice*.

MACLEAN'S
PeOPLE

Edited by Michael Benedict

PENGUIN
CANADA

PENGUIN CANADA

Published by the Penguin Group

Penguin Books, a division of Pearson Canada, 10 Alcorn Avenue, Toronto, Ontario,
    Canada M4V 3B2
Penguin Books Ltd, 80 Strand, London WC2R 0RL, England
Penguin Putnam Inc., 375 Hudson Street, New York, New York 10014, U.S.A.
Penguin Books Australia Ltd, 250 Camberwell Road, Camberwell, Victoria 3124, Australia
Penguin Books India (P) Ltd, 11, Community Centre, Panchsheel Park, New Delhi – 110 017,
    India
Penguin Books (NZ) Ltd, cnr Rosedale and Airborne Roads, Albany, Auckland 1310,
    New Zealand
Penguin Books (South Africa) (Pty) Ltd, 24 Sturdee Avenue, Rosebank 2196, South Africa

Penguin Books Ltd, Registered Offices: 80 Strand, London WC2R 0RL, England

First published in Penguin Canada (hardcover) by Penguin Books, a division of Pearson
Canada, 2001

Published in this edition, 2002

10 9 8 7 6 5 4 3 2 1

Manufactured in Canada.

NATIONAL LIBRARY OF CANADA CATALOGUING IN PUBLICATION

Main entry under title:

  Maclean's people : a gallery of Canadian greats / edited by Michael Benedict.

ISBN 0-14-029769-3

1. Canada—Biography. I. Benedict, Michael, 1947–

FC25.M4453 2002   971.06'092'2   C2002-902391-2
F1005.M24 2002

Visit Penguin Books' website at **www.penguin.ca**

Contents

Foreword, Robert Fulford / ix

Preface, Michael Benedict / xiv

POLITICAL LEADERS

Mackenzie King As I Knew Him, September 1, 1950
Blair Fraser / 2

René Lévesque: Man in the Middle, November 18, 1961
Ken Johnstone / 14

Pierre Trudeau: Intellectual in Action, February 24, 1962
Peter Gzowski / 24

John Diefenbaker: Gifts and Flaws, March 23, 1963
Peter C. Newman / 33

Lester B. Pearson's Puzzling Personality, April 6, 1963
Robert Fulford / 43

John Turner: Once and Future Contender, May, 1971
Christina Newman / 53

Jean Chrétien: Mister No, May 3, 1976
Glen Allen / 62

THE WORLD OF SPORTS

Percy Williams: The Fastest Human, October 15, 1928
Robert T. Elson / 74

Barbara Ann Scott: What It's Like to Be a Celebrity
January 15, 1951
Eva-Lis Wuorio / 85

Is It True What They Say About Gordie Howe? January 1, 1953
Barney Milford (aka Trent Frayne) / 93

Success Can't Spoil Bobby Orr, February, 1969
Stan Fischler / 102

George Chuvalo: Still on His Feet, January 24, 1977
Barbara Amiel / 109

Wayne Gretzky: The Great One, April 26, 1999
James Deacon / 118

TYCOONS

Sir Maxwell Aitken, September, 1911
James Grant / 128

The Molsons of Montreal, September, 1913
Linton Eccles / 136

K. C. Irving: The Last of a Breed, April 18, 1964
Ralph Allen / 145

Conrad Black, Paper Tiger, August 1, 1994
Bruce Wallace / 156

LET ME ENTERTAIN YOU

Mary Pickford: Our Mary, September, 1918
Arthur Stringer / 168

Wayne and Shuster, January 1, 1954
Wayne and Shuster / 179

Oscar Peterson at Home, October 25, 1958
June Callwood / 189

Norman Jewison: The Star's Status Symbol
January 5, 1963
Judith Krantz / 200

Gordon Lightfoot, September, 1968
Marjorie Harris / 210

Donald Sutherland: Funniest Film Actor Ever
September, 1970
Douglas Marshall / 221

Mary Walsh: High Shticking, February 26, 1996
Brian D. Johnson / 231

Shania Twain Revealed, March 23, 1998
Brian D. Johnson / 241

ARTS AND LETTERS

My Memories and Miseries, November, 1919
Stephen Leacock / 252

Morley Callaghan: The Second Coming
December 3, 1960
Barbara Moon / 260

The Apprenticeship of Mordecai Richler
May 20, 1961
Mordecai Richler / 269

Irving Layton: The Man Who Copyrighted Passion
November 15, 1965
Alexander Ross / 281

The World of Alex Colville, August 1, 1983
Gillian MacKay / 291

Margaret Atwood's Triumph, October 3, 1988
Judith Timson / 301

Peter Gzowski's Last Stand, November 18, 1996
David Macfarlane / 311

ROGUES, ROYALS, HEROES AND HEROINES

Mrs. Nellie McClung, July, 1915
May L. Armitage / 322

Billy Bishop: The Allies' Greatest Ace, January 15, 1929
Major George A. Drew / 328

Edward VIII: He Will Be King, January 1, 1930
Richard Dent / 339

The Dionnes: The Quint Question, July 15, 1941
Frederick Edwards / 348

The Inside Story of Gordon Sinclair
December 1, 1949
Gordon Sinclair / 358

My Friend Joseph Albert Guay, the Murderer, May 1, 1951
Roger Lemelin / 368

Queen Elizabeth II: The Girl Behind the Mask
June 1, 1953
Pierre Berton / 379

Prince Charles: Groomed to Fail? March, 1967
Alan Edmonds / 389

Margaret Trudeau's First Hurrah, August, 1974
June Callwood / 396

Princess Di: Our Next Queen, March 9, 1981
Carol Kennedy / 407

Photo Credits / 415

Foreword

AT FIRST GLANCE A profile looks like the easiest kind of magazine journalism, so novice writers sometimes assume that simply organizing the facts of someone's life, while animating them with as many tape-recorded quotations as possible, will do the job nicely. That misunderstanding arises partly because good writers make their work seem obvious, and anything so obvious should come easily.

Moreover, the material in a profile is conveniently limited: it deals with only one human being. But eventually, in learning how to be journalists, we discover that writing profiles is as subtle and toilsome as any other craft. The articles in this book represent the flowering, over several generations, of that special craft, now ancient but still vibrantly healthy.

The ideal magazine profile offers a fresh perspective on its subject, an unfamiliar but persuasive way of looking at what a certain man or woman does. At the same time, it conveys, through incident and example, the tone and texture of that person's life. None of this comes automatically, even after the most patient research. The facts are always important, but not so important as the insights and ideas brought to the article by a writer as skilful as (to take three eminent figures from the history of *Maclean's*) June Callwood, Ralph Allen or Blair Fraser.

When written with intelligence and imagination, a profile puts its subject in a rich context, historical and social as well as professional. A magazine profile is not a long version of a newspaper feature story; when it works, it's more like a short biography. This book's readers will therefore learn not only about a few dozen lives but also about the periods of Canadian history in which those lives were lived and the specialized worlds in which the subjects flourished—such as early-20th-century capitalism, in the case of Sir Maxwell Aitken (later Lord Beaverbrook), or silent films, in the case of Mary Pickford, the world's first movie star, born Gladys Smith in Toronto.

The process of turning profiles into ambitious magazine articles began (like so much in modern journalism) at the *The New Yorker*. Other journals, *Maclean's* included, had published personality sketches for years, and at first there was no reason to think that *The New Yorker*'s "Profiles" department (it appeared in the first issue, in 1925) would be notably different. But by 1927 *The New Yorker* profiles were growing longer and more ambitious, and 10 years later they had developed into a distinct branch of journalism, witty and penetrating as well as meticulously factual. Those pieces, some of them running many thousands of words, became so characteristic a part of the magazine that the editor tried unavailingly to copyright the term "profile"; it became instead a part of journalism's routine vocabulary.

For as long as anyone can remember, *Maclean's* writers have relied on the profile to take their readers through the great issues and amusing topics of the day. This was especially the case in the middle of the 20th century, a period well represented in this book. We who grew up as magazine writers at that time considered the editors and writers of *Maclean's* the elite corps of English-language Canadian journalism. The staff was assembled in the 1940s by Arthur Irwin, who made *Maclean's* the most sophisticated and professional magazine, to that point, in Canadian history. When Irwin left in 1950, he was succeeded as editor by Ralph Allen, who for seven years had Pierre Berton at his side as managing editor. Their *Maclean's* was a fortnightly, which meant it couldn't cover the unfolding news (as *Maclean's* does now) but nevertheless paid close attention to the events of the day.

Irwin, more than anyone, brought a sense of structure and direction to the articles in *Maclean's*. As Berton wrote in his memoirs,

Irwin created a school of magazine writing, a system of editing that involved challenging every paragraph submitted; those who were edited by Irwin, or by people Irwin trained, eventually learned that an article needed to be structurally sound enough to hold the weight of several editors.

We can see some of the quality of that period reflected here in the Berton profile of the Queen, in Blair Fraser's posthumous "Mackenzie King As I Knew Him," in Barbara Moon's account of Morley Callaghan's life and in Eva-Lis Wuorio's piece on Barbara Ann Scott, the figure skater who was the great Canadian celebrity of the early 1950s. In many cases, profile writers in *Maclean's* have brought to their subjects the authority that comes from intimate experience —Peter C. Newman on John Diefenbaker, for instance, or Ken Johnstone on René Lévesque. Sometimes, in what we might call autoprofiles, the writer is on even more intimate terms with the subject, as when Stephen Leacock writes on Leacock or Mordecai Richler on Richler, two of the liveliest pieces in this gathering. Roger Lemelin's brilliant profile of Albert Guay, the Canadian who invented the crime of blowing up an airliner to murder one person, fills a category all its own: it was born when Lemelin, the writer who created the Plouffe family, discovered to his horror that a suddenly infamous criminal was a former neigbourhood acquaintance.

Often, though, a memorable profile results from a writer striking out in territory where he's a stranger: in 1964, having given up the editorship four years earlier, Ralph Allen produced "The Unknown Giant," a remarkable three-part profile of K. C. Irving, who owned much of New Brunswick and controlled the rest. Irving was then truly unknown outside his own province. To my knowledge this was the first of many searching articles on the powerful Irving family in the national media. They eventually became a favourite subject of editors and writers—though never, apparently, to the detriment of the Irvings.

In the faster-moving newsmagazine style of recent decades, the *Maclean's* profile most often springs to life in the hands of a writer highly familiar with the subject's professional arena; the prime examples here are Brian D. Johnson's pieces on Mary Walsh and Shania Twain.

As it happens, I wrote a few *Maclean's* profiles, including one I remember with pride and gratitude and one that left me with an odd residue of conceit and shame. The latter didn't appear under my name. Officially, it was written by Grattan Gray, an amazingly versatile though purely imaginary author to whom *Maclean's* attributed all articles of dubious provenance: those rewritten by so many hands that it was impossible to credit them to one person, those of which the author was for some reason ashamed and those written by people who had no business writing them. My Grattan Gray article fell into the last category.

It was a profile of Lyndon Johnson, published in December, 1963, shortly after John Kennedy's assassination made him president. Peter Gzowski, the managing editor, assigned our Washington correspondent to write a cover story on Johnson and ordered the cover designed around Yousuf Karsh's recent portrait. Gzowski then awaited the arrival of the article. But Christmas was approaching, and our Washington man found that period so emotionally taxing that he celebrated it every year with a titanic binge. After many delays and excuses, and a final promise to send the article one day before it had to be set in type, he failed to deliver.

At the last possible moment, Gzowski broke the news to me: we had to have a profile of Johnson, tomorrow, and the only person available to write it was me, the columnist and sometime articles editor. Gzowski knew what this implied. He was already an expert profile writer, having produced, among others, the prescient article about Pierre Trudeau that appears in this book (later, as a radio star, he himself became the subject of many profiles, represented here by David Macfarlane's elegant account of Gzowski as host of *Morningside*).

I trembled, but set to work, digging through every publication in the office that carried a word about Johnson. I ignored the fact that I hadn't met him and didn't know anyone who had, and had never even visited Washington or Texas. My chief virtue was my exceptional speed as a typist. By three a.m., after the cleaning staff had left the building, I put a manuscript of 3,500 words on Gzowski's desk and went home. When I showed up at the office the next day, I discovered the most expensive cigar in Toronto hanging on my office wall, with a nice note.

After checking the proofs, I didn't read that piece again for a quarter of a century. It turned out to be plausible in its way, but utterly boneheaded. A product of desperate optimism, it surrounded Johnson with an air of benevolence that would have made the article laughable two years after it appeared and sinister three years later. It carried no hint of the angry passion with which Johnson would prosecute the Vietnam war, destroying his career and much of Vietnam while demoralizing American society.

That masterpiece will not be found in this book or, I trust, in any other. But I am represented here by a profile (substantially cut back from its originally published 6,700 words) of Lester B. Pearson. It was written in the spring of 1963, during the run-up to the election that made him prime minister. Since it concerned the Canadian public figure for whom I have felt the most affection (both at the time and in retrospect), it's pleasant also to remember it as the article that taught me more about writing for magazines than any other. It was published in my 13th year as a journalist. Until then, I was still working in the way I had learned during my first newspaper job in 1950: worry about the first paragraph till you get it more or less right, then set down all the succeeding paragraphs in the order in which they will appear in print.

But as I wrote about Pearson, I tried first one beginning and then another, finding each of them unsatisfactory. Soon I had a little pile of failed openings beside my typewriter. As I looked them over I realized that one of them might in fact be useful if placed halfway through the article, another might conceivably be turned into an ending, another might fit in about 500 words after the opening— providing, of course, that I connected them in a way that made sense and smoothed the transitions. This was a great revelation to me: you didn't have to begin at the beginning; in fact, sometimes you can begin at the end. I have been a much happier writer ever since—and most of what I said about Pearson was not wrong. That piece provided something like the truth for our readers and a valuable lesson for the author. What more could one ask of a profile?

Preface

A CURSORY REVIEW OF *Maclean's* tables of contents from the past century reveals several hundred profiles of people such as Mary Pickford and Max Aitken, the future Lord Beaverbrook, whose names are recognizable still today. With that review began the months-long process of winnowing down the list of potential profiles to the 42 found in this collection. The goal: to achieve a historical mix of articles about compelling Canadians from a variety of fields.

Well-written profiles have been the bread and butter of *Maclean's* almost since the magazine's birth in 1905. In fact, in 1908, as the then-monthly publication began to evolve from a compilation of articles first published elsewhere to a fount of original Canadian material, *Maclean's* editor George van Blaricom proudly published 12 profiles in one edition. They appeared under the rubric "Canadians Who Are Doing Things and How." Several of the pieces were as long as 1,500 words—less than half the size of the pieces found here—and profiled such luminaries as Robert W. Service who, while working at the Canadian Bank of Commerce, had just produced his enormously popular *Songs of a Sourdough* and Charles McCullough, who started the Canadian Club movement in 1892.

Maclean's has continued to evolve, but the profile remains an anchor of the weekly output. Hardly an issue of the magazine appears without an in-depth look at a newsmaker, preferably a Canadian. Many profiles receive cover treatment such as the Conrad Black, Wayne Gretzky and Shania Twain articles republished here.

The pieces have been edited for length, but the words that appear are, with few exceptions, as they were first printed. Freelance researcher Michael MacLean updated what happened to the profile subjects and the writers who profiled them. That information appears at the end of each article. (MacLean also ferreted out the secret of Barney Milford, who wrote for *Maclean's* but, in fact, never existed—it was a pseudonym for Trent Frayne.)

The photos are the product of sleuthing by Kristine Ryall, the magazine's estimable associate photo editor who has become as familiar with the National Archives as with our own photo gallery. *Maclean's* library staffers George Serhijczuk and Rosanne Pavicic helped mine our rich written archives, while production director Sean McCluskey transformed those yellowing printed pages to an electronic version that was transformed, once more, to the pristine pages of this volume.

Michael Benedict
Editorial Director, New Ventures

POLITICAL LEADERS

Mackenzie King As I Knew Him

Mackenzie King signing autographs in Ottawa, 1945

By Blair Fraser

SEPTEMBER 1, 1950. Beside a proclamation offering £1,000 for his grandfather dead or alive, Mackenzie King kept a parchment awarding him the Order of Merit. He was proud of both. This revealing paradox shaped the man and helped to shape a nation.

Some people think that last journey killed him—the trip to London in October, 1948, to the Conference of Commonwealth Prime Ministers. He never quite recovered from the breakdown he had there before the conference even began, so that he never actually got to its meetings. Yet, old and sick as he was, William Lyon Mackenzie King did a lot for the success of that conference. It cost him his health, but it may well have been his greatest service to the Commonwealth in his 50 years of public life.

The object of that conference was to bring India into the Commonwealth as a full partner. Prime Minister Jawaharlal Nehru had misgivings on two grounds: How could India join an association based on allegiance to an alien crown? And how could he, personally, after eight and one quarter years in British jails as a political prisoner, become and be accepted as a loyal prime minister?

Mr. King had the answers. Pandit Nehru called to see him in the sickroom at the Dorchester Hotel. Mr. King talked about his grandfather, the rebel William Lyon Mackenzie. He told of the proclamation signed in the Queen's name, offering £1,000 for Mackenzie's capture dead or alive. A copy of it now hangs outside his own study at Laurier House—and beside it the parchment that proclaims him, the rebel's grandson, a member of the Order of Merit. This high order of British chivalry is limited to 24 persons. "My chief reason for accepting the O.M.," Mr. King used to say, "was to hang it beside that proclamation of the price on my grandfather's head."

He told Mr. Nehru of his association with a whole line of sovereigns: he was sworn as a deputy minister under Queen Victoria, as minister of the Crown under Edward VII; he'd served as prime minister under George V, Edward VIII and George VI; he'd been a guest at the wedding of Princess Elizabeth and sent personal congratulations on the birth of Prince Charles. A day or two before, King George VI had called to see him. Yet he had never, at home or abroad, concealed his pride in the grandfather who fled in 1837 to escape hanging. Mr. King could make that story a parable of Canada. For 100 years this country had been struggling for freedom—first the Responsible Government that his grandfather had fought for, then the full autonomy he himself had done so much to win—yet at the same time insisting on retaining its tie with the Crown and the Commonwealth.

Pandit Nehru was deeply impressed. He called again the next day. This time he stayed only a few minutes with the sick old man, but he brought a gift of jade that Mr. King valued highly. Not much was heard after that of Pandit Nehru's personal misgivings.

Meanwhile, Mr. King had been working on the other side, urging that the Crown should not be the principle of the Commonwealth because "the Indians can't accept that." Asked what, then, should be the binding common factor, he'd expound a theory of his own. "The poor British could never understand it," one of his aides said. "I think even Mr. St. Laurent had trouble. It was a bit too mystical for most people."

But I remembered an occasion when he'd made it pretty clear— May 11, 1944, less than a month before D-Day, when Mr. King was in London at another prime ministers' conference. I remembered him walking down the aisle with Winston Churchill (it was astonishing, after all those heroic wartime pictures, to find Churchill and King were exactly the same height) and speaking to both Houses of the British Parliament. It was one of his good speeches, the best I ever heard him make from a prepared text. In one of its paragraphs he said:

> The British Commonwealth has within itself a spirit which is not exclusive but the opposite to exclusive. Therein lies its strength. That spirit expresses itself in co-operation. Therein lies the secret of its unity. Co-operation is capable of indefinite expansion. Therein lies the hope of the future.

If you had to put the guiding principle of his whole life into one word, that would be the word—"co-operation." Mr. King was proud of what he'd done to promote it within the Commonwealth. He was prouder still of his role between Britain and the Commonwealth on one side and the United States on the other. It was a larger role than most of us knew.

One Friday afternoon in August, 1940, Mr. King was at his summer home at Kingsmere. The phone rang; the Prime Minister answered it himself. He recognized the voice at the other end of the line, his old friend Franklin D. Roosevelt.

"What are you doing this weekend?" the President said.

Mr. King realized without asking that Mr. Roosevelt had something definite in mind. "I'm at your disposal," he said.

"Could you come over to meet me at Ogdensburg?"—the little border town in New York State, across the St. Lawrence River from Prescott, Ont.

Mr. King could, and did. The result, so far as we were told at the time, was the Ogdensburg Agreement that set up the Canada-U.S. Permanent Joint Board of Defence.

Actually, the so-called Ogdensburg Agreement was hardly more than an afterthought. Joint defence of the continent required very little discussion; the "agreement" was jotted down by the President on the back of an envelope and issued as a press release to give a plausible account of what they'd been talking about. What they really talked about, from about six in the evening until two in the morning, was the exchange of American destroyers for British colonial bases announced a month later.

One evening at Laurier House (during one of the few private conversations I ever had with Mackenzie King) he showed me a copy of
his cable to Winston Churchill after that Ogdensburg conference. It
was still marked "Secret," though the year was now 1948 and the
secrecy long spent. It was a fascinating document. I realized, reading it, that the British had a hard time understanding President
Roosevelt's worry about encroaching on American neutrality; while
the Americans had no grasp of the British reluctance to alienate
colonial territory. Mr. King, the Canadian, could understand them
both. His job was to explain each to the other and he did it superbly.

One thing that helped, of course, was the network of friendships
in both countries built up in 40-odd years of public life. Everyone
knows of his relationship with the Roosevelts; it's often forgotten
that he and Winston Churchill had been friends for a much longer
time. That went back to 1908; how it began was one of Mr. King's
favourite stories.

He'd met young Churchill briefly in 1903 or '04, when he was out
here on a lecture tour, and he disliked him at sight—thought him a
bumptious, conceited young jackanapes. In 1908, as deputy minister
of labour, King was in England on a mission connected with East
Indian immigration; by that time Winston Churchill had become a
boy wonder of British politics, a cabinet minister in his early 30s.

"You must see Churchill," somebody said. "He knows more about
this than anyone else."

"Anybody but Churchill," Mr. King replied. "I've met him and he's
the last man in England I want to see."

But when he got back to his hotel a few hours later he found a
hand-written note from Churchill asking him to lunch the next day
in terms he could hardly refuse. As King walked into the club lounge
the following noon Churchill met him with a grin and an out-
stretched hand. "We met in Canada four years ago, I think," he said.
"I did make a frightful ass of myself on that trip, didn't I?"

King looked him right in the eye and smiled back. "Well, Mr.
Churchill, there were many Canadians who thought so," he said,
"and I was one of them." With that they sat down to an excellent
lunch; they rose fast friends. The friendship was mutually useful 30-
odd years later.

Introducing Mr. King to the British Parliament in May, 1944, Mr. Churchill said: "I say without hesitation that there was no other man, and perhaps there was no other career which any man could have followed, which would have enabled our honoured guest of this afternoon to lead Canada united into the heart of this world-shaking struggle."

Such words must have warmed Mr. King's heart for they touched on the proudest achievement of his whole career. At his last press conference, on the day in 1948 when he finally retired as prime minister, someone asked him what he regarded as his outstanding work. He said, "Keeping Canada united through the war."

For such men as Sir Wilfrid Laurier and Mr. St. Laurent, members themselves of an ethnic minority, the concept of Canadian unity was part of their heritage; it was in their blood. For Mackenzie King, as for Sir John A. Macdonald, it was not. Both were Scots Presbyterians; neither spoke French at all; neither had any special fondness for French Canadians as such. But both had the wisdom, the penetration to grasp this root problem of Canadian statesmanship, and both had the skill to devise solutions for it. Perhaps "solutions" is too positive a word for the subtle compromises they worked out. Controversy still swirls around the most famous, or notorious, in Mackenzie King's career—his manpower policy during the Second World War. "Not necessarily conscription, but conscription if necessary." Hardly a ringing slogan for a nation at war; hardly a phrase to lift men's hearts.

Yet it worked, in its fashion. To English Canada, angrily demanding a total war effort, it offered a barely tolerable minimum. On French Canada, violently opposed to conscription and furious that the pledges against it should be broken or even modified, it imposed a barely tolerable minimum. Neither side liked it; both put up with it. Whatever you may think of Mr. King's manpower formula there is no doubt what he thought of it himself. He thought it was an achievement. I believe he regarded the conscription crisis of 1944, and his own feat of coming through it with a reasonably intact cabinet and a vote of confidence from Parliament, as the triumphant climax of his whole career.

If that crisis showed his skill as a compromiser it also showed another of his qualities—ruthlessness. That never came out more clearly than in his treatment of the late Col. J. L. Ralston. Grant Dexter, editor of the *Winnipeg Free Press* and an intimate friend of Col. Ralston, published an account of this incident when Col. Ralston died in May, 1948. He referred to Mr. King's announcement of Nov. 1, 1944, that [defence minister] Col. Ralston had "resigned," and went on:

What actually happened is without precedent in this country. Mr. King dismissed Col. Ralston while the cabinet was in session and while both men were seated at the council table. He simply said that the colonel would no longer be the Minister (of National Defence) and that Gen. McNaughton would take over. Thereupon Col. Ralston rose, walked around the table, shaking hands with the men who had been his colleagues, and walked out of the East Block a private member. He did not shake hands with the Prime Minister. He did not become a King-hater, like many others, but from that day forward, he never had respect or affection for Mr. King.

Another colleague, who had a great deal of respect and affection for Mr. King, said, "Don't be misled by appearances. The public thinks this man is flabby, weak, indecisive. In fact he is tough, hard as nails, and absolutely ruthless when he wants to be." It's a paradox, one of the many in his complex character, that this "tough, hard, ruthless" man should also be the Great Conciliator, a genius at bringing men of opposite views together and composing their differences.

When he was deputy minister of labour he handled about 40 industrial disputes; only two developed into strikes. Working for the Rockefeller Foundation during the First World War, he smoothed out labour troubles in several of the biggest war plants in the United States. His 1918 book *Industry and Humanity*, if rewritten into less ponderous prose, could still be used as a textbook in personnel relations.

To the end of his days, Mr. King considered himself a radical; nothing annoyed him more than people who thought there was no difference between the Liberal and Conservative parties. About five years ago, a friend of mine introduced to him David Lewis, then national secretary of the CCF. "I'm very glad to meet you," said Mr. King. "You know, we ought to be in the same party. All the progressive people should be together."

Take a look at the King records: Fair Wages Resolution, 1898 (to forbid sweatshop practices on government contracts; this was introduced as a result of Mackenzie King's articles in the Toronto *Mail and Empire*). Railway Disputes Act, 1903. Industrial Disputes Investigation Act, 1907. Bill to establish eight-hour day on public works, 1910 (Mr. King introduced it and it passed the Commons, but the Senate killed it). Combines Investigation Act, 1922. Old Age Pension Act, 1927. Unemployment Insurance Act, 1940. It may have taken a long time, but it adds up to a lot.

Here's a paradox again, though. This man who spent so many years improving the lot of the working man was, himself, a very hard man to work for. He was the first Canadian statesman to seek legislation for an eight-hour day, but he worked his own staff like galley slaves, night after night. To some extent he could plead necessity; after all, a prime minister has to be busy, especially in wartime. But he had a total disregard for a man's family obligations or private plans; nothing mattered but work.

At the same time he required his staff to be very considerate of him—not just efficient, but obsequious. One young secretary fell permanently out of favour when he failed to turn up to welcome the prime minister home from a journey. When the same man forgot to see him off on the occasion of the next trip he very nearly lost his job.

Yet this same Mackenzie King, notorious as a hard master, was famous for acts of consideration and kindness, even to the merest acquaintances. One Christmas Eve not long ago, a couple who knew Mr. King only moderately well came home to find a large bunch of flowers on their doorstep, with Mr. King's card. Christmas morning the P.M. himself rang up: "I was so sorry not to find you in when I took those flowers over last night. I'd got so many I didn't know what to do with them all, so I made up a few bunches and took them around to friends."

Not long ago he gave an interview to a visitor from out of town who'd lost his wife a few months before. The visitor didn't know Mr. King very well and it was no surprise to him that Mr. King made no mention of his bereavement. Next morning, by special messenger, came a hand-written letter from Mackenzie King, two pages long. Mr. King hadn't known of his visitor's tragic loss, had learned of it only after the man had left. Then followed a message of condolence which was a masterpiece of good taste and genuine sympathy.

In 1943, a Conservative editor, who'd fought Mackenzie King continuously and bitterly for 30 years or more, got word that his son was missing in action overseas. It happened during the first Quebec Conference with Mr. Churchill and Mr. Roosevelt. At midnight the telephone rang; it was Mr. King calling from Quebec to express his sympathy and concern. This was one situation where his thoughtfulness was absolutely unfailing; it extended to friend and foe. His heart went out to any acquaintance, however slight, who'd suffered any bereavement, however remote or even trivial.

I once owned an Irish terrier that ran off and got lost. I put an ad in the paper, stating the breed of the dog and giving my name and phone number. About 10:30 that evening the phone rang. "Fraser? This is Mackenzie King speaking. Have you found your dog?"

That was the only personal call I ever got from Mr. King and I was more than surprised, I was astounded. For weeks I kept it dark, thinking it might have been some Press Gallery wag with a gift for mimicry. But when I finally plucked up courage to tell one of his secretaries about it, he said, "Oh, that was the P.M. all right. He does that kind of thing all the time."

On the Monday after Mr. King died, the *Ottawa Citizen* alone carried seven by-lined stories by different staff reporters, all on the theme "I knew Mackenzie King." The degree of acquaintance varied a good deal, but all these stories are absolutely genuine. Mr. King wasn't the hermit he was painted.

Except for his old friend Sen. Charlie Bishop, who'd known him as a green young deputy minister in 1900, he had no intimates among reporters here. But the rest of us did see a bit of him from time to time, in spite of our constant moans about how seldom he met the press. We didn't see him casually or easily. Mr. St. Laurent can be buttonholed as readily as any other minister. He walks alone to work every day, often goes alone to lunch at the Rideau Club and sits at the nearest club table that has a vacant chair. Mr. King never did things like that. We saw him by appointment, and rarely.

But when a reporter did get a private interview, Mr. King treated him as a guest. Often the appointment would be at Laurier House, for tea in that famous top-floor study. If you were especially lucky it might even be out at Kingsmere (that never happened to me, but it has to some people). Or it might be just a brief chat in the office at the House of Commons or the East Block. Wherever it was, Mr. King always behaved like a host, never like a busy executive.

If the talk was off record, as it usually was, Mr. King would some-times talk with astonishing frankness. I remember one time in his last year as prime minister, a colleague had just brought in a highly controversial measure. Mr. King, as head of the government, was just as much responsible for it, in theory, as the sponsoring minister, but he said quite bluntly that the whole thing was a great mistake. "I don't blame the minister so much, I blame his officials," the Old Master said. "You know, Fraser, ministers listen far too much to their advisers nowadays. That's something I learned not to do when I first went into Sir Wilfrid's cabinet . . . " and he drifted off into anecdotes of political life 40 years before.

To meet Mr. King at close range like that, to listen to him talk, was to realize the charm he had and to know why he was such a forceful personality at international gatherings. In public he was both cold and dull. In 50 years of practice he never learned to read well from a prepared text; his oratory, on these formal occasions, was usually stiff and artificial. Privately he was just the opposite. His public speeches were all wrapped up in cocoons of qualification and reservation; his private talk was blunt, forthright and memorable.

He could be very witty, too. The funniest, the best, and in a curi-ous way the most moving speech I ever heard him make was at the Press Gallery dinner in 1948, when he told us for the first time his full plans for retirement. For the first 15 or 20 minutes he gave a burlesque of himself—first an ambiguous sentence, then a demon-stration of all the fantastic meanings editorial writers would read into it. We all laughed until our sides ached.

And then, almost imperceptibly, he grew serious. I don't remember what he said, and it was all off the record anyway, but I do remember the quiet that fell on a rather rowdy and bibulous audience and the ovation he got when he sat down. No man who could talk like that would ever lack invitations, even if he weren't the prime minister. Mr. King would have been a welcome guest anywhere.

So in that sense the picture of him as a friendless man is quite false. He had hundreds. I saw the heaps of his mail on his 75th birthday: baskets and baskets of it from all over the world.

Still, it is significant that he was sensitive on this point. Nothing hurt his feelings as much as the statement, often printed, that he was a man with few friends. It hurt because, in a different but very real way, there was some truth in it. I don't think many people were really close to Mr. King, or he to them.

Partly it was the penalty of his job. When the late Robert Manion became Conservative leader in 1938, Mr. King invited him out to Kingsmere and offered him just one piece of advice: "Try not to see too many people. There is nothing more fatiguing. You must ration very carefully the number of people you see each day, or you can't carry on as a party leader."

Partly, too, it was his own choice. Some years ago, talking to a Liberal official of gregarious habit, Mr. King said, "You're seeing people too much. I've always found I can control people better if I don't see too much of them."

It's usually said, and I think rightly, that the Rt. Hon. Ernest Lapointe was the closest friend he ever had among cabinet colleagues. Mr. King used to call Mr. Lapointe "Ernest." But Mr. Lapointe, to his dying day, never called the prime minister anything but "Mr. King." That's why there were few mourners in the nearest, deepest personal sense when he died. Most of his immediate family were already dead and so were the old dear friends. Of those still living, the men who'd been closest to him physically were the very men who knew how far he had kept himself away from them.

Nevertheless, he was mourned.

While his body lay in state in the Hall of Fame, a friend of mine overheard a mother who'd brought her little boy to see him. The child didn't know who Mackenzie King was; the mother was trying to tell him. "He was a great prime minister," she said, "and he was prime minister longer than anybody ever was before. He did great things for Canada. The things he did will make Canada a better place for you to grow up in. He was . . ."

Quite suddenly she stopped talking and began to cry, and then she turned and went away. Of all the millions of words poured out in tribute to Mackenzie King none gave him surer promise of immortal memory.

Blair Fraser, who drowned in an Ontario canoeing accident at 59 in May, 1968, was Ottawa editor of Maclean's *from 1943 to 1960, and then again in the later 1960s. He was editor of the magazine from 1960 to 1962.*

René Lévesque: The Man in the Middle of Quebec's New Deal

René Lévesque at an election fund-raising dinner in Montreal, 1962

By Ken Johnstone

NOVEMBER 18, 1961. Quebec is currently entering the first stages of an economic revolution, and René Lévesque, minister of Natural Resources in the Quebec government, is its spark plug. This appraisal is shared by enemies and supporters alike of the controversial and outspoken gadfly of the Liberal cabinet of Premier Jean Lesage. Lévesque is probably Quebec's best-known, best-loved and worst-hated public figure.

The new leader of the Union Nationale, Daniel Johnson, has solemnly and repeatedly warned Lesage against "the crazy socialistic ideas" of Lévesque, and Gerard Pelletier, editor of Montreal's big daily, *La Presse*, told me, "He's the one man you can trust; he has sincerity and resourcefulness, and he won't miss the bus."

When, in the summer of 1960, Quebec's long-entrenched and well-oiled but corrupt Union Nationale election machine finally crumpled under the onslaught of a rejuvenated Liberal party led by Jean Lesage, many people in that province, impressed by the Liberal party's progressive platform, looked for a new deal for the long-suffering populace. The subsequent reforms introduced by Lesage swept like a fresh breeze through the province, amazing

some, confounding others, and leaving a skeptical knot of unbeliev-
ers still convinced that it was too good to last. Hospital insurance
was introduced and a new deal in education making it possible for
students to attend school without fees all the way to Grade 12.

But for René Lévesque and an impressive number of young
French-Canadian intellectuals who share his views, the foregoing
was simply a mild preliminary to the real struggle for economic
emancipation on the part of the 85 per cent of the Quebec population that owns less than 10 per cent of the province's wealth. "We're
at the same stage as the Cubans," Lévesque says, "but we've already
got shoes. Two pairs." The struggle has already been joined, and the
intellectuals believe its course will have important consequences for
the rest of Canada as well as for Quebec.

René Lévesque told me: "Either we will have a planned program
for promoting the French Canadians economically, or there will be a
blow-up. The French Canadians will no longer tolerate the status of
second-class people in their own province. The days of empire building and big company domination in Quebec are over.

"Big companies are in here to exploit the resources, and this is
right and proper. But they should never have control over the townships, the police, the politicians, the lives of the people. And their
operations must be modified and conditioned by the welfare of the
people in the province. The big economic decisions in the future
must be made by the provincial government with this interest in
mind, and of course with the co-operation of the interested parties.

"But if the aspirations of the people are thwarted, the situation
can change rapidly. They are roused to demand their share in the
country's wealth. When I, for one, can rouse them further, I do."

The man who offered this flat challenge to the economic over-
lords of Quebec is a thin wiry figure of 39, five and a half feet tall,
with a broad-domed balding head, sharp gray-green eyes, a strong
nose, thin humorous mouth and firm chin. He gives an impression of
instant awareness, and candid intelligence.

When René Lévesque speaks for Quebec aspirations, he speaks for
the most advanced and articulate section of that province's lively
middle class. Sharing his views in great part are people like Pelletier,

André Laurendeau, editor of the small but influential *Le Devoir*, Jean-Louis Gagnon, editor of the aggressive new *Le Nouveau Journal*, educator Father Georges-Henri Lévesque (no relation), labour leader Jean Marchand, influential writers like Jacques Hébert and Pierre Trudeau, Abbé O'Neill, co-author of a trenchant treatise on political morality that helped dig the grave of the Union Nationale government, and Maurice Lamontagne, top French-Canadian economist and economic adviser to Liberal leader Lester Pearson.

Lévesque originally became widely known to the people of Quebec through television, first with *Carrefour* (Crossroads) back in 1954, and then with a succeeding program, *Point de Mire* (Focus). They were news feature programs in which Lévesque undertook to examine the background of current issues, both domestic and world-wide, and his lucidity and simplicity in dealing with these issues and making them clear to the simplest housewife or backwoods farmer made his face and name familiar across the province. His outspoken handling of ticklish issues roused the ire of the Duplessis government and made him at the same time one of the most reviled and respected figures in the province.

While Lévesque is a favourite target of the Union Nationale (antichrist and communist are their favourite epithets for him), he is also an object of suspicion and worry for some members of his own party, who see in him the spearhead of a young and aggressive wing which aims at the total abolition of all the familiar disreputable practices of the past. Lévesque describes the situation candidly:

"The big problem is that the party, like every other party, has its people who believe in the program, and others who wish that the party would behave like its predecessor and dish out the gravy. These latter people, if they can't be re-educated, have to be discouraged or die off. They are an older element who are cynical about politics generally; an attitude which they usually describe as 'being realistic.'"

As minister of Natural Resources, Lévesque has made it perfectly clear that he thinks the government, for a start, should take over most of the electrical power resources of the province. Hydro-Quebec has already started buying out sections of private power companies, and under Lévesque no further concessions will be granted private industry in this field.

Lévesque told me: "The economic development of Quebec must be planned and decided by the government through a method whereby the people of the province can participate as shareholders and not just as employees."

The bitter truth is that Lévesque may find himself almost isolated if a showdown comes within the cabinet. According to most observers the showdown is not far off. If they're right, Lévesque will make sure his departure is noisy. "If the government doesn't stick to its program, if it becomes like previous governments," he warns, "then I'll quit—and everyone will know why."

This gadfly preparing to sting the flank of big business was born in New Carlisle, Que., on August 24, 1922, the son of Dominique Lévesque, who was an early associate of Ernest Lapointe and a devoted supporter of Sir Wilfrid Laurier. René was the first of four children; his brother Fernand is a journalist on the staff of *La Presse*, his brother André is a lawyer in Quebec City, and his sister, Alice, also in Quebec City, is married. As a youngster, René was noted for his tough independent character. At four, he roamed around so much his father tried tethering him to a tree with a rope. When a passerby commiserated, the tot told him to mind his own business.

René started his radio career as a 14-year-old summer replacement with CHNC in New Carlisle where he was an announcer and wrote news bulletins. His interest in radio continued while he attended university in Quebec City (the family moved to Quebec City after Dominique Lévesque's death in 1938). René obtained his BA there and took two years of law at Laval before he gave this up to go overseas as a radio reporter during the war. There, in Alsace, after a series of bouts with laryngitis, he lost his normal voice and returned in 1946 with the hoarse raspy whisper that he was to make so well-known subsequently over the air in Quebec.

Back in Canada he spent five years in the International Service of the CBC; later he did a stint as a CBC war correspondent in Korea. When television started, he helped prepare the first CBC French-language news feature programs, and out of these the popular *Carrefour* and *Point de Mire*. On the latter he spent about 100 hours a week in research, documentation and on-the-spot coverage. His job took him all over Canada and to the news-making centres of the world.

His first trip to Russia was with the newspapermen covering the visit of [external affairs minister] Lester Pearson in 1955. Pearson was invited to visit Khrushchev at his summer home in Yalta, and though the press was invited along, only Lévesque and a Toronto newspaperman accepted the invitation. Lévesque carted along a portable tape recorder, and when Pearson and Khrushchev held their first conversations the two reporters were permitted to stand at the door and look into the parlor where the meeting was held. Khrushchev spotted Lévesque's equipment, and called him over.

"Radio?" he asked.

Lévesque used his only Russian. "*Da, da*," he answered.

Khrushchev invited Lévesque to turn on his equipment, and Lévesque was delighted to oblige. Then Khrushchev launched into a violent attack on NATO, which gave Pearson some difficulty in finding effective answers. Lévesque recorded the exchanges as they were translated. When he got back to Moscow with his exclusive recording, he allowed the English and French newspapermen there to listen to the exchange, and it made headlines in Paris and London. He shipped it air express back to Montreal, but when he got back to the CBC he found the recording gathering dust on a shelf. It had been decided that since Pearson had not fared well in the exchange, the recording would not be released. "My scoop wasn't good enough for Canada!" he lamented. (Parts of the recording were later broadcast.)

Point de Mire came to an abrupt end with the CBC producers' strike in March 1959 when Lévesque entered wholeheartedly into the strike on the side of the producers and proved, to the surprise of himself as well as the strikers, to be a very effective orator. The strike was long and bitter and it took place in the middle of winter, involving people who had absolutely no experience of such actions. Yet they stuck it out till final victory and a most important factor in maintaining the morale of the strikers was the moving yet always well-reasoned speeches of René Lévesque. They usually ended each mass meeting and sent the strikers away determined to hang on.

CBC discontinued *Point de Mire* soon after the strike. It was then that Lévesque, approached by the Liberals to study their new platform for the forthcoming provincial election, decided that the platform was worth fighting for. Although this would be his first experience on the hustings, Lévesque was no political tyro. Because of his raspy voice he had never been used in any of the commercial shows presented by CBC; instead he had been sent to cover political conventions and elections. Thus he covered the 1952, '56 and '58 conventions and elections in the United States, the 1953, '57 and '58 Canadian federal elections, and the 1952, '56 and '58 Quebec provincial elections. Parties and programs were an old story to him, and, of them all, he liked the 1960 Quebec Liberal platform best. "It was a good beginning," he said later.

The 1960 election was fought with no holds barred, and Lévesque was a particular target of the Union Nationale. Not only did he have to contend with all the traditional ballot-stuffing, impersonation and telegraphing which is traditional in Quebec elections, but he was singled out for special attention by the Union Nationale leadership. Much of this backfired. A vicious personal attack, which was launched against him by means of a record circulated privately among the clergy, and recounting his alleged marital difficulties, actually won a great number of scandalized priests to the Liberal cause in protest against this tactic.

Strong-arm tactics are also commonplace in Quebec elections. One day, about two weeks before the election, a burly man walked into Lévesque's headquarters in the Laurier district of Montreal, a northeastern section of the city with a large Italian population. He was Johnny Rougeau, wrestler by profession, and a local hero. He told Lévesque: "You're an honest guy, but you're going to need some help or you're going to get hurt. Let me know when you need me."

As the tension increased, Lévesque went everywhere with the broad-shouldered wrestler by his side. Nobody bothered him. On election day, however, Lévesque learned that a gang of goons was terrorizing the voters in the polling booths around Danté Street, and that the police were reluctant to intervene. He got into a car with Rougeau and drove into Danté Street, where he was immediately surrounded by a mob of more than 50 roughnecks who promised to tear both of them limb from limb if they stepped out of the car. Deliberately Lévesque and Rougeau climbed out of the car, and Rougeau begged for the first offering in the cause of political partisanship. During all the milling and pushing the police suddenly arrived with a squad of paddy wagons; more than 50 members of the goon squad spent the rest of the day in the cells. Since Lévesque won the election by the narrow margin of 129 votes (increased to 179 in a subsequent recount), he likes to think that the foray at two o'clock in the afternoon played a major part in spiking the guns of Union Nationale telegraphers.

Immediately after the election, Lesage appointed Lévesque minister of Public Works and minister of Hydraulic Resources. Lévesque lost no time in applying the Liberal promise to eliminate graft and payoffs. Within nine months he was able to show a saving of $4 million, mainly by starting open-tender bidding and renegotiating contracts which had been let by the previous government through "letters of intent." He also eliminated such quaint discrepancies as a squad of "bridge-watchers" who had drawn some $60,000 in salary for making sure that the communists didn't blow up the Three Rivers bridge, as Duplessis had insisted was their fixed intention. He dismissed a waterworks commission which had been appointed by Duplessis in 1948 to study water pollution, had spent $312,000, but had never brought in a report.

Then, when the Department of Natural Resources was formed this spring, Lévesque was appointed minister to head it up. The *Montreal Star* observed: "This will probably give sleepless nights to those who are astonished at Mr. Lévesque's cheerful admission of leftist leanings, yet his previous record is a good testimonial to his ability and dedication."

René Lévesque has lost his raspy voice; it's now a pleasant baritone. He told me that his voice suddenly started to come back to him in the midst of the election campaigns after he had delivered three speeches in one night. "All that shouting," he explained, "was just like an operation. That's what medical friends of mine have told me."

Lévesque puts in backbreaking days at his work. On Mondays he is usually at Hydro-Quebec in Montreal, where officials still haven't gotten over the shock of finding him on his first visit quietly having a cup of coffee in the employees' cafeteria. Tuesday to Friday he spends at his office in Quebec or in the House when Parliament is in session. He usually stays at the modest Clarendon Hotel in Quebec: "There I miss the lobbyists who always check in at the Chateau Frontenac." He leaves Quebec City on Friday night to be in his office in the Laurier constituency early Saturday morning, where he stays all day listening to constituents with grievances, problems and advice.

He is sure of spending only Sunday with his wife and three children, Pierre, 13, Claude, 11, and Suzanne, five. René tries to take his family on trips out of Montreal; in winter he skis with them and in summer he tries to spend his vacation with them near salt water, an old love for a man born on the Gaspé coast.

After his father's death, his mother decided to study the culinary arts more thoroughly, so she enrolled in a course at university. After a year she decided she was learning nothing new there. She went to Paris for more intensive instruction, then decided to learn Italian, and spent a year in Florence and Bologna. When René became involved in the controversy over his reporting on Russia, she decided to go to the USSR to find out for herself. She came away after two weeks convinced that her son had been scandalously maligned but, a good Catholic, she made a pilgrimage to Jerusalem afterward to make sure she hadn't been contaminated by the Reds. She lives now in Quebec City where she is currently working on the translation of a long article on investment corporations which she thinks may be helpful to René.

René Lévesque needs all the help he can get. Jean Marchand, head of the Confederation of Catholic Workers, told me: "He is strong, honest, bright, but he has a terrible job; I wonder if he can pull it off?"

"I have faith in Lévesque. He meant the difference between victory and defeat for the Liberals. But if his experience is bad, what will happen afterward?"

René Lévesque resigned from the Liberal party in 1966 to establish a soveriegnty movement, which became the Parti Québécois two years later. In 1976, the PQ won the provincial election and Lévesque became premier. Although he lost the 1980 referendum with 40 per cent of the vote, his PQ was re-elected the following year. Lévesque resigned as premier in 1985 and died two years later of a heart attack in Montreal at 65.

Ken Johnstone was an assistant editor at Maclean's *from November, 1955, to September, 1956.*

Pierre Trudeau: Portrait of an Intellectual in Action

Pierre Trudeau at home, 1962

FEBRUARY 24, 1962. In a civilization where the influence of the thinking man is generally confined to his advice on filters for cigarettes, Quebec stands out as a place where the intellectual has had some part in a recent and vital political victory—the toppling, in June, 1960, of the Union Nationale regime. How big the part was, of course, is impossible to know for sure. But it is quite obvious that the part of the Liberal platform that appealed to uncommitted voters, and swung the balance of electoral appeal from the UN to the Liberals, was the part inspired by a small group of men who were and are, undoubtedly, intellectuals.

A few of these men had been harping on the themes eventually picked up by the Liberal party—the themes, to oversimplify for a moment, of political and social reform—for as long as 10 years before the actual changeover of power. The principal place where they were doing so was a small magazine called *Cité Libre*, which published its first edition on June 15, 1950.

Cité Libre began with a circulation of 500. By the election of 1960 it had passed 5,000, but its influence could never be measured in numbers. Shortly after its inception, the eminent and acerbic journalist André Laurendeau wrote in *Le Devoir* that *Cité Libre* was saying things "out loud" (about Duplessisism and Quebec) that until then "others have only whispered." By the mid-1950s, other people and other publications (including *Le Devoir*) were saying them too—but only after *Cité Libre* had shown the way. Its influence was so widespread that one reader remarked that if he hadn't known *Cité Libre* was published only four times a year (it's a monthly now), he would have thought from the frequency with which it was quoted that it was a daily newspaper. Some bishops forbade their charges to read it (though its editors were all Catholics) and many university professors refused to write for it on the privately admitted grounds that they were afraid they would lose their jobs if they did.

Yet, for all its influence, *Cité Libre* has always been an amateur magazine. Its first capital was $300, which was subscribed by the six men who started it. Those six men, and the four who joined the group shortly after its inception, were involved in other things as well. Some of them have since achieved some prominence: Pierre Juneau is executive director of the National Film Board. Roger Rolland is regional program director of French networks for the CBC. Charles-A. Lussier is in charge of Quebec House in Paris. Gérard Pelletier is editor of French Canada's foremost daily newspaper, *La Presse*. And all of the original 10 have been very much the intellectuals, engagés, being involved with the law or the labour movement, or writing in other publications and generally offering a strong contrast with the traditional English-Canadian intellectual who huddles in an office somewhere and writes occasional essays for the *Queen's Quarterly*.

One of *Cité Libre*'s original six, and the one who, with Pelletier, has been its moving force, is Pierre Elliott Trudeau, a wiry, gentle-spoken 42-year-old bachelor who at once typifies the group—and the thinking man engagé—and breaks all its rules for membership. On the typical side, Trudeau is about as intellectual as one can get, having completed a bewildering number of courses in law, economics and political science at the universities of Montreal, Harvard and Paris, and the London School of Economics, from which he graduated at a very erudite 27. He is, like most of the *Cité Libre* people, well left of centre in his politics, though he has never been, for one reason or another, a card-carrying member of either the CCF or the NDP.

Trudeau is the author of what is generally regarded as *Cité Libre*'s most important single article, *"Un manifeste démocratique"* ("A democratic manifesto," published in October, 1958), and the editor of *La Grève de L'Amiante* (*The Asbestos Strike*), a book published in 1956 under the imprint of Les Editions *Cité Libre*, which, in the guise of an examination of the events of 1949, directed a blistering attack on the status quo in Quebec: most blisteringly on clericalism, the education system and electoral practices. Unlike any of his confrères on the magazine, and unlike virtually all intellectuals, engagés or otherwise, Trudeau is a millionaire, or close to it. He is currently living with his mother in a large and very comfortably appointed house in the city of Outremont on Montreal island. Each morning, he drives either to his Sherbrooke Street law office, which has been described as a "free clinic for anyone with an interesting case," or to l'Université de Montréal, to whose staff he has recently been appointed, and when he leaves for work he chooses between a black Mercedes-Benz sedan and a 300 SL sports car. He is a brown belt at judo, master of three languages (French, English and Spanish) and jack of several others, world-traveller, skin diver, skier and bad amateur pianist. He is a formidable debater and, as one of Montreal's most eligible bachelors, an authoritative judge of wine and women.

Where clothes are concerned—which is somewhere, in fashion-conscious Montreal—Trudeau is a creative thinker, whose costume varies between conservative Britishism and corduroy slacks and sandals. He has been observed swimming in a pool in Ste. Adèle while snow fell around him during a meeting of the Institut Canadien des Affaires Publiques, which he helped found, and he once tried to row a boat from the Florida Keys to Cuba.

In 1952, Trudeau attended an international conference of economists in Moscow. There, to the great chagrin of his guide and interpreter, he was discovered throwing snowballs at a statue of Stalin. "I have since wondered if I should write Khrushchev and show him how far ahead of him I was," he says, "but then it was not the thing to do. However, I told them, truthfully, that I used to go to Ottawa all the time and throw snowballs at Laurier's statue, and I was let off with a warning."

Such tactics—whose results have not always been so amicable—have sometimes led to Trudeau being dismissed as nothing more than a clown. He is, of course, much more. Democracy and democratic practices have few more eloquent spokesmen in Canada and, through what Trudeau calls "the dark years" of the 1940s and 1950s, they probably had none more determined in the province of Quebec. Nevertheless, Trudeau himself admits that some part of his life as a social critic—"if you want to look at it psychoanalytically"—has been motivated by a desire simply to throw snowballs at authority.

Sometimes, "authority" has meant not so much the people in power as the reigning popular sentiment. Trudeau's willingness to be on the unpopular side has seldom been so evident as it is in French Canada this winter, when he is standing squarely against the wave of nationalism and separatism that is sweeping the province. Asked a few weeks ago to expound on why he stands so strongly against separatism, even when he admits that the feeling may be stronger in French Canada now than it has ever been before, Trudeau said:

I am against any policy that is based on race or religion. Any such policy is a reactionary policy and—while the bases of race and religion don't necessarily lead to evil—it is true that for the last 150 years nationalism has been a retrograde idea. There may be some countries where separatism is the only solution to current problems, but Canada is not one of them. By a historical accident, Canada has found itself approximately 75 years ahead of the rest of the world in the formation of a multinational state and I happen to believe that the hope of mankind lies in multinationalism.

If I were an English-Canadian Machiavellian, I'd encourage the separatists. I'd give them as much publicity and pay as much attention to them—or have the public pay as much attention to them—as I could. I would think that if I could keep the bright young men coming out of the universities worrying about separatism, I could hold them back for another 10 years. While they were arguing about separatism, my sons would be getting the kind of education that would help them in tomorrow's world, and when the next industrial revolution came along—the cybernetics revolution—it would be, once again, my sons who were equipped to be the effective leaders. A nation of people only has so much intellectual energy to spend on a revolution. If the intellectual energy of French Canadians is spent on such a futile and foolish cause as separatism, the revolution that is just beginning here can never be brought about.

Trudeau is no less comfortable in English than in French, so that he misses completely the frustrations of having to use a language in which he is not at home when speaking with members of Canada's majority. The two languages were interchangeable in his childhood home; they have remained so interchangeable in the family that Pierre habitually speaks English to his sister, a Montreal matron, and French to his brother, an architect. In school, he recalls: "The professors used to tell the stories about French-Canadian triumphs with great dramatic flair and when they would come to the climax of a battle that we won the students would burst into applause. That rather amused—and annoyed—me, and when we got to the result of the battle of the Plains of Abraham, I remember, I broke into applause myself. I was alone."

In the war years, Trudeau was neither so alone nor so removed from his French heritage that he could forgive the government for its conscription policy—a phase of political history that he is still bitter about—and like many young French Canadians of his eminently eligible age, he simply continued his schooling. Since then, however, he has seen his share of fighting. In 1948, after he had finished at the London School of Economics, he set out, at first with a motorbike and later simply with a knapsack, on a year-and-a-half's tour of the world. His itinerary during that time sounds like a catalogue of trouble spots. He was arrested in Jerusalem, in Arab dress and without papers, shortly after the assassination of Count Bernadotte: friends vouched for him, after some harrowing hours. He saw street fighting in the suburbs of Rangoon during the Burmese civil war and travelled across Cambodia and Vietnam in an army convoy at the height of the Indo-Chinese wars. He was arrested—and later released—crossing the India-Pakistan line shortly after partition and he crossed the Khyber Pass while tribesmen from Afghanistan were conducting regular raids on Pakistani villages.

In Paris, Trudeau met Gérard Pelletier, who had been an acquaintance at home and who was there with the World University Service—"giving American money to countries that were about to go Communist," as Pelletier puts it. The two of them, with occasional visits from other temporary expatriates, began talking about the need for change in Quebec, and out of those conversations came both the idea for *Cité Libre*—"we knew we needed a place to put our ideas forward, and we knew the traditional places wouldn't be open to us"—and the bases of the unconventional (for Quebec) ideas that have dominated Trudeau's thinking ever since.

Where Trudeau differs from the traditional left is that he is not yet convinced that French Canada is ready for a "social revolution." "The ideas we were putting forward," he says, "may seem self-evident now—ideas like separation of church and state, electoral reform, a re-evaluation of our educational system—but they were not self-evident then, at least in Quebec." And it is the frustration he felt in trying to make his desire become reality that has led to such petulant generalizations as this: "Historically, French Canadians have not really believed in democracy for themselves; and English Canadians have not really wanted it for others."

Armed with these convictions, or at least the beginnings of them, Trudeau returned to Canada in 1949, "determined," as he says, "to see how the cogs of democratic government worked." Through some academic connection in Ottawa, he was able to latch on to the very hub, the Privy Council, and for nearly three years worked there as an "economic adviser," summarizing interdepartmental arguments for cabinet decision and generally oiling the cogs. But those were also the first years of *Cité Libre*, to whose meetings Trudeau was commuting regularly, and "although the work with the Privy Council was fascinating, I knew that the place I wanted to be was Quebec."

Gérard Pelletier, who along with several other members of the *Cité Libre* group was then in the labour movement, urged on Trudeau the notion that the unions in French Canada could use his legal and economic training, and in 1952 he moved to Montreal and opened a law office. He has kept one open ever since, and from it has offered advice—often free—to scores of people involved in everything from habeas corpus to property suits, but his chief interest through that time was labour legislation and labour-management bargaining. "I would not like to give the impression that I was trying to use the unions," he says, "but I felt that for the kind of change I wanted to see in Quebec—an awakening of democracy—the unions were the best vehicle. At the same time, because of my training, I was able to advise both the Catholic syndicates and the international unions, who were often at loggerheads, and I was able to act as a sort of bridge between them."

Trudeau prepared briefs, served as union nominee on arbitration boards and argued union cases before other arbitration boards. "It was amazing," he says, "how much technical advice the unions needed. Again, I blame the system, the lack of education. For years, the unions had been calling strikes just when the companies wanted them to, when supplies were stockpiled and the market was crowded. Without economic advice, the unions were often just suckers."

Through the 1950s, *Cité Libre* increased in stature, if not in practical wisdom. Those who appeared regularly in its pages automatically cut themselves off from the political Establishment, and in those days the political Establishment reached everywhere. Trudeau's experience is as good an example of this phenomenon as anybody's. Four times during the Union Nationale years he was offered a job by the faculty of social sciences at l'Université de Montréal. Four times he accepted and four times the offer was retracted. Why he was not hired during this period, in spite of his obvious qualifications, was never clearly stated to him, but the inferences are obvious.

Then, in the autumn of 1959, Maurice Duplessis died and Paul Sauvé ascended to power, bringing with him a clean breath of reform to the Union Nationale. But on January 2, 1960, Sauvé died and the UN seemed on the brink of a return to a Duplessis-type regime. The Liberals, realizing there was no route to power through orthodoxy, moved to outflank the UN on the left. In so doing, they attracted such small-L liberals as René Lévesque, now minister of resources. (They were, apparently, prepared to move even farther to the left: Pelletier, and a couple of others as far left were also offered a chance to run. Trudeau was not, perhaps because he had independent means. Unlike, for instance, Lévesque, who has been growing noticeably restless under the pressures of Liberals seeking to return to the old ways, Trudeau could bolt any job the party could offer him at no risk to his livelihood.)

After the defeat of the Union Nationale on June 22 the theories of Trudeau's *manifeste démocratique* seemed borne out: the old regime was toppled by a single force. Is the "democratic revolution" under way? "Of course," Trudeau said not long ago. "As one example, this province is obviously on its way to developing one of the best educational systems on the continent, if not the best. But the margin of victory was very narrow. We still do not know if democracy is firmly planted here. And think how much faster this revolution—for it is a revolution—would have gone, if there were more people like Lévesque in power, if all the forces of democracy were represented in the government now."

Pierre Elliott Trudeau was prime minister of Canada from 1968 to 1979, and from 1980 to 1984. He died in his Montreal home on Sept. 28, 2000, at the age of 80.

Peter Gzowski, one of Canada's foremost broadcasters and writers, was the magazine's Quebec editor when he wrote this piece. He was managing editor from 1962 to 1964 and editor for nine months in 1969.

John Diefenbaker: His Powerful Gifts and Glaring Flaws

John Diefenbaker in Ottawa, 1958

By Peter C. Newman

MARCH 23, 1963. The political convulsions of the last few weeks—the embittered cabinet resignations, the attempted *coup d'état*, the sudden fall of Parliament, the calling of an election which few voters really wanted, and the rowdy campaign that has followed—all these events have left many Canadians disturbed and baffled. At the centre of their perplexity are two particularly puzzling questions:

Is John Diefenbaker the villain or the victim of this debacle?

And if he's the villain, how did he manage to get himself—and *us*—into such a mess?

To people who've seen Diefenbaker only as a platform campaigner or a television performer, the two roles in which he's supremely effective, the vilification to which he has been subjected in the past two months is particularly bewildering, because it seems so sudden. But those who have observed the prime minister closely and have come to know him well realize that the torrent of accusations against him have not been prompted by an overnight transformation in his personality.

It's not John Diefenbaker who has changed; it is the times.

For most citizens it was the mix-up over Canada's acquisition of nuclear warheads that first revealed the extent of Diefenbaker's indecision. But ever since he took office it's been well known in Ottawa that he suffers from an almost morbid inability to make up his mind. (At one point in 1959, for example, 47 senior federal government appointments—all of them the prerogative of the prime minister—were vacant, simply because Diefenbaker couldn't decide among the suggested nominees.)

Although the resignations of Douglas Harkness, George Hees and Pierre Sévigny from Diefenbaker's cabinet early in February were the first intimation most Canadians had of dissension among his ministers, it has been common knowledge on Parliament Hill for years that his ministers exist in a state of undeclared revolt, kept in constant turmoil by Diefenbaker's threats to change their portfolios.

Much of the current confusion in government affairs has been blamed on the prime minister's lack of administrative skill. This is not a recently acquired failing. Diefenbaker took office at the age of 61, too late to erase the habits of a lifetime. His 20 years as a defence lawyer in the rough tomorrow country of northern Saskatchewan have indelibly coloured Diefenbaker's approach to all that he does. He came to the toughest job in the country without having worked for anybody else in his life; he had never hired or fired anyone and never administered anything more complicated than a walk-up law office.

Then too, it may be hard to understand how the country was allowed to get into such a state when it's well known that Canada's civil service is one of the most competent in the world. The explanation is that Diefenbaker has never fully trusted his civil service advisers. He knows that nearly all of them rose to positions of responsibility during the two decades of Liberal administration, and he regards everything in this world with a political bias.

Neither is Diefenbaker's current campaign against Bay Street really surprising. The sight of a Tory prime minister condemning Toronto financial interests is indeed a strange one in Canadian history. But then Diefenbaker has always been a maverick in his own party. When he was in opposition he shocked his fellow Conservatives by advocating that businessmen convicted of monopoly practices should be jailed, not just fined. His overriding consideration in power has been to ally his office and himself with the welfare of "the average Canadian." He is unalterably convinced that the identification of the Conservatives with big business (and therefore, at least by implication, against the little man) could hurl his party back into the political wilderness, where R. B. Bennett's associations with Bay and St. James streets pushed it for 22 years.

But the most puzzling question of all about John Diefenbaker's present behaviour is this: why, when the odds are so heavily stacked against him, does he insist on clinging to the prime ministership, thus risking not only his own humiliation but permanent damage to his party? The answer is buried deep in the complexities of his character and the experiences of a harsh lifetime in politics. Even now, no matter who or what goes against him, he adheres with scarcely diminished faith to an old belief that he is bound to win on April 8 because he is somehow *meant* to have power.

This assurance in everything he does—that some greater providence than personal ambition is guiding his career—is Diefenbaker's predominant characteristic. Unlike most Canadians in public service, he went into politics not by chance but by choice. It was a choice so stubbornly maintained that he was willing to spend 15 years in the desultory scuffle of unsuccessful electoral combat before gaining office of any kind, and a further 16 years as an impotent opposition backbencher before he finally captured the leadership of his party.

When, on Dec. 14, 1956, he strode down the centre aisle of Ottawa's Coliseum behind two pipers blowing "Cock o' the Walk," to be hailed as the new chief of the Conservative Party, Diefenbaker must have felt that his entire life had been ordained for this moment. And when, six months later, he was sworn in as the nation's 13th prime minister, it must have seemed that at long last his destiny had been fulfilled.

No politician in Canadian history ever rose so steadily through a succession of personal defeats. But Diefenbaker knew how to wait and he had a nose for power. Virtually alone in his confidence that he would eventually achieve his lifelong dream of becoming prime minister, Diefenbaker fought the 1957 campaign on metaphysical grounds, insisting that he had an "appointment with destiny." That spring of 1957 when the man from Prince Albert first soared into our collective awareness now seems curiously long ago. Watching Diefenbaker on the hustings today—saying essentially the same things in the same way he did then—it's not easy to remember just how he managed to win our loyalty. The man and his message were the same, but the circumstances were far different. In 1957, as voters prepared for Canada's 23rd general election, there was widespread uneasiness across the country. Sated with the easy materialism of the lush Fifties, many Canadians were groping for some deeper national purpose. John Diefenbaker successfully drew upon this widespread frustration to create a shared vision of a more vigorous and more noble future.

While Louis St. Laurent stumbled across the country reading his speeches like legal briefs that he had never seen before, Diefenbaker pummeled his audiences with highly evocative pledges of momentous (and quick) action on their behalf. ("We have a choice! A road to greatness in faith and dedication—or the road to nonfulfillment of Canada's destiny.") His strongest attacks were on the Liberals' shameful handling of the 1956 pipeline debate. He pledged that he would "restore Parliament to the people" by appointing a "permanent" speaker, abolishing the closure rule and reforming the Senate.

During the six years he's been in power he hasn't redeemed any of these promises, but in 1957 he seemed to mean what he said. The turning point in his campaign came as he entered the Georgia Street Auditorium in Vancouver on May 24. A surging crowd of 3,000 gave him the loudest ovation of his career. Another 2,000 supporters milled around outside, sitting on curbs, car fenders and tree branches, listening over outdoor loud-speakers. In the awed tones of a prophet witnessing a miracle, Diefenbaker declared: "It is a deep inspiration for me to see this vast audience. This is the kind of thing that gives me the strength to continue to work on behalf of the average men and women of this country. From the bottom of my heart I thank you. I won't let you down."

In the fall of 1958, however, the political atmosphere began to change. Unemployment statistics for November showed a walloping 22 per cent jump in the number of jobless Canadians since the same month of 1957; the cost of living was rising sharply; the Unemployment Insurance Fund was doling out funds at such a rate that it hovered near bankruptcy; members of the RCMP and the armed forces were restless because their pay increase requests had been flatly rejected. At the Six Nations Reserve near Brantford, Ont., the Iroquois Indians invited television crews in to record their revolt against federal authority and a delegation of 1,000 western farmers was being marshaled for a march on Ottawa to demand $300 million in deficiency payments.

Much of this growing disenchantment with Diefenbaker was due to the impression he had fostered in two election campaigns that there would be jobs for all. "I'm an artist for Diefenbaker, I draw unemployment insurance," became a common unfunny quip in those areas of the country where the number of jobless was climbing to new post-Depression highs. Between 1950 and 1956, unemployment in Canada averaged 3.4 per cent; the average during the Diefenbaker years has been 6.4 per cent—nearly twice as high.

While much of this high unemployment was due to structural weaknesses in the economy, most economists agree that the Conservatives made an error in attempting to combat it by attacking its effects instead of its causes. According to many experts, one of the chief reasons for the sour job picture between October, 1958, and December, 1960, was former Bank of Canada Governor James Coyne's policy of tight money, which pushed interest rates to their highest levels in 40 years. At the same time, the Diefenbaker government was running huge budgetary deficits designed to generate economic expansion. The two policies tended to work against each other. Instead of trying to overrule the obstinate governor, the Diefenbaker government merely absolved itself of responsibility. "Under Canadian law," Donald Fleming, then minister of finance, told the Commons on April 27, 1959, "the federal government does not exercise control over the money supply." The carnage created by the manner Diefenbaker finally chose to remove Coyne in the summer of 1961—a phony charge that Coyne had tried to raise his own pension payment—probably was the turning point for the prime minister.

Investors outside our borders saw the Coyne affair as evidence that Canada's national affairs were no longer being properly managed, and began the slow withdrawal of money from this country which culminated in the currency crisis of June, 1962. At home the business community interpreted the government's attitude as final proof that Diefenbaker was not a man who could be trusted. Most important of all, Diefenbaker's incredibly inept political handling of

Coyne's firing instilled new hope in Pearson's dispirited Liberals. For the first time, John Diefenbaker and his immense parliamentary majority began to look vulnerable.

Diefenbaker seemed to treat the Commons with the impatience of a ringmaster not quite in control of his troupe. Baiting by the opposition—at which he himself had been such a master—seldom stirred him to bold, imaginative replies. It just aggravated him. His temper frayed often in the House, but never more noticeably than on May 25, 1959, when he overruled the speaker, Roland Michener, who was trying to make him sit down according to parliamentary rules. "Will you allow me to finish now!" Diefenbaker snapped at the speaker, and it was Michener who sat down.

As Diefenbaker's difficulties mounted, it became increasingly evident that he was hampered not by external forces but by the peculiarities of his own past. Everything he has done as prime minister has been profoundly influenced by the formative years of his life, spent pleading before impressionable juries in the dusty courtrooms of prairie towns. While his forensic talents were an asset on the hustings, they soon proved to be a liability in office.

The lifelong habits of a lone-wolf defence lawyer made it difficult for him to delegate authority—an essential of cabinet government. His intimates insist that throughout most of his regime he has regarded himself as a beleaguered figure, continually threatened by would-be successors. Cabinet ministers complain that the prime minister often leaves over for renewed debate subjects on which there has been more than ample discussion and even decision. "Instead of discussing 'what should we do next,' we'd spend most of our time arguing 'how do we get out of this one,'" a former Diefenbaker minister says now.

The trappings of Tory philosophy which had survived for nearly 100 years were swept away as the backwoods Baptist from Prince Alberta laid down his personal testament of what Canadian Conservatism meant to *him*. By picking Diefenbaker as their leader in 1956, the Conservatives committed themselves to an ideological and emotional upheaval. But the transfiguration Diefenbaker has brought about in his party is far more extreme than even his own supporters anticipated. He thinks of himself as the sacrosanct head of a people's government and distrusts most of the great power groupings in contemporary Canada.

Diefenbaker has tried in every one of his election campaigns—and in none harder than the one he's fighting now—to appeal over the heads of both his cabinet and his party directly to "the average Canadian." He sees himself as a genuine folk hero in direct, spiritual communion with this mythical "average Canadian." On Nov. 15, 1961, for instance, he participated in a realistic civil defence exercise which called for him and six ministers to huddle in the basement of his official residence, and go through the motions of invoking the War Measures Act. Since it was obvious that if the practise alert had been real the prime minister would have been killed, reporters asked him whether he really intended to remain at 24 Sussex Drive if war came. "This is one of those decisions not subject to change," was the reply. "I would not take any more precaution than is available to the average Canadian."

Despite his deep and genuine affection for his "fellow Canadians," the 1962 election campaign seemed to prove that Diefenbaker thought he understood the average people of this country better than he actually did. During his previous five years in power, he had managed to spread government spending into many constituencies and in his electioneering he took it for granted that the voters would repay him with their ballots. This left the impression with many voters that the prime minister no longer cared whether votes were bestowed on him with passion or indifference, just so long as they were bestowed.

This was a grave misjudgment of the national mood. In 1957 and 1958, Canada's citizens were full of optimism and eager for the kind of imaginative leadership Diefenbaker seemed to be promising. But in 1962, after five years of his administration, they were becoming disillusioned and frightened by the uncertainties of the future. On election day, last June 18, Diefenbaker lost 91 seats. [Diefenbaker emerged as head of a minority government with 116 out of 265 seats; the Liberal Opposition had 98.]

He found himself in office but not in power. For the first few weeks after the election he seemed in a state of uncomprehending shock. From that time until now, everything he's done has somehow gone wrong. In the fall he went to the London Commonwealth Prime Ministers' Conference in good faith, only to become the victim of bad press relations which made it appear in Canada as if he was completely out of step with all the other Commonwealth leaders. Then came the week of Oct. 22, when President Kennedy virtually declared World War III against Russian missile installations in Cuba. The United States requested the Canadian government to order an immediate military alert. Under Canada's NORAD agreement this would have included landing U.S. nuclear-equipped fighters on Canadian bases, allowing an unlimited number of U.S. bomber overflights, and bringing our own forces to something close to a wartime footing. The Conservative cabinet hesitated for the first vital 44 hours before complying, thus drastically enhancing its reputation for indecision. Finally, Liberal Leader Lester Pearson's defence policy declaration of last Jan. 12 brought out into the open the split on nuclear warheads within the Diefenbaker cabinet, which culminated in the resignations of three key ministers.

Now, as he moves into the last phase of the current election campaign, John Diefenbaker remains convinced that the political instincts which have carried him through his life are still holding true. He firmly believes that he will attract to his colours a majority of Canada's uncommitted voters. This is the real dimension of his task, since the 1962 election proved that his 1957 and 1958 victories failed to alter the fundamental political character of the country. There are still many more Grits than Tories. To win, the prime minister has to prevent the nation's electors from returning to the voting habits temporarily obliterated by his personal popularity in that triumphant campaign of 1958.

At the same time, of course, Diefenbaker must somehow retain Canada's traditional Conservative vote. Although he rescued Canadian Conservatism from two decades of decay—and no other man could have done it—under his leadership the party compromised many of its traditional principles without developing any new ones. After six years of Diefenbaker's stewardship, the ordinary Canadian Tory who used to believe that his party stood for individual responsibility, the British connection, national sovereignty and free enterprise, must wonder whether these ideals are not, in fact, in greater danger than they were during two decades of Liberal administration.

Although he has behind him a period of governing Canada with the most powerful administration its citizens have ever elected, Diefenbaker now stands almost as alone as he did more than two decades ago, when he first came out of the west. But John Diefenbaker has always felt that he stood alone. He fought his way into the party leadership by himself, tried to govern the country alone, and now he faces the climax of his life, still alone, and still fighting.

John Diefenbaker lost that 1963 election, winning just 95 seats. He also led the party during the 1965 election campaign, but failed to dislodge the Liberals. As a result, he was forced to call a leadership convention in 1967, which he lost to Robert Stanfield. Diefenbaker remained an MP, *dying in his Ottawa home on Aug. 19, 1979, at age 80.*

Peter C. Newman was Maclean's *Ottawa editor when he wrote this piece. He became the magazine's editor in 1971 and presided over* Maclean's *transformation into a weekly newsmagazine in 1978. Since stepping down in 1982, Newman has continued to write a* Maclean's *column as well as his best-selling books. He now lives in Vancouver.*

Lester B. Pearson's Puzzling Personality

Lester Pearson campaigning in Toronto, 1963 election

By Robert Fulford

APRIL 6, 1963. There is nothing about Canadian politics in this remarkable year that is more remarkable than the personality of the Liberal leader, Lester Bowles Pearson. At the age of 65, the time when most men escape into retirement, Pearson is once more asking the Canadian people to make him their prime minister. He has offered himself twice before—in 1958, when he was utterly rejected, and in 1962, when he was nearly accepted—and now he is again making his way across the country, telling everyone who will listen about the benefits a Liberal victory will bring on April 8. In this role Lester Pearson has grown familiar, but he is still a puzzling phenomenon. He is possibly the most misunderstood of all the modern Canadian political leaders.

Pearson attracts a wide-ranging collection of followers, all of whom exhibit a curious habit of assuming he shares their own views and then demanding that he live up to them. Pacifists and bomb-banners have for years believed that he is secretly their friend, even though he helped found NATO, the most powerful military alliance in history. Despite this, he was still in a position to say to me recently: "I've become a kind of symbol for a lot of the woolly ideas people have about peace and defence." He said it sadly, like a man who feels he is never really understood, and never will be.

It is not only bomb-banners who fasten on Pearson. Intellectuals tend to believe he's an intellectual, though his favourite reading is the sports page. Diplomats believe he's a diplomat, not a politician, though he has been a working politician for 15 years. The left wing of the Liberal party looks on him as an ally; so, strangely, does the right wing, or a large part of it.

For many people Pearson is a kind of mirror for their own ideals and anxieties, just as Mackenzie King sometimes was. For others, particularly for the young men he has drawn into the Liberal party, he is a symbol of Canadian excellence, of the first-class world status that many young Canadians want for their country. For young Liberal politicians he fills the role that Glenn Gould fills for musicians, or Bruce Kidd for athletes.

These strangely mixed followers, who might in some cases seem to be mutually exclusive, may all be attracted to Pearson by a single quality: in Ottawa, a city of obsessive talkers, Pearson is a good listener. He believes, with an almost religious conviction, that he should hear every possible opinion before making a decision. One result of this is that he's a very bad chairman: meetings chaired by Pearson tend to drone on endlessly. A happier result is that people who meet him privately tend to go away thinking that they, and they alone, have his ear. Even reporters who come to him with tough questions end up telling him about their own careers and throwing in their political opinions for good measure. The mirror-like quality of Pearson is itself a reflection of his mind. He almost completely lacks ideology, and he possesses nothing that could be called an obsession. His beliefs are eclectic, a compound of the best thoughts available.

In some ways Pearson is the most *unlikely* politician who ever seriously proposed himself for the office of prime minister. In private he displays a manner that is so stunningly casual and so unlike that of most politicians that it falls just short of being undignified. He has less self-importance than the average small-town alderman, and a good deal less than any other major figure in federal politics.

Though he now wants badly to be prime minister, he has never shown the usual signs of desperate ambition, possibly because power and influence have always in the past sought him out. His employer for two decades, the Department of External Affairs, steadily promoted him from junior foreign service officer to first secretary in

London, to assistant undersecretary, to minister counselor in Washington, to United States ambassador, to deputy minister. In 1948 he entered politics with ease, at the request of both Mackenzie King and Louis St. Laurent, and became minister of external affairs. By the time he was made Liberal leader, in January, 1958, he had already won international esteem and the Nobel Peace Prize which is as precious as anything the Canadian electorate could give him.

Pearson's public image, as opposed to his private manner, is the unconcealed despair of his friends and advisers. Ironically, the man Bruce Hutchison called "the first Canadian in history who has ever printed a clear image on the mind of the world" is still unable, after working at it for five years, to imprint a clear image of himself on the mind of Canada. Pearson allows the young men around him to advise him on what kind of necktie to wear, how to talk, and how to appeal to French Canadians, but no one has ever discovered how he might convey to the voters the warmth and good humour that his associates experience in his presence.

A researcher for the Liberal party told me: "if Pearson could sit down and talk privately with every voter in the country for five or 10 minutes, we'd win in a landslide." After having spent a little time with him, I don't doubt it. But he can't. Instead he must reach the voters through TV and radio and public meetings, and in these media he is seriously handicapped. "There are some things in politics I don't like, never have liked, and never *will* like," he told me recently. "The hoopla, the circus part of it, all that sort of thing. It still makes me blush."

Chants of WE WANT MIKE appear to make him nervous, and he accepts fulsome praise without much grace. At moments like these his face plainly shows his attitude: he regrets that all this nonsense must be endured before he can get on with the real business of politics, which is government.

Pearson's attitude to crowds does not flow from any intellectual aversion to lowbrows. His high professionalism in his own field was proven decades ago, but he is not an intellectual in any of the usual meanings of that term. Like most specialists he reads a great deal in his field; like most politicians, he devours newspapers, from *Le Devoir* to the *Times* of London to the Toronto *Globe and Mail*. But his reading for pleasure consists usually of books by writers like Agatha Christie and Ian Fleming; his private concerns are not those of an intellectual. "To my wife's disgust," he told me, "I am also an undiscriminating TV viewer." He likes baseball games, hockey games, and Wayne and Shuster, but he'll happily take *Ben Casey* or *Dr. Kildare* and he has a special affection for Marshal Dillon, of *Gunsmoke.*

The political attitudes Pearson carries into this campaign, and will carry into office if he is elected, began to develop between October, 1956, and March, 1958, the most crucial period of his life so far. In those 18 months, Pearson experienced the best and the worst moments of his career.

At the United Nations, in the fall of 1956, Pearson was given the chance to fulfill himself in a way that no other Canadian and few other diplomats ever have. When the armed forces of Britain and France entered the war between Israel and Egypt, they split the Western alliance down the middle, brought the Commonwealth to the worst crisis it had ever endured, and came close to causing a world war. Pearson, as external affairs minister, went to the UN, took charge of the Canadian delegation, and began putting to work all the skills he had carefully developed over 28 years as a diplomat. Pearson did not make peace all by himself; what he did was, first, work hard and successfully to develop formulas which would bring together the countries which Suez had split apart, and, second, press for a UN emergency force to keep peace on the Gaza Strip.

The prestige he had built carefully for himself and Canada proved strong enough to accomplish this much. His efforts didn't heal the wounds of Suez—there is bitterness yet, in Britain and elsewhere— but today there is still a kind of peace between Israel and Egypt, and a kind of unity among the Western nations. For those two accomplishments, Pearson will always receive much of the credit.

In the election of the following June, the Liberal government fell and John Diefenbaker assumed power. The following winter, in the space of six weeks, these things happened to Pearson: on Dec. 10, 1957, in Oslo, he received the Nobel Peace Prize and heard himself praised for "his personal qualities, his powerful initiative, strength and perseverance"; on Jan. 16, 1958, in Ottawa, he was easily elected leader of the Liberal party; on Jan. 20, 1958, in the House of Commons, he received the most abrupt and humiliating defeat any new party leader ever had to endure. "No one ever started off worse than I did," he has since acknowledged.

Before he went into the House that day, to take his new place as leader, he was persuaded—mostly by Jack Pickersgill, but also by [former prime minister] St. Laurent and C. D. Howe—to move a motion of nonconfidence in the government. At this point the worst thing that could happen to the Liberals was an election. The 1957 defeat had all but destroyed the party's spirit; even among those Liberals who had held their seats, a good many were then deciding not to run again. The party had no money, and no new candidates, and no argument to take to the voters.

One friend who saw Pearson both during the Suez crisis and just after the disaster in the House of Commons says now: "He was an entirely different man. There he was in 1956, dealing with all these terrible problems at the UN, working 18 or 20 hours a day, his eyes looking like red circles, and he was *happy!* He was doing what he knew how to do. But when I saw him after Diefenbaker tore a strip off him in the House, he was miserable. His confidence was shattered." Pearson was miserable not because of anything Diefenbaker had said but because he himself had performed badly; he was a professional who had blundered into a world in which he was an amateur.

Twelve days later Diefenbaker dissolved Parliament and called an election. Without experienced advisers or much help from St. Laurent, Pearson ran a makeshift campaign. The Conservatives won 208 seats, the Liberals 48, and Lester Pearson settled down to learn how to be an effective leader of Her Majesty's Loyal Opposition.

During his first year or two in office, Pearson often seemed curiously apathetic. The rumours of his impending retirement which cropped up frequently were never true, but they were seldom groundless. Some of them followed private conversations in which Pearson made no secret of how weary he was, and how stale and flat his new job seemed to him. He hung on, his friends suggest, mainly because he couldn't stand the idea of Paul Martin taking over the party. This period in his life ended when several of the party's backers demanded that he either stop talking about his dissatisfaction or quit the job. He agreed to stay, but only when it was promised that he would get enough money to make the party solvent. Then he stopped talking about his unhappiness.

Ever since then, the Ottawa press corps has made a habit of describing new, improved versions of Pearson: there must now be few correspondents who have not at one time or another announced to their readers that Lester Pearson has made a new man of himself. Beyond question, Pearson's public style has changed. Most of the change is in his manner in the House of Commons: he has grown steadily more confident. By the summer of 1961, when the government bungled the firing of James Coyne, the Bank of Canada governor, Pearson was ready to exploit every advantage. "He handled that beautifully," a reporter who watched the incident told me recently. "He was completely in charge of his own party, and he was sure of just what he wanted to do—make the government look very bad— and he did it." By the following winter, Pearson was close to being Diefenbaker's equal in the cut-and-thrust of Parliamentary debate. On Jan. 23, 1962, when Diefenbaker tried to interrupt him, Pearson brushed him off with a contemptuous "Sit down, Mr. Prime Minister, sit down," and a few seconds later: "Be calm, sir." He had come a long way since January, 1958.

For his part, Pearson is not conscious of any major change in his personality. "I'm only sure my *awareness* of these jobs has changed. At the start I was uncomfortable in the House—I hadn't been subjected to much rough and tumble before. I had to become more aware of the political side of the job."

Pearson's loyalty to the party men around him, and his willingness to listen to them, has had the curious effect of making some of his lieutenants feel, to their great personal satisfaction, that they have made Pearson what he is. At times this feeling is reflected in a tone almost of condescension in the conversation of the men who help write his speeches (he writes many of them himself, and edits all of them), run the party organization, and generally push Pearson towards the office of prime minister. "So I told him to wear the bow tie if he feels like it, or not wear the bow tie he doesn't feel like it," one of his advisers said recently. "He's improved a lot on television, he was pretty bad before. His lisp is still there, but it's improved. His voice isn't so high-pitched any more. We don't want to *change* him, really, just merchandise him."

They talk, sometimes, as if Pearson were the creation of his assistants. It is true that he's had professional speech lessons, that he has sat down with advertising men and heard his TV manner criticized as if he were reading soap commercials, and that sibilants which will bring out his lisp are carefully pruned from his speeches. But these are marginal changes: the qualities that will win or lose this election for him are qualities he has possessed for years; they owe nothing to the professional image-builders. Far from their having created him, Pearson has carefully and coolly made *them* what they are. They all exist in national politics because Pearson decided they should.

Walter Gordon, who would be minister of finance in a Pearson government, is an old friend whom Pearson elevated to a high level in the party. Tom Kent was a business executive and former newspaperman whom Pearson chose as policy adviser and speechwriter. Keith Davey, the national Liberal organizer, was the advertising manager of a Toronto radio station when Pearson chose him. Richard O'Hagan, Pearson's executive assistant, was a public relations man to a Toronto advertising agency. These people, and a good many others, were brought out of private life and into full-time politics because Pearson thought they would be useful to him and to the party. They all seem to fit a pattern of organization Pearson carries in his head; certainly he manipulates them more than they manipulate him.

From the pure politician's point of view, Pearson still retains a nasty habit of seeing more than one side of an argument. Just how little the years in politics have fundamentally changed him was demonstrated by a luncheon meeting he had a year ago with Red Kelly, the hockey player. The party leaders, including Pearson, had decided that among their candidates they needed some celebrities, and Kelly looked like a possibility. Several prominent Liberals had spoken to Kelly about running for Parliament, and now Davey and Pearson met him for lunch at the Park Plaza Hotel in Toronto. After some conversation about hockey the candidacy was mentioned. Kelly said that though the idea was attractive, he didn't really believe he could comfortably combine hockey and a seat in Parliament. To Davey's astonishment, Pearson agreed it *would* be too much for one man. The meeting broke up on that note, and it took a lot of talking to get Kelly interested again.

But the inability to put his political impulses ahead of all his other impulses—the inability, in fact, to *have* political impulses—has not prevented Pearson from becoming in some ways an expert politician. The unity of the Liberal party as it went into the 1962 election was in itself a tribute to the skill Pearson brought to the leadership. "It is easy enough," Jack Pickersgill told me, "for a party leader who is also prime minister to hold a party together—or it should be. He has all those loaves and fishes to distribute to the faithful. But Mr. Pearson has held this party firmly behind him, *out* of office." There has not been a serious dump-Pearson campaign since 1958, and no campaign against him or his policies has gained any momentum.

Recently I asked Pickersgill how he would compare Pearson with the two prime ministers Pickersgill worked for, St. Laurent and King. "In the way he reaches his political decisions," Pickersgill said, "he grows more like King every day."

He explained that St. Laurent, with his sharp lawyer's mind, made a decision by removing the human element from it and working it out like an algebraic equation. Then he tried to make it fit political reality. Neither King nor Pearson has exhibited such a sharp mind. King listened to all political viewpoints first and then produced something like a consensus. Pearson does the same.

The comparison, I understand, does not delight Pearson—in foreign affairs King was much too timid for Pearson's taste, and Pearson has written without much affection about the isolationist policies Canada pursued under King in the 1930s. But the comparison serves as an accurate description of the kind of domestic politician Pearson has become.

It has been obvious for a long time that Pearson will never be either a radical social reformer or an emotional spellbinder. He will never possess the magnetism of a Roosevelt or a Kennedy—or a Diefenbaker. In a curious, shy way, he would probably dislike himself if he ever succeeded in becoming that kind of politician. But five years ago he took over a Liberal party which had almost died of obesity, under leaders who were supposed to be first-class politicians. Today, he stands at the head of a party which is rich, lean, eager, and ready for power. He achieved this not only with charm and intelligence but also by learning, slowly and painfully, the difficult, necessary art of the professional politician.

Lester B. Pearson went on to win the 1963 election, albeit a minority with 128 out of 265 seats. He narrowly failed to get a majority again in 1965 with 131 seats and resigned as prime minister in 1968, when he was replaced by Pierre Elliott Trudeau. Pearson died on Dec. 27, 1972, at age 75.

Robert Fulford was a columnist and articles editor at Maclean's *from 1962 to 1964. The widely respected Toronto critic and author edited* Saturday Night *from 1968 to 1987.*

John Turner: The Once and Future Contender

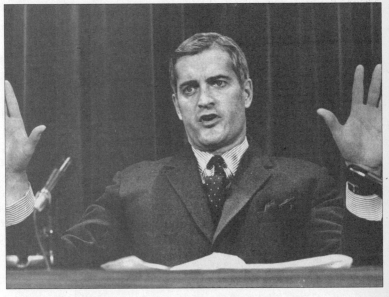

John Turner as justice minister, Ottawa, 1970

By Christina Newman

MAY, 1971. For dedicated politician watchers—those of us who are fervid voyeurs at the keyholes of power—probably the most fascinating aspect of Pierre Trudeau's method of governing Canada is the very nearly total control he exercises over the Liberal Party.

One clear measure of that control is a catalogue of what's happened to the men who only three years ago last month were Trudeau's opponents in the race for the Liberal leadership: Robert Winters is dead, having given up politics forever on the day that he was beaten; Paul Hellyer is a mute backbencher whose resignation as deputy prime minister met scarcely a shrug of concern; Eric Kierans, Joe Greene and Allan MacEachen are quiescent privy councillors, part of that faceless pack who thump their desks when the leader raises his hand; and Paul Martin has disappeared, grey-haired, into the somnolent hush of the Senate.

In fact, of the seven vanquished contenders who stood shouting hoarsely behind Trudeau on the platform that night when he was anointed in 1968, only one is still hoarse, still shouting—and still a man to be reckoned with on his own rather than on Trudeau's terms.

He's John Napier Turner, the minister of justice and attorney general of Canada, certainly the most personable and probably the most visible of the Trudeau cabinet ministers. Through a combination of furious activity and cautious moxie, Turner has managed, in the years since his defeat at the convention, to obliterate his old image as a pretty-boy celebrity—the sexiest thing on the squash courts, the handsomest man at the ball—by turning his traditionally soft portfolio into a place to take a tough stand. When he went into Justice in the summer of 1968, Turner was determined to function not as the government's legal counsel but as a zealous and genuine reformer of the law. To the astonishment of those who used to say he was nothing but a lightweight, he has already proven so successful at this task that within the legal profession, among men of all political persuasions, he's being called the best minister of justice since Confederation.

For a start, he has revamped the old pork-barrel system of appointing judges by insisting that all the men he elevates to the bench be the best qualified lawyers available; he has set up a complicated system for reforming and reviewing the law on a continuing basis, and attracted to this task a number of impressive legal experts whom he calls "young tigers, guys between 25 and 35, who are old enough to have made their mark and young enough to still have juice." He has already steered through the House, or has ready for introduction, several solidly progressive bills—on such contentious issues as bail and arrest, expropriation, wiretapping, no-record convictions, legal aid—the main thrust of which is to balance citizens' rights against those of the state. In his frequent public speeches, he is given to quoting such remarks as Oliver Goldsmith's "Laws grind the poor, and rich men rule the law" and to pledging, by implication, anyway, that he, John Turner, young tiger, is out to redress this ancient inequity.

Turner's critics—and it's perhaps a mark of his political importance that he has so many—are saying that his new liberal-reformer stance is just another phase in a long drive to become prime minister. "I tell you," an Ottawa Liberal told me recently, "this guy has been programmed to be PM since he was 12. If he figures the smart politics of the moment calls for a reformer, then a reformer is what he'll be. I once said to him that people would like him better if he'd only be more spontaneous and he looked through me with those blazing baby-blues and I got the feeling he was going to punch out 'Be More Spontaneous' on a piece of cardboard and feed it into a slot in his gorgeous middle."

The justice minister responds to questions about his long-term future with a careful "I intend to stay in politics as long as it's challenging because when it's challenging, it's interesting" and the astute among his advisers point out that in the Trudeau-dominated Liberal Party, the whole contender question is irrelevant. Jerry Grafstein, a Toronto lawyer who used to be Turner's executive assistant, responds to it testily with, "Look, if you say after Trudeau it will be Turner, what does this mean? Trudeau has everything as prime minister—power, privacy, accessibility to the greatest minds in the world. Why would he want to give it up? And when he does give it up, the whole game could be different. Turner might then be a rich old man in a boardroom, for all we know."

Still, in the past few months in Ottawa—during the winter of the War Measures Act and the Montreal Five, the bilingual obscenities and the seasonally adjusted unemployment—when it began to look as though Trudeau might have human failings after all, there was a good deal of not-so-idle talk about alternatives, more flexible approaches, different men with different ideas. In these conversations, Turner's name and Turner's ambitions came up more frequently than anyone else's.

This fascination with Turner and his prospects has been evident ever since he took time out from his Montreal law practice to enter active politics as the "dreamboat candidate" in the general election of 1962. At the time he was described jealously by his political foes as "the young pol every old pol would like to be"—the man who had everything. And still has. Superb good looks. Money. Youth. An impressive scholastic record. The Canadian championship in the 100-yard dash. Vast political experience. A rich and pretty wife. Handsome children. Fluent French.

Turner's childhood was privileged, though not exactly in the way that the mythmakers would have it. His mother was a graduate of Bryn Mawr, an important government economist and a familiar of the Ottawa Establishment in the Thirties and Forties. But she was also a miner's daughter and a widow, bringing up two young children on a civil servant's salary. (Turner's father, an English journalist who wrote for *Punch*, died in 1931.)

"What my mother was able to give me," he says, "was a good education (at St. Patrick's College and Ashbury College, an Ottawa private school) and a real sense of the excitement of public service." When Turner was a preadolescent during the war, he used to wake up in bed at midnight and hear men like C. D. Howe, Robert Fowler and Donald Gordon arguing economic policy in the living room and sometimes, when he was out walking his dog in the twilight, he would be joined by Mackenzie King ("No guff! In the flesh!").

His mother was a formidably intelligent and ambitious woman. ("Sort of early Women's Lib," says Turner zestily. "You dig?") She demanded excellence of her son and excellence is what she got. By the time she remarried in 1945 and moved on to become a powerful figure in B.C. society as the wife of the Vancouver industrialist Frank Ross, Turner was 16 and ready to enter university. He spent four febrile years at UBC as a frat man, track and field star, sportswriter, jive-talking hep cat ("Hey there, snappy pair of kicks, who ya featurin' tonight?") and student in political science. When he won a Rhodes scholarship in 1949, the student newspaper sent him warmly on his way with an editorial that said he'd been "the most popular student on the campus."

From Oxford, Turner went on to the Sorbonne in Paris, where he became fluent in French and then came back to Canada to practise law in Montreal. For most of the next decade, he was the very model of a socially acceptable bachelor, taking out the prettiest girls, working for the okay cultural and charitable causes, belonging to the Junior Bar and getting himself into the headlines in 1958 as the man who danced with Princess Margaret at a ball given in her honour by his stepfather, who was then lieutenant-governor of British Columbia. For the next 18 months, British and Canadian papers tried hard to turn this into a hot romance, reporting that Margaret had "summoned Turner to her table" at later parties on her Canadian tour, that he was "a secret caller at Clarence House" and even that he was the subject of "formal discussions with the Queen."

He *was* the only non-official Canadian guest invited to her wedding in 1960 and the whole dancing episode, which Turner remembers as "a lotta fun," gave him an extra gloss when he went to Liberal gatherings in Kingston, Ont., later that year and in Ottawa in 1961. Shortly afterwards, he was persuaded to stand as a candidate in the

Montreal St. Lawrence–St. George riding "during one long lunch at the Reform Club" as John Payne, a Montreal public relations consultant and Turner adviser, remembers it. In the 1962 campaign, he took the seat away from the incumbent Conservative, Egan Chambers, in a blur of campus debates, apartment blitzes, stylish liberalism, pretty girls, outdoor marquees, floating blimps and vigour. And then John Turner went to Ottawa and encountered the hard realities. He found out that while the voters might be dazzled by him, the professional pols were not, that the energetic attitudes that had been endearing in a vital young Montreal lawyer were called "pushy" in parliamentary circles and that in the grey corridors and back rooms of the capital all that glitters is suspect.

"I served a rough apprenticeship under Mr. Pearson," Turner says. "He had this sort of avuncular attitude toward me. He'd known me since I was five and felt I was too impatient, that I needed to understand the administrative process, to be in what he called 'the kitchen of government' for a while." So Turner served time as a backbencher, a parliamentary secretary, a minister without portfolio with "special responsibilities" to the quintessential Old Grit, Jack Pickersgill, and finally as a full-fledged minister in the unrewarding new portfolio of Consumer and Corporate Affairs. "If Turner had been nothing more than the glamour boy that the backbiters said he was, he would have buckled in those years," says Sen. Keith Davey. "But he didn't buckle. He learned. And what he learned is what he knows so well now—how to be a politician, how to be a winner, how to roll and punch and roll again."

And, it might be added, how to build a power base within a political party, although this lesson didn't sink in until Turner had endured the final stage in his apprenticeship, as a losing contender in the leadership race of 1968. "That convention was the last glimpse anybody will ever get of the young John Turner," says John Payne. "It was a kind of crucible for him. He saw how deals were made, how power is traded. He never looked better than when he was making his policy speech on the night before the voting and yet he knew he couldn't win. It was a toughening experience."

It was also an experience that created a certain coolness between Turner and Trudeau, although no one in either man's camp will admit to this. But it was Turner who lost the most when Trudeau decided to run for the leadership a month after Turner himself had declared. He lost his appeal as the youth candidate: he lost support he'd counted on in Quebec; and he lost his hard-won toehold in the old Liberal Establishment, to which he belonged despite its supposedly stern treatment of him. What he gained was a reputation as a fighter and a certain grudging respect from the Trudeau-ites when, refusing to release his delegates, he hung on thin-lipped until the last ballot, which saw Pierre Trudeau win, Robert Winters come second and John Turner come third. After the voting, Turner was heard to remark to a supporter that he just couldn't figure out "what the hell this guy's got on the ball," and then he shut up, as all good Liberals must, and came to the aid of the winner.

His method seems to be to work feverishly on all fronts at once covering all contingencies, plugging all loopholes, cultivating all comers and never, ever getting into trouble. ("In nine years in federal politics," says Brian Mulroney, a young Montreal Tory, in wonderment, "he's never made a mistake that anybody can pin on him.")

When he wants to introduce a piece of legislation, for example, he starts first with the caucus of his own party, craftily canvassing everyone to find out if they have any objections to his plans. Then he talks to the Opposition to find out what they might find offensive in his draft. He has become so adept at behind-the-curtain negotiating that when a Turner bill is before the House, the Opposition customarily give him full co-operation, sometimes even curtailing their speaking time for his convenience, a situation that has played an important part in the fact that Turner has been responsible for more major legislation than any other minister in the Trudeau regime. He also maintains, oddly enough, a warm friendship with John Diefenbaker, who makes a point of being in his seat when Turner is up and who is given to saying moistly, "Young man, you'll be prime minister, one day, you mark my words," and to talking about the fact that they are, both of them, "Commons men to the core."

Outside the House, Turner prides himself on paying attention to the old-fashioned courtesies, making sure he informs the appropriate chief justice before announcing a judicial appointment, sending congratulatory messages to the chairmen of government inquiries, and explanatory letters to anyone who takes public issue with his stands. He talks regularly with people across the country, phoning around in the early morning to seek advice from such supporters as John Payne in Montreal, Jerry Grafstein, Irwin Cotler, Dave Smith in Toronto and Lloyd Axworthy in Winnipeg. He has kept in close touch with what he calls the One-Nine-Five Club, the 195 voting delegates to the 1968 leadership convention who stayed with him on the last ballot. ("Think of it," says Turner, with fresh amazement, "the loyalty of those guys! They stuck with me even though they knew there was no way I could win.")

He's even painstaking in attending to the affairs of his current riding, Ottawa-Carleton, which has been safely Liberal since 1881, handling hundreds of complaints from federal civil servants who live in the constituency, fixing up appointments, attending association meetings. The seat was opened up for him in 1968 after Turner had lost his Montreal riding in the redistribution process. Turner's detractors say hopefully that taking on this riding may have been a mistake since it can't be used as a regional power base as a B.C. constituency might have.

Turner's chief reason for running in Carleton seems to have been that he himself lives there in a Rockcliffe house that's filled with solid antiques, pale chintzes, polished silver, an English nanny, three children between three and seven and his very attractive blond wife, the daughter of David Kilgour, until recently president of Great-West Life. Turner met Geills Kilgour, a graduate of the Harvard Business School, when she worked on his first campaign. He married her the next year in a big peau-de-soie-and-Alençon-lace wedding in Winnipeg, where she went to private schools and her family still lives. Mrs. Turner is a rare woman in political circles; she says what she thinks, she attends every possible function that she can squeeze in; she knows in exquisite detail House rules, party policies and political manoeuvring, and she refuses to let anybody make political hay, or press pictures, out of the Turner children or their personal lives. For his part, her husband keeps his weekends free so he can be at home most Saturdays and Sundays, scheduling his frequent speeches to student groups, bar associations and chambers of commerce so they don't conflict with family plans.

The charge that his initiatives, however admirable, are made with self-aggrandizement resolutely in mind, is one that's made constantly about Turner. His supporters find it hardly worth refuting ("What the hell," says one of them, "John's so good a lot of little guys are bound to snipe.") and claim it's irrelevant in any case. What is relevant, they sensibly point out, is that Turner has come a long way in his stated ambition to make the Canadian legal system among the most contemporary, flexible, compassionate and easily enforceable in the world.

One senior civil servant who came into close contact with Turner for the first time last fall says, "I went to talk to him rather skeptical, imbued with the sour attitude that most public servants who don't know him have—that he's just too much, too good to be true. After a couple of hours, I found myself first liking him and then wanting to defend him, to tell people that he really believes what he does. Partly it came out of a feeling I got that inside him there still lurks an anxious boy, trying desperately to please a lot of demanding, accomplished adults. I suspect that this anxiety will only be stilled when he makes it to the prime minister's office."

Will he make it? "Well," answered the mandarin inscrutably, "Disraeli used to say that the secret of success in politics is constancy of purpose." Or in a phrase that Turner himself might turn: dig you later in the East Block, baby.

John Turner made it to the prime minister's office in 1984, defeating Jean Chrétien in a leadership race following the resignation of Pierre Elliott Trudeau. But Turner was prime minister for only 79 days, losing a general election to Brian Mulroney later that year. Turner, now a Bay Street lawyer, fought Mulroney unsuccessfully again in the 1988 election and resigned as Liberal leader in 1989.

Christina Newman was an associate editor at Maclean's *from 1971 to 1974. She was nominated for a Governor General's award for* Grits, *her 1983 study of the Liberal party and won the prize in 1990 for* Trudeau and Our Times, *co-written with her husband, Stephen Clarkson.*

Jean Chrétien: Mister No

Jean Chrétien in his Ottawa office, 1976

By Glen Allen

MAY 3, 1976. Jean Chrétien, president of the Treasury Board, stern keeper of the nation's purse, permitted himself a chuckle. He had just settled the hash of Richard Malone, publisher of the Toronto *Globe and Mail*. Brigadier General Malone, a conservative and the very pasha of Canadian journalism, had delivered a speech to the Canadian Club, a magnificent tirade against government spending. He said it was time to halt the rot in Ottawa. On Feb. 24, the *Globe* reprinted the speech under the heading, "A case of tragic misman-agement." Though his name was not even mentioned, Chrétien ordered his staff to ready a reply: Malone's volley would not go unanswered. Chrétien's long, dry, point-by-point defence of Liberal financial policies was sent to the *Globe* on March 11. Weeks went by and nothing happened, so a copy of the letter was sent to Claude Ryan's *Le Devoir* in Montreal. Ryan, no friend of the *Globe* these days, printed all but a few sentences of it. His headline blared across the full width of a page: "A letter the *Globe and Mail* delays publish-ing." The very next morning the minister's letter was in the *Globe and Mail* and Chrétien—the fastest gun in the East—had won another round. It is becoming a habit.

Jean Chrétien came to Ottawa 13 years ago, before French Power was ever heard of, before Pierre Trudeau, before Jean Marchand—and he will probably be there long after they are gone. He is a survivor. He has survived political pestilence: in the early Sixties the Liberal benches were rampant with scandal, and nearly everyone in trouble had a French name. He survived his political mentor (Mitchell Sharp). He survived his looks (think of a tall Willie Pep). He survived his small-town Quebec background, one that put him in double jeopardy: an outsider to the Outremont–St. Foy Quebec Liberal establishment and, by definition, a figure of folklore, if not sheer fun, to many English Canadians. He survived six years as minister of Indian Affairs when there had been seven ministers in the seven years before him. Somehow, perhaps alone among francophone ministers, he has survived the bloodlust of the English mandarinate, who are almost embarrassingly fulsome in their appreciation. Says one of the dozen senior civil servants in the Treasury Board: "He's open, relaxed, fun, smart and easy to relate to." He seems to be surviving his current post, as president of the Treasury Board, which is only slightly less perilous than being solicitor general when the country wants to hang. And he came out whole after the dial-a-judge affair in March. One minister (André Ouellet) looked sneaky, another (Bud Drury) foolish and a third (Marc Lalonde) at the very least overzealous, but Chrétien—he was the man so jealous of his integrity he'd fight like a wolverine to protect it (both Judge Kenneth Mackay and the *Globe and Mail* retracted allegations that he had acted improperly).

Joseph-Jacques Jean Chrétien was born in January, 1934, in a community on the outskirts of Shawinigan, then called Belgoville (for the Belgian who built both the town and the pulp mill below it). Chrétien was born a Liberal. His father, Wellie, a mill machinist, was a Liberal. His grandfather was a Liberal. Chrétien's Liberalism is so distinguished it carries the imprimatur of Maurice Duplessis's scorn. "I was just a kid when I met Duplessis, and he said to me: 'Aren't you the grandson of François Chrétien?' I said I was, and Duplessis said, 'Well you're a goddam Liberal' (*Christ de rouge*)." Chrétien says he first got thinking about politics when he was 16, though a brother, Guy, now a Shawinigan pharmacist, remembers Jean at 14 locked in loud debate in the town poolroom with Duplessis supporters two and three times his age. As a student at the seminary in Three Rivers, he was strong in the sciences and weak in deportment. "I got thrown out four times," says Chrétien. "My father told me there had to be a black sheep in every family and I was it." But he remained a good Liberal. When he was 18 he was squiring his 16-year-old wife-to-be, Aline Chainé, to Liberal meetings, and at 22 he was a chief Liberal organizer in the 1956 provincial election. After Laval (president of the Liberal student group, national vice-president of the Liberal university graduates), he and three other lawyers founded a law firm in Shawinigan. Their offices were above the new Steinberg's store, the grandest building in town, and Chrétien says he did well.

But law was just one more entrée to politics. The only question was, "Shall I go provincial or federal?" The provincial legislature seemed more inviting. Jean Lesage was building his "Quiet Revolution," and Chrétien's townsmen felt much closer to Quebec City than to Ottawa. Besides, he spoke about four words of English (a friend says they were "Hello," "Goodbye," "Yes," and one that was to become important in his lexicon. "No"). But federal politics won. "You remember Marcel Chaput? He had been kicked out of the federal civil service for expressing his views. There was a lot of emotion over that," explains Chrétien, especially in a town like Shawinigan, where at one time every plant manager, indeed anyone with any money, was English. "I didn't agree with Chaput's views, but I found myself on his side, and I was mad. But at one point one of my friends who had spent some time in English Canada told me: 'You talk about the Anglos like that, and you don't know a thing about them.' He was saying I was narrow-minded. I thought about it again that afternoon when I was driving back from Trois Rivières in my car, and he was right." Ottawa it was.

Chrétien got the Liberal nomination in St. Maurice–Laflèche in 1963, and wrestled the seat from the Créditiste who just the year before had won by 9,000 votes. In Ottawa he found himself sitting off in a back corner with some other MPs as young and callow as himself: Gerry Regan (now premier of Nova Scotia), Ron Basford (now justice minister) and Rick Cashin of Newfoundland. At his first caucus meeting Chrétien was handed a questionnaire. The prime minister was asking all backbenchers what their interests were. Chrétien put down "finance." He didn't know a thing about finance, traditionally an English field, just as ministries like Public Works and the Post Office were French. But he was the only one to claim such an interest ("I thought at least I'd learn something"), and Pearson promptly put him on the banking committee.

In 1964, there was a provincial by-election in his riding, and René Lévesque, then the Lesage government minister in charge of finding candidates for the Quebec Liberal Party, met with Chrétien. He asked him to give up his Ottawa seat and, according to Chrétien, said there wouldn't even be a central government in five years. (Lévesque, now president of the Parti Québécois, says Chrétien is "screwy" if that is what he remembers.) "For a minister of a federalist Liberal Party to say that was intellectually dishonest," says Chrétien. Seventeen of his 19 organizers urged him to run provincially, but after meeting with Pearson he decided against it.

Chrétien was made Pearson's parliamentary secretary in 1965, and six months later he became parliamentary secretary to then minister of finance Mitchell Sharp. In 1967, the same day a Montreal professor named Pierre Trudeau was named minister of justice, Chrétien entered the cabinet as a minister without portfolio. Eight months later he was minister of national revenue, and then, in 1968, minister of Indian Affairs and Northern Development, where he was handed a ticking bomb. The department's administrators had been hard at work on a new policy for the Indians, one they called an "end to apartheid." But the Indians labeled it "cultural genocide" and, until it was finally abandoned, Chrétien was forced to defend it across the country. In 1974 he was named president of the Treasury, the central planning agency that regulates government spending.

All this time he scoured the country, making lively attacks on the English for their attitudes toward the French, on the French for their feelings toward the English, and once, in Inuvik, on "the Toronto-Montreal professional northerners." At election time he did his bit in other ministers' bailiwicks and tended his own garden.

The interview with Jean Chrétien goes badly. He seems distracted and somehow suspicious. Every now and then he lifts an eyebrow in the direction of one or two executive assistants sitting in, as if to ask how long it is going to go on. And he would rather speak English than French to the English reporter. He says all that is wrong with his English is that he puts the accent on the wrong syllable (putting the accent on the wrong syllable of "syllable"). It's true, his English has improved—NDP House leader Stanley Knowles calls him "a sharp debater" in the language—but it's still bad. His French, on the other hand, is rich and colloquial, marked by a trace of that accent peculiar to the Mauricie district—a profusion of breathy h's and consonants dropping faster than the leaves in autumn. There's a chocolate rug on the floor of Chrétien's big first-floor Commons office. At one end sits a desk without a shred of paper on it, at the other a tweedy sofa and two chairs and a case full of Eskimo sculpture under glass. On one wall is a photograph of the side of Prime Minister Pierre Trudeau's head, signed "with cordiality" by the PM, and on another a stunning Eskimo tapestry. Some ministers spent $10,000 or $50,000 or even $100,000 on similar offices, but the decorators gave this one no more than a lick and a promise—these furnishings cost the taxpayer only $1,959. The only thing to look at, anyway, is Chrétien's face. It is endlessly interesting. The steep forehead almost overshoots the eyes, throwing them into shadow. The angles and contours of the complicated nose would defy a geometer. There's a slight lilt to the left side of the mouth—something, said a friend, that once bothered him enough to seek therapy for it. It is by far the most interesting face in the cabinet. The French would make a movie star of this face: this is not Willie Pep, after all, but Jean-Paul Belmondo.

Two days before, Chrétien had been in Welland, Ont., pushing bilingualism, and the next week he was off to Béziers, France, to speak to the 26th annual meeting of the France-Canada Association where, according to a dispatch from Agence-France-Presse, he told France to send more immigrants to Canada and gave away some Eskimo art. But now he has a few minutes, and talks first—a little wistfully—about his time in Indian Affairs, "my most productive years."

"There were all kinds of stories that the Indians of Canada were second-class citizens, that they were victims of legal discrimination. But I said, 'Okay, you don't like the Indian Act, then we'll scrap it.' My white paper was rejected, of course, but now if they have reserve land it's because they want it. If they have the Indian Act it's because they want it. It brought the thing out in the open." Chrétien calls it "my white paper" and, true enough, he had some hand in putting it together. But the Indians said that Chrétien was a puppet in the hands of his bureaucrats. "None of this was new with Chrétien," says Harold Cardinal, president of the Alberta Indian Association and one of the principal spokesmen for the Indians then. "He was a professional politician who did his work well. I don't think he ever knew what we were talking about. But at least he made life interesting."

Chrétien badly needed a motherhood issue in Indian Affairs, and he found it in national parks. In his six years as minister he increased the number of federal parks from 18 to 28, including, for the first time, two parks in Quebec, one just a long flip of a coin away from his home town. In the 35 years before Chrétien, Parks Canada had grown by only six parks. But that, too, is returning on Chrétien, who is still lobbying for a third park along Quebec's Saguenay River, even though he's long gone from the ministry. The whole notion of federal parks in Quebec offends many younger Quebeckers, who see their history as a succession of colonizations by the English, English Canadians, Americans and now, if they can believe what they see, by French-Canadian federalists.

"Look," he says, sniffing conflict in the air. "I believe in national parks. Beautiful places have to be put aside. Never before were there national parks in Quebec. Everyone tried. They [the Quebec nationalists] feel it's hurting them. If the federal government does something good, it's bad for them. So much the better. I'm a helluva fighter. People want to benefit from all the services of their federal government. And the people of the Saguenay will not be shy to see the Canadian flag fly over the Saguenay River."

Speaking of the flag, the people of Chrétien's own riding can barely lift their heads without seeing the Canadian maple leaf flapping away above them. Guy Germain, a Shawinigan lawyer who ran against Chrétien for the Tories in 1968 and again for the Créditistes in 1972, says: "Chrétien has accomplished some very concrete things for this riding. He's a very good member, I can't deny it." There's La Mauricie Park. There's going to be a new federal building that will employ at least 100 white-collar workers. There's the $4 million the federal government gave for the TransQuébécois superhighway that sweeps north out of Trois Rivières and through Shawinigan. In fact, hasn't the minister been—well—especially good to his riding? Chrétien replies that he's tried to look after his people, and says it's part of his job. "You know, I even phoned a judge."

One October day in 1971 Chrétien called Quebec Superior Court Justice Harry Aronovitch to ask when a judgment on a bankruptcy case he had heard at the end of September would be ready. A Montreal textile manufacturer named William Sears who had a factory in Grand-Mère near Shawinigan wanted to lease part of the plant not being used, which to Chrétien meant jobs for his constituency, where unemployment was as high as 20 per cent. Sears told Chrétien he could not lease the Shawinigan factory, however, until a complicated suit involving a Spanish maker of weaving machines in Montreal was settled. The conversation, as the judge was to tell his colleagues, was "very short." He told Chrétien the judgment would be coming out when he was good and ready. In fact, it was handed down on November 9; Sears rented part of the factory and later (you guessed it) got a DREE grant to help him out.

"It was crazy," says Chrétien. "All those guys on the other side acting like offended virgins. When I called the judge I said, 'I'm Jean Chrétien, member for St. Maurice.'" Didn't he think the judge might have heard the name before? "Well, when I became a minister," replies Chrétien, "I was not any the less the member for St. Maurice." As morality, the argument may seem a little tortured, but as style it both disarms and overwhelms. Chrétien gambles that the explanation will either end the matter or end him. Lorne Nystrom, the NDP MP from Saskatchewan, himself in parliamentary combat with Chrétien over the salaries of senior civil servants, has been watching Chrétien with growing interest. "On this judges thing he just came out and said, 'Look, this is what I did.'"

Chrétien was in trouble a few years ago over a road contract award for his riding's national park. A feisty little weekly named *Quebec-Presse* found out that a Quebec City–area builder had made the lowest bid but that the contract had been given to a Shawinigan contractor whose bid was $3,000 higher. Chrétien waffled a bit but then told Montreal's *La Presse*: "In all honesty I can say I would prefer that the contract go to a fellow in my own riding." What do you say after you say you're not sorry?

But if it's "yes" and "yes" again to his lucky constituents, it's "no" for everybody else. As president of the Treasury Board, Chrétien works in tandem with Finance Minister Donald Macdonald, a man whom, according to associates, Chrétien both likes and respects. If Macdonald plans the great sweep of Canada's economic policies, it is Chrétien who plays the heavy, the hired gun. Ottawa must hold the line on federal spending now that it is limiting wages and prices, and it is Chrétien, in charge of spending close to $40 billion a year, who must do it.

But holding back government spending is like Canute holding back the waves. Spending is still up 16 per cent over last year. It is still outracing the rise in the gross national product. It has gone up by 388 per cent in 10 years. And, according to a 300-page supplement of the auditor general's most recent report, Ottawa is barely in control. The report's main conclusion is devastating, in a quiet sort of way: the federal government's financial control systems "are significantly below acceptable standards."

The federal civil service is the single largest work force in the country, with more than 300,000 employees (not counting the army or public corporations). It keeps getting bigger, because life gets more complicated, because there are more things for inspectors to inspect out there—because, as Chrétien puts it, "There are more Canadians sending in tax forms." Chrétien's power, on paper at least, is awesome. He decides how much money those people make, when they have their lunch or go home to their 300,000 husbands or wives and one million children. He decides everything from how much to pay a civil servant who uses his motorcycle on public business (half the rate for cars, or 8.75¢ per mile) to the size of the fuel allowance for a bureaucrat working in the high Arctic ($1,105 if he's married, $663 if he's not).

Chrétien defends the civil service at every opportunity and says one of the greater myths in Canadian society is that civil servants do less for more money than other Canadian workers. "My own deputy minister—a man who has to supervise the spending of $42 billion and make sure it's well-administered—is making less than $60,000.

In business he'd be making a bundle." But the civil service is a state within a state, with a life of its own. (As Harry Truman once said of the civil service and his successor, General Dwight Eisenhower: "He'll sit there and say, 'Do this,' and 'Do that,' and nothing will happen. Poor Ike, it won't be at all like the army.") And when the government's anti-inflation directives pinch the bureaucrats, the showdown will be one to remember. Survivor meets survivor.

Jean Chrétien lost the 1984 Liberal leadership race to John Turner, but won the job six years later. Chrétien became prime minister after winning the 1993 general election and was re-elected in 1997 and 2000.

Glen Allen joined Maclean's *as a member of its Montreal bureau in 1975. When he left the magazine in 1993, he was working in its Ottawa bureau. He now lives in Toronto.*

THE WORLD OF SPORTS

Percy Williams: The Fastest Human

Percy Williams sprints away, 1932

By Robert T. Elson

OCTOBER 15, 1928. One day in July the Prime Minister of Canada, stirred by news from overseas that a Canadian high school boy had won a dual Olympic championship cabled congratulations. The next morning, this cablegram was received by a slim-shouldered boy who sat propped up on a white cot in a bare bedroom in the Hotel Holland, Amsterdam. All about him on the bed were cablegrams, but as he opened this one, he exclaimed in excitement: "Why it's from Premier King . . ."

Thus Percy Williams, Canada's Olympic champion, on the morning after the winning of the 200 metres—his second victory in four days and one of the greatest victories in running history—still a little dazed by the world-wide attention which swamped him, was still more amazed that he should attract the attention of the nation's chief executive. "You see," he said later, "over there in Holland after it was all over it was just like winning a race in the high school meets at home—only at home the reporters didn't come to interview you and there were no cables.

"Through it all," he continued, "it was hard to believe that I was here at the Olympic Games. Gee, when we were kids we used to read and talk about the Olympic Games, but I thought only heroes competed there."

And there you have the key to the character of this young boy who brought back to Canada this summer a championship almost unparalleled in the history of the modern Olympiads. You have also the secret of his popularity at home in Vancouver, where they call him "Vancouver's Lindbergh." There is also good reason to believe that today all Canada likes this young champion just as well as they do in his home town. Yes, the "fastest human" is now a Canadian, but best of all he is just the same likeable Canadian boy who went overseas a commonplace member of the Olympic team.

Yet, if there is any Canadian boy who has the right to be proud of his record, Percy Williams is that youth. There he went overseas, aged 20, just out of high school, alone and unheralded, to take the Olympic crowns away from the champions of a decade. So frail that some declared he could not last a single round of Olympic competition, he ran eight heats in four days and won the 100 metres and then the 200 metres—the second victory being over fresh men who were concentrating on that event alone. It was the second dual victory in the history of the Olympics and probably the greatest of all time according to the fields of competition.

Bobby Kerr, of Hamilton, the man who won the 200 metres in 1908 at London will tell you, too, that as this victor came across the track after that terrific 200 metres the first words he gasped out were: "Well, won't Granger be pleased? Golly, I owe most of this to him."

Bob Granger is Williams's coach, the man who for three summers taught him his form and his style so greatly admired overseas. He had not given Williams his speed or that fighting heart which enables him to race on to the finish while other men wither before the strain, but to Percy it was Granger who had done it all, and he had been merely the instrument of victory.

Now, Percy, tired of running, wants to drop out of the limelight for the winter and renew those old friendships in Vancouver which a summer of athletics so badly interrupted. It is a hard thing for a winner to do, but the better you know Percy Williams, the more sure you feel that if any man can do this, he is that man. He is that kind of a boy who is naturally unaffected and it will take a great deal more than an Olympic championship to shake him out of his routine.

Just as Gene Tunney was such a different type to the ordinary run of the prize-ring, so different is Williams to the running champions of the past 10 years—Paddock, Abrahams, Scholz, Murcheson, McAllister. It is hard to recognize him as an athlete in his street clothes, and as a champion you would have to look twice to be sure of yourself—the Amsterdam crowds found that out.

For instance, on the afternoon of his victory in the 200 metres, 1,000 or so stragglers lingered outside the dressing rooms hoping to catch a more intimate glimpse of the champions. There must have been 200 or 300 enthusiastic Germans, 100 or so Americans and a big crowd of Hollanders. First the German runners appeared, Kornig and Lammers leading, and up went the shout of "Allemand!" for they were still national heroes, even in defeat. Then Paddock, smilingly led teammate Scholz out and the Americans cheered them, somewhat faintly, but the crowd followed them with interest—both had been in the athletic limelight for years. Next came London, Britain's man, and he got a cheer, too. Then there was silence and the crowd awaited the winner.

There appeared at the door a slight, good-looking young fellow, wearing golf knickers and a black sweater. His sport shirt was open at the neck, and he swung a battered brown bag. With him appeared a couple of other ordinary-looking youths, and together they cut through the waiting crowd. After a minute or so the watchers grew tired and drifted away. Percy Williams the Olympic champion had come and gone. But in the words of an American coach who got his first close look at the boy hours after the victory—"Why, he simply doesn't look like a champion."

And later on, when they came to examine this victory a little more closely, they found it just as difficult to explain his running ability. They found, for instance, that he is the lightest man ever to win an Olympic championship—he weighs but 125 pounds. And when they came to enquire into training methods, the orthodox held up their hands in despair. In experience, his record showed that before coming to the Olympic Games he had only competed in two meets which could be considered of first-class competition, and that the foundation of his championship had been laid on a rough grass track. Furthermore, his pale face, narrow shoulders and slight build gave no evidence of levels of energy on which he must have drawn to keep him going on to victory while others faltered to defeat.

Some say now that he was only a flash in the pan, that he met and defeated the Americans when they were off their regular form. Canadians, however, know better, for they know that if he continues running, he will be an even greater sprinter than he is today. And why shouldn't he be, if at the age of 20 he is world's champion, has thrice equalled an Olympic record for 100 metres, has done the 100 yards under 10-flat, and all this though he has been in first-class competition but twice before the Olympiad? What, they ask, will he be after a few more years have given him maturity to add to unparalleled experience?

While it seems certain that Williams will remain in Canada—he has not replied to any of the dozen offers he has received from the United States, which reached him the day of victory—it is not so certain that he will continue his running. Just before he left Canada for the Olympiad he said he would just as soon drop out of running after the games, but whether victory has changed his mind no one knows. Victory has made him more reserved than ever, for since he has been made a champion he has been inundated with advice, and he is rather afraid to make a statement now for fear of being misunderstood.

Percy Williams really only started running about four years ago in the first year of his term at King Edward High School, Vancouver. But in commencing track and field work, Williams was advised to go slow by his doctors because a serious illness some years previous had made it inadvisable that he place any severe strain on his heart. It was during this first summer that Bob Granger, his coach, who has been such a faithful campaigner in his cause, met the boy. Bob persuaded Percy not to drop running altogether that summer and go to the track for a few hours practice in the afternoon. As it turned out, these summer afternoons on the grass of Vancouver's practice field at Brockton Point were more devoted to sun baths and play than to serious training.

After a winter's rest, he again came out for track and field, but Bob held out no bait of championships. He is an enthusiast for the game's sake, and expects others to be the same. During that summer, Williams did learn much about sprinting, for when entered in the Caledonian Games against George Clarkson, of the University of Washington, then considered one of the best collegiate runners on the coast, he beat him in the fast time of 10 and 3/5th seconds. These victories delighted Bob, and even then he commenced to talk of the Olympic team of 1928.

So far as anyone knows, these victories did not seem to make the slightest impression on Williams, who still remained only lukewarm toward his best sport. His chief complaint was that it cut into his swimming—a sport forbidden by Granger on the ground that it affected his speed.

With these victories behind him, he entered the season of 1927 in stronger form than ever. Then, in his first appearance that year, he justified all hopes by breaking the 100- and 220-yard records for British Columbia within three hours of each other. In the 100 yards, his performance was exceptionally good—he equalled 10 flat, running over a rough turf course. This success encouraged Granger a great deal more than it did Percy, and when vacation came, Williams had hardly a moment's peace as Bob drove him to the track. They worked harder than ever before, not so much on speed trials, but on starting, on arm action, lengthening stride—the drudgery that takes hour after hour of nerve-racking time and which seems so unimportant at the time but counts for so much when you are sprinting against a field of your peers.

Williams again entered the Caledonian Games of that summer, and facing three crack sprinters brought up from the University of Washington, he trimmed them all. Almost within the hour after this race, Granger commenced to press Williams to be sent back to the Olympic trials and Canadian championships. The local track funds were at the lowest ebb, so a collection was organized in the stands that afternoon. It brought one-third of the desired amount. Bob Brown, backer of the Vancouver Amateur Athletic Association, for whom Williams has always run during the summer, made up the rest of the fund out of his own pocket. But the money raised merely made up enough to take Williams east and included no funds for Granger.

Granger felt that, it being Williams's first long trip away from home, without someone with him he would be lost. He went to the head of one of the railroads in Vancouver, obtained a job on a dining car and paid the rest of his expenses out of his own pocket. Unfortunately, however, the start east was made late on a Monday night, which meant that Williams would not arrive east until Saturday morning—the very morning of the trials. It was a tough break and, coupled with the fact that Williams—in an upper berth in the middle of summer—did not sleep very well, it was almost enough to keep him out of competition. Bob and Percy got away from the station about an hour before the meet. In the 220 yards, Williams won the first heat and in the final ran neck and neck with four others until the last 10 yards, when he faltered and was unplaced. It was his first defeat, and it came as a disappointment to friends in the west, but not to Williams himself. In his own quiet way, Williams returned home and attributed defeat to the conditions under which he ran. "The champions did not seem to run so much faster," he said. Bob Granger came home with his head full of notes regarding this Waterloo, and he laid his plans for this year accordingly.

Spring came late in Vancouver this year, but not any later than Williams's training. He delayed so long getting into regular work that even Granger despaired. As captain of the High School of Commerce relay team, one of the fastest produced in British Columbia, he was entered in the out-of-city 100 for high school boys at the Washington Relay Games, Seattle, his first race of the season. There, with but a few weeks starting practice, he ran to overwhelming victory in the 100 yards, equalling the track record of 9.9 seconds set by Paddock. This bit of work stamped him as the west's outstanding candidate for Olympic honours.

Then came British Columbia's Olympic trials and one of the most remarkable feats of Williams's career—he equalled the Olympic record of 10 and 3/5th seconds for 100 metres over a rough grass track which had a slight incline against the runner. Later at Hamilton, and in one of the heats overseas, he did the same thing, but both these latter times, track conditions were prepared for it. Afterwards Percy said that if he had a good track on that day he might have made it one-fifth faster.

Public subscription saw Percy to Hamilton for the final Olympic tryouts, but again finances were so limited that there were no funds for Granger. But Bob, determined to see Williams through again, worked his way east and paid his own board in Hamilton during the training. How Williams earned a place on the Olympic team by winning both sprint events there is an old story now. It is enough to say he won by margins decisive enough to leave no doubt that here was a different Williams from the train-tired boy who had failed the year before. But even then there were few who would have predicted Olympic victories for him; although Bob Granger had the courage to put in writing for a western newspaper his belief that Williams would win the Olympic 100 metres.

Just before the Olympic team sailed, however, another financial crisis threatened to separate Williams from his coach. The Olympic Committee had no funds to take private coaches along, and Granger's funds were exhausted, although Pat Mulqueen promised Granger that if he came overseas at his own expense, the Olympic Committee would see that he was housed. At home, Pinky Stewart and Williams's pals, aided by Percy's mother, gathered a few hundred dollars to help Bob out, but it arrived in Montreal too late. Bob followed in the third class of the next boat, arriving in Amsterdam three days after the Olympic team.

There followed that dazzling achievement which sent the whole athletic world gasping and the Canadian flag to the masthead twice within two days. The story of that achievement has been written, but there were a few things behind the scenes overseas which give you just a little closer insight into it all.

For instance, on the day the Games opened, there had been the long wait till the afternoon when competition commenced. Most of the men were trained to the breaking point. Phil Edwards, the 800 runner, could barely eat his lunch, and afterwards we in the dining room could hear him pacing the floor like a caged panther. And there was John Fitzpatrick, Percy's teammate, solemn as a churchwarden as he ate that Sunday dinner. Granger sat at the same table and he simply didn't eat; he just toyed with his lunch. But with Williams it was different. He was a little dazed and quieter than usual, trying to remember that he really was at the Olympics. He still preserved that outward calm, however, that later saved him ounces of energy as others strained at the leash counting minutes between races. And it was the same in the dressing room later where he lay quiet on his table, unconcerned by the stir and bustle, listening to Granger's nervous words as Bob massaged his legs. It was Bob who sent him out for the second semi-final in which he equalled the Olympic record for the third time—with the words:

"Remember it's only a Sunday school meet."

It was Granger who needed that advice, not Percy—who lined up alongside the champions in the same way he used to do at Brockton Point. But inside of him his nerves were racing too—he let us know that after a reporter had asked him how he felt before a race.

"What a fool question," Percy exploded, "how does anybody feel before a race—scared as blazes."

Then came the semi-final of the 100 metres, when McAllister, America's flying cop, led him to the tape in 10 and 3/5ths. Then even the stoutest Canadian hearts faltered, because he seemed so frail for victory beside that husky American. Bob Granger was frowning as he left for the dressing room after that race, but when he came back he was smiling. "Percy says he got left on the mark," he said, as he returned, "he's still got a chance."

What chance did he have? They lined up way down the chute from the press stand. There was Lammers, Germany; London, Britain; Wycoff and McAllister, and then Williams. How could he come out ahead of these giants? From the press stand we saw them start—just a flash of them, and then that frenzied crowd pushed to the rail and they were lost for a second in a maze of waving arms. Then they shot into the last 40 yards and Williams was in front and he was running to win. London, of Britain, was coming up but McAllister was faltering and Wycoff was done. The German was another stride behind London.

Anyone's word is as good as mine about what happened then, but what I saw was Bob Granger standing alone up in the tiny Canadian section of the stand, tears streaming from his eyes and his hand all bloody from where he had beat it on the barbed wire, shouting for Williams to come on. Then I saw Bobby Kerr break from the judges' consultation stand and throw his arm about the shoulder of the new champion—1908 and 1928 were reunited. The band played "The Maple Leaf Forever" and nobody remembered the words. Who cared? The Canadians were still cheering. Out in centre field, Williams struggled with the desire to pull his sweat pants over his knees and the duty to stand at attention.

Coming home on the Canadian bus that night they cheered and cheered until they hardly made a sound, throats were so hoarse, but Williams sat alone with Doral Pilling, Alberta's javelin thrower, who threw a husky arm about his shoulder and did the cheering for them both. That night the reporters found Williams in bed and asleep for the 200 metres of tomorrow. Next morning the deluge of cables kept Percy's mind off the 200 metres.

That next day was the day they ran Borah, Kornig and Williams together in a qualifying heat and eliminated the American in one of the greatest 200 metre races in history. It was also the race in which the Canadians sat back about to see Percy defeated after Borah led him to the last 20 yards and then rose to cheer as he repassed the American at the tape—still in the competition. That was also the time when big Bob McAllister, the flying cop beaten the day before, rose in his seat and pointed at Williams. "There goes the greatest sprinter in the world today—Now I can say that I have beaten the world's best once anyway!"

The victory in the 200 metres final the next day was of a different kind. There was a smell of rain in the air as the final drew on with two Canadians—Fitzpatrick and Williams—still in the competition. But an air of gloom hung over the Canadian camp, for the experts had spoken and they had said that the 200 race of yesterday had tired Williams. Surely he could never come back again to win after yesterday's trial. And Bob Granger said: "Yes, yesterday's race was pretty tough."

One by one the champions made their appearance early this day, for they needed warming up; even up to the last minute there was no Williams. He was down below in the dressing room, we found out later, buried under a pile of blankets, Bob Granger's way of warming him up to prevent him losing precious energy. Then there was a delay at the start—they all stood around on the far side for a moment, some nervously prancing. But there Williams stood, still in sweatshirt and pants, still waiting calmly. He took these off eventually with exasperating slowness.

"He'll be rushed at the mark," said someone.

But he wasn't. He came off the start with the rest of them. Then around the one turn, with them all strung out as they had started in the staggered lanes. The stretch, and Fitzpatrick was out of first place. But where was Williams? He was still behind. Then, in those last 40 yards, he seemed to shoot forward and his hands beating their perfect time in that peculiar arm swing of his. And with a roar we saw him finish first.

Percy Williams entered the 1932 Olympics in Los Angeles, but withdrew after pulling a thigh muscle and never raced again. He lived with his mother for most of the rest of his life in relative obscurity in Vancouver, selling insurance, and committed suicide in 1982 at age 74.

Robert Elson, who trained with Williams, had a successful journalistic career, finishing with Time *and* Life *magazines. When he freelanced this article for* Maclean's, *he was working for the* Vancouver Daily Province *and was the only Canadian journalist to cover Williams's Olympic heroics. Also an author, Elson once described Canada as "a triumph of politics over geography and economics—and sometimes, it seems, over common sense." He died in 1987 at age 80.*

Barbara Ann Scott:
What It's Like to Be a Celebrity

Barbara Ann Scott, Feb. 1, 1948

By Barbara Ann Scott
As told to Eva-Lis Wuorio

JANUARY 15, 1951. Sometimes I feel like a freak or a monkey in a zoo—if that's what people mean about being a celebrity. And sometimes I feel like crying because absolutely strange people are so nice to me. Sometimes when I'm walking down the street people stare at me and whisper until I begin to wonder and worry if my slip's showing. Sometimes when I'm shopping I turn around and look into the eyes of people who have been peering over my shoulder. And sometimes when I'm skating I can feel the good will of all those thousands of people watching me and this makes me want to try harder to give them a good show.

I guess being a celebrity is partly being unable to do what you want to do when you want to do it. You put the people and things they expect you to do first. You put yourself and what you like to do second. In a slightly scary way I sometimes feel as though I, Barbara Ann, didn't exist at all. I often seem to be something people have conjured up in their minds, something they want to believe I am, something a little bit better than perfect—which no one can be.

In the main, though, the same sort of things happen to me that happen to everybody else. Right now my mother and I have settled for the first time for a winter-to-ourselves in a little flat in Toronto. I haven't had an ordinary ordered life at home since I was nine years old, and I'm 22 now. True, I have had a wonderfully exciting time and I've loved it, but it's been far from a normal home life. First it was practising the same figures over and over for eight, nine hours a day at the Ottawa Minto Skating Club in the winter, at Lake Placid, N.Y., or Kitchener, Ont., or Schumacher, Ont., rinks in the summer. After a day like that you're too tired to do anything else. Then it's been traveling to competitions and exhibitions. And in the last few years, since I turned professional, it's been traveling with shows.

People I meet seem to think it all very glamorous. Well, it is in a sort of a way, but besides hard work it's also living out of suitcases and being ruled by curtain times and train schedules. I've always tried to be an orderly person. I get that from my father, who was an Army man. Even on my dressing table backstage I like to have all the make-up I use just so, lined up like soldiers on a clean white towel. I like having my suitcases and drawers always in order. But still, living out of a suitcase can never feel like normal life to me. You never feel when you sit down in a hotel chair the relaxation I'm sure people must feel at home. You never feel, "This is my chair, this is my place, I can stay here as long as I like."

I've never worried about people liking me or not liking me because I've always liked them. But sometimes I'm frightened when I'm alone on the street or in a crowded room. Frightened and sort of lonely. I wish then that just one friend would turn up who liked me and knew me and expected nothing, someone I'd know well enough to relax and have fun with, like other girls.

Sometimes people seem to say extravagantly nice things to you and you feel they've been saying just the opposite to others. Those remarks come back to you and you wish they hadn't bothered saying the nice things to you in the first place when it wasn't sincere.

Having people interested in me and in the things I do was hard to get used to at first but now I've come to accept it as part of my life. It began when I was six and first started to skate and they noticed me then, I guess, because I was so tiny. I stayed tiny until I was 12 and when I skated people often stopped to watch; it seems they're always interested in some little person flitting around. Now when people look at me and then stop me on the street it's often just to say they've seen me skate or wish me luck or ask me for an autograph.

Sometimes grandmothers ask what kind of skates to buy their grandchildren. Little children are full of questions. When they ask me how to get to be like me they seldom wait for an answer. Thank goodness, because I could only say it's much better just to be oneself.

Autographs can be embarrassing. The other night I was dancing at the Royal York Hotel in Toronto and in the middle of a dance a man asked me for an autograph. Happily, my escort didn't mind, but some boys don't like that at all. Another thing is the way people are always thinking and saying I'm engaged if they see me with a boy. Then they phone Mother to ask about it. She's heard it so often she usually asks right at the start of the conversation: "Who's Barb engaged to *now?*"

Sometimes people I don't know write and ask me to marry them. There's one farmer who's been writing my mother since 1945 and suggesting that they get together and have me marry his son. He's quite complimentary. He has often written: "After all the strict training she's made herself do I'm sure she could manage my boy." And there was the man last summer who used to call me long distance and write letters saying that he'd got my message and I was the only person who could help him. It seems he imagined he heard these messages.

We had a small cottage in Brockville, Ont., and in the evenings we often visited friends nearby. One stormy night Mother and I drove home quite late. The pines on the drive bent and shook with the wind and the rain. There were just the two of us at the cottage. Sometime after midnight Mother was awakened by pounding on the front door, then the kitchen door. She went down and shouted through the locked door: "Who is it?"

"Is that you, Barbara Ann?" a man's voice called. "Only you can help me."

Those were the words he'd used on the phone, and written, so Mother knew who it was. "She's not here," she called. "You'll wake everybody in the house." She hoped he'd think there were a lot of strong men around.

Then, while he kept running from door to door and banging and shouting, and the rain kept slapping the windows and the thunder rolled, she called the town police. I'd awakened by then and came down calling: "*What* are you doing, Mother?"

"Get back," she called. She thought he might have a gun.

There was lightning right then, and it flashed through the hall windows and he saw me and began shouting: "I see you, Barbara Ann! Only you can help me!"

Mother was standing with a toy baseball bat in her hand.

And then the police came and he ran away. Later a young Brockville policeman came back and told us the man had been caught and he was a little mental.

But those things don't happen often. Mostly nice things happen to me. Once I was invited to an Army-Navy football game in Philadelphia by some cadets who wrote and asked if all of them could be my escorts. I couldn't go because I didn't know any of them but it was fun to get the invitation. The stewardess on the plane from England last year wrote and asked if I'd go to a dance with her brother, a West Point cadet. And sometimes the boys at Royal Military College at Kingston, Ont., have sent me invitations, but I never could accept them because I always was skating or training.

Fan letters sometimes come directly to me, to the theatre or stadium where I'm playing, or to home. Usually they're sent to Ottawa to Mrs. Eileen Hodgson, who used to be my father's secretary. She answers all the mail, and sends out photographs (she orders them in 5,000 lots) when people ask for them. She lets me see the letters she thinks I should see. We get about a dozen a day even when I'm not in a show. She always laughs and says it's $10 in postage a month in the quiet times.

There was a letter the other day from a man in Germany who said he was living in a two-room shack and wanted to move for the winter and would I send him money. A Czech boy wrote that he needed a motorcycle to go between his university and home. A woman in northern Ontario once asked me to help with the mortgage on their farm. Sometimes people just write: "Send me $5,000; I know you have it." All these requests go to the St. Lawrence Foundation which manages my business affairs.

I've always worn funny little bonnets for skating and practising and children often write asking for these, or for skates and boots. But there just wouldn't be enough for everybody so we thought it better not to send any. When I had a hat with a little umbrella sticking out of it, and there were pictures in the newspapers of me wearing it, several women's groups wrote that they'd like to have it as a prize for their raffles. (I gave it to my niece Judy.)

Then, too, I get requests to sponsor things. These go to the people who look after my business affairs. I've sponsored sweaters, skating bonnets, skates, dolls and cosmetics.

People have given me a lot of wonderful things too. The most impressive was the yellow Buick convertible the city of Ottawa gave me when I came back from winning the world and European championships in Sweden and Switzerland. But I was going on to the Olympics then and when there was talk about it interfering with my amateur standing I returned the car. But when I turned professional in June, 1948, the city gave it back again, this time painted a light blue, my favourite colour.

A little boy in the Alberta foothills sent me his most prized possession, a knife carved out of horn. A former German prisoner-of-war sent me a silver ring given to him by a German general. He said he'd liked Canada so much he wanted me to have the ring. Others send me bits of handicraft, shell brooches, handkerchiefs, hand-knitted socks and Dutch bonnets, flowers and toy animals.

People give you many gifts when you're a celebrity but they expect a lot too. You are readily praised and more readily blamed. And sometimes they're pretty quick to judge without knowing what has really happened. I'm thinking of Edmonton last winter.

We were on the cross-Canada tour of the Skating Sensations. In Vancouver I caught flu. Then I began to have an awful pain in my side; it would hurt to laugh or take a deep breath and it was really terrible when my partner had to lift me. In Calgary, after one lift in the middle of the show, I could hardly move. We called a doctor. He said I had a broken rib and taped me and I finished the show.

Afterward he examined me. "You not only have a broken rib but a bad cold and pleurisy," he said. "To bed for two weeks you go."

"But that's silly," I said. "I can't. We're all booked and I haven't got an understudy." He said if I *had* to skate I was not to do anything extra for at least two months. A lot of public appearances had been arranged but he said these had to be cancelled. He gave Mother and the manager of the show a letter to that effect. The first cancellation went to a Calgary department store where I was supposed to sign dolls.

The same thing was supposed to have been done in Edmonton. But when we got there and had been received by the mayor, the car started for a department store. Mother said: "I'm sorry we can't go there. It's doctor's orders." We were told a lot of children were waiting. I suggested we should drive by the store and wave at the children, which we did twice.

I turned the radio on when we got to our hotel room. An announcer was saying that I certainly must have changed to have such an obvious disregard for little children. Then the newspapers came out. One headlined my bad manners, another had an editorial about what did I think I was since I'd turned professional. I was terribly upset.

When I went out of the hotel and walked down the street I felt like a criminal. At a press conference you could have cut the atmosphere with a knife. But after I had explained the true facts of the matter several radio stations interviewed me to give me a chance to explain in public.

We were to skate the next night. Everybody in the company expected to see no audience but perhaps some flying eggs and tomatoes. The place was packed. I was grateful to the people for being so understanding and the crowd was just about the most enthusiastic of the entire tour. Later that week we gave a free matinee for Edmonton children under 10.

People sometimes ask why I turned pro. Well, I was nearly 20 then, and there were no new competitions to enter. I'd worked very hard all my life and I'd have had to keep on doing the same old things over and over. I talked to my mother and to the friends of my father who since his death have been very kind. On their advice the St. Lawrence Foundation to help crippled and underprivileged children was founded. It is my employer. Everything I earn goes directly to the foundation. I receive an allowance, the size of which depends on what I'm doing. The rest goes in donations to deserving causes. I've never received a pay cheque for what I've done.

J. S. D. Tory, a Toronto lawyer, is the head of the foundation. Then there is R. V. Hicks, a lawyer in Tory's firm; C. F. Lindsay, a banker and a friend of my father; and H. H. Caldwell, of the Caldwell linen mills, in Prescott, Ont. They look after everything. Except for a few short holidays I can't remember ever having had time to loaf. That's why I'm enjoying this winter with no shows to do. It's a holiday for my mother too, who works as hard at my career as I do. I'm going to see all my friends and make new ones and I hope they won't think they have to talk about skating. But next summer, unless there's a war, I'm going to go back to England to skate in another musical play on ice. Last summer I skated with Michael Kirby in *Rose Marie* at Harringay Arena in north London, and I never enjoyed anything as much.

Even though my life has been sort of artificial, it's been fun. I'd like to work for a couple more years and then I'd like to settle down and have a home of my own. That will be wonderful too.

Barbara Ann Scott skated professionally for seven years, until 1955, when she married Tommy King, an ice-show publicist. They lived in Chicago for 43 years, where he owned a commercial real-estate company and she groomed, trained and showed horses, directed a summer theatre, and was involved in charitable organizations. In 1998, the Kings retired to Florida.

Eva-Lis Wuorio was a writer and assignments editor for Maclean's *from October, 1947, to April, 1951, when the Finnish-born journalist returned to Europe, where she wrote short stories, novels and children's books.*

Is It True What They Say
About Gordie Howe?

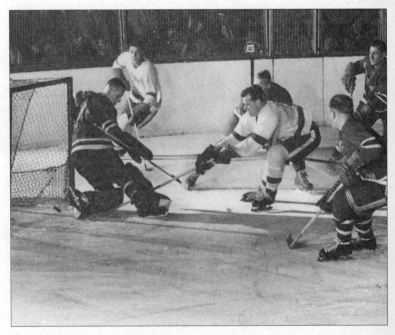

Gordie Howe scoring number 215 in New York City, Nov. 11, 1953

By Barney Milford

JANUARY 1, 1953. Clarence (Hap) Day, the assistant general manager of the Toronto Maple Leafs, flew to Detroit one day last October to discover if the Red Wings and the Montreal Canadiens had picked up any new hockey tricks since he'd viewed them last season. The Wings were booked to play Day's Leafs four nights later in Toronto and the Habitants were on the agenda the following week so Day put on his dark glasses and false beard, took a chair behind the Detroit bench and proceeded to scout two of Toronto's more detested rivals.

As generally happens when Detroit plays Montreal it was a spirited wrangle between two of the National Hockey League's most colourful teams. For two periods Day had virtually nothing to place under his retreating hairline for future reference. Both sides looked brisk and polished and vigorous and accomplished and this was nothing new to the Leafs. But in the third period, with Detroit nursing a 2-1 lead, the game blew wide open and here is how it happened:

Gordie Howe, the Saskatoon youngster who is Detroit's All-Star rightwinger, broke across the blueline with the puck near the boards and was immediately hounded by Doug Harvey, Montreal's All-Star defenceman, who was endeavouring to force him into the corner. He seemed to have succeeded, too, for he had pushed Howe to such an angle that the rightwinger's shot was blocked easily by the Montreal goalkeeper, Gerry McNeil, and it bounced out four or five feet in front of the goal.

Harvey still had his right shoulder dug into Howe's left side as they circled toward the back of the net, with Howe's stick rattling against the backboards as they scooted along. He was in no position to reach the loose puck until suddenly he straightened, lofted his stick high in the air with both hands, slid the butt-end of it into his right hand as he brought his arms across Harvey's hunched shoulders and then, shooting left-handed, reached out for the loose puck and drove it across McNeil's chest into the net. The Canadiens were so shaken by this legerdemain, and the Red Wings so ecstatically buoyed (hockey players are an emotional band), that Detroit had no difficulty adding three more goals for a 6-1 triumph. Hap Day, in his report to Leaf coach Joe Primeau the following morning, described the play with a noticeable quaver in his voice and concluded that it was "the most brilliant goal I ever saw."

Things like this make many people believe that Howe, who will not be 25 until next March 31, is the best hockey player alive today. Almost everyone in the NHL who makes his living thinking has a favourite Howe play to describe, usually so poignant that it requires gestures, and the stories seldom overlap. The common denominator is Howe's versatility.

Invariably, hockey men begin their orations by noting that he can do everything well. Then, their heads shaking unbelievingly and their audience as silent as the Montreal Forum when the enemy scores a goal, they launch into a detailed account of this or that fragment of how Howe won them. Of this young man they point out that he can skate, he can fight, he can backcheck, he can stickhandle, he detests defeat and therefore has great spirit, he can kill off penalties, he can make plays, he can think, he can shift, he is durable and, most important of all, he can put the puck in the net. He can do it right-handed or left-handed, an exceedingly rare accomplishment.

There is no known way that a rival coach can stop Howe consistently. Sid Abel, his centre on the great Detroit line that had Ted Lindsay at left wing, was asked soon after he became coach of the Chicago Black Hawks this season if his experience in playing beside Howe had provided him with a theory on how to stop him. "Naw," replied Abel gloomily. "What I'd like to do is put a saddle on him and let somebody ride around on his back."

Howe's leading booster, not unnaturally, is Jack Adams, general manager of the Red Wings, who does not spar around with reservations. "He's the greatest player I've ever seen in hockey," Adams remarked on the eve of the league's annual All-Star game in Detroit last fall. This was shocking news to supporters of Maurice (Rocket) Richard, the idolized Montreal rightwinger who recently established an all-time scoring record when he wiped Nels Stewart's 324 from the record book. For two years there had been considerable controversy over the relative merits of Howe and Richard. Dick Irvin, coach of the Canadiens, apparently held the trump card for any such discussions with this observation: "When Howe scores as many goals as Richard has then I'll consider it time to start comparing them."

At the start of the current season Howe had scored 160 goals in league play, compared with Richard's 319. However, as we shall see, the remark by Irvin was not as conclusive as it first appeared. For one thing, over the last three seasons, Howe not only scored as many goals as Richard but actually scored 13 more—125 to 112. For the long-range view, Howe is seven years younger than Richard, who is now 31, and therefore can conceivably last seven years longer. He needs to average only 23 goals a season, or approximately half of his present output, to overtake the Rocket.

The pro-Richard faction got its first great shock two years ago when Lloyd Percival, director of Canada's Sports College, released a detailed analysis of the two players after watching each over a 17-game period and recording various statistics revealed by stop-watches, graphs and charts. In noting 17 points about their play, Percival's researchers concluded that Howe was superior in 16 of them, including such items as "carries puck out of defensive zone more often," "completes more passes," "hands out more body checks," "backchecks more often and travels faster when so doing" and "shows greater variety in scoring plays." Research showed Richard superior in only "acceleration from a complete stop." Percival confided that the tests "point out Howe's great versatility and Richard's lack of team play without regard to their individual scoring."

Howe earned $9,000 in bonus prizes last season. He got $1,000 from the league and $1,000 from the Red Wings for winning an All-Star berth, the same for winning the scoring championship (for the second successive season) and the same for winning the Hart Trophy, which goes annually to the player voted by hockey writers as the most valuable to his team. And, like each of the Red Wing players, he got $3,000 as his share of the play-off pool as Detroit won the Stanley Cup. On top of a reported $12,000 salary, which this season is believed to have been upped to $15,000, Howe thus observed his 24th birthday last spring with earnings of $21,000.

The money could scarcely have come drifting down on a more modest young man. When Howe established an all-time NHL scoring record of 86 points during the 1950–51 season he was asked to explain his sudden arrival among hockey greats. "It was just luck," he related. "The big reason must be because I'm on a great team and have Abel and Lindsay to play with on a line." When asked for his reaction to the Percival analysis which showed him superior to Rocket Richard in 16 out of 17 departments, Howe told a nationwide radio audience: "I feel very honoured to be mentioned in the same breath with as great a hockey player as Richard." Linked romantically with Barbara Ann Scott a year ago by an overzealous publicity man, Howe remarked: "It was just a big joke. I was pretty surprised to see my picture there in the paper beside hers."

Rough and tough on the ice, Howe, a six-foot, 194-pounder, is quiet-spoken, retiring and shy between games. He very rarely swears, in or out of uniform, and is a stickler for physical condition.

Early this season, with Detroit in first place in the wake of 7-0 and 6-1 victories over Chicago and Montreal, Howe was riding along in third place in the scoring with four goals and three assists. The day before the team entrained for Toronto for its next game, the Red Wings coach, Tommy Ivan, dropped into the dressing room in the Olympia a few hours after practice. He found Howe, garbed in sweat clothes with a heavy towel piled around his neck, working alone on the stationary bicycle.

"What's your trouble?" he asked Howe in surprise.

"Aw, I'm not going so good," a perspiring Howe retorted. "I should be putting more in the net."

Bachelor Howe, who once remarked that girls "make me feel nervous," spends his summers in Saskatoon in the two-storey house he bought for his parents after the 1950–51 season. He is an outstanding baseball player and was batting .374 in the Saskatchewan Senior League late last summer when the Detroit management, fearing an injury, requested that he stop playing ball.

Gordie is the fourth youngest in a family of nine in which there are five girls. As a youngster he endeavoured to overcome a lack of minerals in his infancy, which had left him with a weak spine, by working for a building construction company, mixing cement, and by hanging from the archway of doors and swinging his hips endlessly. As a result, he has a thick upper body, with big arms and strong wrists.

Howe has a thick neck (he wears a 16 1/2 collar) but it looks skinny because it is long and because his shoulders have a long gradual slope which actually gives his upper body a coffin shape. He dresses nattily, his trousers sharply draped and the coats long on his hips, and he drives a powder-blue hard-top convertible Oldsmobile. He wears old pants and crew-necked sweaters at home in the off-season but, like all the Red Wings, never goes to the dining room of a hotel without a jacket and necktie (it's a club rule that also applies to railway dining cars).

He's a patient, easy-going lobby-sitter, an asset for a hockey player who must spend many idle hours waiting around hotels during road trips. Most stops are overnight and the players either lobby-sit or shop or take in a movie until 3:30 p.m. when the Red Wings, at least, go to the hotel dining room for a steak, baked potato, one vegetable and ice cream. When the game ends they hastily shower and change and grab taxis for the railway station and the overnight ride back home or, occasionally, to another road stop. Howe, who doesn't smoke and has only an occasional relaxing beer, tries to get at least 10 hours' sleep every night.

Howe gave no thought to professional hockey as a boy, playing the game as a midget and juvenile mostly because every other youngster in Saskatoon with the normal number of legs played it. But when Gordie was 14, Russ McQuarrie, a great promoter of minor leagues in the city, sent him to Winnipeg to attend a New

York Rangers' tryout camp. It was the first time Howe had been so far from home but he has little recollection of his week in Winnipeg. "The only thing I knew," he remarked not long ago, "was the route from the hotel to the Amphitheatre rink." He was on the ice only four or five times and because he was an underdeveloped six-footer he got scant attention from Lester Patrick, then boss of the Rangers. "Lester kept asking me my age," Howe recalled recently. "Nothing else ever happened."

He went back to Saskatoon where the late Fred Pinkney, then a Detroit scout, picked him up for the Red Wings. He'd filled out a little by the following fall and Jack Adams, the Detroit general manager, liked him and urged him to work on his physique and to return to Windsor the following year. Howe did and Adams, desirous of having him develop under Detroit supervision, sent him to the Galt, Ont., juniors, then sponsored by Detroit and coached by Al Murray, former New York Americans defenceman. But, because he was being transferred from one branch of the Canadian Amateur Hockey Association to another, Howe was compelled to stay out of hockey for one year. Nevertheless, Adams kept him at Galt where he played exhibition games and practised daily under Murray. He quit school ("I was embarrassed a little; all the kids my age were about half my size") and got a job in Galt.

Howe did so well in fall training when he was 17 that Adams decided to make him a professional and sent him to Omaha in the United States Hockey League where Tommy Ivan was the coach. Howe, who therefore never played junior hockey, scored 22 goals and had 22 assists but he did more than that to indicate to the Detroit brass that he was a real find. Playing in St. Louis one night he became involved in an exchange with defenceman Myles Lane, a former NHLer and a very rugged performer. The exchange developed into a fight and Lane knocked Howe down with a right-hand wallop. Howe scrambled to his feet and Lane knocked him down again. Once more Howe got up and this time he tore past Lane's punches and gave the big defenceman a lacing. That night, Tommy Ivan phoned Jack Adams in Detroit. "Jack, we've got something here," he said. "This big skinny kid, Howe, has the guts of a burglar."

Thus, when Howe was 18, he was ripe for the NHL. To that point he'd been fairly free of injuries, although he had a rupture operation after his season in Omaha. But, early in his first year with Detroit, he was checking Bryan Hextall in a game in New York and he felt his left knee twinge. The cartilage had popped and it came out several times during the season. Nevertheless, playing with Adam Brown and Billy Taylor, he got seven goals and 15 assists and played 58 games.

Howe had the cartilage removed from his left knee in a post-season operation and in his second season, by now operating beside Lindsay and Abel, he doubled his points output with 16 goals and 28 assists. He seemed headed for big things the following season but early in December he was belted by defenceman Pat Egan and tore the cartilage in his right knee when he bounced into the boards. Two weeks later it was apparent the knee couldn't be mended and the cartilage was removed before Christmas. He worked hard to strengthen his knee and made a remarkable recovery to return to the lineup in just over a month. A shoulder injury later sidelined him for four games and altogether he missed 30 games of the 70-game schedule. He came back to shine in the play-offs, leading all point-getters with eight goals and three assists and that outburst was indicative of his future. In the play-offs the next season, 1950, Howe received his gravest injury of all.

In an incredibly vicious series with Toronto, Howe raced across the ice to check Ted Kennedy near the end of the first game. Kennedy, cruising near the boards, pulled up short as Howe slammed toward him and Howe crashed headlong into the boards. He crumpled to the ice, blood streaming from his nose and eye. A brain specialist ordered an immediate operation to remove fluid causing pressure on the brain. Also, he had a fractured cheekbone and nose. After a 45-minute operation Howe's condition still was serious 24 hours later and headlines in the three Detroit newspapers shouted that his life was in danger.

This added animosity to the riotous hockey series and seemed to add to Detroit's determination to whip the Leafs, which they did in seven games. Then, with the fast-recovering Howe able to leave the hospital 10 days later, they won the Stanley Cup by beating the New York Rangers in the final. Howe, his head heavily bandaged, joined his team on the ice after the game when the fans began to chant, "We want Howe!"

He recalled the occasion recently. "That was the biggest thrill I've ever experienced. The folks sure made me feel that I wasn't forgotten."

Of Kennedy, whom the Detroit papers had flayed unmercifully after the accident, this paragon of modesty observed: "Ted isn't the kind of player who would deliberately injure an opponent."

Howe hit his top stride after that, setting a new league scoring record the following season. A small hole had been drilled over his right ear in the operation and the management insisted he wear a helmet to protect his head. Howe wore it for a time, then discarded it. "Makes me sweat," he explained.

Gordie Howe went on to play 32 seasons in the NHL *and* WHA *before retiring at 52. When he hung up his skates in 1980, he was the* NHL *career leader in goals, assists, total points, games and years played. Howe now lives in Traverse City, Mich., about 400 km northwest of Detroit.*

Barney Milford was, in fact, Trent Frayne writing under a pseudonym when he had another piece in the same issue. Frayne first wrote for Maclean's *in 1941 and has written hundreds of articles for the magazine since then. He lives in Toronto with his wife and fellow frequent* Maclean's *contributor, June Callwood.*

Success Can't Spoil Bobby Orr—
It Worries Him Too Much

Bobby Orr fishing at his Little Nahant, Mass., home, 1969

By Stan Fischler

FEBRUARY, 1969. There was music in the turnstiles at the Boston Garden station of the Metropolitan Transit Authority. It was late on a Sunday night in November and the ribbon of fans curling out of the ugliest arena in the National Hockey League moved quickly, springily, onto the platform. They always play up-tempo tunes at the Garden when the Bruins win. And the fans seem to move with a special rhythm on a night when Bobby Orr is playing *his* game; and they talk in "didjas."

"Didja see that kid's shot?" a youth in a Boston University jacket was explaining to his girlfriend. "Didja see him set up that goal?"

They were legitimate "didjas" because on this night 20-year-old Bobby Orr, the pride of Parry Sound, Ont., once again delighted 14,653 aficionados. His opponents were the Chicago Black Hawks and in the first period Bobby Hull scored for the visitors. But the fans could tell this would be Orr's night because he was skittering around the ice like a water bug on a pond. It meant his knees felt good and, given time, he'd work toward the Chicago goal. "I'm always nervous in the first few minutes," he explained, "but after I get hit—or I hit somebody—I start moving."

On this night it took him 21 minutes of playing time to start moving. It happened after Pat Stapleton of the Black Hawks was whistled down for a penalty. Bruins' coach Harry Sinden, who appears young enough to be Orr's brother, looked down the bench. Orr looked back. There was no need for words. Orr braced himself atop the boards, leaped over and skated hard to his position at the blue line.

The puck was dropped. It skimmed to Orr. His stick curved back in an arc, then cracked against the rubber and it flew on a straight trajectory over the arm of Chicago goalie Denis DeJordy. It was in the net and the score was tied, 1-1. Less than five minutes later Dallas Smith of the Bruins passed the puck to Orr. With one arm Orr brushed aside Pit Martin of Chicago as if he were flicking a fly off his wrist. He saw teammate Ed Westfall camped alone near the net. There was a quick pass, a shot, a goal. The Bruins were ahead to stay in a game they eventually would win 5-3.

Like so many nights at Boston Garden, this one belonged to Orr. He wore a huge, contented grin as he dressed and explained the goal-making plays to reporters. He looked like an ad out of *Gentlemen's Quarterly*. The glistening blond hair curved slightly down his brow. He wore a red-and-blue-striped tie that dipped into the recesses of his new grey suit with blue pin-stripes. This was Bobby Orr, the *wunderkind* of hockey, the best defenceman in the NHL, saviour of the Boston Bruins and highest-paid player in the world. At a glance, you'd never know that this man has problems.

His problems stem from a fact remarked by his hometown chum, Bob (Homer) Holmes, who was visiting Boston on this night: "You can take Bobby out of Parry Sound," said Holmes, "but you can't take the Parry Sound out of Bobby."

It's true. Orr, hockey's newest Golden Boy, is a victim of his success. He worries that stories of his $400,000 contract will disturb the Bruins' morale. He fears adoring fans will turn against him when he plays poorly. He cherishes the small-town life of Parry Sound and desperately tries to match it in Boston. He wonders whether his fragile knees, so often under surgery, will carry him through another season. "I was scared when I came into this league," he said, "and I'm scared now."

He is not really frightened but rather concerned, just as he would be concerned at home in Parry Sound if somebody denounced him as a "big shot." The consequences were apparent at the start of the season when his defence partner, Ted Green, walked out on the Bruins and threatened to retire unless management renegotiated his contract. Orr obviously was the cause of Green's displeasure.

Green, who in his robust way is a valuable member of the Bruins, had a point. If Orr is worth $400,000, why shouldn't Green, who is at least half the player Orr is, be worth $200,000? Other Boston players could have used the same argument and Orr knew it. As he walked through the dim recesses of Boston Garden after the game with Chicago, Orr talked of his concern about dissension on the team.

"I'd rather give those players my money," he said while signing autographs and trying to make his way to the parking lot near the Charles River. "Yeah, I'd rather give away the money than have any unhappiness on the team; that is, if there is any unhappiness. I don't know if there is, or was, any. If there is, I'd just as soon not know about it."

Fans followed Orr and his friend Homer and the reporter all the way to the parking lot and the 1968 Meteor hardtop. Orr gunned the accelerator. "Let's get outta here," he said, "I hate the city. The fact is, except for Toronto, I'd never been in a big city until I came to Boston. And if I stayed here in Boston, I'd never get any privacy; the people recognize the players. I couldn't stand living in an apartment; that's why we took a place on the ocean."

He turned the car north, through Sumner Tunnel, then past Logan Airport, along Route 107 to Lynn, then a sharp right turn at Lewis Street. Now he was on the causeway called Nahant Road that leads to the hamlet of Little Nahant, which juts out into the Atlantic just north of Boston Bay. He stopped the car in front of the three-bedroom house he shares with John Forrestal, the Bruins' assistant trainer, and teammate Gary Doak. The house sits on the lip of Massachusetts Bay, facing the historic towns of Salem and Gloucester. "This," he said, filtering sand through his fingers as if it were gold dust, "is the super life. I walk out the door, I'm on the sand, toss out the fishing pole and haul 'em in. Cripes, that's super."

But the house in Little Nahant is only a temporary sanctuary. Twice a week he reports for the games at Boston Garden, and then there are practices—and always the fans who are as ready to puncture him as pat him on the back. The butcher, the accountant and the welder who are lucky to make $10,000 in any year expect perfection from the kid with the $400,000 contract. "One of their favourite lines," Orr went on, "is, 'Who the heck are you, getting that kind of money when other players deserve just as much?' A girl once wrote me that, but she had the guts to put her name and address on the envelope. At least I could write her back. I tried to tell her that all the love in the world won't pay my bills."

He got up and walked to the kitchen, opened the refrigerator and poured himself a glass of beer. "Another fella wrote me and said I'm a heck of a guy and the Bruins are a great hockey team, so would I please send him five dollars. That was early in December. Next day I write him back that I make a policy not to send money in the mail. A week later he writes me again and says, 'The Bruins still are a great hockey team but *you* don't have any Christmas spirit.'"

He was tired and begged off to go to sleep. The team had a day off the next day, and he and Homer would fish, relax and trade stories about Parry Sound. Orr was up at 11 a.m., and on the phone at 11:30. It was his lawyer, Alan Eagleson, calling from Toronto. Eagleson, founder of the NHL Players Association, helped negotiate Orr's contract and handles all his business. Orr owns a car wash, some land near Toronto, and co-owns a sports camp, near Orillia, Ont., with Mike Walton of the Toronto Maple Leafs and ex-Leaf trainer Bob Haggert. After finishing the phone conversation, Orr made it clear who handles the business problems. "Every once in a while Al will call and tell me he's bought something for me, and I'll say, 'Al, that's great.' Why not? We're quite close, and he's put a lot of money in my pocket."

Now, Eagleson was considering several bids by publishers to have a book ghost-written by a sportswriter but with Orr's by-line on the cover. It would be helpful to Orr, but Eagleson suggested there was no point starting on the book until it was certain Orr's legs would stand up through this season. They agreed to wait. Orr clearly isn't as concerned about the book as he is about his knees and his hockey. "Cripes," he said after tossing his fishing line into the ocean, "there's no easier way to make a living than playing hockey. It's just a question of the knees holding up."

If he does turn out to be a fragile hockey player, he will return home and become an active partner with his brother Ron in the family sporting goods store. To some players exposed to the big-city life, returning home would be unthinkable—Montreal-bred Rod Gilbert, for one, makes New York his year-round base—but Orr finds central Ontario appealing. "Only 6,000 people in Parry Sound," he said, "but that's where the good life is. Plenty of bass, pickerel, right on Georgian Bay. We've got this cabin on an island in the bay. Paid 150 bucks for it and we've had a billion dollars' worth of laughs. Homer's got a dog that climbs trees. I've got a dog that keeps running away from home. The people are great. But mainly I love it because it's small, there's no traffic, no noise."

The best he can do to approximate that life is rent the home in Little Nahant and hold reunions when his parents, brothers Ron and Doug and sisters Pat and Penny visit Maple Leaf Gardens. As he walked back to the house he remembered that the Bruins would be visiting Toronto in a week and there would be a big Orr get-together, but that his next business would be with the Philadelphia Flyers on Wednesday night. This turned out to be Orr's game again. He helped spark the Bruins to a 7-1 win over the visitors.

And when it was over, the MTA subway turnstiles seemed to be singing again and the jubilant mob was waiting for Orr outside the dressing room. "The way Bobby's playin'," a fan in a corduroy jacket said, "he could be mayor of this town." Patiently, smilingly, Orr signed the programs and the eight-by-10 glossy photos of himself. When somebody suggested he wanted him to run for mayor, Orr laughed. "Tell 'em I'll always go back to Parry Sound."

A half-hour later he pushed his way back to his car. A companion asked him if all the chasing and signing bothered him. He said it didn't; the fans are paying his salary and he respects them. "Look at it this way," he said, heading north for Little Nahant, "I can't write a story and I can't fix a tire. I eat the same food as everybody else and I chase girls just the way other guys do. I'm really no different than anybody else, except that sometimes I get my name in the paper."

In the end, Bobby Orr did not return to Parry Sound, and now lives outside Boston where he is a partner in Woolf Associates, a sports management company. In that 1969–70 season, Orr broke scoring records for defencemen with 21 goals and 64 points. In the following year, he led the league in scoring with 120 points and led his Bruins to the Stanley Cup. Orr had 11 knee operations as a player and played only nine full seasons before retiring in 1978. He later fell out with Eagleson, who subsequently was jailed after pleading guilty to fraud and theft.

Stan Fischler is an American sports writer and broadcaster who wrote regularly about hockey for Maclean's *in the 1960s and 1970s.*

George Chuvalo Is Still on His Feet

George Chuvalo landing a punch on Muhammed
Ali, Toronto, March 29, 1966

JANUARY 24, 1977. The trouble was that hardly anyone showed up. The press conference to announce the March 7, 1977, fight between heavyweights George Chuvalo and Bobby ("Pretty Boy") Felstein was held in the posh motel ambience of Toronto's downtown Holiday Inn. The two trays of canapés and the three silver chafing dishes cradling some indeterminate pasta casseroles were laid out neatly next to the cutlery and paper napkins and the makeshift bar had seven bottles—rye, gin, vodka, scotch, vermouth and red and white Canadian wine—all lined up next to one another waiting for a thirsty press contingent.

A fellow from the suburban *Mississauga News* did arrive. A consultant from the CBC's local French station, CJBC, appeared and placed his 200-plus pounds of St. Urbain Street bulk, draped with amulets and necklaces, on one of the little folding chairs lining the room, and proceeded to punctuate the stillness with heckling. "Ain't nobody coming, eh," he shouted to the nervously pacing promoters. There was no one present from the three major Toronto newspapers, so all the attention was focused by default on one press heavyweight, local CBC broadcaster Brian Williams. Williams, who carefully avoided the bar, stood stoically on the sidelines gnawing sporadically at the crackers with shrimp paste, gearing himself up for what to him the situation obviously called for—some tough questioning. The promoters of the fight sat stiffly at one end of the room like the parents at a mixed faith marriage—in attendance for the children's sake, but wearing black. Chuvalo and Felstein circled the food warily, sucking in their stomachs and ample portions of pasta. As he paused at the doorway of the suite, George Chuvalo grumbled *sotto voce*, "Jesus," he said, "this is some half-assed press conference. They called it for 12:30 to 3:30 p.m. What kind of a dumb thing to do is that?"

"How do you expect us to take this fight seriously?" asked an intense Brian Williams, looking from the paunchy 40-year-old Chuvalo, who last fought more than two years ago, to the soft white contours of Felstein, 34, spilling out between the jacket and pants of his burgundy leisure suit, telling more about his three years of fighting inactivity than any sports column.

Fighters and promoters looked at one another. They had money to make and deals that stretched far beyond the water-and-spittle-soaked corners of a boxing ring. The comeback of George Chuvalo? Well, that was of some interest to George himself and of some minor short-term concern to his promoters, but only a moment in the larger scheme of things. And to Canadians, the return of George Chuvalo, our best heavyweight ever, should mean something else as well. It is a sign of what boxing has come to in this country and of what to look at if you want to understand not just the *symptoms* that ulcerate boxing—the mobsters, the rounders and the con men—but more importantly, the disease itself that has all but wiped out the sport in English Canada.

He was our Great Canadian Hope. George Chuvalo, the flat-faced, high cheek-boned son of Herzegovinian parents whose forefathers had survived the massacres of the Turks, the hostilities of the Serbs, and made it from Yugoslavia to the relative paradise of Toronto's west end. His mother was so good at plucking chickens that her boss let her bring her only son to the chicken-processing factory where she worked. So it was that Irving Ungerman, the poultry czar of Ontario, came to rock George Chuvalo's baby carriage.

By 17, Chuvalo was Canadian amateur heavyweight champion. At

21 he was a professional and the Canadian heavyweight champion. But being heavyweight champion brings in something slightly below the salary of your average chicken plucker in a country like Canada. Chuvalo just didn't have the connections or the cash to move into the big leagues and promote himself. So in 1964 Ungerman became his manager. Fueled by a desire to see not only George's name in lights but his own as well, he went about spending the money necessary to break into the big time. The big purses. The big names. Joe Frazier. Muhammad Ali. Sonny Liston. As much as $65,000 a fight for Chuvalo and little more than expenses going to Ungerman, together with the adrenalin rush of being in there talking it up and negotiating with the Beautiful Black Cats.

Ungerman and Chuvalo. They came close, but they never quite made it to the top. They were always one fight away from the big payday, the wipe-out with the million-dollar purse and the closed circuit TV rights worth a few more million with the ringside mink-and-sequin dudes betting sweet money. *If* he had beaten Ernie Terrell. *If* he had won against Patterson.

All the same, he was ours. The first Canadian boxer to be in the running. A man who couldn't, *wouldn't* be knocked down. "A punching bag," said *Ring* magazine, not entirely without a note of respect for the Canadian fighter who seemed impervious to pain, whose thighs would wobble and knees buckle, seem indeed to turn to jelly, but who then would move forward again, even when, as in the fight with Frazier, one eyeball had been knocked out of its socket and the other eye was a slit so that all he could see was a flickering shadow. "Quit in a fight?" says Chuvalo. "You never quit. That's the most humiliating thing in the whole world."

He made money, too. "About $500,000, maybe a little more," says Ungerman, trying to add up Chuvalo's income in 10 years of fighting. Not bad for a kid with a grade 12 education. And in spite of the 95 fights (76 wins—including about 70 knockouts—17 losses, and two draws), all he had to show for it was a couple of small scars beneath one eye and around the bridge of his nose, faded and masked by swarthy Herzegovinian colouring. No stumbling speech, slurred words, just the quick staccato talk common to prizefighters who seem to feel a compulsion to speak in double time just in case they get knocked out before completing a sentence.

Still, the money situation was always uncertain. Chuvalo was a top heavyweight—at his peak during the Sixties, *Ring* magazine rated him number three in the world—but in North American pro boxing it doesn't really count unless you're number one. A dentist, a lawyer, even a hockey or basketball player can get by just being good, but in boxing you don't make it as a contender. Half a million bucks looks nice made in just 10 years, but it spreads pretty thin over the next 20 or 30 when going 15 rounds is 13 too many, and when, if you're not at the top, you're nowhere.

George Chuvalo is in training for his March 7 fight in Toronto's Lansdowne Youth Athletic Club. The name is somewhat euphemistic since the only "youths" ever likely to frequent the club are Chuvalo's eight-year-old daughter and a Slavic-faced fighter who looks exactly like a young Chuvalo and now sits playing cards at the back of the gym. This kid, it is claimed, could have been a great fighter, but his contract is said to be held by "the boys from Hamilton," a euphemism for the mob. When this young fighter ran out on a New York City fight, no one in Canada would touch him with a 90-foot pole. "I said I want to hear that you're free of your Hamilton connections before I'll arrange a fight for you," says Irving Ungerman. The kid goes back to playing cards. Breaking such contracts in tennis or golf would be a matter of polite discussion among lawyers. In boxing it's not just the contracts that might get broken.

The Lansdowne gym is one of two or three professional gyms in Toronto and it's there that Chuvalo has always trained. The gym is above an auto body shop that never appears to be open, but the smell of gasoline fumes permeates every floor of the building. Once upon a time the gym had windows, but now they have been bricked up and covered with posters of boxers, nudes and rock stars. In the yellow electric light of the Lansdowne it's always night. Chuvalo began training for his comeback in November. George would lug in his equipment, spend 20 minutes or so in three rounds with a punching bag and a bit of skipping and knee jerks that looked highly unlikely to make much of a dent in the near 270-pound frame he was hauling around (three weeks after training started he had put *on* about five pounds).

Having sweated, wheezed and snorted his way through the 20-minute training session, Chuvalo gets ready to leave the gym and make a few deals. For Chuvalo, life *is* deals. The $2,000 Sansui stereo rig in his house is a "deal" in return for showing up to sign autographs at a local Dodge-Chrysler dealership where an old friend, former boxer "Irish" Tommy Burns, works (though that particular deal is somewhat soured by Mrs. Chuvalo's propensity for wrapping deal-cars around lampposts); the jeans he wants to go and buy for his kids are "deals" at a wholesaler out in the east end and the muffled conversations held in doorways, showrooms or on telephones—all rendered mysterious by a boxing patois incomprehensible to the uninitiated—are deals. The fight on March 7 is another deal, and Chuvalo is personally working on the right angles. But he's worried about the promoters. This time Ungerman has checked out. He's not involved with Chuvalo's comeback. As far as he's concerned, Chuvalo shouldn't be boxing anymore and, besides, he's worried about the people getting involved in this particular deal.

Whoever these people are, they fill the vacuum created by the wholesale abandonment of boxing by responsible members of the community. Amateur boxing programs, the breeding ground for professional fighters, have dried up in Canada. High schools, colleges, the YMCA, Kiwanis clubs and police associations have all dropped or are cutting back on any regular boxing programs. It may have been a chicken-or-the-egg situation, but the anti-boxing movement, which sees boxing as (a) a brutal sport and (b) the special domain of mobsters, certainly contributed to the cold-shouldering of boxing by the respectable community at large and the corruption and decay of the sport in Canada.

Boxing, wrote legions of editorial writers, was an activity that manifested the worst aspects of man's nature. "Does any intelligent man or woman," asked the Toronto *Globe and Mail* in one of its several ban-boxing-diatribes, "still accept the badly bruised proposition that there is some connection between manliness and the ability to give and receive the legalized assault and battery of the ring?" It would have been hopeless to point out that man's impulse to stand up and fight—which enabled him to survive in the first place—seemed less reprehensible than some other impulses in human nature such as envy, avarice, hypocrisy or selfishness.

The Toronto promoters of the Chuvalo-Felstein fight incorporated themselves as Gemini Promotions, Inc. They estimated that the fight would cost about $30,000 ($10,000 in prize money to Chuvalo; $5,000 to Felstein), with at least half of that needed up front. While Gemini was planning on using the fight to establish its credibility and then quickly move into the more lucrative field of rock concerts, George Chuvalo was planning to use the fight to push his latest venture. It had been some time now since George had hustled a business of his own and he wanted to "start something that would run itself." But what?

Enter Arnold Foote.

In his native Jamaica, where he headed his own marketing and promotion firm, Arnold Foote wielded a great deal of power until Michael Manley was first elected prime minister and Arnold became *persona non grata*. There was the little matter of his passport being temporarily lifted by authorities, who seemed peeved that Foote had run the advertising campaign for Manley's opponent in Jamaica's 1972 election, former prime minister Hugh Shearer. Foote's clients in the Caribbean read like *Fortune*'s top 500 list, but when he came to Canada two years ago with his Canadian wife about all he had was a scrapbook of awards and citations and a good deal of marketing know-how. Just how this polished Jamaican aristocrat of careful tastes in wine, and a penchant for old mahogany furniture and good silver, met up with Chuvalo is one of those little peccadilloes of fate that neither seems to want to explain. But meet they did, and Foote grabbed the obvious. "Chuvalo's Fruit Punches!" he exclaimed.

The Foote-Chuvalo team set about developing a line of fruit drinks in lightweight, middleweight and heavyweight sizes and enlisted a well-known independent Canadian food processor, SunPac

Foods, to help them. In the tiled laboratories of SunPac, suitable amounts of fruit concentrate and chemicals were sniffed, filtered and tasted to produce the appropriate tastes.

Food marketing is not a simple business. Developing a fruit punch is one thing. Getting the chain stores to list it on their computers is quite another. That requires capital, a good broker and a good gimmick. The gimmick was clearly Chuvalo's name, but he had been out of action for some time and his currency needed some updating. A title fight for the Canadian heavyweight boxing championship would solve that, but the Canadian Boxing Federation wasn't about to sanction a Chuvalo-Felstein match as a title bout. Chuvalo could see the commercial potential in a fight even if it weren't a title match. "Listen," he counseled his promoters in a whispered phone conversation, "we could go for the controversy with the federation. You know what I mean?"

By January of this year, the Chuvalo Fruit Punches were still not in the stores and production was already two months behind schedule. And by January, Chuvalo had at least 40 pounds to lose to get into fighting shape, and two months in which to do it. But in spite of the dire predictions of food brokers ("these guys are in for a big shock if they think the Chuvalo name will get them on the shelves"), the haphazard training program for the fight, the sleazy occupants of the boxing gyms and the cynical sports columnists, there remained some gold among the dross and that gold was George Chuvalo himself.

Making and missing appointments, beginning businesses and coming back to start new ones all over again, moving, wheeling, dealing and smiling with a genuineness that sorted out the nickel-and-dime sentiments of temporary camp followers and along-for-the-ride business associates, it was Chuvalo who would go the distance. In all his fights they had never knocked him down. Commentators could make fun of stolid Chuvalo standing there, legs apart like a mindless Colossus, taking, taking endless physical punishment, but there remained a dignity about a man who would not throw in the towel and take the easy way out. There was a quality of spirit that sneering observers (who themselves would wither at the glance of a spinster schoolteacher) could never understand. And in life, as in the ring, Chuvalo will survive with some personal decency. Whether he goes into the ring March 7 to make one last stand, or to flog some fruit punches, or just to pick up a needed $10,000, he will do it with charm and with guts.

George Chuvalo knocked out Bobby Felstein in the ninth round and retired as Canadian champ in 1978. Subsequently he had to fight personal tragedy, losing his first wife and three sons in drug-related deaths, but is now a respected anti-drug crusader living in Toronto.

Barbara Amiel was a senior writer for Maclean's *from 1976 to 1981. She has been a regular columnist for the magazine since 1978, although a guest column appeared in 1966.*

Wayne Gretzky: The Great One

Wayne Gretzky waves goodbye to Ottawa fans in his
final game in Canada, April 15, 1999

By James Deacon

APRIL 26, 1999. Hollywood will no doubt make a movie about Wayne Gretzky some day, and it will have to include the scene where he plays his last game in Canada, in Ottawa against the Senators. It happened like this last week: Gretzky and his New York Rangers, who had already been eliminated from playoff contention, were playing the home team to a draw, thus denying the Senators a chance to boost their own playoff position. Yet with 4:45 left in the third period, during one of Gretzky's shifts, the crowd began to chant, "One more year! One more year!" Then, minutes later during a stoppage in play, the big-screen scoreboard above centre ice replayed highlights from Gretzky's career, and the PA system played Carly Simon's "Nobody Does It Better." The crowd rose in tribute, and players on both benches stood, too, banging their sticks against the boards and on the ice in the quintessential hockey salute.

When the game finally ended in a 2-2 tie, the Senators lined up, one by one, to shake Gretzky's hand. As for the Corel Centre fans, they stood by their seats long after they would normally have scattered for the parking lots, cheering, whistling, clapping. This from the opposing team's supporters. Most had come to the game wondering if the rumours were true, that the Great One was actually leaving the game he had so profoundly changed. Now, it seemed, they knew, and they were not going to miss their chance to say goodbye. Prodded by his teammates and by the unwavering applause, Gretzky emerged from the dressing room for a curtain call. It was too brief for the crowd, which didn't stop until, a few minutes later, he returned again, without equipment but with his soaked jersey draped over his narrow frame. He stepped out to the bench and waved up into the seats in all directions, but he was too overwrought to bask in the adoration, so he quickly disappeared down the tunnel to the dressing room.

Such is the esteem in which Gretzky is held. For weeks, he had wrestled with whether to finally call it quits, and he had waged the battle mainly by himself. Normally, he would have consulted his father, Walter. But he didn't want even a hint of his plans to leak, and, as one family associate said: "Wally's incapable of telling a lie, so it would have gotten out." Why the secrecy? Modest by superstar standards, Gretzky feared the farewell fuss that would inevitably have occurred at every arena in the league. Nor did he want to distract his teammates when they faced more pressing issues. "I thought about this for a long time," he explained later, "but I kept it extremely quiet because we were in a playoff hunt and I did not want it to disrupt the team."

A team player to the end. Gretzky holds every meaningful NHL goal-scoring record, yet his greatest hockey talent was his knack for setting up other players to score. And in a lengthy list of career accomplishments, one of the more remarkable is that the man who played on a level no one has ever achieved, and who was a leader even when someone else had been designated captain, somehow managed to be "just one of the guys" in the dressing room. So out of respect for the Rangers, Gretzky did not make his retirement official until he returned to New York City, when he could be among his teammates in his last hockey home. It was also no surprise that he deflected the lavish praise, crediting everyone from teammates to locker-room attendants for so much of his success. And he had an easy explanation for his unfailingly gracious demeanour during 21 years as a pro: if he had become a role model off the ice as well as on, it was because he was Phyllis and Walter's boy, then and always.

His retirement leaves the hockey world feeling more funereal than joyful. What, after all, was the NHL without the Great One? For two decades, he was the shining constant in a hurly-burly sport that too often bashed itself in the head. He helped lead the transition away from the thuggery of the mid-1970s, when the Philadelphia Flyers ruled by the fist, to a more skilled game that embraces players from around the world. That internationalization is in part why Gretzky insists the sport is thriving and can absorb the loss of its most compelling character. "I've always said no player is bigger than the game," he said, adding: "The game is in great shape."

Maybe so, but try telling that to fans around the NHL, who even in Gretzky's less productive seasons have cherished every sighting. Tell it to the rink rats who secured 99's signature because he was one of sport's all-time great autograph-signers. Tell it to the NHL marketing department, for whom he is still the only player with transcendent appeal in the United States. Tell it to ABC, the U.S. TV network which just bought the league's broadcast rights for five years and $800 million (U.S.), starting next season.

Then explain it to his family. Gretzky was never just Wayne—Janet, the kids, his dad and his dad's Brantford, Ont., buddies were all fixtures at every big event, just as they were at Madison Square Garden for the last hurrah on Sunday. "There is going to be a lot of emptiness," Walter told *Maclean's*. "My friends always watch the games with me at our home and, gee whiz, we won't have that anymore. Emptiness." Janet was similarly wistful. She hoped her husband would have a chance to go like Michael Jordan had—with a freshly minted championship. "I didn't want him to leave on a down note," she says, "but he reassured me a thousand times that he was happy with his decision, that this was the right time." Still, she will feel the loss, too. "I'm happy for him, but I'd be lying if I said I won't miss it," she said. "I love to watch him play."

And tell it to the man himself. A significant part of Gretzky's appeal was the childlike joy he took in the game. He loved the company of fellow players, the goofing around in practice and, above all, the competition. The decision to give up hockey had been a long, agonizing process. Hockey had been his life for 35 of his 38 years, and even while he stood in the Madison Square Garden theatre insisting his last days as a player ought to be fun, he said so with a voice that quavered, with eyes that were red and glistening, and with body language that suggested hockey's loss was no match for the sadness Gretzky would feel when he unlaced his skates one final time. "I am going to miss every single part of the game," he said. "But life goes on."

Gretzky was 10 years old when he got his first tip on how to handle public life. As usual, it came from his dad. "You've got to behave right," Walter told his son back then. "They're going to be watching for every mistake. Remember that. You're a very special person and you're on display."

Why saddle so young a boy with so great a responsibility? The younger Gretzky was a prodigy, hockey's Mozart, whose first symphonies were composed with goals, assists and victories, and whose exploits were being chronicled in national publications. In 1971, Gretzky led his Brantford peewee team to 68 straight victories on the back of his whopping 378 goals (the league's next-best scorer had 40). Despite adding 120 assists that year, Gretzky sparked resentment not only among vanquished opponents but also among some parents of his teammates, who accused the phenom of denying their children a chance to shine. Former Detroit Red Wing goalie Greg Stefan, who played on that peewee team, denies that Gretzky put personal glory ahead of team goals. "Wayne was so competitive," recalls Stefan. "Some of the parents would call him a puck hog, but he would do what it took to win."

Gretzky outgrew hometown hockey and left at 14 to play in Toronto. At 16 he joined the major-junior Greyhounds of Sault Ste. Marie in the Ontario Hockey League, and at 17—a year before his NHL eligibility—he signed with the World Hockey Association's Indianapolis Racers, owned by Vancouver businessman Nelson Skalbania. After eight games, he was traded to the then-WHA Edmonton Oilers. Some veterans were suspicious of the newcomer with the big reputation. "He was just a kid with acne, a scrawny little guy," recalls Al Hamilton, the Oilers captain then. "We wondered what was all the ranting and raving about. We soon realized he had a unique talent, and each time you saw him play you saw something new." His teammates also saw passes coming—like they had never seen them before. "He had an uncanny knack," says Hamilton, "of knowing where the puck was going to go to, and of finding guys—the puck would end up on your stick."

Gretzky's NHL career began the following fall, after the WHA folded and the NHL absorbed the Oilers and three other teams. As a 19-year-old rookie, he tied longtime star Marcel Dionne as the league's top scorer with 51 goals and 86 assists, totals that were mere appetizers. In Edmonton, aided by other talented young players—among them centre Mark Messier, defencemen Paul Coffey and Kevin Lowe, goalie Grant Fuhr and winger Jari Kurri—Gretzky reached unheard-of heights. He scored 92 goals in 1981–82. Four times he finished with more than 200 points for a season. "He didn't just break records—he blew them out of the water," marvels Dallas Stars winger Brett Hull. "These were records that people had thought were untouchable, and he made a mockery of them."

The team trophies came, too. The Oilers won the Stanley Cup in 1984, 1985, 1987 and 1988, and Gretzky led Canada to two Canada Cup triumphs in the 1980s. He recalls Game 2 of the rivetting, three-game series against the Soviets in 1987 as perhaps his greatest-ever game, and he capped Canada's Game 3 triumph by setting up Mario Lemieux's series-winning goal in the dying moments. A magician on the ice, he was no choirboy off it—but he was discreet. "He had his party times," says longtime Oiler broadcaster Ken Brown. "There are legendary stories here in Edmonton, but he knew when to do it and how to do it."

Gretzky was firmly in control of the hockey universe in those last years in Edmonton, and his splashy Edmonton wedding to American actress Janet Jones was the stuff of royalty. What Gretzky didn't know was that the Oilers' owner, Peter Pocklington, was struggling in his other businesses and was getting ready to cash in his most valuable asset. On Aug. 9, 1988, only 25 days after the Gretzky-Jones wedding, Pocklington abruptly shipped his star to the Los Angeles Kings for $15 million (U.S.) in cash.

There were other players involved in the deal to make it look like a trade, but Gretzky wasn't fooled, and still refers to being "sold" rather than traded. He felt betrayed and so did Edmontonians, who raged at Pocklington for dispatching their pride and joy—the man who put Edmonton on the international map—down to the States. The deal made Gretzky wary of the business of hockey, and he needed to be. While the Great One made hockey a hit in Hollywood, Kings' owner Bruce McNall ran out of money and was later convicted of fraud and sent to jail for four years. Subsequent Kings owners had money problems, too, and Gretzky grew tired of the corporate instability that undercut the quality of the team. In 1996, he asked for a trade and was dealt to St. Louis, where he was briefly teamed with Hull, the Blues' great sniper. When St. Louis opted not to re-sign him that off-season, Gretzky joined the Rangers for what would be his last three seasons.

With age and without much of a supporting cast, Gretzky experienced lean times in New York. Worse, Team Canada failed to win the 1996 World Cup on home ice or the 1998 Olympic title in Nagano, Japan. He was crushed by both defeats, and his apparent misery reflected the feelings of his country. But part of what made Gretzky such a compelling leader was his great perspective. No one took the Nagano loss harder than he did, but he was not about to let it ruin his Olympic experience. Following the final game, Gretzky returned to the athletes' village and found his teammates, morose and quiet, sprawled in the lounge. Speed skater Catriona Le May Doan came in about the same time, and recalls watching Gretzky adroitly turn the mood around. "Come on, guys," he barked. "It's not so bad that we can't go have a beer." So they all did.

His father, in fact, was the first to denounce the theory that Gretzky could not be replaced. "When Gordie Howe retired, everyone said, 'What is going to happen when Gordie is gone?'" Walter said last week. "Someone took Gordie's place, and when Wayne goes, there will be others that will step in. It's such a great game."

Others need to be convinced. He may not be leaving with a freshly won championship, as Michael Jordan did last year in basketball, but Gretzky is unlacing his skates while still, undeniably, the most important player in hockey. "It's a big blow to the game," says Dick Irvin, the respected *Hockey Night in Canada* broadcaster. "These people (at NHL headquarters) are sitting there thinking, 'We're in trouble—who is going to take his place?' There isn't anyone."

Irvin has a point. Gretzky's value to the NHL is far more complex than Howe's was, largely because professional sports are vastly different businesses now than they were even 15 years ago. Gretzky became a marketing vehicle—for sponsors' products, for league visibility and expansion, and for TV ratings. The NHL that he joined in 1979 was poorly managed, had no U.S. network TV contract and had few prospects for growth. Since then, the league has expanded from 21 to 27 teams, and league officials attribute much of that to Gretzky's impact—to the success of the Los Angeles Kings and the subsequent profile it gave the game. Entertainment giants like Disney and Blockbuster suddenly wanted to play, so teams in Anaheim, Calif., and Miami, respectively, were born. Thanks in no small part to Gretzky, the NHL, under new management, could bill itself "the coolest game on earth" without blushing. Speaking of Gretzky's retirement, NHL commissioner Gary Bettman said: "We always knew that we would have to deal with this day. We just hoped it wouldn't be this soon."

Gretzky's remarkable clout has helped sponsors, too. Directed by his longtime agent, Michael Barnett, he saw his off-ice income begin to rival the $8.5 million (U.S.) a year he was getting in Los Angeles. He has helped sell pizzas, camcorders, clothing and, of course, hockey equipment. His first-ever endorsement, in fact, was with Titan hockey sticks, initially for $5,000 a year and all the lumber he could splinter. When he first started using the sticks, the then-Finnish company was No. 15 in the North American market. When Gretzky took up another brand in 1989, Titan was No. 1 in the world and had built a massive manufacturing plant in Cowansville, Que. "Wayne was responsible for us building that factory in Canada," said Bob Leeder, sales director for Titan. "He made Titan hockey sticks."

What will Gretzky do now? If he knows, he's not saying. "First and foremost, I want to give the time to my family that I haven't been able to give before," he said. No one doubts he will. "You can't underestimate how important his family is to him," says teammate Adam Graves. "He always had his kids at the practice rink, or wherever he was going." But experts who consult with athletes say the first year after retirement is difficult. The sport provided the rhythm in Gretzky's life, his days structured by practices, meals and games, his years reduced to two seasons—hockey and summer. He thrived in that environment, and now he must live by a different beat. "I'm not too concerned about that," he said. "I have a tremendous family, and they will keep me busy."

He is not hurting for cash. A conservative investor, he has socked away millions over his career, enough to consider an ownership position with a team, if he wanted. "I made more money than I ever imagined," he said, "but I know I earned it, and I know I made money for some other people, too."

In the end, it was the effort it would take to be Wayne Gretzky that prompted him to retire. Despite an off season, Gretzky remains one of the league's elite players and could certainly play effectively for another couple of seasons. But he is similar to the late, great Joe DiMaggio, who once said that he had to play his best baseball every day because someone might be seeing him for the first time. Over the past few months, Gretzky began to doubt that he could perform at an acceptable level for another 82-game season. And rather than slip below his own remarkable standards, he decided to go.

He was the greatest player in the game Canadians care about most, but he was also Wayne Gretzky from Brantford, a regular guy who happened to earn riches and fame without forsaking family or roots. He was the best playmaker hockey has ever known, but he rarely displayed arrogance or conceit. And going into last Sunday's final game, when he saw the effect of his announcement on his teammates' morale, he did his best to cheer them up. "He wants us to be happy for him," defenceman Brian Leetch said gloomily. "But it's hard for us not to feel sad."

Same goes for Canadians.

Wayne Gretzky is now part owner of the NHL *Phoenix Coyotes and executive director of the men's Olympic hockey team for the 2002 Salt Lake City Olympic Games.*

Sports editor James Deacon has been profiling athletes at Maclean's *since 1990.*

TYCOONS

Sir Maxwell Aitken

Max Aitken as Lord Beaverbrook during the First World War

By James Grant

SEPTEMBER, 1911. This is the story of a man—half boy and half man—who set out to build himself a great castle, and when he had pulled great stones together ready for the raising of the walls and the towers of the building, and when he had even raised some of the walls to a height which showed how great a castle it was to be—he suddenly left off at his castle-building and went away with men who told him that there was a greater work to be done; who told him of a land of dragons, and who said that it would be much better work to go in for killing the dragons than for finishing the walls of the castle. For the castle, they said, would be but a selfish work, whereas to rid the country of a pest would be a work done for the whole people and would make the world remember him always as a man who had done it a great service.

This refers to young Sir Maxwell Aitken who set out to become master of the financial situation in Canada, which is equivalent to the building of the castle aforementioned; but who has been turned aside to champion the cause of the Unionist Party and the Imperialists of England who seek to destroy the dragon of Liberalism and Imperial indifference. A large number of people in Canada have overlooked the most interesting fact about Sir Maxwell Aitken. They have been arguing as to whether he made his millions out of watered stock or whether he merely took opportunities which they were too slow to see. It does not matter whether Sir Maxwell Aitken made his money by stock manipulation or by saving up the interest on a post office deposit; in the procession of great men who walk down the main street of the earth every day, he is a curious figure— a strange figure, and the only question is, will that figure grow greater or will it dwindle?

Of course, there is also the question of Sir Max Aitken's courage. He knew he was a good castle-builder. He knows, and fair-minded Canadians know, too, that if he had remained in Canada he would have been probably one of the greatest financial forces in the Dominion. But he has quit finance for politics and imperialism. Has he the courage to keep on, or will he go back and complete his career as a financier? Or—will he stand by his fate as a politician, whether it be to die as a back-bencher, or to lead a nation—more than a nation—an empire.

Before 40, the New World grudges a man serious publicity. It reads accounts of boy prodigies who play pianos or violins or sing sacred solos in church choirs; or, in athletics, it is glad enough to hear of champion bowlers, pitchers, runners or lacrosse players who developed at an early age; but in the realm of Politics and Finance men of 35 are children—to be seen and not heard. Therefore, although Max Aitken at 23 had merged two banks, although before he was 30 he had bought and redeemed a dying trust company, although he had exploited railways and power companies in tropical latitudes—little was heard of him in Canada. His own generation was jealous, the older generation was suspicious. He himself chose to work quietly. His influence was underneath the surface-showing of older merchants and financiers, and it is to be feared, undid the foundations of many of them who were too proud and too slow to match their wit against a youngster's. Even since he formed the greatest mergers in Canada, the cement trust and the car trust, he had been little known among the general public until the Canadian Associated Press in London cabled to Canada last December that "Mr. W. M. Aitken" was creating almost a sensation in his election campaign in one of the Manchesters.

Canadians in eastern Canada, where Aitken was born, said: "Max Aitken! Max Aitken running for member of Parliament in England!

Who is he? What Max Aitken is it?" And then they remembered. "Oh, that little fellow who used to be old man Stair's secretary! Well! well! We thought he was dead when Stair died. Isn't that odd! Member of Parliament in England!"

Other Canadians, except for a few business men who had not taken Max seriously enough in time and who rubbed their noses reflectively, knew even less about him, and asked for further information. Upon which they were told that Max Aitken was a young man who had done well in Canada and who was now *buying* his way into popularity in the Old Country—of course, they said "buying." It is only recently, when Sir Sandford Fleming in the Canadian Senate attacked him for alleged stock-jobbing in connection with the forming of the Canadian cement merger, and later, when it was announced that King George, at his coronation, had been pleased to make him "Sir" Max Aitken, that Canadians really began seriously to consider him.

One should, of course, begin with a story of Sir Maxwell's early struggles. His father was a Presbyterian minister in a small town in New Brunswick. "Max" was educated at Dalhousie College, and after leaving there read law in (then Governor) Tweedie's office. He read more of it in R. B. Bennett's office in Calgary. But these facts throw little light on his career. He earned his living for a time by short-hand and insurance. Even today, when he wishes to dispose of a letter quickly, he writes a memo in Pitman's system on the bottom of it for his secretary.

Between this 20th and his 25th year he was a considerable figure in Maritime Province finance. He became secretary, but afterward partner, of John S. Stair, a leading business man of Halifax. The lean-faced secretary soon wielded as much business influence in Halifax as the average successful man wields at 50. At 23, he brought about the consolidation of the Union Bank of Halifax and the Commercial Bank of Windsor. At 25, he was building railways and lighting plants in Cuba. Then he bought three-quarters of the stock of the Montreal Trust Company, and, changing his residence to Montreal, took charge of that institution, so that it recovered its health and thrived, despite the panic of 1907. In 1909 he was listed as one of Montreal's millionaires. That year he bought the Rhode-Curry Car Company, and, associated with Mr. N. Curry, formed the Canadian Car & Foundry Company. A year or two ago, with Rodolphe Forget and E. R. Wood, he formed the Canadian Cement Company. Meanwhile, his enterprises continue to do well, while he has become an English MP and a Knight.

I interviewed him at his home in Worplesdon, Surrey. I will not say that he was difficult to interview, nor easy. You could tell that he had not been interviewed very often before, and that he did not view with any pleasure, nor with any displeasure, the prospect of his being "written up." He was of medium height and sallow complexion. On first impression he appeared to be a man of light build, with little colour and thin hair, nervous hands, and a voice that sounded as though he was recovering from a cold. He looked like a thousand other respectable men of intelligence, but he looked also—over-worked. This thin hair was tousled on the top of his head as though he had been lying down and reading. There were some questions to be asked:

"Do you believe that trusts are bad things?"

"No. I believe in 'consolidations.' They are more efficient. They give better service to the customer. In a large country such as Canada, they reduce the distribution costs. They are good for the consumer."

"You admit that they centralize power and that they offer oppor-tunities for unscrupulous men?"

"Of course. So does a police force."

We were in the library. All around him were the things which would have taken an ordinary man a lifetime to collect. Out there, through the deep windows, the lawn ran away and hid under the skirts of the oaks and behind the clouds of rhododendrons. A swag-gering wind insulted the roses which climbed modestly over the condescending bows of an oak. In the house itself was every neces-sity and every luxury, was order, was good taste, was the savour of a gentler presence somewhere, and the presence of children. There, in a deep chair, was the master of these things, this boy, Sir Max Aitken.

"Humph!" he said, moving uneasily. "We need rain. We need it badly."

Rain was all that one could see him needing. Everything else was there that the ordinary Englishman could want. An ordinary Englishman of wealth would have been content and would even have left it for the rector to wish for rain.

Before Max Aitken left Canada he was selling more than $13 million worth of bonds every year. In the early part of last year, having already formed the cement merger and the Canada Car Company, and having been the prime mover in a score of industrial concerns all over the Dominion, he bought the Montreal Rolling Mills Company for $4 million. In July, he sold to the Steel Company of Canada.

That month he went to England. His health had given out.

It was here that he met the men who caused him to change the direction of his ambitions. It is said that the two chief influences toward this end were Rudyard Kipling and [prominent Conservative who was elected party leader in November, 1911] Bonar Law. Kipling and Aitken had met years before, just after Kipling had been given an honourary degree by McGill University. The author of *Mulvaney* and *Kim* and *Puck of Paak's Hill,* was then riding on a 15-cent excursion steamer on the River Mirimachi, in the east. Aitken was a fellow passenger, and it was there that the friendship had started. Mr. Bonar Law had played with Max Aitken when the two lived in the vicinity of Newcastle in their juvenile days. Law's father was a clergyman, as was also Aitken's. Their interests in those days had been more or less in common.

He was bitten in England, as many another Canadian has been bitten, by the germ of Imperialism. Men talked to him of the needs of the Empire, of the work that is to be done to make the Mother Country and the Colonies realize the meaning of the word Empire. With millions already in his possession, he turned his back upon his plans for financial conquests and enlisted under [Conservative Opposition leader] Mr. Balfour.

It is an old story now how Sir Maxwell went into the election last December and how, although the seat was rated as a difficult one for a Unionist to win, he won it by a substantial majority. At that time the great London dailies devoted great space to his campaign. He was discussed pro and con by all the papers. Bonar Law, in an election address, described Aitken as "the most capable young man I know." The Toronto *Globe*, having made sure just who he was, contributed a fatherly editorial in which it admonished him to be as successful in his new line of life as in his old, the penalty, it hinted, being greater obscurity than if he had been only an ordinary man and failed. But Max Aitken was in no position to pay any attention to the people who had ignored him before he went to England, and who were compelled to recognize him after the people of England had "discovered" his abilities. He retired to his new home in England, a sick man. There followed a time when he was scarcely expected to recover, so much strength had he expended in his first political battle. But he had won it.

The question is: How much ability has Sir Maxwell Aitken? And what kind of ability is it? If one could answer these with certainty, then one might be able to guess how far Sir Maxwell will travel in the new sphere which he has chosen. The attacks which have been made upon him in connection with his career in Canada, and the things which have been insinuated against his knighthood, have little bearing upon the case. Some few papers wanted to know why certain other Canadians had not been honoured in Sir Maxwell's place, forgetting that the honour was not given to Sir Maxwell as to a Canadian, but as to a valued citizen of the British Empire, living in England. His ability as a man of business has not been proven to be any less by the attacks upon him. His knighthood was undoubtedly a recognition not only of his own worth as a citizen of England, but of the high family with which Sir Maxwell is connected.

Now, these are some of his qualities, as one might read them in looking over the facts of his career and in meeting him. He has ambition, determination, tenacity of purpose, keenness of insight, alertness, quickness of decision, and quickness in action. He works very hard. He rises early and goes through his mail. He sees business callers and gives business directions during the day. In the evening he enjoys the same relaxations as other men, but when they have gone to bed, when the lights downstairs have been put out, Sir Maxwell lies in bed and reads into the early hours of the next day. He reads quickly and digests the information. He is one of the best-informed men of the day.

Sir Max Aitken has a great deal of the primitive man about him. Perhaps this is why Kipling is said to admire him so. Perhaps it will help him in politics; perhaps not. In his instinct for retaliation he is like a boy. If he is hurt a little, he will say nothing; if he is hurt to the quick his impulse is to strike straight back, without a cry, without warning—but to strike! He is a man with the highest moral sensitiveness, but I would guess him to be ruthless in the heat of the game. He would not willingly hurt anyone, but when he is running he sees nothing but the goal. He bends all his energies toward it. He has an appetite for work and an instinct for success. These qualities have probably assisted him in his career as a financier.

Finance, however, is a primitive game, calling out the primitive instincts. Politics is more subtle. Although a statesman may be self-seeking and an opportunist, he must disguise it. He cannot succeed merely by overcoming his enemies, he must make his enemies overcome themselves so that their defeat looks, in the eyes of the people, more like the hand of Providence than the hand of a political general. Sir Maxwell Aitken may possess these subtler qualities. At all events, he has the wit to find out for himself the rules of the new Game and adapt himself to them, rather than force the new Game with old methods.

He stands with three courses before him: If he leaves politics in time he has yet the key to the financial; if he remains in politics he may succeed, he may become a great name throughout the whole Empire; or he may become only one of the House of Commons of England—an honourable enough post, but in Max Aitken's place it would be tragedy, and time for someone to write another psychological novel.

Max Aitken bought his first of several newspapers in 1916, became Lord Beaverbrook in 1917 and a cabinet minister the following year in David Lloyd George's coalition wartime government. A longtime friend of Winston Churchill's, Aitken left politics after the First World War, but Churchill brought him back into his Second World War cabinet as minister of aircraft production. He continued to take an active interest in his papers until his death at 85 in 1964.

The Molsons of Montreal: Pioneers of Steamship Traffic on the St. Lawrence River

John Molson Jr., 1862

By Linton Eccles

Editor's Note—The family sketches that have appeared in Maclean's *from time to time have been one of its leading features. These articles are not intended to give some fulsome praise or to laud the genealogical tree of some favourite of fortune, but rather to carry the reader into the early lives and surroundings of the founders of the family in order to ascertain, if possible, some of the shaping characteristics that have counted for much in the making of fame and fortune later on. To this end our writers have endeavored to make an unbiased appraisal of their talents and accomplishments.*

SEPTEMBER, 1913. If you were to stand at the northwest corner of St. James and St. Peter streets, Montreal, and look diagonally across at the opposite corner, you would see a dingy old building that your utilitarian sense would tell you ought to have been pulled down long ago and to have made way for something as near to a skyscraper as the city's old building laws will allow, which is 10 storeys. Certainly the dingy old building is solid enough, and looks as if it will stand for a century or so yet. But upon this gilded location stands a modest three-storey building that might have been commodious, or even handsome, 50 years ago, but is obviously wasting space in these days of golden real estate cornersites.

There is a story told on the street that one day a New Yorker, newly representing his firm's interests in Canada, stood on that northwest corner, and looking across saw the dingy old building. "Here's a chance to do business," he thought; so he took a notion he'd go over and see the president and ask him why he let the grime accumulate on his building when he could have it cleaned "as good as new" for a matter of $30. This young man came to Montreal with the reputation of a salesman, but he sold nothing to the Molsons. Instead, he was shown politely to the door, and a month or so afterwards he had been in the city long enough to grasp the fact that the grime of the Molson's Bank Building was not the least considerable of its assets.

Running a bank sounds a whole lot more fashionable than running a brewery, but if there had been no Molson's brewery there would have been no Molson's Bank. It is over 130 years since John Molson, a young Englishman, landed in Canada. He was a blacksmith by trade, and by ambition, being an immigrant, a fortune-seeker. The total population of this country then was recorded at 127,845, and the chief thing happening was the resistance of the neighbouring Vermonters to American union. Molson came on to Montreal, where something like a sixth of Canada's aggregate of people was centred. He started to work at his trade in a foundry on Notre Dame Street, which, if it were standing to-day, would be opposite the present Molson's Brewery.

When John Molson, after four years breaking in as a Canadian, made up his mind to start brewing beer for his fellow citizens, he had no farther to look for a location than across Notre Dame Street from the foundry. We do not know even whether he had had any experience in brewing before he came to Canada, but he certainly started on the right track by learning to brew well.

But the brewing business by no means filled all the ambition of John Molson. Machinery and the handling and improving of it was an older passion with him, and like all good engineers he had a bent for inventing contrivances to save human labour. At the significant time when James Watt in England and Robert Fulton in America were working on the steam engine, and puzzling out how it could be adapted to propel a boat, Molson was busy along parallel lines. He never met, and so far as is known now never had any communication with either Fulton or Watt, but he studied out the steamboat problem for himself. He was hampered, as provokingly as were his two better remembered contemporaries, by lack of financial faith of others in his speculative undertakings, and he had to rely almost solely upon his brewery profits to prosecute his engineering advantages.

Still, Molson was made of stubborn stuff and he had a firm belief in the coming power of steam. He went on brewing good beer, and from what was left over in the revenue he paid his help at the foundry, and built a steamship, which he called the *Accommodation*. This ship was launched ready for business on Nov. 1, 1809, about two years after Fulton sailed, or rather steamed, at the Hudson in his "puffing billy" boat, the *Clermont*. True, Fulton's steamer preceded that of the Montrealer, but its engine was built by James Watt in Britain, whilst John Molson both designed and erected his own engine.

No sooner was the *Accommodation* successfully floated at Montreal than Molson with the few associates who were prepared to place their lives in his hands, was ready to try her out. On Nov. 3, 1809, she started on her maiden trip to Quebec. The *Accommodation* measured 85 feet over all and was fitted with a six horsepower engine of the early locomotive type, just resting on the framework of the boat, and unprotected from the weather. Her builder figured that, going downstream, he could make the ancient capital within 36 hours, but he reckoned without his pilot and the strong current. After hairbreadth escapes from being wrecked, they anchored off Three Rivers for the night, and arrived at Quebec on the morning of the third day after leaving Montreal.

The *Accommodation* had room for 20 passengers, but only half that number ventured on the initial passage with her designer. Whether they held a prayer meeting en route or upon landing safely at Quebec is not recorded, but John Molson had seen enough of his experiment to know that it had succeeded in the essentials. He had built and handled the second passenger steamer in the world, and the first one built entirely in North America. But not for a hobby had he prosecuted this experiment. Molson was a man of business first and a philanthropist afterwards. He knew that if the *Accommodation* was capable of establishing a regular sailing on the St. Lawrence, the prospective passengers were capable of paying for the trip. Twenty was his limit, but he charged each of them for the passage, including berth and meals and with a limit of 60 pounds of baggage, two pounds 10 shillings—which was worth considerably more than $12.50 will buy to-day.

On August 20, 1812, he added a second vessel to his fleet and launched the *Swiftsure*. Recognizing now that he meant business the government granted him a monopoly of steam navigation on the St. Lawrence, and Molson reciprocated, during the War of 1812, by placing his ships at the disposal of his adopted country, and they were used for transporting troops.

Good commercial men always, the Molsons have found scope and opportunity to be good philanthropists. Away back in 1815 we find the founder of the family figuring at a meeting called to inaugurate the Montreal General Hospital, towards which object he contributed several hundred pounds. The war of a year or two before had demonstrated the need of such an institution, and John Molson had seen for himself scores of sick and wounded soldiers quartered upon the charity of private residents of the city.

The following year we learn of him extending his steamboat service to Lake Ontario, and, with other businessmen interested in shipping, petitioning the legislature to undertake the deepening of the river's channel between Montreal and Three Rivers. On Nov. 3, 1816, the Bank of Montreal was opened as a private bank, and John Molson was one of the original subscribers to the starting-out capital of £87,500. The Bank of Montreal was incorporated on May 18, 1822, and Molson became president of the institution seven years later.

By this time his reputation as pioneer of steam navigation and as a prosperous commercial citizen was well founded. His being a most retiring man did not prevent the honours that were forced upon him. He donated heavily towards the new building of the General Hospital which was completed on May 1, 1822, at which date the city's population was given as 18,767. In the early 1830s, when there were around 25,000 people in the city, came the plague of Asiatic cholera—3,500 persons died within five months, and the General and other city hospitals were filled to the doors. Old John Molson, who had done much to set it on its feet financially, died in 1840.

Besides the brewery and the foundry, he had started a paying tug and freight carrying service, as well as opening what must have been about the first wallpaper manufactory on the continent. He also experimented with a sugar refinery and a distillery, but dropped these when he found they did not pay.

Whilst the whole Molson family has had, and has, a finger in the bank pie, the brewery seems to have been the special preserve of the eldest son for the time being. When the turn came for Mr. Herbert Molson, the present proprietor, and great grandson of the first John Molson, to take it over, the condition of his father's will was that he should pay into the family estate the sum of $75,000, which was a cheap price to pay for a property of two large blocks assessed by the city at half a million dollars—or nearly as much as the sacred bank itself—and for a business that turns out every day 10,000 dozen bottles of beer, which, it is claimed, is more than all the other bottled beer trade of the country.

John Molson, junior, who became the Honorable John by virtue of his seat on the executive council of Quebec, and who followed his father in building up the brewing trade, was a soldier practically all the time he was not busy on his various money-making projects. He commanded a regiment of volunteers in the Rebellion of 1837. In 1862, when there was great excitement over the Trent affair, he formed the Hochelaga Light Infantry, which afterwards was merged in the 1st Prince of Wales Rifles. Also he handed over for barrack purposes to the Tenth Regiment of British Infantry a college for boys which he and his father had founded in conjunction with St. Thomas's Church, and which had not succeeded in its original purpose very well owing to its being situated in the French section of the city.

John's brother, William, was the first president of Molson's Bank, which enjoying its franchise under the Free Banking Act, first opened its doors on Oct. 8, 1853. Two years later it became chartered, and had $300,000 of paid-up capital. William Molson had the reputation of being a staid, safe character. It is Molson's Bank history that you could time the clock by him. He never left the office for luncheon until the tick of one, and a minute after he could be seen descending the steps to St. James Street. His other habits were just as punctual, and the staff had to follow suit or quit. William Molson, who was the bank's president for the 20 years preceding his death, is remembered as one of the earliest benefactors of McGill College. His epitaph from the late Judge Day was, "He was one of those who know the value of money, yet whose hearts are ever open to the appeals which are made to their benevolence."

Thomas Molson, who died in 1911, and who was the grandson of old John Molson, and father of Herbert Molson, the present proprietor of the brewery, had a kink of eccentricity in his character. After his prime he became a Unitarian, and some time after he had taken this step he donated to Trinity Anglican Church the interest on $10,000 upon the condition that the Athanasian Creed was never recited in the church. This income was enjoyed by the Anglican body for several years, and then a new rector was appointed who was none other than the Bishop Mills of Ontario of today. The Rev. Mr. Mills declined to cut out anything that was contained in the Prayer Book ritual, he stopped his ears against all talk of compromise, and ordered the treasurers of the church to return the money to Mr. Molson, which was done.

Previous to his Unitarian days, Thomas, with his father the Hon. John Molson, had founded St. Thomas's Anglican Church, and had given the site. When the church trustees decided to move to more fashionable Sherbrooke Street, Thomas bought back the original site for $10,700, and he also contributed $20,000 towards the building of the new edifice. He afterwards gave to the church further sums of $20,000 odd, making his total donations to St. Thomas's $51,700. His later gifts were made following his change of creed, and around the latest of them is told an interesting story.

There was a mortgage of $10,000 remaining on the church, and an emergency meeting was called to consider how to raise the amount of the interest, which was overdue. The church wardens were in a fix, and none, but one, could see the way out of it. This one was Mr. John Campbell, city accountant, who had in his pocket a cheque which he had received that afternoon from his lifelong friend, Thomas Molson. The cheque covered the total of the mortgage and interest to date, and Mr. Campbell created a dramatic surprise when he announced the fact. There came a strong kick from the temperance section of the vestry, which section objected to taking money from brewery profits and wanted to return it to the sender, but the objection was overruled by the majority.

The Molsons were one of the prominent Montreal families bereaved by the *Titanic* disaster, when Mr. Henry Markland Molson was drowned. He was a grandson of the first John Molson, and son of William Molson, first president of the bank. Markland Molson, born three years after the Molson's Bank started, left an estate of several millions. He was on the boards of so many concerns that it was a wonder even to office acquaintances that he found time to look into them all. Molson's and City and District Banks, the National Trust Company, the R. & O. Navigation Company, Canada Paper Company, Crown Life Insurance Company, Canadian Transfer Company, Standard Chemical Company, the Blaugas Company of Canada, Canadian Rubber Company, and the Montreal Cotton Company were among the most prominent of his directorial undertakings.

Dr. John Elsdale Molson, who is now the largest individual shareholder in the Molson's Bank, lives the life of a country gentleman in the country of Sussex, England. He is another of old John Molson's great grandsons. Dr. Molson, who is 50 years old, married early in life the daughter of one of his physician professors. Like most of the Canadian Molsons, Dr. John Elsdale is a Conservative in politics, but so far he has not been successful in his ambition to get into Parliament, the London constituency of Bethnal Green, North East, having turned him down at the general elections of 1909 and 1910. Even in the old country, where dignity and wealth run easily together, Dr. Elsdale Molson is known as a dignified personality, and he has a natural charm of manner that makes him a popular guest at country house parties.

Dr. Molson really is the development of type which was presented by John Molson, the Canadian immigrant of 1782. The old man's word was reckoned fully as good as his bond, and he was proud and jealous of the trust placed in it and in him. Farmers who teamed into old Montreal week by week after the harvests to bring him their grain knew him for a straight dealer. They had no need to ask him for documents in return for their barley; they knew that one of the last things John Molson would think about would be to beat them out of a bushel. He wanted the best grain, and he paid promptly for the best.

In addition to being a straight business man, John Molson had something Napoleonic in his make-up. No ordinary man, away back in those pioneer days, could plan and scheme and think in advance of his times as he did. Witness his imagination in grasping mentally the idea of steam propulsion and then his practical ability to go ahead and work out his theories to demonstration point. With it all he had the great standing virtue of punctuality in his habits and in his keeping of engagements.

The Molsons who have followed after the founder of the Canadian family have no reason to be ashamed of their antecedents. The old man set the pace of succeeding steadily by fair methods and giving everybody with whom he dealt an honest deal. It is a reputation that not many crowned heads, not many princes of finance, can justly claim, and it is to the credit of the Molson family in general that they have lived up to the reputation established by their founder. They are a people of many possessions, and if the average wealthy family of today can show as much clean money as can the Molsons, then the financial world must be a great deal more morally sound than an outsider or even an insider can judge.

The Molson Bank Building still stands, now protected as a heritage structure, but the bank merged with the Bank of Montreal in 1925. The Molson family still controls Molson Breweries whose chairman is Eric H. Molson, a great-great-great-grandson of John and grandson of Herbert.

K. C. Irving: The Last of a Breed

K. C. Irving striding in front of his new Saint John, N.B., oil refinery, 1964

By Ralph Allen

APRIL 18, 1964. A few weeks ago, when I was assigned to go to New Brunswick to do a story on the fabled and—according to one school of thought—the fearsome K. C. Irving, I felt the same twinge of apprehension with which I had embarked in 1961 to do stories on Moise Tshombe in Katanga and Hendrik Verwoerd in South Africa and, in 1962, on Fidel Castro in Cuba. The few things that have been written about Irving the individual as contrasted with Irving the corporation offered little reassurance. I was assured by several inhabitants and former inhabitants of his vast Atlantic fief that it would be a total waste of time to try to see him in person. To seek any candid observations or insights from his employees and his neighbors would be equally futile, I was warned; even his enemies are loath to discuss him except in privacy, among themselves, like *maquisards* hiding out in cellars.

When I did get to see Irving, briefly, on the day after my arrival, he told me politely but firmly that he would not be interviewed that day or any other. Before I left Saint John two weeks later I had four lengthy talks with him—although there was no explanation or hint of an explanation for his change of mind. It is true that he told me almost nothing, but even in his most guarded moments he fell far short of the advertised figure of the icy, arrogant feudal lord or even of the more conventional tough-guy boss of a tough, hard-driving business juggernaut. Throughout our conversations, even when I brought up matters which he clearly believes are nobody's business but his own, he was as polite and cordial as though I were an elder of his church. In addition he arranged for me to see as much of his industrial operations as there was time to see, including his oil refinery, his two pulp mills, two of his four sawmills and some of his two million acres of pulp and timber land.

All this supported my growing conviction that Irving is far from an easy man to simplify. It is almost never safe to guess what he is thinking or is apt to do about the events, circumstances and people around him. That he inspires a great deal of admiration and respect in his native province is a fact beyond mistaking. This admiration, however, is frequently tempered by a sort of *yes-but* syndrome. "Yes, but if he weren't so *bloody* big!" There's another semi-stock saying, particularly among politicians who know by experience that if you get the reputation of being against K. C. Irving you can easily get the reputation of being against Progress; among business rivals who don't care to tangle with him head-on if it can possibly be avoided; and among the hundreds of thousands of ordinary workers, consumers, newspaper readers, television viewers and bus riders to whom Irving is not merely a symbol but a constant living presence, the man who signs the paycheck, the man who sells the oil for the furnace and the gas for the car, the man who owns the papers and the TV station, the man who runs the bus lines.

Irving shows no inclination to be cut down to size by anyone. A few of Irving's encounters with those who do not see eye to eye with him have had a peculiarly intimate, almost neighborly character. One of these involved a skirmish outside his Saint John oil yard, away back in 1948 when Irving was still in his 40s. He had refused to accept a unanimous conciliation board recommendation for wage-and-hours adjustments, and nearly 50 of his men went on strike. The same day Irving walked up to the massed picket line outside the plant, pulled off his topcoat and yelled: "You may be tough but I'm tougher." Then he mounted the cab of one of his stranded trucks and drove it through the picket line himself. (Years later Irving told an interviewer that he hadn't been looking for trouble, but only obeying a principle that "it never pays to talk with your coat on.")

In simple accuracy it must be reported that Irving seems to be more at home against tougher opposition. When, in July, 1961, before the company was taken over by Shell, an official of Toronto-based Canadian Oil made the careless boast that his firm was the only Canadian-owned oil company operating in the Maritimes, Irving issued an outraged statement pointing out that his own big oil company was not only Canadian-owned but Maritimes-owned. "Let's not forget," he reminded the Atlantic provinces—and for once they were united and unanimous behind him from Shag Harbour at the southeast tip of Nova Scotia to Flowers Cove at the northwest corner of Newfoundland—"that in some cases Upper Canadians are the worst type of foreigners."

If Irving holds any government in awe he has never betrayed the fact. In the 1951 hearings on the Irving Pulp and Paper Bill, one of his lawyers announced casually to a committee of the provincial legislature that the Irving mill was pumping several million gallons of waste-contaminated water into the St. John River every day. One witness to the hearings read a section of the fisheries act forbidding the throwing of debris or "mill rubbish" into any salmon river (which the St. John unquestionably and, in its good years, magnificently, is). The then premier, John B. McNair, sidestepped the question of pollution on the ground that it was a federal affair. The rest of the Irving Pulp and Paper Bill went through unanimously, including clauses giving the company exemption from suits for creating a nuisance as well as the right to divert any watercourse needed for its operations.

Ten years later, during the hearings on the East Coast Smelting and Chemical Company Bill, Irving was an interested spectator in his capacity as one of the chief owners of the company and its affiliated base-metal mines. There must have been moments when he imagined he was listening to a tape recording. The president of the Miramachi Salmon Association said the pending bill presented "a great danger to water and fisheries resources" and another brief went further to warn that "if every company is to be exempt in the matter of pollution the province might as well say goodbye to the salmon-fishing industry." Irving himself appeared as a witness long enough to reaffirm the Magna Carta of big industry in New Brunswick: its special rights and immunities, he argued, are designed only to protect it from "petty interference." "Some people might have the opinion that the industry was of no value and might be prepared to cause us a lot of trouble," he said. "The industry just feels we should not be annoyed without good reason." The East Coast Bill passed unanimously.

Perhaps the most exacting legislative fight of Irving's career was waged partly in support of a non-Irving firm. In 1935 he sold 35 per cent of his pulp and paper company to Kimberly-Clark, the U. S. tissue manufacturer. At the same time he prepared to build a new Kraft mill himself and undertook to negotiate water and tax agreements which would help Kimberly-Clark to build and operate an adjoining tissue mill. In due course Kimberly-Clark would become the biggest single customer for Irving pulp.

Irving personally steered a 30-year tax and a 25-year water agreement through the Lancaster and Saint John city councils. These preliminaries involved little more than the normal horse-trading that accompanies such negotiations anywhere. But when the tax agreement went before the legislature's municipalities committee for approval, a strong rear-guard action was mounted by, of all people, the mayor of Lancaster. Although his council had approved the agreement, the late Parker D. Mitchell hadn't ever liked it and he went to Fredericton to say so one final time; it wasn't the amount of the taxes that he opposed, it was the length of the fixed-rate term and the lack of protection against further depreciation in the value of the dollar and further increases in the rate of the city's spending. Who could tell in 1958 what Kimberly-Clark's and Irving's 1988 dollars would be worth? Who could guess in 1958 what the city's budget would be in 1988?

Irving had intended to let his battery of lawyers do any talking necessary, but again he intervened in person. In so doing he supplied a textbook summary of the take-it-or-leave-it basis on which all big industries—not Irving industries alone—have always hammered out their initial tax and utilities contracts with New Brunswick and its industry-hungry towns and cities. The Saint John area, he pointed out, is not an ideal location for a paper mill. It just wasn't true that Kimberly-Clark would settle its new mill there regardless of the inducements offered. "Anybody who thinks this is a pushover is wrong. We need the assistance of this tax bill. I don't see why we should have so much concern about the future. The future will take care of itself."

The next day Irving's Saint John newspapers—in one of their rare combat missions in direct and unmistakable support of the owner— fired a massive whiff of grape square across the bow of the difficult Mayor Mitchell. The *Morning Telegraph-Journal* led off with a front-page editorial calling the mayor's protest against the tax bill "a sorry spectacle ... obstructionism." The newspapers—the editorial was repeated in the *Times-Globe* the next evening—went on to a more generalized lecture: "When outside interests are privately and without fanfare to consider establishing a major plant here, the first thought that seems to arise is not how to welcome development but how to block and frustrate it ... Every encouragement should be given to real opportunities for new industries, so that the further progress of the area will match strides with the rest of Canada."

The legislature approved the bill, but it did grant Mayor Mitchell the semblance of a victory—the reality of which can only be decided by the legislature of 1973. It cut the period of the tax agreement from 30 years to 15, with the option of renewal "if approved by legislation."

Ruminating on the whole tortuous episode a while ago, a prominent but slightly bruised Saint John politician ended up on the standard *yes-but*: "It's too bad we haven't got half-a-dozen more K. C. Irvings." What, for the sake of argument, I asked him, would happen if a candidate for public office decided to campaign on a straight platform of down-with-K. C. Irving? "He'd get clobbered," the politician said glumly. "And I guess"—he said this glumly too— "he'd deserve to get clobbered."

Industrial history has no control groups. The ceaseless debate of the Maritimes—"suppose there had never even been *one* K. C. Irving?"—is as far from resolution today as it was 55 years ago when as a small boy in the village of Buctouche Irving was looking for a market for his first ball of saved-up binder twine. But impossible as it is to guess what might have happened without him, it is easy enough to demonstrate what's happening *with* him. Except for one brief shutdown caused by fire, the pulp mill—or now the two mills working in tandem—hasn't had an idle day since Irving took over in 1946 and its output has increased from around 90 tons a day to 500 tons a day. (Charles Lynch, a bleach-plant operator who also happens to be a steward of Local 30 of the Pulp, Sulphite and Paper Mill Workers Union, was getting 65 cents an hour for a 48-hour week when Irving bought the plant 18 years ago. Now he gets $2.16 an hour for a 42-hour week. "No, I'm not satisfied. I hope I'll never see the day when we're satisfied. But taking everything, Irving has been a good man to work for. One winter there was no sale for pulp. But he wouldn't close down. He hired warehouses all over town and began stockpiling and kept the plant going.")

Although a scarcity of orders brought some midwinter layoffs at the Saint John shipyard and dry dock, even abstainers from the larger debates about Irving are impressed by the life he's pumped into a plant that five years ago was dying on its feet. The Brunswick–East Coast base-metals complex has already meant, in the estimate of *The Financial Post*, that hundreds of residents of "one of the most hard-pressed areas in Canada . . . have traded the subsistence of local-assistance payments and marginal industries for steady employment and weekly paychecks." Irving spells jobs in a dozen other major plants and areas, and in New Brunswick jobs spell life itself.

Although my misgivings about venturing into Irving's empire without, so to speak, a visa or a sponsor, proved largely unfounded, the adventure was not without its hazards. Interviewing Irving can be a frustrating task, though not for the reasons I had been led to expect. The difficulty is not that he is rude but that he is polite. His personal manners bear so little resemblance to his corporate manners that some of the people who have seen him lose his temper or heard him hurl his clipped insults toward his permanent or temporary foes have put it down to business tactics rather than blood pressure. During my four meetings with him I saw the polite Irving only: the same Irving his loggers, his clerks and his foremen see, the

Irving in whom old-fashioned courtesy appears to be as deeply imbedded as his Presbyterian code of morals. Although, in the course of duty, I felt I had to ask him two or three rude questions, he never offered a rude answer:

Q: It has been said, by people who think they know, that you are worth between $300 million and $400 million. Have you any comment?

A: I have no comment whatsoever.

Q: Many people believe you are the power, financially and otherwise, behind the Liberal Party in New Brunswick and the party repays your favor in kind.

A: Nothing could be further from the truth.

Q: It is often charged that you drive harder bargains than anyone else in taxes, special legislation, expropriation rights, exemptions from lawsuits and the like.

A: Any tax agreements or other concessions that we have received have not been out of line with those extended to other large industrial employers when they established their plants.

Sometimes, on a difficult question, it took—what with the constant interruptions of the telephone and his private radio network, complicated by what I believe was a kindly desire on his part not to hurt a stranger's feelings by being unduly curt with him—as long as 10 or 15 minutes even to arrive at a no comment.

Q: Everyone who has had dealings with you, from inside your firms and from outside, says you have a phenomenal memory. How have you trained it?

A: If I do have an extraordinary memory it's a gift. I've never consciously trained it. With industries that you build from scratch you just naturally know certain facts that you can always use as check-points.

Q: What is the future of New Brunswick generally?

A: New Brunswick is the best province in Canada. I just plain think it has a wonderful future. Up to now we've had more or less rigid national policies for the whole of Canada. If we're going to prosper in New Brunswick, Ottawa must to some extent modify its thinking and adopt more regional policies. We have been handicapped, as I said in my radio speech in January, by a national monetary policy with its periods of a premium dollar, tight money and high-interest rates, by a national shipping act which has been detrimental to New Brunswick and by a national energy program which has in the last three years created prosperity in the west and chaos in the east.

Behind this podium-like stance I caught just one glimpse—or thought I did—of the hidden streak of romance and quiet humour that Irving locked up for himself, his family and, at most, two or three particular friends. One afternoon, by some electronic freak the telephones and the radio were silent for a stretch of almost five minutes. Irving started talking about the time he almost left Canada, away back after the first war.

"Addie McNairn, another fellow from Buctouche, and I had been in the Royal Flying Corps together. We never got into action but we met a lot of people from faraway places, Australia and New Zealand and South Africa. A couple of years after the war, Addie and I went west on a harvest excursion but our real destination was Australia. Western Canada was an eye opener in itself. We shocked 160 acres of oats and another 160 acres of wheat for a Mr. Simpson near Milestone, Sask., and we did well enough that Mr. Simpson sent us on to a Mr. Thompson near Weyburn. We started spike-pitching, real hard work for I think it was $4 a day, but one of the lady cooks looking after the harvest gang got sick and I took over in the cook-wagon. If I'm not mistaken I got $10 a day for that. What struck Addie and me was how different farming in western Canada was from farming back home. Mr. Simpson, the Milestone man who gave us our first job, was originally from Virginia and he told us he spent one winter out of every two in Virginia and the other one in California. In all the time it took us to shock his 320 acres he spent not more than half a day with us in the fields. What an eye opener that was to me and Addie. Farming to us—even if you owned the farm—meant getting up personally at four o'clock in the morning to feed the stock and milk the cows and then looking after the crops or working all day in the woodlot when the weather was right for it. This unbelievable look at life in the wide-open spaces made us all the more determined to go on to Australia, and as soon as the harvest was over we went to Vancouver and started looking for a boat."

There was a long-distance interruption from Montreal but in a minute or two Irving was back in Vancouver in 1920. "While we were waiting to find the right boat we stayed with a friend of my father's, Uncle Bob Brown. I never did find out for certain but I have a feeling Uncle Bob might have gotten in touch with my father about this Australian thing because suddenly Addie—who was four or five years older than I was and the unchallenged leader of the expedition—began putting it off and putting it off. After a while it was November and Addie was still saying we'd get a better boat and a better fare if we waited just another few more days. And then one day he said: 'Well, here it is winter. Let's go up logging in northern B.C. Then we can go to Australia in the spring.'

"'Addie,' I said, 'if I'm going logging I can go logging in New Brunswick,' and I got on the next train and went home to Buctouche."

Irving smiled. "I often wondered why Addie McNairn changed his mind."

"Then you never saw him again?" I asked.

"Oh, yes. I saw him all the time. An average of at least once a week for the next 40 years or more. He came back to Buctouche too. I often thought of asking why he suddenly decided we weren't going to go on across the Pacific but I never did; we were the best of friends and I suppose I thought if I asked him it might embarrass him or give him the idea I was mad at him. Addie died three years ago and so now I'll never know."

I asked Irving another question. Looking back after that long gap of years—as he obviously must have done more than once in the time that intervened—had he ever regretted missing the boat to Australia?

"Oh no," he said. "You never regret the things you don't do. If the things you've done turn out to be mistakes, you try to correct them or at least learn from them. But no, you don't regret the things you haven't done. There just isn't time for that."

K. C. Irving, who Forbes *later described as the world's third richest non-monarch, continued to build his empire until it encompassed more than 300 companies. To avoid succession duties, he moved to Bermuda in 1971, but still spent as much time as possible in New Brunswick where he died in 1992 at age 93.*

Ralph Allen, who died of throat cancer in 1966 at 53, was editor of Maclean's *from 1950 to 1960.*

Conrad Black, Paper Tiger

Conrad Black in his Toronto office, 1998

AUGUST 1, 1994. The Garrick Club is 163 years old, which is not old at all by the standards of London's private clubs. It was founded as a place for actors to meet gentlemen, actors not being considered gentlemen in Victorian England, and it remains devoted to that mission in two respects: its membership is drawn heavily from the arts community, and its doors remain open to gentlemen—only. So a small dining-room in the Garrick seemed an appropriate place for the esteemed publisher Harold Evans to hold court one day last month on the evils of his former boss, Rupert Murdoch.

The Australian-born Murdoch is the world's pre-eminent media baron, whose empire stretches from newspapers to movie production and satellite television. But he is best-known—and most reviled—for publishing tabloid papers that mix stories about sex with stories about sin. Evans worked for Murdoch at *The Times* of London, but quit in 1982 after one year and one collision too many with his boss. Murdoch, he now says, is a liar and a doublecrosser who tried to drag the stately 209-year-old *Times* down market to the level of what Evans likes to refer to as his "bordello of papers."

Only one of the 11 other London media executives lunching around the mahogany dining table in the Garrick Club spoke in Murdoch's defence: Conrad Black, publisher of *The Daily Telegraph*, London's largest quality newspaper, and a press baron of considerable heft himself. Rupert may print trashy newspapers, said Black, who was the only one present to refer to the demonized publisher by his first name. But he is a brilliant businessman who has been good for the British newspaper industry.

Black's defence was remarkable given that the very next day he would lead The Telegraph PLC, the public company that owns the newspaper, into the kind of no-holds-barred circulation war with Murdoch that Britain had not seen since the heyday of the 1930s press lords. Last year, Murdoch audaciously slashed the cover price of *The Times* from 45 pence (94 cents) to 30 pence. For 10 months, Black held the *Telegraph*'s price at 48 pence, content to fight for readers with promotional gimmicks rather than matching the price cut and doing deeper damage to his profits. But when Telegraph PLC executives phoned him in Toronto during a business trip in early June to tell him that the previous month's circulation figures were particularly bad, Black had to act. *The Times*' daily circulation had climbed to 517,575 from 356,000, at a time when the *Telegraph*'s own numbers were slipping below one million a day, a level they had not gone under since 1948.

When Black finally slashed the *Telegraph*'s price to 30 pence on June 22, the fallout was ugly. Fears that the price war would vaporize newspaper profits caused Telegraph PLC shares to fall by more than a third on the London Stock Exchange the next day. That left the company's investors—some of whom had bought $153 million worth of Telegraph company stock from Black's own company, Hollinger Inc., just three weeks before—feeling especially burned. City of London authorities absolved Black of any ethical misconduct, saying that there was no evidence that he planned to cut the *Telegraph* price when he sold the shares. But many investors remained furious. Cazenove & Co., one of the City of London's most venerable firms, resigned as The Telegraph PLC broker on June 30. And some investors muttered that it would be a long time before Black would be able to come back to the London exchange to raise money.

Meanwhile, Murdoch kept up the pressure on Black by hacking another 10 pence off *The Times*' price. His "enemy," as he had made perfectly clear a year earlier during a meeting with Australian investors, was the *Telegraph*. Leave the *Telegraph* to me, Murdoch told Sir David English, whose company publishes the rival *Daily Mail*. "I'll put them out of business for you."

Black was more blunt. "Rupert is opening his arteries; he is trying to kill us," Black told one interviewer. In Australia, Murdoch's tabloids published stories suggesting that the *Telegraph* would lose money this year, and questioning Hollinger's solvency. Black's *Sunday Telegraph* responded with a story about Murdoch headlined "Falling star?" speculating on how his Asian satellite television network, Star TV, was gobbling up hundreds of thousands of dollars in start-up costs. Both sides were heaving hardballs. "There will be blood on the carpet," warned *Telegraph* editor Max Hastings. "Stop behaving like a Serb, Rupert," scolded Paul Johnston, writing in the pages of the Black-owned magazine *The Spectator*.

It must be understood, the barons insist, that none of this should be taken personally. "I yield to few people in my respect for Murdoch," says Conrad Black, sitting in his darkened 15th-floor office in London's Canary Wharf on a smoggy July afternoon. "Indeed, up to a point, he is a friend of mine. He invited us to his daughter's wedding, and we are reasonably friendly with him socially. I've always been a defender of his, unlike most people you encounter in this business."

Black continues: "But he's a funny guy. He's a cynic. When you get right down to it, Murdoch thinks the average person is a slob, with his belly full of beer, falling asleep in front of a pornographic movie on television, and if you just bring things down far enough he'll buy it. It never sits very easily with Rupert to run a quality product. And by making all these ridiculous, indiscreet remarks about putting us out of business, he has offended a lot of people, and made it possible for us to seem like a giant killer just by staying alive and holding our position."

It is three weeks into his battle with the world's most fearless and predatory media baron and Black says he doesn't know why everyone thinks his position is so awful. New underwriters are knocking on his door. Sure, the City investors are upset, but they'll come around. Black has been making the rounds, seeing them all privately, and he says that many investors are getting over their early jitters

about the effect the price war will have on the Telegraph's corporate
bottom line.

But the conventional wisdom in business circles from London to
Sydney still revolves around the concept of "deep pockets," and
Murdoch's, most people believe, are deeper. The theory is that
Murdoch's News Corp. International, far wealthier than Black's
Hollinger, is able to subsidize a long price war during which time
The Times can challenge the *Telegraph's* dominance. Black isn't buy-
ing it: "a load of bunk," he calls the scenario. The current circulation
battle is costing Murdoch so much money, says Black, that "before
he can put significant pressure on us, his pockets are going to have
to be well below his ankles."

Indeed, most of the harm done so far has been to Black's prestige
and image, so carefully cultivated over the last decade. When he
arrived in London in 1986 to take control of *The Daily Telegraph*, he
was a little-known colonial who was greeted with great suspicion.
The first profiles in British papers, many written by Canadians,
were unflattering. And the *Telegraph's* outgoing owners, the Berry
family of Wales, which had owned the paper since 1927, had tried
desperately to find someone, anyone, else to sell the paper to.

But Black's stewardship of the *Telegraph* proved wildly successful.
He quickly restored the paper to profitability. He worked hard to
allay investors' fears that he was just another in a long line of head-
strong, debt-addicted media tycoons, and convinced them to let him
take the Telegraph public. He then used the newspaper's cash to
expand Hollinger's holdings into one of the world's great newspaper empires. Although the recent price war may have altered the
equation, Hollinger's stake in the *Telegraph* was recently responsible
for almost 75 per cent of its earnings.

Since the late 1980s, Hollinger has acquired the daily *Jerusalem
Post*, 19 per cent of Southam Inc. in Canada and a controlling 25-
per-cent stake in Fairfax. Last April, Black bought the *Chicago Sun-
Times* for $160 million, adding it to Hollinger's American publishing
group of otherwise small dailies and weeklies. In all, Black publishes
490 daily and weekly papers, reaching nearly five million readers a
day. All the while, he breathed the rarified air of London social and
business circles as befits the publisher of the most powerful Tory

newspaper in Britain. On the cusp of turning 50, Black was even able to publish an autobiography with the not-so-humble title *A Life in Progress*.

The events of the last two months have tarnished that image. The gravest wound was the tumble in the Telegraph's stock value so soon after Hollinger sold 12.5 million of its shares. Many investors did their bellyaching in public. "The credibility of the management is somewhat suspect and their reputation has been severely damaged in the eyes of the City," says Richard Peirson, investment director at Framlington Group PLC, a small but longtime Telegraph shareholder. "He has pissed off the establishment on this one," says Hylton Philipson of Pall Mall Ltd., who has done several North American deals with Black.

The harshest blow may have been Cazenove's resignation as the Telegraph's broker, a decision that Black insists was mutual. Cazenove is the bluest of blue-blood firms, and dropping The Telegraph PLC—the first such act in "recent memory," company officials said—is a stain on Black's reputation. A Cazenove official told Black that the company felt it had to do the "honourable thing," but Telegraph company executives were outraged. "Cazenove's behaviour was extremely disappointing," says Telegraph vice-chairman Daniel Colson. "When a client runs into flak, you don't run for the tall grass."

Meanwhile, Murdoch's executives—or what Black calls "his numerous spear carriers and bootlickers"—argue that Black displayed a glaring lack of business judgment in failing to match *The Times'* price cut right away. "Black has already made the crucial error in this war," said one senior Murdoch executive who did not want to be named. "In the history of newspapers, all the great proprietors never let the grass grow under their feet. They reacted right away." Indeed, the blueprint for *The Times'* strategy is the successful price war launched in 1930 by *The Daily Telegraph* itself, when it cut its price in half from two pence to a penny. Circulation nearly doubled in six weeks, sending the *Telegraph* on its way to becoming Britain's largest daily.

Imagine accusing Conrad Black, who prides himself as a historian, of not knowing his history. Black allows only a "maybe" when pressed on whether he should have matched *The Times'* price cut immediately. "If you speak of military history"—and Black loves to—"it is always useful to get your opponent to commit as much resources as he can before you have to fire any live ammunition yourself," he says. He used the time to retire some of Hollinger's debt. And by delaying the price cut for 10 months, he says, The Telegraph PLC is richer and better armed for battle.

"Look, it is no time for complacency," says Black. "We are dealing with a formidable adversary; Rupert is a bold man. He is like—and I make this comparison in one sense and one sense only—the early Hitler, always wanting a *ruse de guerre* because he always thought his opponents were ninnies who would react too late and indecisively. He was hoping that we would be so attached to our cover price that we wouldn't move to meet the threat when it came. But he's not vain. When something doesn't work, he abandons it and tries something else.

"Murdoch's not mad, you know."

By circumstance and tradition, the publisher of *The Daily Telegraph* is a powerful player in British Conservative circles. Years ago, the paper was virtually the party organ. Now, its blend of right-wing politics, well-reported domestic news and healthy sports coverage is still the paper most favored by core Tory voters, the choice of middle managers on their commute into London. Black inherited the power that comes with the station of *Telegraph* publisher, and he exercises it with clear joy.

"If I look back over the newspaper publishers I have known, it is only Beaverbrook with whom he compares," then-Tory Defence Minister Alan Clark wrote flatteringly in his diary after first meeting Black in 1990. The comparison to Lord Beaverbrook—New Brunswick's Max Aitken who rose to become a powerful British publisher and adviser to prime ministers in the first half of the century—is often invoked, no doubt because both are Canadian. But both men also enjoyed owning their papers for social and political clout as much as for profit. "I run the paper purely for the purpose of making propaganda," Beaverbrook told the 1949 Royal Commission on the Press. Beaverbrook insisted that he controlled the content of his papers by hiring editors who agreed with him. And if they disagreed on an issue? "I talked them out of it," said Beaverbrook.

Black, devoted to profits and alarmed at suggestions that he is a meddling proprietor, would probably cringe at some of the comparisons to Beaverbrook. (For one thing, when asked to name his favorite songs as a guest on the venerable British radio program *Desert Island Discs*, Black listed "Londonderry Air" by American gospel singer Paul Robeson. Robeson was one of the people on Beaverbrook's blacklist of names that could never appear in his papers.) Black is still more likely to write a letter to his own paper when he disagrees with something it has published, a practice that his London book editor Ion Trewin says "the British public find endearing."

But he is not above issuing orders to editors. This year, he insisted upon, and recruited the writer for, a positive profile of South African Zulu Leader Mangosuthu Buthelezi. Black has long supported Buthelezi for his anti-Communist position, although the Zulu leader was widely perceived in the West as an obstacle to the country's peaceful transition to majority rule. (The story did not completely satisfy Buthelezi, who wrote to Black, thanking him but pointing out some "errors" in the piece.) But Black is mostly content to hire editors who share his conservative views and then leave them alone.

Still, Black grew concerned this year that the *Telegraph*'s editorial pages had lost their sharp conservative focus. The same day that he cut the *Telegraph*'s price, deputy editor Trevor Grove, perceived by the Thatcherite wing of the Tory party as too "wet," was fired and replaced with Simon Heffer, an uncompromising right-winger. Hardline Tories had been screaming for Grove's head since the late 1980s ("I'm not Conservative enough for them because I will vote Tory only once at elections, not three times," Grove joked to associates), but, in the past, Black and respected *Telegraph* editor Max Hastings had protected him.

Black says that he told Hastings to correct the paper's editorial drift, and that it was Hastings who sacked Grove. But some *Telegraph* employees suspected that Grove's firing was the work of the invisible hand of his wife, outspoken columnist Barbara Amiel, who gives no ground on her conservative views. "Things started to go sour after he married Barbara," said one former *Telegraph* employee. "We suddenly started to get phone calls in the middle of the night from Black, complaining that there was too much political correctness in the paper."

Black's eyes narrow when asked whether Amiel steers his guidance of the *Telegraph*. "I was aware that there was a myth that had floated around—though I thought it had died by now—that my wife was exercising some Mephistophelian influence on my relations with the editor," he says. "I can assure you none of that is true."

But parts of English society revel in repeating stories—true or exaggerated—about Black and Amiel, the uncouth colonials loose in London. They tell of a time when Black and Amiel rushed to fill empty seats in the second row at a Sir Georg Solti concert so that they would be positioned directly behind the Royal Family. Or of a time that a long-winded Black lectured then-Prime Minister Margaret Thatcher at a 10 Downing Street reception on the history behind trooping the colour, while she impatiently repeated: "I know, Conrad."

"The key to any large city with a complicated social structure is not to get too identified with any one group, or else you get associated with a disagreeable amount of gossip," says Black with a sigh. But Black is far more comfortable in London society than Murdoch. "Black has a strong connection with the English and has been easily accepted," says respected journalist Hugo Young, who is also chairman of the Scott Trust, which funds *The Guardian* newspaper. "Murdoch despises and detests the English. He has an image of England as a tired, old anti-meritocracy."

Black and Amiel drift between social sets, from cultural leaders like Sir David Frost, to financial buccaneers, to the Royal Family. (It was the discreet support of the Queen and the Queen Mother, after some cajoling by Black, that cleared the way for the striking Canada War Memorial to be erected in Green Park, across from Buckingham Palace. Government bureaucrats had opposed placing the granite memorial to the one million Canadians who fought for Britain in two world wars in one of the royal parks in the centre of London.) The couple are particularly close friends with a crowd of what might be termed renegade right-wingers, which includes wealthy businessman Sir James Goldsmith, a leading crusader against European integration. "I don't agree with most of what Goldsmith says on that subject, I'm a free trader," smiles Black, although he worries that closer European union will bring the continent's socialist tendencies to Britain.

Still, Amiel hosted a much-discussed party at London's Ritz Hotel when Goldsmith was elected to the European Parliament in May. (Goldsmith's approach to dismantling the European federation is the same as Lucien Bouchard's approach to Canadian federalism: destabilize from within.) The party's guest list was an impressive array of London's elite, including Princess Diana. "Black and Amiel have a high social cachet," says a breathless Ewa Lewis, social editor of the glossy *Tatler* magazine. "Amiel makes him more known. She's glamorous and bright. Before they married, he was just a chunky newspaper proprietor."

Lewis adds: "They are power and glamor. They are not perceived of as Canadians at all."

It is hard not to get the impression that life in Britain has lost some of its sparkle for Conrad Black. Even before the price war blew up, he was focusing on the American end of his business. *The Daily Telegraph* may still be Hollinger's flagship, but the American publishing arm is now more profitable than the British side, he says. Perhaps it is the spectre of a Labour government that is souring him on the United Kingdom. "The United States is a more commercially and politically reliable country than Britain," he says. "I like it here in London and I'm well received here, but I am not one of those people who aspires to become English."

He dismisses the trials of the last two months with a wave and a casual acknowledgment that he has endured worse in his business career. "If I have to, I'll take the *Telegraph* private again once the dust settles and I can be certain that there won't be a public relations problem," he says. But Murdoch has thrown a twist into Black's careful plans. The *Telegraph*, his bastion, the spiritual heart of his empire, is under attack by a man who, in Black's assessment, "loves the high wire." He is sober at the thought.

Then he brightens as he starts to run through his options, listing the many weapons still available to him. "We would have to be unprecedentedly inept to lose this," Black finally concludes. *The Times*, he argues, must be 10 pence cheaper in order to steal readers from the *Telegraph*. "Watch," he says with a wink as he ushers a visitor past the oil paintings of naval battles on his office walls to the outer door. "I could drop my price to 25 pence tomorrow and then we'd really wax Rupert." He chuckles at the thought, and is still smiling as he turns and shuffles back down the hall towards his office.

Conrad Black and his Telegraph *survived the newspaper war with Murdoch which effectively ended in 1995 when a 50 per cent increase in newsprint costs forced all publishers to increase prices. In 1996, Black acquired the Southam newspaper chain and two years later launched* The National Post, *but in 2000 he sold Southam and a 50 per cent interest in the* Post *to CanWest Global for $2.29 billion.*

Bruce Wallace worked for Maclean's *from 1985 to 2000, starting in the magazine's Montreal bureau and becoming bureau chief there, in London and Ottawa. He now is the European correspondent for Southam News, based in London.*

LET ME ENTERTAIN YOU

Mary Pickford: Our Mary

Mary Pickford, circa 1915

By Arthur Stringer

SEPTEMBER, 1918. For Mary Pickford was born to rule. That imperial instinct cannot be smothered beneath Little Lord Fauntleroy masquerades and tomboy antics and Brete Harte comedies. Her success has not been an accident. It has been a campaign, and a conquest. The chariot that has carried her to her triumph has been the motion-picture, not so much that the motion-picture suited her as that she suited the motion-picture. But it was a chariot, remember, clattering, resplendent, spectacular, involving none of the undulations of the cantilever-spring.

I have called Mary Pickford the best-known woman in the world, and with equal truth I think I can call her the best loved. Those significant phrases, those affectionately appropriating epithets, "Our Mary" and "Little Mary" have not clung to her without reason. And associated with her name is that emotional affiliation which at first sight appears almost fanatic. It is the unquestioning adoration which in times more legendary was bestowed upon saints and in days more barbaric was lavished upon conquerors.

Through this new instrument of emotional refreshment which has been made from the throwing of shadows across a cotton sheet, through this new-fangled combination of sunlight and shutters and nitrate of silver, the personality and the pictured person of Mary Pickford has crept about this earth of ours, so that today she is known to the coolie-workers of Kimberley as well as to the flat-dwellers of Harlem, to the peons of Mexico and the pearl-fishers of Sambalong. Her face, plastered on the hoardings of Madras, is not unknown to the Parsee of Gujarat; it is recognized by the Basuti Kaffir and the sampan-paddler of Hong-Kong and the miners of Alaska and the *fellaheen* who still plow the plains of Sharon with the same crude share that Elisha once used. And that brings us back to our queen in question, whose slightly puzzled face plainly implied she was awaiting and fortifying herself against the customary fusilade of questions.

"I'm not going to ask you, Miss Pickford, what your hobbies are, or why you went into the pictures, or whether you like them or not, or any of those familiar old questions."

"Then this isn't to be an interview, after all?" inquired Little Mary, with a doubtful look creeping up into that lucid blue eye of hers.

"I'd like to make it another sort of interview," I protested, for as I've said before, I wasn't so interested in the Pickfordian method of hairdressing as I was in the cerebrum behind the coiffure. "All right," I said, a little humbled. "Let's begin that way. Let's get it over with, and off the slate. What, Miss Pickford, do your hobbies happen to be?"

"My work," was that young lady's prompt reply.

"This isn't customary," I reproved. And Little Mary laughed.

"I know it isn't, but it's the truth. It's all I have a chance for, all I have energy for, except from what I can crowd in for my Red Cross work. People, I know, should have a hobby. But I don't seem to have the time to do what other people do.

"I was born on the eighth of April, in the year of our Lord, 1894, and as my father's name was John Smith, I was christened Gladys Mary Smith. It was late in life I took the name of Pickford, which was a family name. I was born in Canada, as you know, in the City of Toronto.

"My father died in February, 1898, before I was quite four years old. He died leaving my mother with three children, myself and my younger sister, Lottie, and Jack, the baby, who is just 21 years old now. He didn't leave much else, I'm afraid, besides us three children. Mother—and always, you must remember, Mother has been and still is my world—found it pretty hard to keep that little home intact.

"My childhood memory of Toronto is of a very strict city, for my father when he was alive wouldn't even let me ride a bicycle. But at the age of three I'd taken part in a cake-walk. I wore a gorgeous cos- tume, and it was up on a big platform somewhere, I can't remember where. All I know is that it was my first amateur performance in public. I made people laugh and I loved it. So in less than a year I became the bread-winner of our family by learning to play the part of Little Eva in *Uncle Tom's Cabin,* and actually doing it on the pro- fessional stage. That was with the Valentine Stock Company.

"These, of course, were all what the profession called 'kid parts,'" continued Miss Pickford. "And I kept on at that sort of part for eight years. But when I was almost 13 years old something hap- pened. It was something which marked the Great Divide in the whole continent of my girlhood. It was a small thing, as so many of life's vital things seem at the time, but it swept the bandage of con- tentment from my eyes. It brought about what I've often been prompted to call a second birth that day in San Francisco, where I happened to be playing in one of Hal Reed's melodramas, the one called *For a Human Life.*

"That awakening came one afternoon through a talk with another woman, a talk in a dingy little dressing room. The woman was Jean Patriquin. She was an older actress. She disliked me—at least she disliked me at first, because I overheard her say, 'That precocious stage kid!'

"It hurt. It startled me. I went to her to have it out, for stage life is terribly confined and competititive, and even the stage child soon learns to stand on guard, jealously on guard, over her own little territory.

"We had it out, Jean Patriquin and I, but in a way very different to the way I had expected. We sat down and talked things over. I woke up to the fact that I didn't know so very much, compared with that older woman, and that I was facing a woman who knew life, who had an infinitely broader vision of things than I had. She awakened something in my soul, something that had been sleeping there like a seed.

"She made me unhappy and restless and ambitious for better things. And from that day on, I started to study in earnest with a real hunger for knowledge. I wanted to improve, to be different.

"You know what stage people are like. They're the most naive and self-conscious, the most obstinate and generous, the most sensitive and insensible, the most clever and yet the most contracted guild of workers in all the wide world. And it was no little battle to break away from those old ways of thinking and living. But the seed had sprouted and I couldn't stop its growth."

"When did you first turn to the moving pictures?" I inquired.

"It was two years later, in 1909," was the reply.

This story of how Our Mary broke into the movies has been told in many versions and with many embellishments, and the straight truth, I am afraid, will come as a bit of a shock to those persons who make a habit of sacrificing verity on the altar of romance. But the Pickford family, be it recorded, had been "on the road" and when Mary went on the road in those early days it was essential, of course, that her mother should go along with her. And it was equally essential, under the circumstances, that Lottie, who was two years younger than Mary, and Jack, who was the baby, should be taken along with their mother. It was a condition which involved sacrifice, and entailed discomfort, but when Little Mary the breadwinner moved from place to place, that itinerant little family circle moved with her, constituting a triangle of sustaining guardianship which easily enough merged into a quadrangle of companionable adventuring.

The season on the road ended, as seasons have the habit of doing. Thereupon the Pickford family, as theatrical families also have the habit of doing, returned to New York to cast about for a new engagement for Little Mary. A humble abode was found up in the Bronx. Agencies were consulted, the managers' offices were visited, the old and much-trodden tracks of the theatrical aspirant were explored and re-explored. But for once the star of Mary Pickford was not in the ascendant. The carefully guarded savings of the road-trip began to dwindle. The summer grew old; the producers made ready for the opening season. Still there was no engagement for Mary Pickford. Finally, in that little home of over-strained hope up in the Bronx, the last of the season's savings were gone, the last with the exception of one tragic and lonesome nickel. Mary Pickford studied that solitary coin of baser metal for some time. Then she took a deep breath and went to her mother.

"Mother," she announced, "I'm going to gamble our nickel."

"How?" demanded a parent much too worried for frivolity.

"On the movies," was Mary's answer.

She announced it quite bravely, with her shoulders back. But she gulped a little as she passed that lonely little ultimate coin in through the wicket for her subway ticket. It would be a nine-mile walk back, and the heat of midsummer still lurked in the heavy and humid September sea-air of Manhattan. But she buckled on that invisible armor-plate in which many a timorous genius has cuirassed herself for the storming of Broadway, and headed straight for the Biograph offices. Then her heart sank. For on the inner side of that threshold she found herself in a waiting-room crowded with girls, all of them just as eager and ambitious as she was herself, and many of them much more magnificent as to outward apparel.

But there was a difference. It was hidden perhaps, behind the tired eyes and the slightly frayed little frock and the pallid cheek from which the subway air had taken the last of the colour. But it was there, as inextinguishable as the spark of true genius. And that weary and nervous and over-worked official whose task it was to pick out the "extra people" for the old Biograph Studios had not said 20 words to the hollow-cheeked girl from the Bronx before he spotted that difference.

"You, kid, I'll want you," he announced with a nod of approval.

Whereupon Mary, with the iron hoops of anxiety loosed from her heart, smiled. She smiled for the simple reason that she couldn't help smiling. And you, gentle reader or sour-mapped reader, or whatever you may be, you very well know by this time what that Mary Pickford smile is like. It made the Biograph man stop and meditatively scratch his ear. "And instead of working with those extras, I guess I can slip you in at a real job. Be back here at 10 in the morning. Next, there!"

The director's call put a stop to our talk. There was a scene to be "shot." It is not permitted me to describe that scene in detail. But one thing that impressed me as Miss Pickford faced the camera was the sudden and unthinking transformation of character on her part. In almost the flash of an eye the Jekyll vanished and the Hyde asserted itself, unwilled, apparently, and without effort. It reminded me of the dualism of the artist of that multiple personality which can be packed away in one body. For I had witnessed an ingenuous and sensitive girl suddenly translated into an adroit and far-seeing artist. I was reminded, too, of the mental strain involved in the making of a big picture, the mental strain unknown to the general public that sits before the finished product.

It is a matter of record and common enough knowledge that at the young and tender age of 17, Mary Pickford took the running broad-jump into matrimony. It amounted to practically a runaway match, for it is probably the first and the last step which Little Mary took without the advice of her mother. Nor was Mary altogether carried away by the romance of the situation when she slipped away with her young leading man and returned a radiant and happy bride of 17. This leading man, let it be remembered, was her first. And he was an Irishman, one of a family of more or less famous actors. He was the possessor of a distinctly Hibernian charm which had its corporeal basis in Irish blue eyes, black hair, and a light and debonair manner. And he not only tumbled head-over-heels in love with Mary but during long and onerous workdays in the studio he was both kind and considerate with the less experienced new comer. It was Owen Moore, in fact, who schooled Mary Pickford in many of the tricks of the new trade.

The trail of the screen-star, however, is not a macadamized road. It cannot be deemed either unfair or ungenerous, I think, to point out what the world in general now knows, that Mary Pickford's marriage with Owen Moore has not turned out a happy one. For several years, while not exactly agreeing to disagree they have at least elected to follow separate paths.

Later, as we resumed our conversation, I remarked, "You were saying that you regarded marriage as one of the big things in a woman's life."

"Don't you?" asked Mary.

"Of course," I acknowledged, and the hazel-blue eyes inspected me closely, apparently to make sure that I remained as sincere as was merited by the matter in hand.

"And success, on the other hand, can be an equally big thing in a woman's career," continued Miss Pickford. "No, not an equally big thing, but a tremendously absorbing thing. It would be a pose, of course, for me to say that I've not been successful, successful at least in certain things. I have, I suppose, in a way. But you know how it is. It's always the next turn ahead, the view over the next hill-top, the hunger for the height we can't quite get to.

"I've done certain things. I imagine the world knows pretty well what they are. As I've told you before, I've succeeded, and I'm not going to be hypocritical enough to scoff at success, for from the time I was a pretty little tot I've been working hard for it. But there are some things work won't bring and money won't buy. You can't go to market and carry home contentment or happiness, and every woman has a craving for those things, just as every woman wants love. No work and no profession and no calling can take its place. There's an ache in every girl's heart for it. We all demand it, the old-fashioned, simple, honest, human love that keeps the world going on.

"I have been poor much longer than I have been the other way. And being poor taught me to appreciate the things that I've been able to get. Now, don't imagine that I'm going to moralize over the virtues of poverty. I've no intention of doing that. I'm merely stating a fact—if you're born with everything you want you've missed the fun of the biggest game there is, the elemental old joy of accomplishment, the human satisfaction of going after a thing and roping it down. When you get it, of course, it's not going to be what you expected, and it's not going to make you any happier than you were before you got it. I suppose it's only the going on that counts."

"But is it a case of going on?" I asked. "I mean, do you look for continuous progress in the matter of motion-picture work?"

"There has been a steady advance in motion-pictures," explained Miss Pickford, "from about the time I first went into them. And that advance gives every promise of continuing. When I did my first work in the movies, back in the old Biograph days, I swung into that field just about the time of the birth of the silent drama. It was about the time when the first serious attempts were being made to do something better than merely portray human beings in action, with no definite story-interest to unify that action."

"I was told the new Pathé company recently offered you $25,000 a week, on a long-term contract," I suggested.

"I did not accept that offer. And I never make long-term contracts. I never, in fact, sign a contract for more than six months."

"Why not?"

"In the first place, because everything about the photoplay world is in such a state of change. Tastes change; the public changes, conditions and methods change. I've always felt it wouldn't be fair to my management to tie them up for more than six months at a time."

The little star looked at me with laughter hovering about the over-wistful eyes. They were not the eyes of a light-hearted and carefree girl. They were the questioning and shadowed eyes of the woman who has sounded life and life's temporalities. "Who knows that the tide isn't going to turn tomorrow, or the day after tomorrow?"

In so far as I have been able to observe and judge, this business of being a motion-picture star is about the most competitive business on the face of this essentially competitive earth of ours! Since the regime of the efficiency expert in every large studio each star is charted and watched and kept under record. Day by day and week by week elaborate ledgers are kept of every high-salaried actress, to make sure that the actress in question is returning value for value. House reports are assembled and tabulated, the figures from the distributing agencies are recorded and considered, and the fluctuating barometer of that star's popularity is scrutinized by expert eyes and rendered into easily comprehensible form on the duly prepared blanks of expert accountants.

And when you are not an ordinary star, but a star of the first magnitude, sufficiently radiant to be recognized even as a dictator of your own contracts, there devolves on your shoulders not alone the need for sustaining past records for "keeping up your batting average" as Miss Pickford so aptly phrased it, but the necessity for finding fit vehicles, and the assembling of casts and costumes and properties, and the employment of adequate directors and assistants, and, above and beyond the studious guardianship of name and personality, the somewhat forlorn treasuring of that bodily strength which is the basis of your camera-value, of your pictorial appeal to the eye.

"Why couldn't any decent-looking girl make a hit in a picture?" I demanded.

"She could," was Little Mary's prompt and somewhat unlooked for reply. "Any such girl could become a star. But that is very far from saying she could remain a star. A shrewd director can always tell such a girl what to do. There are even cases where the stupider you are the more satisfactory you prove. But the final test in such things, it seems to me, is not being skyrocketed into fame by some one spectacular production, but in sustaining your average, in doing as well tomorrow what you did today. That, I think, proves whether you're an accident or an artist."

Mary Pickford has enjoyed both the distinction and the advantage of being the conspicuous first-comer in the garden of screen achievement. She was still without ponderable rivals when she caught and carried off her first worm of triumph there. She was the first to make a success of the portrayal of child parts, being little more than a child herself at the time. So unqualified has that early success proved that the world has insisted on the repetition of the tried and tested note of juvenility until what was once a matter of triumph has devolved into something approaching strangely close to a matter of martyrdom. For what the unthinking general public still demands of Mary Pickford is *ingenue* charm, the "Little Eva" of the 19th century transposed into the "Little American" of the 20th century.

Mary Pickford's beauty, defying even an indisputable irregularity of feature, is a beauty that is rooted in brains and does not pass away.

That face will always retain its pictorial appeal, its indecipherable allurement, even when time has turned the furrows which time must turn. At any rate, I concluded as a courier announced to Miss Pickford that her car was waiting, there is a tremendously interesting experiment in human psychology awaiting the world during the next decade or so. It will tell whether or not those loyal and long-reaching queues are to lose their old-time idol. For even now, we must remember, their Mary is no longer Little Mary. She is a woman facing the complexities and profundities of life, waiting to clarify them through art, as art itself is clarified through life. And unless the powers behind her awaken to this fact, unless they take advantage of this fact, a great field will remain untilled and a vein of the brightest metal will remain uncovered.

In 1919, Mary Pickford, along with D. W. Griffith, Charlie Chaplin and Douglas Fairbanks, established United Artists, still a leading movie production company. A year later, she divorced Owen Moore and married Fairbanks, but they divorced in 1935. Pickford then married actor Buddy Rogers in 1937 and they remained a couple until she died at 86 in 1979.

Her film career continued until 1933 with a total of 194 movies. Pickford successfully made the transition to talkies, winning a best actress Oscar in 1929 for her part in Coquette. *After her retirement from the screen, Pickford continued as a producer and vice-president at United Artists until she sold her shares in 1951. Despite her enormous wealth, she became increasingly reclusive in her latter years.*

Arthur Stringer was a prolific—and popular—novelist and poet who grew up in southwestern Ontario and later moved to the United States where he died in 1950 at age 76.

Wayne and Shuster:
It's No Fun Being Funny

Johnny Wayne (left) and Frank Shuster preparing
their weekly radio script, 1954

By Johnny Wayne and Frank Shuster

JANUARY 1, 1954. One time when we were fishing in a Muskoka lake, a friend pulled up to our canoe in his outboard long enough to say hello and to introduce us to someone in the boat with him. When he gunned off for shore he made the common mistake of thinking that he couldn't be heard above the noise of his motor. As a result, when he was a few yards from us, he sat there shouting to his passenger in a voice audible for about 20 miles: "That's Wayne and Shuster, the radio team. You know, off the air, they're the dullest characters I've ever met."

It's not often we get it so clearly. But it just about sums things up. People get the idea that a comedian is a bagful of gags in a loud check suit, that a gag man is a gag man 24 hours a day.

Actually, we're a couple of Babbitts. We live within three blocks of one another in Toronto's Forest Hill district, surrounded by flowers, shrubs, lawns, taxes and children. The nearest we come to acting like comedians is when we trip over tricycles in the driveway.

We work at home, regular office hours, five days a week, eight hours a day, with an hour and a half for lunch. The half-hour weekly Wayne and Shuster show that is our bread and butter is broadcast Thursday evening, over 33 stations on the CBC's Trans-Canada network. Thursday afternoon we take the script we've written to the studio and go over it with the other people in our group: Terry

Dale, our vocalist; Samuel Hersenhoren, our musical director; Johnny Dobson, our arranger; Jackie Rae, our producer; Don Bacon and Dave Tasker, our technicians; our actor-announcer, Herb May; and feature player Eric Christmas. Every other working day the two of us meet at 9 a.m. dressed like any other businessmen, make dull remarks to each other, like "Hi, John," or "Morning, Frank," and go through that coma of blinking and warming up to the day's labour.

One of us yawns, sits down at the typewriter and peers at the rough script where we left off the day before. Say it's the parody we did on *Lost Weekend: Comic Books Anonymous.* The one at the typewriter says something like: "Well, we're up to that part where the Disneymaniac has become a slave to comic books and his friend tries to snap him out of it." He quotes the last lines we have written—

SHUSTER: *You have to break this habit—it's destroying you.*

WAYNE: *Go on, I can read you under the table any time.*

SHUSTER: *No you can't. You must make up your mind that you've got to give up comic books.*

WAYNE: *Well, can I just have one for the road?*

We sit in silence, wondering where we should go from there. Finally, one of us says: "What about getting him home and then having his mother hide his comic books?" We do this and then we have the Disneymaniac crack up. We have to figure out what he should do when he cracks up. We decide he should start pleading for a smell of a newsstand. The one at the typewriter puts a new sheet of paper in the machine and types:

WAYNE: *Let me smell a newsstand, Mom! Just let me smell a newsstand!*

We cross our fingers and hope that this will rate a laugh and move on to the next gag, debating, racking our brains, pacing the floor. The only time we laugh at our own script is late in the afternoon when we're hungry. We laugh then, to try to convince each other that what we've ground out is funny enough to give us the right to quit and have dinner.

We work from a series of roughs. One of us gets an idea and punches it out on the typewriter. We act it out. If we both like the gag, we feel fairly safe with it. If we don't, one attempts to talk the other into it. Mostly, we look as gay as a couple of accountants who can't get the same balance.

Our older kids, Michael Wayne, 6, and Rosalind Shuster, 7, are so used to seeing us like this that they don't quite believe we *are* Wayne and Shuster. Once Rosalind said, "Wayne and Shuster were on the air last night. Boy! Are *they* funny."

She and Michael then gave us dirty looks, as though they wondered why they had to pick such a dull pair of clods for fathers. Eventually we'll probably get the same kind of looks from our younger kids, Jamie and Brian Wayne, aged 3 and 2, and Stephen Shuster, 4. And they'll all have to endure the ordeal of being the offspring of comedians.

For popular ideas die hard, including the one that a comedian is something irresponsible in baggy pants and a false nose. One time right after we'd moved to our present homes our wives were out for an afternoon walk, pushing baby carriages, when a nice old lady stopped them, welcomed them to the neighbourhood and settled down to a little gossip.

She pointed across the street and said: "See that house over there. Do you know who lives there? Frank Shuster. They tell me he's drunk from morning till night."

Our wives had just left us knee-deep in encyclopedias, musical dictionaries, cigarette butts and the modal music of medieval England. The wackiest bit of burlesque has to have its roots in fact, or it isn't funny. If we do a piece of satire about climbing Mount Everest we have to know something about the technique and terminology of mountain climbing before we start playing around with it. A lot of the time when people think we are handing out exploding cigars, we are right back where we started from eight years ago, when we were post-graduate English students at the University of Toronto—sitting in the reference library looking worried.

We go home, spread out our notes and start working for gags. We pace the floor, chew our nails, teeter, peer out windows, frown, shake our heads and sometimes get stymied and just sit there for hours on end looking at one another without saying a word.

Sometimes we carry the blank stare into overtime. We stare at our families and friends, still thinking of the unfinished script. Our wives are used to it. When they see the expression, they say, "Leave him alone, he's writing."

We get about one page of finished script to every eight pages of copy. We work at each joke till it's right; pruning it; reworking it, shifting the emphasis, reading it back and forth till we get the right ride to it. A joke has to scan properly. It's like Virgil. Not that it has to break down into iambic pentameter, but—well, take that joke that has become a test pattern for comedians: " 'Pardon me, do you have 20 cents for a cup of coffee?' You say, 'Coffee's only a dime.' And he says, 'I know—won't you join me?' "

That has cadence and rhythm. Suppose he said, "I know. I would like you to join me." It isn't funny. Maybe you don't think the first one was funny either; but the point is it's funnier than the second, purely because of the sound, the impact it has on your ear.

There's an old story among comedians about this technique. It's about a group of professional comedians sitting around knocking one another out by just mentioning jokes by number. "Seventeen," someone says. Everybody laughs. "Forty-four," another one says. They fall off their chairs. Then a new member of the group tries it. "Thirty-six," he says. Nobody laughs. When he asks afterward what happened, they explain: "It's not the joke, it's the way you tell it." A comedian develops a sense of pace and timing that's an important factor in humour. We use the audience to help it along. We don't wait for laughs as most people think. We use laughs as punctuation—we think of them as colons and semicolons. We can time them and control them to build up a good pace.

Every time we go in to our tailor, he says, "Man! I've got a real suit for you. Something really sharp. Long jacket, green-and-yellow check. Wear it with a red shirt and a blue bow tie and you'll stop people like a traffic light."

He wants to dress us like show people. Good advertising, he says. We tell him that isn't what we want. He looks baffled and asks what we *do* want. We tell him we want to dress like gentlemen, and he bursts out laughing and says, "That's a wonderful gag," and starts hauling out suits with baggy pants.

Writing a half-hour of humour to a weekly deadline, hot or cold, whether you feel good or have a toothache, isn't done with long jackets and red shirts. Our show goes into about a million and a half homes. Our audience is made up of people of every age, type and taste in humour. We have to try to make them all laugh. We work for a kind of humour that's based on simple familiar things. An example would be the bit we worked into one program when we announced that we were expecting a very special guest, the manager of a drive-in theatre. The announcement was followed by the sound of a car roaring up the aisle and squealing to a stop. That sounds easy: the sort of thing you'd think up in a minute. It isn't.

In that particular case we had to figure out what to do with the imaginary car and its passenger once the gag was over. Not that anyone would really think there was a car in the studio, but humour has to produce a certain illusion of reality or it falls flat. Leaving that fictitious car there without doing anything about it would have spoiled the feeling. Nothing else would have made sense. It would have been just as if a mystery-story writer had built up an important character then, without explanation, dropped him halfway through the book. The thing had to be solved—with a laugh.

We kept coming back to that one all day, without getting anywhere. We had another go at it after supper. We tried one idea after another but they didn't jell. We tried having the manager come up on stage, with Herb May taking the part, but it upset the rest of the program. We didn't want the theatre manager in the script; we just wanted him out of the studio. We worked till three in the morning without getting the right gimmick. We finally gave up and went to bed.

Next morning, driving downtown, we got the answer. It was simple. We saw a guy get stuck at the corner of Avenue Road and St. Clair, blocking the path of a turning streetcar. He backed up his car. We had the answer. We'd just tell a bad joke and have the manager of the drive-in slap his car into reverse and shoot out of the studio.

Transforming everything into show material becomes a subconscious process. It goes on all the time, when we're in restaurants, talking to friends, having lunch, sitting at a ball game, walking down the street or sitting in a show.

In our search for gags we have to keep clear of those that will offend someone. Jokes based on any form of affliction are taboo; the only people we make fun of are ourselves. We can't even use jokes like the wartime favourite about the short-sighted doctor who, when the expectant father said, "What is it, doc?" answered, "A baby." There are too many short-sighted people in the world.

Even then you never know when you're going to make somebody mad. One time we did a show about a dentist's office. The patient was nearly murdered. We had a lot of fun. So did the studio audience. Right after that we got a letter from a dental organization. It said: "So far, we've spent $1.5 million trying to convince the public that the dentist doesn't hurt. You've offset all our work in one night. Thank you. Yours very truly ..."

Some people don't even wait for the gag. They start laughing anyway. If one of us says, "Both my kids have chicken pox," somebody says, "Jeez! that's funny."

Mechanics hand us bills for $175 for gaskets, gears, fuel lines, fittings, bolts, nuts and top lube and stand there chuckling while they wait for us to look funny. When we just look sick, like anybody else, they figure we're having an off day.

Sometimes it works the other way. People are so disappointed that we're not funny that they get sore. There's a stock joke in show business about a comedian who came out of a night club feeling sick and asked the doorman to call him a cab.

"I've got a headache," he said.

The doorman sneered, "What's so funny about that?"

A comedian doesn't feel funny all the time. Not only that, he's never sure he's funny any of the time. We're never absolutely sure what's going over and what isn't. In sheer desperation we put what we thought was one of our worst gags in a parody of [1951 drama] *The Brave Bulls*. The toreador grabs the bull by the horns and the bull goes beep-beep like an old-fashioned auto horn and we crack, "Well, what do you know—an Oldsmobull!" For some reason, that brought a terrific gale of laughter from the audience.

What we thought was one of our better gags didn't even prompt a smile. It was in *Henry the Twenty-Second*, a take-off we did on *Henry V*. The script went like this—

WAYNE: *Men, we shall fight this war even it takes 100 years.*
SHUSTER: *One hundred years—that's awful.*
WAYNE: *Oh, I don't know, think of the veterans' benefits.*

Well, we thought it was funny anyway, even if nobody else did.

We used to try our gags on our wives, but we don't any more. Wives aren't typical radio listeners. They like everything. We wouldn't want it any other way. Criticism we can get; good honest criticism by people who would like to slit our throats. We like our wives to think we're wonderful.

Anyway, as soon as we try a gag on someone, he isn't a normal audience. He becomes a judge. It's like handing someone a drink of water and asking him if it's good or not. The minute he has to think about it, he's lost.

We like our work and feel that we've made a reasonable success of it. Not only that, we did it without selling newspapers at the corner of Toronto's King and Yonge. According to most Canadian success stories, that corner must have been so crowded with newsboys in the good old days that pedestrians had to walk on the road to get past them. Our parents gave us a university education.

From the time we got together in Varsity days with a show called *Wife Preservers*, we've been lucky. We've never had one of those music-comedy sponsors who keeps his talent trembling with the breakfast-table opinions of his wife, daughters and spaniel. Our sponsors have all left us alone. But we've had to produce, on schedule. We've been able to so far. One of the reasons is that we long ago decided it would be tough producing humour with ulcers. We decided we weren't going to have any.

In the meantime, we have a lot of laughs out of people who think comedy is a matter of moods and mad inspirations. It does us good. Last May we did a show that went wrong. We knew we had a poor house from the minute we got the "on the air" signal. We ignored it: one of the golden rules of show business. We plowed through as if the whole audience was in the aisles. If you keep going as if nothing had happened, and try to give everything just that much more socko, you can usually get an audience back with you. We never take that tack of insulting the audience. Get them mad at you and it makes things worse. We haven't been hit by any eggs yet, but we're not taking chances.

Anyway, a poor house doesn't necessarily mean your stuff is off. Maybe somebody fainted in the audience before you came on. If that happens, an audience can't shake its mood.

But that night we went home not feeling too good, for several reasons. One of them was the poor house. Another was that our kids' teacher had just congratulated our wives on having normal children, indicating that she'd expected them to wear false noses, squirt their playmates with trick flowers and give them exploding bubble gum. In our business, you can be sensitive about this sort of thing and a remark made with the best of intentions—such as the statement that your children are nice and normal—can get under the skin.

As we were coming up our street a couple of children stopped us and started clamouring, "Tell us a joke." They always do that. It's hard to get jokes to please kids but we told them the one about how you can't starve in a desert on account of all the sand-witches. They said what they always say: "That's terrible." This is a tradition with kids, like catching frogs.

As we reached home it was raining and it was May 24, and we'd promised our youngsters we'd set off fireworks, so we felt worse than ever. We waited, but instead of easing off, the rain turned into a steady downpour.

A promise is a promise, and we didn't want to disappoint the children. So, although nobody else was lighting fireworks in our neighborhood, we got dressed up in sou'westers, oilskins and rubber boots. With the rain beating in our faces and trickling into our rubber boots we braved the torrent, went out on the lawn, fumbled with wet matches and sent a couple of soggy rockets skyward. They didn't work very well. The other junk didn't work very well either, but at least we felt we were being good parents and not letting the kids down.

In about 10 minutes we happened to look around and saw a small traffic jam out on the street. All the drivers were grinning. It dawned on us that they weren't giving us credit for being good parents. They had that too familiar expression: "There're those maniacs Wayne and Shuster. Those guys are mad—absolutely mad." They were waiting for a show.

It began to strike us as funny. Suddenly, we felt a lot better. We put on a show there in the rain. We danced the sailor's hornpipe, we bellowed nautical commands above the gale, we did everything but hold Roman candles in our mouths. And the audience was with us. We had a good house, there in the rain. Nobody knew it was one of the few shows we hadn't written, from nine till five with an hour and a half for lunch, and when we went indoors finally we decided it wasn't so bad after all, having people think you're funny. And we'd picked up a couple of ideas for next week's show.

Wayne and Shuster became a Canadian institution through three decades of CBC-TV *comedy specials. They also made a record 67 appearances on* The Ed Sullivan Show, *but resisted pressures to move to the United States. Johnny died of brain cancer at 72 in 1990, but Frank still lives in Toronto.*

Oscar Peterson at Home

Oscar Peterson with one of his boys, 1954

By June Callwood

OCTOBER 25, 1958. Oscar Peterson, rated by many the best jazz pianist alive, spends his working hours in the lemon-blues world of jazz music, bowing in his tuxedo and cummerbund to applause in Carnegie Hall or the Hollywood Bowl, watching cigarette smoke drift through thin spotlights on nightclub bandstands in New York and Chicago, goading himself to perform brilliantly in the embalming environment of recording studios. He sleeps restlessly by day, rising in the full afternoon to eat breakfast, and rides airplanes between concert bookings in Europe or the Orient.

Few careers offer so many obstacles to the likelihood of a cohesive marriage and sound family life, but Peterson has both. He lives with his pretty wife and five merry-eyed children in a four-bedroom bungalow in suburban Toronto. His friends know him to be a loving and stern father, insisting on better behaviour than most parents can exact from their children, a sensitive and positive husband whose 11-year marriage is weatherproof, and a conscientious citizen. He once astounded Montreal police by reporting an unwitnessed minor collision with a parked car.

Peterson is celebrated, not always joyously, for his honesty. A musician who was a close friend of his once asked in smug anticipation. "Oscar, what do you think of my piano playing?" Replied Peterson promptly: "I'll tell you, you're not a pianist."

I visited the Petersons recently to get some equally candid answers. Along with them, we got some good conversation and a wealth of common sense. We arrived around one in the afternoon, as Oscar was sitting down to breakfast with the youngest and most gamin-like of his five children, five-year-old Norman.

"He always waits to have breakfast with me whenever I'm home," explained Oscar. Six-year-old Oscar Jr. approached shyly and his father turned to him. "You want some too?" The boy nodded quickly.

"He's already eaten," protested Mrs. Peterson, coming from the kitchen with two plates of scrambled eggs.

"I'll give him part of mine," Oscar told her. The boys joined their father at the table and ate neatly, watching the adults with silent fascination.

Both Oscar and his wife, the former Lillie Fraser, are 32 years old. He is a huge man, over six foot one and weighing 240 pounds; she is small, trim and quiet. When they are together, Oscar does the talking. Both credit this, a manifestation of the balance of their relationship, with the success of their marriage. After the boys had finished and had disappeared in the direction of their bedroom, the Petersons discussed marriage.

Their three daughters—Lynn, 10, Sharon, 9, and Gay, 8—were born so close together that Lil had, for a time, a sense of being trapped. In the lull before the birth of the boys, she suggested to her husband that she get a change from her household chores by taking a job.

"We don't need the money," Oscar stated, feigning incomprehension.

"I know," said Lil. "I just want to get out for a while, that's all."

"Your place is right here with those babies," Oscar informed her stiffly. "Just forget any other notion you might have."

For some years now Lil Peterson has been enthusiastically resigned to this role. "I don't know how those marriages where the husband is henpecked work out," she commented wonderingly. "They're unnatural; both the husband and wife feel terrible."

"Another thing that causes a lot of trouble in marriages is that both aren't more honest with one another," interposed her husband. "They have suspicions or problems and they don't get them out in the open. I had to take you to Europe to get you to really talk to me, tell me your grievances."

Lil laughed at the recollection.

In return for what both regard as Lil's proper containment, Oscar is extraordinarily devoted. He awed fellow musicians one day at New York's Idlewild Airport, when the group was transferring from a transatlantic plane to one taking them to Chicago for an engagement the next night.

"I'll meet you there," Peterson announced. "I'm going home first."

"You haven't got time to go to Chicago by way of Canada!"

"Yes, I have," he retorted calmly. "I can get half a day with my family. It's worth it."

"He does that all the time, even if he can only be home a few hours," observed Lil gratefully. "If his tour is going to be a long one, he arranges for me to join him halfway through. And when he comes home, he's loaded with gifts. He brings unusual, unexpected things, like a carved teak chest from Hong Kong."

The Petersons led the way downstairs to the basement recreation room where one wall is filled with records and the rest of the room bristles with the latest equipment for hi-fidelity and stereophonic listening, film projectors, tape recorders and an ebony grand piano someone in Denmark once gave him. Lil Peterson observed that the Danish piano is far removed in quality from the one Oscar first knew. He was born in Montreal a few years ahead of the depression in a family severely afflicted with poverty. One of five children of Daniel Peterson, a railway porter, Oscar was a sickly child who spent a year in a sanitarium recovering from tuberculosis, and so did one of his sisters. They remember the period as a time of sanctuary from their father's harsh discipline.

"He decided as early as I can remember that I was going to be a musician," Oscar recalled. "I was playing a cornet in the family orchestra when I was five and he made up his mind that I had talent. He went right out and bought a piano, I'll never know how. He must have gone without things to pay for it. From that time on, my sister and I practised—or else."

"His father used to beat them with his belt," explained Lil, smoothing her skirt. She had settled on a narrow bench along one wall of the room, in the attitude of a spectator. "His sister Daisy used to get it worse than Oscar. She told me about a time when their father was going out on the railroad and he assigned them both a very complicated concerto to learn. They knew they would have to play it without a mistake before he got back. Well, Daisy practised for three, four hours every day, just terrified. Oscar didn't touch the piano, lolled around and read comic books or something. The day before their dad was due home, he went over to the piano and played the whole thing through perfectly. His ear is fabulous."

The Peterson children had no toys but played with what they could find around the house: boxes, clothes pegs, spoons. Only one child had a doll and although she is now an adult, she treasures it still. "We were poor, too," Lil added. "My dad was a porter on the railroad, too, but we weren't as poor as the Petersons." Oscar remembers with burning vividness the shame he felt on his first day in high school, wearing patched pants.

"One thing about it, though," Lil observed seriously. "Those kids really got a lot of love. They were very close as a family. Their mother used to try and protect them from their dad's beatings. He loved them too, in his way. He just wanted a lot for them."

"That's a mistake I won't make with our children," commented her husband, moving around the room absently in search of his cigarette lighter. "I have no ambitions for them at all. People sometimes ask me if I want them to be musicians. I say, 'If they want to, sure.' They can be whatever they like; I won't push them. I've seen too much misery when that happens."

As a reaction from his father's brand of discipline, which descended like an avalanche before the culprit could stammer an explanation or denial, Oscar is meticulously fair with his children. When he does spank them, after due enquiry, he suffers an agony of remorse. The Petersons tolerate no rudeness or show of disrespect for adults from their children. In his implacable insistence on honesty and courtesy, Oscar sometimes detects in himself a glint of his father's steel. "I have to watch myself," he confessed. "It turned out to be a good thing for me to be raised that way, but I don't want it for my kids."

He also has more than a trace of his father's stubbornness. "I remember the first time I ever heard a jazz piano," he mused, shifting his bulk in his chair. "I was about 12 and this sailor off a West Indies boat was playing. I listened and I decided I wanted to play music like that, only play it better."

The boy returned home and grimly began to practise jazz, getting a feel for the cleverness of the idiom. He rested his instinct for the music on a heavy foundation of classical training. When he wasn't in school, he practised from eight in the morning until noon, from the time he bolted his lunch until six, from after dinner until after midnight—for a year.

"When that sailor came back the next year, we had it out at the piano," grinned Oscar.

"How did you do?" He was asked.

His grin widened. "I made out all right."

As a youth he won a radio amateur contest and his father used the prize money, $250, to buy a newer piano. Eventually Oscar found work in dance orchestras around Montreal. His father used to clock him, allowing no more than 40 minutes from the moment the final "Good Night Ladies" was due to be played until Oscar was expected at his front door. The pianist didn't dare be late.

"Lil and I started going around together when we were both 16, isn't that right, Lil? We got married when we were 21. Then my wild period started."

Oscar's leap into wild oats was on a scale appropriate to his size. He stayed up until dawn playing jazz with any musician with sufficient staying power, drank his share, was impatient and irritated at his wife's complaints. He had no intention of trading one taskmaster for another.

"Then one day I went to see our minister," Oscar related with an appreciation for the drama of the story. "And he straightened me right out."

"What did he say?"

"Nothing, that was the beauty of it."

The minister, Rev. Charles E. Combes, must have been startled to find Peterson on his doorstep early one morning, giving strong indication that he had not yet been to bed. He invited him in, urged him to have a cup of tea and asked the purpose of the visit.

"I told him everything I was doing, all the crazy terrible things. I left nothing out, *nothing*. I was going a way I didn't want to go and I didn't know what to do about it. When I stopped talking, after a long time, Rev. Combes said politely, 'Is that all?' 'Why, yes,' I said. 'I don't have to worry about you,' he told me. 'You know the difference between right and wrong.' That was all he said to me. I just stared at him. After that, I had to live up to his faith in me."

Lil grinned at him. "Remember how you used to get sick every time I did, all the time I was pregnant?"

Oscar laughed. "I really did. She used to get sick at odd times, not just in the morning. Once I was walking down the street and I suddenly was violently ill, right there on the sidewalk. Later I discovered Lil was ill at the same time."

Oscar Peterson's big break as a musician would have broken a lesser man—he made his United States debut in Carnegie Hall, at a jazz concert that starred people like Ella Fitzgerald, Roy Eldridge, Coleman Hawkins. The jazz impresario Norman Granz arranged it, after asking if Oscar was game.

"Go ahead," Peterson told him. "After a break like that, I'll never be able to whine that I didn't get a chance."

One September night Granz introduced the unknown Canadian to a sold-out audience, mystifying them because Peterson's name wasn't even on the program. "Play whatever you like, for as long as you like," Granz told him. Peterson started with "I Only Have Eyes for You" and went on, amid applause and cheers. Since then he has made 30 to 40 record albums and has won world acclaim.

"The best thing that ever happened to me," Oscar reflected, unconsciously staring at his hands, "was when I heard that Art Tatum had named me as his favourite pianist. He played the greatest piano in the world, that's all. Vladimir Horowitz is maybe second. And Tatum said that about *me*. That's the best tribute I'll ever get."

Frank Sinatra is also a Peterson fan. Once Peterson and his trio were appearing at a Las Vegas hotel at a time when Sinatra was singing just down the street. On the final night of his booking, Sinatra ended his act early. "I don't know what you people plan to do now," he told his audience, "but I'm going to hear Oscar. It's his last night and I don't want to miss him."

Oscar chuckled as he remembered the occasion. "Frank came to see me all right," he smiled, "and he brought half of Las Vegas with him."

In the pause that developed, Lil murmured idly, "Remember that first tour, the Jazz at the Philharmonic tour?"

"Yeah," Peterson recalled. "Granz knew that as a Canadian I wouldn't have any idea about how a Negro is treated in the South. He offered to let me skip those dates, but I said I'd go."

"You phoned me and said you were starving," Lil inserted, moving an ashtray nearer her husband. "Your voice sounded just sick. All you were eating was hamburgs. You couldn't go into restaurants; either the white musicians would bring you out food to eat in the car or else you could stand at the back of the restaurant and they'd pass it out the kitchen door."

"I couldn't eat that way," Peterson explained. "Traveling in the south, it feels like you're not just in another world, you're on some other planet."

"Once you had to play with a tire chain at your feet, to protect yourself in case anyone in the audience came over the footlights to attack you," added Lil.

"Yes, but I've known discrimination in Canada too."

"Hamilton," said Lil tersely. Oscar nodded. A few years ago a Hamilton barber refused to cut Peterson's hair. Oscar argued for a time, then went to the nearest newspaper office and the subsequent publicity brought a score of phone calls to the Peterson home from barbers who denounced the bigot and offered to cut Peterson's hair any time.

"Oscar has a reputation for being so nice all the time that people suspect he is two-faced," Lil smiled. "I've heard them say, 'Don't trust Oscar, he's just *too* nice!' They don't know him. He doesn't often lose his temper but when he does, he really blows."

Discrimination triggers his temper occasionally. The earliest example of it was when Oscar was about nine or 10, in a classroom with another coloured boy. The teacher, in trying to find out which student had thrown a ruler, snapped, "I'll bet one of the niggers did it." Oscar leaped to his feet. "You apologize for that!" he screamed. His indignation led him to the principal's office; the teacher subsequently left the school.

The Petersons believe that there is a general bettering of toler-ance, despite recent ugly disturbances. As proof, their children haven't felt any discrimination. Although their district in Toronto has few Negro residents, several neighbors hurried to welcome them during their first week there.

Another source of annoyance to Oscar is the theory he sometimes encounters that it isn't the least surprising that a Negro should be a good jazz musician. "They explain to me that it is a black man's music, so naturally I can play it. That's nonsense. I'm a Canadian. I learned jazz in a country whose atmosphere is slightly sterile for a jazz musician. It has nothing to do with colour. I know a lot of tone-deaf Negroes."

While the Petersons talked, the five children were playing some-where in the house so quietly they couldn't be heard. The oldest, Lynn, appeared at her father's command to search for his lighter. She went out, came back a few minutes later holding it. He thanked her politely, she said, "You're welcome, Daddy," and went out again silently."

"Are they good students?"

Both Petersons considered this and nodded together. "I encourage them," remarked Oscar, "but I never praise. They aren't doing me a favor by getting good marks, or themselves either. It's just expected of them, just normal procedure."

"I hear you don't allow rock-'n'-roll music in your house."

Oscar looked surprised. "It just happens that way, doesn't it, Lil? The girls have radios but they never turn them on. They like classi-cal music and jazz, sometimes some of my records, or Don Shirley or Anita O'Day. They are all taking music lessons and I think that accounts for it. Once you learn something about music you don't fall victim to subterranean rock 'n' roll."

The discussion led from rock 'n' roll to jazz, and jazz musicians. There was a comment on the high proportion of dope addicts among jazz musicians and Peterson's voice went down in tone and up in volume.

"That's another of those generalizations that annoys me," he says irritably. "I know a doctor who became an addict. They put him in a private institution; no one even heard about it. But if I took a shot of heroin, police sirens would clang, headlines all over the place. I'd be branded for life. Very few musicians are addicts, but the whole profession suffers."

Peterson's dislike of dope in all its forms is pronounced and forthright. Recently he was a guest at a home where the host lit a marijuana cigarette. "What's the matter, Oz?" he was asked. "You can't come in *my* home again," said Peterson frankly. The argument that ensued lasted for hours.

"I noticed a good friend getting the habit while we were on tour a few years ago," Peterson recalls. "After a while, he mentioned to me he was worried his wife would find out. I told him, 'How could she miss? It's written all over you, you're a junkie. You're also a weakling.' He quit the habit."

"Are you ever nervous?"

"Never about myself. I have faith in myself. I know I can play. I believe that talent is a manifestation of ego. Sometimes with a musician it may be the only ego he has and he's terrified when he's doing anything else but playing. The only thing that bothers me, sometimes a musician I don't like will come in to hear me and suddenly I play marvelously, way over my head. It makes me wonder what kind of a phoney I've been, playing at the other level most of the night."

"Are you improved now as a musician over a few years ago?"

Oscar and Lil exchanged an affectionate look. "I think so. I've stopped trying to prove a point demonstrating technical ability all the time." He paused and thought through what he was about to say.

"You enter the scene," he resumed carefully, "and you're battling greats. You have to find a wedge to get that door open. So you look over your assets and pick the strongest one to use to bludgeon the doorkeeper."

He hesitated, hoping not to be misunderstood. "I've got my membership now, I'm inside. I can say something with one note, if I want to."

Oscar Peterson is one of the most decorated jazz musicians of all time. Among his almost countless international awards are eight Grammy awards, two Junos, a Governor General's lifetime achievement award, the UNESCO *International Music Prize and a Japanese lifetime achievement* *award worth more than $200,000. He still performs occasionally, has recorded 95 albums under his own name, more as an accompanist, and has received 14 honorary degrees.*

He and Lillie Fraser divorced in the early 1960s, and Peterson now lives with his fourth wife in Mississauga, Ont.

June Callwood is an award-winning journalist and author who contributed her first article to Maclean's *in 1947. Callwood, who lives in Toronto with her husband, fellow writer Trent Frayne, has written more than 15 books on a wide variety of topics.*

Norman Jewison:
The Star's Status Symbol

Norman Jewison on the set, 1966

JANUARY 5, 1963. Norman Jewison, an even dozen years away from driving a Diamond cab on the night shift in Toronto, is at work in Hollywood these days directing his second movie, *The Thrill of It All*. This is a $3-million comedy starring Doris Day, the biggest female box office draw in the business. As soon as the picture is completed, Jewison will direct his first Broadway show, a new musical comedy by Meredith Willson, the author of *The Music Man*. Before Jewison went to Hollywood in 1961, he had established himself in New York as the highest-priced director of the highest-priced musical variety shows in all television. As a former Canadian colleague, Ross McLean, says, "Having Jewison as director became a star's status symbol."

Since 1952, when Jewison was first hired by the CBC, he has succeeded far more spectacularly than any other television director on either side of the border. This includes a number of men quite as creative and capable as Jewison is. And it raises the question again of what, in addition to real talent, it takes to make the *big* big time in show business.

In the interesting case of Norman Jewison, what it has taken is luck and charm. His luck is demonstrable and he has a very special kind of charm, compounded of truly monumental self-confidence and equally great friendliness which, in combination, enable him to handle performers with exceptional ease. In Jewison's rise as a director, luck and charm have probably been fully as important as talent.

One form of Jewison luck, his former Toronto TV colleagues maintain, was his marriage to his wife, Dixie, a tiny brunette Toronto model. Dixie, a determined young woman, is credited with pointing her husband's talents toward the places where they would be most likely to be conspicuously recognized and handsomely rewarded—New York and Hollywood.

It's likely that success won't change Norman Jewison, since he has been running his career with the psychology of success from his first professional days. He seems to have been born with unconquerable scrappiness, irrepressible cockiness and an overflowing belief in his own instincts. He radiates a take-it-or-leave-it attitude which contrasts amusingly with his slight physical presence. On a movie set, surrounded by grave, middle-aged technicians and assistants, he looks like the messenger boy who just arrived with the hot coffee. He dresses with dash and an informality which somehow proclaims his status: his denim pants fit beautifully, his sweaters are hand-knit in Rome and as only a man who is very sure of himself could do, he goes to work in white sneakers. Jewison breezes through life, a 35-year-old Peter Pan, forgetting his wallet, his script, even forgetting where he parked his Jaguar to which he has, in any case, forgotten the keys. Someone always takes care of him.

On the job Jewison almost explodes with exuberance and enthusiasm. His ex-secretary, Barbara Geist, recalls that he had an "almost hypnotic effect" on the casts and crews of his television shows even though "he was a great one for getting there late and then keeping everybody working around the clock." A performer at heart, Jewison acts out every part in the script "with such delight and love that everyone connected with the show would get wildly excited." He has, at most times, a joyous quality which makes even television executives relax. Jewison's former boss at the Columbia Broadcasting System in New York remembers that "it was a good idea not to have a hockey stick or a puck in your office when he arrived because no matter what the crisis was, you could be required to defend your goal for an hour before talking business."

There is general agreement among people who have worked with Norman Jewison that no other director anywhere can get as much out of a star in co-operation, effort and performance. Perry Lafferty, producer of many of the television shows Jewison directed, says, "He does no ritual dances around the performers. He realizes that the bigger the stars, the more scared they are. He has a child-like directness in his way with them—like a kid who gets a bead on a lollipop and goes after it. And the stars get courage from working with someone like Norman who is marching right up the centre of the street."

Jewison can be as tough as anyone in the business when necessary, but with his short stature he looks so young and defenceless that he never seems to represent any sort of threat—a great advantage in dealing with people as insecure as most entertainers. He says: "They see me and I look like a Canadian newsboy. But performers need a father figure, someone to lean on, and believe me, it doesn't take them long to start leaning."

Jewison takes frank delight in telling stories which show how his charm works—the mechanics are never concealed, presumably because the charm itself is real, not manufactured for the occasion. For example, when he directed a Judy Garland television special that co-starred Frank Sinatra and Dean Martin, he was informed that Sinatra only rehearsed by the side of his own swimming pool. Jewison was determined to get him out to the inconveniently located sound stages at Burbank. "I was ready to quit if Frank wouldn't come. I called him and just explained the problem—for a half hour or more. Eventually he agreed, but only if I'd have the rehearsals catered by Romanoff's."

In addition to sweet talk, Jewison has a way of withdrawing his moral support at a crucial moment in an argument—like a superior nanny—which is amazingly effective with show business people. "Judy Garland can be the most amusing, intelligent dame you ever met and then suddenly she'll be a seven-year-old. I'll tell her, 'Now you're being a child—I don't even want to talk to you anymore.' I had no problems with her because I know how to handle her."

Sometimes his technique is a little more elaborate. Doris Day always looks at the daily rushes of her pictures, a practice to which Jewison is firmly opposed since he knows that she is notoriously neurotic about the way she is photographed. "Doris," I said, "*look* at the rushes if you feel that insecure about them—go on, *look*. How do I feel about it? You're talking about me? Oh, I'll be terribly, terribly upset, of course … it's never happened to me before … not with Judy or Belafonte or Gleason or Julie Andrews … but if you must, you must. But how can you *stand* to do it on top of all the other work you have to do? What a responsibility! Gosh!" The picture has been in production for many weeks, and so far Doris Day hasn't seen a foot of film.

Charming and lucky Norman Jewison was brought up in modest circumstances on Queen Street East in Toronto. His family, strong Methodists of Protestant Irish stock, owned a small dry goods store where, after school, Norman helped sell girdles and ladies' stockings. He went to Malvern Collegiate and then to Normal Model School, to which his adored maiden aunt, a schoolteacher, paid his tuition. He served in the navy as an ordinary seaman and, on navy credits, he graduated from Victoria College at the University of Toronto. From the age of six, when he first learned to recite all 11 verses of *The Shooting of Dan McGrew*, Norman, a born ham of the most relentless sort, had pounced on every opportunity to sing, dance, act, write and direct any school theatrical production going.

Trying to break into television in 1950, he took the advice of CBC executive Stuart Griffith who told him to go to London to look for work. There Jewison lived meagrely on his own rabbit stew for two years—he tells, with Dickensian relish, that he was once reduced to stealing a stray turnip from the floor of a greengrocer's—and eventually got a few odd jobs at the BBC.

On his return to Toronto, Griffith hired him for a CBC training program. Ross McLean, who was involved in the same program and now admires Jewison's work, remembers that "it was not too easily perceived then what Norman had to offer beyond a wild abundance of energy. It was a fantastic sideshow to watch him working in the control booth. From the beginning to the end of the show his whole little body would vibrate while he gurgled, babbled, whistled, screamed, jumped up and down and spoke every performer's lines. But at no time was I conscious of any special talent or taste or tidy results from him. He didn't seem ambitious—there just wasn't that much direction to what he was doing. No one perceived that Norman was going anywhere."

Those early days of Canadian television were the perfect training ground for future directors, since everyone learned how to do everything and a director's job involves a multitude of complex techniques. He must be able to work constructively with the scriptwriter, decide on casting, tell the set designer and lighting man what effects he wants, put the show together physically in rehearsal and "call" each carefully planned camera shot from the control room while the show is actually going on. In the six years Jewison worked for the CBC he directed, and eventually produced, many shows with moderate success.

But he wasn't happy. He had frequent battles with the CBC brass, about whom he is still outspokenly bitter, over the amount of control he insisted on exercising over his shows. Jewison is a ferociously, in fact a fanatically, independent man. Before he had any recognition or reputation to speak of, he found it impossible to tolerate the slightest infringement on his rights as creative boss of a show. As an example, he resigned a choice job as director-producer of the Sunday night *Showtime* when General Electric, the sponsor, wanted to make suggestions about the show and the CBC wouldn't back up Jewison's refusal to listen to them.

"By 1958, when I was doing *The Barris Beat*, I felt there was no leadership at the top of the CBC. The executives were afraid of anything that smacked of good showmanship or theatricality. And I'd gotten to the point where I didn't even really care."

It was at this stage of his career that the Jewison luck began to function. Larry Auerbach, an agent at the William Morris office in New York, one of the two largest talent agencies in the world, saw some tapes of *The Barris Beat*. This was a short-lived variety show Jewison directed and which, at that time, was only broadcast locally in Toronto. Auerbach spotted Jewison's work, put together an 18-minute kinescope of some of the best numbers and asked Jewison to come down from Canada for job interviews.

At that particular moment a CBS program vice-president named

Mike Dann was in what seemed to be an impossible bind. The *Hit Parade* program had just moved to CBS after 10 years at NBC and there wasn't a good musical variety director available in New York. Auerbach showed *The Barris Beat* kinescope to Dann and in fine, fairy-tale tradition Dann decreed, "Send for that man." Jewison, as it happened, was waiting in Dann's outer office. Dann hastily called in a quorum of other vice-presidents and then summoned Jewison.

"In walked what appeared to be a 17-year-old pixie in blue jeans, wearing sneakers and an open shirt and needing a haircut. We couldn't believe our eyes. We were terrified at giving such a big assignment to such a young boy (Jewison was then 30) but we were desperate."

This particular *Hit Parade* assignment was a startling stroke of luck for a totally unknown Canadian director, and enabled Jewison to move into American television under the best possible conditions. The *Hit Parade* had been doing so badly that any change at all could only look good. But, far more important, CBS gave Jewison its finest team to work with. The producer of the show, Perry Lafferty, is a highly respected television veteran, a calm, cool, polished professional who ran the over-all operation perfectly and backed Jewison up at every turn. In addition Jewison asked for and got the services of top Canadian talent: writer John Aylesworth and music arranger Jack Kane. His CBS technicians, from the camera to the grips, were the best in the business. This entire team did 26 successful weeks of *Hit Parade* and then went on to do a 12-week Andy Williams summer program. These two series were what really established Jewison's name in television; all his future success stems from them. Perry Lafferty says today: "Norman got great credit and so he should, but perhaps he got *more* credit than he really deserved since the shows were team efforts." (To be accurate, Jewison didn't do *all* 26 *Hit Parades*. After the 10th show he suddenly announced, "I'm tired," and he and Dixie took off for Algonquin Park in mid-northern Ontario, which is Jewison's idea of paradise regained. After four exhausting days of camping, tramping and portaging a canoe through the wilderness—"Dixie can portage a mean canoe or more than her own weight in gear," Jewison admiringly observes—he returned refreshed to Manhattan.)

Jewison's next CBS assignment, *The Big Party*, was the turning point of his career, not because he did such a good job but because he walked out on it. Sponsored by Revlon, it was the most expensive and highly touted production of the season, in which just plain folks like Tallulah Bankhead and Rock Hudson got together and entertained their just plain friends like Sammy Davis Jr. and Jerry Lewis. Disaster struck early in the person of one Mort Green, whose job it was to relay the "suggestions" of Mr. Revson, the president of Revlon, to Mr. Jewison. Mr. Revson expects the same obedience to his suggestions as did the King of Siam some 100 years ago. Unable to function, furious, frustrated, embroiled in a dozen skirmishes, Jewison resigned before the first show even went on the air, although it was then too late in the season for him to expect to get another good assignment. The show was one of the most memorable debacles in all television history. Perry Lafferty, who remained with *The Big Party* for the full 13 hideous weeks, says, "There were 92 chiefs and no Indians. It frightened Norman, and from one point of view it was much easier for him to leave than to stay."

Freed of *The Big Party* by good sense, Jewison went onward and upward by good luck: as a free agent, he could now make his break into television "specials"—lavish productions in which the sponsor often spends as much as half a million dollars on a single show. Only a few days after he left *The Big Party* Jewison was interviewed by Harry Belafonte, who was looking for a director for his first television appearance. Belafonte says, "I saw a spark of imagination in Norman's work. I felt that, of all the directors I'd considered, he was the one who would best be able to take a live image, put it through a mechanical device and retain its strength and the artistic level."

Belafonte picked Jewison in the teeth of his sponsor, Mr. Revson of Revlon Incorporated. "I *loved* the rebel in Norman. I find that very sympathetic to my own emotional point of view." The show, which won several awards, was, for Belafonte, "the happiest experience I've had in television. It was unique for me because of Norman's ability to adapt himself to the world of Negro art. It was amazing how he knew, better than anyone, how to light that beautiful black face of Odetta's, how he'd ask about the meaning and sub-meaning and sub-sub-meaning of the words of the songs."

The Belafonte show set Jewison up in the TV-special trade: he did several more, including *The Fabulous Fifties*, produced by Leland Hayward. But frequently Jewison lost juicy assignments because of his refusal to work when he couldn't call the turns. David Susskind, who was producing an Art Carney special, wanted Jewison to direct. He turned down the job because he couldn't also produce it.

"Susskind's directors do all the work and then he comes along in the last three days and takes all the credit," he said later. "He doesn't pay well either—who put him on the throne?" Jewison missed a chance to direct Ingrid Bergman in a dramatic show when he demanded that CBS bring the British playwright John Mortimer over from England for two weeks of rewriting. CBS declined. "I *refuse* to get involved in something that isn't right—I don't care who's in it," Jewison says.

A conflict over script changes brought about his biggest loss, that of a very close friendship and a good working relationship with Danny Kaye, whose TV special he had directed. The executive producer of the show, the redoubtable Sylvia Fine, who is also Mrs. Danny Kaye, edited the tape of the show *after* it had been edited to Jewison's satisfaction, causing him to make a formal complaint against her to the Directors' Guild. Very few people in show business have ever dared to go to the mat with Sylvia Fine.

In spite of these setbacks Jewison turned down far more shows than he accepted ("A Connie Francis special—*that's* special?") and he refused to do any more weekly series since he had decided that he couldn't get the kind of perfection he wanted without wildly expensive weeks of planning and rehearsal, luxuries which don't exist in television outside of specials. At the peak of Jewison's television reputation he went without work for an eight-month period when no specials were available on his terms. Mike Dann of CBS says, "I offered him over half a dozen projects when I knew he needed work and money, but he didn't accept. There are other directors who have as much integrity but they are a lot richer and older."

Jewison's attitude turned out to be as astute as it was hazardous. His name was associated only with top-notch shows but he had, to a degree, priced himself out of the market and his career was standing still. Finally, in 1960, he asked CBS to release him from his contract since many of the shows he might want to do were scheduled for NBC.

As a free lance, Jewison has turned down many lucrative offers, including the Garry Moore, Perry Como and Andy Griffith series. He directed only four big shows, the Danny Kaye special, a second Belafonte special, the much applauded Judy Garland special and a star-filled extra-special called *The Broadway of Lerner and Loewe*. During this period he made $80,000, but there is no doubt that he could have earned considerably more if he had chosen to. Now his strategy of excellence is beginning to pay off. Last spring he was signed to direct his first movie, *Forty Pounds of Trouble*, starring Tony Curtis, solely on the strength of the Judy Garland special. Since it had long been plain that there weren't going to be enough specials on television to keep him working steadily, Hollywood was the obvious step. Today, while he works on the Doris Day picture for Universal-International, two other studios, Metro and Columbia, are after him for other films and his first Broadway musical will be on the boards sometime next fall.

Charming, lucky, talented Norman Jewison. On one page of his personal, leather-bound copy of the script of his current movie he has doodled these words: Hapi, Happi, Happy, HAPPY. Smar, Smart, SMARRT.

Norman Jewison soon established his movie reputation with three consecutive hits: The Cincinatti Kid *(1965),* The Russians are Coming! The Russians are Coming! *(1966) and* In the Heat of the Night, *which won the Oscar for best picture of 1967. He returned to Canada in the late 1970s and in 1988 founded the Canadian Centre for Advanced Film Studies in Toronto.*

Judith Krantz wrote for a number of American women's magazines before moving to Toronto in 1959. During her 18-month sojourn in Canada, which she remembers fondly, she wrote several freelance pieces for Maclean's. *In 1978, her debut novel,* Scruples, *became the first of 10 international blockbusters. She now lives in Bel Air, Calif.*

Gordon Lightfoot

Gordon Lightfoot on tour, 1968

SEPTEMBER, 1968. The trip north from Toronto with Gordon Lightfoot was an Arcadian dream: there was Lightfoot, a beautiful man, driving the car through the special luminous twilight that comes to Ontario in May, over roads that undulated with the land, just as the steam rose off the black earth like smoke. The funny Victorian-Gothic farmhouses and villages perched intact on the horizon, temporarily immune from the urban sprawl. This was, in fact, Gordon Lightfoot country. He came from Orillia, 40 miles northeast of the little town of Alliston where we were heading that night for a concert in the high-school gymnasium.

Alliston's houses belong to the 19th century but the Frederick Banting Memorial high school is aggressively 20th century—a sterile saltbox. It was imbued with a different spirit that night, however. Gordon Lightfoot was the first genuine *star* to play the town in years and every one of the 2,000 folding chairs in the cavernous gym had been sold. The crowd that started lining up at eight o'clock was mostly under 25, uniformly clean-cut, scrubbed and innocent-looking. No hippies here—no sideburns or turtlenecks, no weird clothes or wild makeup. There were knots of newly wed teenagers, pregnant young girls, talking about finishing grade 13, about babies, about drinking Southern Comfort and Coke and getting *very* sick, and about Lightfoot: "He's pretty big, you know."

Gordon Lightfoot is pretty big indeed. He's 29 and he's had more songs recorded by other artists in the past five years than any songwriter in North America except Bob Dylan. "For Lovin' Me," one of his earliest songs, has been recorded by more than 100 artists. His albums sell phenomenally well in Canada. His second album, *The Way I Feel*, has sold more than 125,000 copies and won him a gold record. He went from singing in a bar to filling Vancouver's Queen Elizabeth Theatre in a matter of months, strictly on the hits other people had made by recording his songs. He composed honest tunes with an astonishing variety of textures. His lyrics are straightforward and touching, without obscurantism or flatulent philosophy.

At precisely nine o'clock, John Stockfish, electric bass, sporting a pre-Elvis pompadour, and Red Shea, acoustic guitar, looking like a shambling Paul Newman, took their places on the vast naked stage. Then, in a blizzard of buckskins, Lightfoot was front and centre singing "For Lovin' Me."

The buckskin jacket, with its rows of fringes, was a surprise, a holdover from his early Country-and-Lightfoot days. The rest was hip: bell-bottom jeans, brightly coloured shirt with a Californian-style scarf loosely knotted at the throat. The soft curling blond hair gave him the appearance of a minor Greek god. He's paler and heavier than your average Greek god, but sexy in a vulnerable kind of way. The crowd loved him. They whistled and stamped their feet at every song, building up an empathetic rhythm as he sang.

The star quality was all there: the presence, the pacing, the confident patter, even corny jokes. The kids dug whatever he said. "A few weeks ago I was in the Princess Hotel in Edinburgh, Scotland. I met a girl named Marie Christine Dupuis. She couldn't speak English, and being a Canadian I couldn't speak a word of French. We spent five lovely hours together. This song is about a woman compared to a ship."

Lightfoot moved into "Black Day in July." He wrote it just after the Detroit riots last year. It's solid musical journalism, documenting America without putting it down. His sense of that violence is graphic:

Black Day in July: Motor City madness
*   has touched the countryside.*
And thru the smoke and cinders you
*   can hear it far and wide.*
The doors are quickly bolted and the
*   children locked inside.*
Black Day in July.

Black Day in July: and the soul of
*   Motor City is bared across the land.*
And the book of law and order is taken
*   in the hands*
Of the sons of the fathers who were
*   carried to this land.*
Black Day in July.

The audience shouted their approval. "I wish I had some answers," he replied.

Between sets, he relaxed by reminiscing about his early career. He sat with his leg slung over the arm of a chair, his long elegant fingers fiddling with his ring. "Alliston's a lot like Orillia physically—a small, pretty town. I'm not sure what I feel about Orillia—that was 11 years ago and I got out. When I first went to Toronto I was a real hick. I was a clerk in a bank for $40 a week—some financier. I lived with another guy from Orillia in a boarding house in the east end."

Unlike many folk singers and young composers who can think up tunes and lyrics but have to get someone else to transpose them, Lightfoot is the complete composer. He's come the whole disciplined route: singing and drumming in the high-school band, operettas, studying piano, forming his own singing groups and bands; a barbershop quartet that almost won a national championship until the bass quit and the group collapsed. When he graduated from high school in 1957, he studied at the Westlake School of Modern Music in Los Angeles to polish all his techniques. Now he can identify any note played and can sight-sing.

After the show was over, the crowd dispersed reluctantly. About 30 girls waited for autographs. Through the middle of them strode a tall, heavily built girl in an orange dress. It was the ultimate groupie, or group follower, Lynn Ackerman. She is the most devoted and obsessive of all Lightfoot's fans. "It doesn't matter where we play," Lightfoot explained, "if it's in Sudbury or New York, she'll show up."

It's hard to understand why. She has almost no contact with him, although occasionally he shouts from the stage, "Is Lynn out there?" Nothing is quite as sad as watching Lynn watching Lightfoot zap off out of a parking lot. I wondered how she'd get back. "By bus, or hooking a ride with someone," Lightfoot said. "I don't know, I can't get myself involved in her bag."

We roared along the highway drawn by the prospect of greasy chips—the first food anybody had had since noon. "Man, I worked bars for two years after I learned how to play guitar. I mean, when the Village Corner Folk Club thing was happening for Ian and Sylvia, all I could pick was four-string axe—the simplest there is. I was writing all the time and had started singing some of my own songs. The first time I really broke out with *something* was at the Toronto Teachers College in 1964. Steele's Tavern, where I was playing, let me off for an hour. The thing at the Teachers College was all me. I went over well and I knew it. It *did* something to me."

It did enough to give him confidence in his own songs, and he incorporated them into his repertoire. One night a few months later, Ian Tyson came into Steele's with John Court, Albert Grossman's partner and record producer. Tyson liked Lightfoot's songs and later recorded several; Grossman, *the* New York agent for folk and pop singers, signed Lightfoot. That did it. Calls for concerts started coming in. "Peter, Paul and Mary did 'For Lovin' Me' and they were on my bandwagon for months. They'd shout my name out at concerts."

The next day, Lightfoot was faced with two shows in Cobourg, Ont. In spite of fatigue and indigestion from last-night's hamburgers, he headed out to visit some old friends between shows. In drizzling rain we pulled up front of a ranch-style bungalow huddled uncomfortably between some elegant old, brick Victorian houses.

Gordon Lightfoot

The vast living room of the house was covered in about a quarter of an acre of beige carpet. Lightfoot politely removed his pointy cowboy boots. Everyone followed his example, to the host's astonishment. We sat down to tiny sandwiches and a drink. "We've followed Gord's career closely for 10 years," the host said. "When we realized that Gord was in the chorus singing and dancing on *Country Hoedown*, 18 of us got together and sent a petition to the CBC demanding that they give Lightfoot a chance to sing by himself. All they did was send back a picture of King Gannam, the star of the show."

"When I started out on *Country Hoedown*," Lightfoot recounted, "the producer said, 'You're a clumsy son of a bitch, but you've got potential.' I did every one of those 250 shows terrified that I'd forget my lines or the dance steps."

We left the house at 6:30. Lightfoot, Shea and Stockfish needed time to tune up for the evening performance—a holy, private ritual for musicians. The dressing area for the band was in the school's music room. The hall was filled to capacity: 1,024 tickets at $2.50 and $3.50 each had been sold.

Lightfoot got thunderous applause when he ran on stage and swung into "For Lovin' Me." The pacing of this show was faster than the afternoon and the night before. An electric quality was building up all during the show. The crowd swayed in time with his music, they responded to every movement of his body and every song he sang. Lightfoot was digging it—he kept nodding affirmatively and smiling at Shea and Stockfish. At one point he said, "We're really together tonight. Lord, let it stay like this."

The evolution of Lightfoot's lyrics has been from very simple, charming songs like "The Way I Feel":

The way I feel is like a robin,
Whose babes have flown to come
* no more.*

to more complex historical songs like the "Canadian Railroad Trilogy":

215

There was a time in this fair land.
When the railroad did not run,
When the wild majestic mountains
Stood alone against the sun.
Long before the white man and
*   long before the wheel,*
When the green dark forest was
*   too silent to be real.*

This remarkable song has the quality of Francis Parkman's histories of Canada. You can *feel* how empty and lonely it was—no wisp of smoke over those incredible forests.

Barnstorming is an exhausting way to pay the bills. "You have to travel with your own PA system and expect the worst about lights. Small-town promoters don't realize you can get up there with the wrong lights, bad sound and make an ass of yourself in front of 1,000 people."

In Hamilton the following day, the seating arrangement was bad, the lights were terrible and the promoter wanted Lightfoot to cut the afternoon show short. "I can't do that, man," Lightfoot shot back. "They've paid good money for a Lightfoot show and that's what they'll get—a complete show, and a good one." He was right. It was a good one.

When the pressures of perfectionism and performing dry him up aesthetically, Lightfoot takes off for England. It started in 1963, when he took his Swedish bride Brida and spent the summer in London. He'd suffered a fearful, arid period in his writing for almost two years. Before that, songs had been pouring out of him. Some were good, and some, like "Two Kids from Cabbagetown," were awful. Through a fast-talking agent he got on British television with a show called *Rancho Vegas*, featuring live horses and Rodgers-and-Hart early Americana. Even though the show was a seedy affair and he felt numbed by it, Lightfoot wrote 30 songs. During a more recent fallow period, he went to England and rode around in train compartments by himself. Sixteen new songs came to him swiftly and he started writing poetry as well. Perhaps England frees him from his small-town background and the dominating Canadian landscape. *Now* he's articulating urban fear and violence and the enormous burden of Canadian history.

The following day the group flew to Washington, D.C., to open for a week at the Cellar Door Club. It was a relief after barnstorming. A gig in a club means that the performer isn't being eaten alive by all the fiddly details of being on the road. The Washington week turned out to be an enormous success. The club was filled every night in spite of racial tension, the Poor People's March, a transit strike and bad business all over town. "The first night, I went through five songs without saying anything and I told the crowd, 'You know it's good, don't you?' and they've been coming back ever since."

At 7:30, there was a tour show: students from out of town get a dinner and a show for the price of a ticket. These kids were from Detroit and to their mutual astonishment they'd never heard of Lightfoot. He played it cool until he came to "Black Day in July." "This is a song about your city. I'm sorry it has to be this way." There was an awkward pause when he finished and then they let loose with their most enthusiastic applause of the evening.

One kid yelled, "Who wrote that?"

"I did," said Lightfoot. "These are all my songs."

"Did you record that one?"

"Yes, I did," he replied, warming up to one of his hobbyhorses. "But CKLW in Windsor won't play it. It's being played on FM markets, but the top-40 stations in the States won't play it. I don't blame them. They're not ready for that sort of thing. They've got their ratings to think about."

His distress at this situation is kept hidden most of the time. But CKLW is another matter. Later, as he stabbed at a steak sandwich, he said, "It's number one in Detroit and it's the Canadian station. It's the only place in Canada to break a record in the U.S. I'm not asking for a hype. I've accommodated myself, played their clubs, their hops—and *nothing*. I'm Canadian, man, and they won't even listen to me." Almost everyone has had a hit out of Lightfoot but Lightfoot himself.

But his bitterness disappeared when he got on to his own songwriting and Canadian history. Don Harron, writer of this year's

Canadian National Exhibition grandstand show in Toronto, wanted Lightfoot to perform in it. "It's not the right thing for me to do," Lightfoot said. "Mine's very simple, man—all I do is go and sing my songs. I don't want to be part of a production." So Harron asked him to write a song for Catherine McKinnon and lent him books on Louis Riel. The books have completely captured Lightfoot's imagination. He's not trying to write a document of the period, but get a feeling for it. "A song has to have a point of view, a philosophy to hold it together. I get about 100 songs a year sent to me by amateurs. But they don't have a point of view. For instance, I don't write anything on the road. I make a few notes *maybe*. I've got to feel it first, then I know what to write."

The nine o'clock show, as did all their shows, started precisely on time. I sat with a couple of girls, typical of that audience, who said, "We know more about his songs than we do about him or his singing."

John Stockfish and Red Shea walked on in their super-straight clothes, and took their positions. Lightfoot sat on the stairs, holding his axe, waiting for his introduction. In a burst of energy, he leaped from the stairs, bounded onto the stage and was into the second bar of "I'm Not Sayin'" before the applause caught up with him. He smiled winningly into the smoky blackness and introduced the next two songs with, "Here's a couple of old chestnuts for you"—"Ribbon of Darkness" and "Spin, Spin, Spin." He sings these old songs well, but there's an irony in his performance of them. They lack the passion, his own performing passion, that he projects into his newest songs. The old ones seem merely to evoke pleasant memories.

When he finished the set, we went upstairs to the manager's office to cool off. We talked about the poetry he'd been writing in England. "In some cases he spends less time writing a poem than he does his tunes," Shea said. "Well, songs take infinitely more time," Lightfoot chipped in. "After writing 135 songs, then it seems pretty easy to sit down and crank out 40 poems. If you can put poetry into the songs, that's where it's really at. Bob Dylan has it. I'm aware I do it."

In a storm of energy they ran back to the stage at 11:30. Right into "I'm Not Sayin'": Lightfoot dipped his head and guitar in acknowledgement of the applause. He poured charm past the pale-blue spotlight into the blackness. He moved into "Walls" *("I'm not ashamed to say I've loved you well").* His eyes closed, he started enjoying the warmth of the crowd and the pleasures of performing. The light switched to a soft red, and Lightfoot's features seemed more sculptural than ever. "People have to get used to me," he's said. "They don't get my songs the first time they hear them. They may have to hear them three or four times and they know it's good. I may not be recognized until after I'm gone—in a mass sense, I mean."

The crowd at the Cellar Door was recognizing him right now. "Black Day in July" drew the longest applause. The show took a dramatic rise in intensity at this point. He came on very strong, milking every scene in the song for its terrible consequence.

"Does Your Mother Know": He started to sweat slightly. The sensuality of his performing held the audience completely still. Nobody bothered to touch their drinks. He leaned back, straining, pushing the words out, working his jaw slightly. It was impossible for any female not to love him a little bit.

Then "Bitter Green": *Bitter Green they called her/Walking in the sun/Loving everyone that she met.*" He stared into the blackness, waiting for the intense loneliness of this new song to settle on the audience, to make the Young Ones moodily introspective. It all came together meltingly: the mikes, his voice, the instruments. The audience could feel every emotion he sang about, see it in his face. The emotional level just reached the drowning point when he started into one of his novelty songs. The audience twitched and laughed nervously in reaction. He'd brought them down too fast. They applauded for a long time and he started an encore to the show without moving from the stage. He turned to Shea: "I think you know what I want to do." They started "Rosanna" together, played 10 bars. Then Lightfoot lifted his guitar over his head. "Cut it, cut it. It's not working." Then he switched into "The Mountains and Maryann." He put them right back up there—traveling.

Dawn was trying to break through the rain when I finally left the club. I hung around because it was too hard to leave the source of that much excitement. But there was a plane to catch and all the Scotch of the long evening was catching up with my head. I went out to the airport alone and never felt closer to a Lightfoot tune in my life. He *knows* what it's about.

> *In the early morning rain*
> *With a dollar in my hand,*
> *With an achin' in my heart*
> *And my pockets full of sand,*
> *I'm a long way from home,*
> *And I miss my loved ones so.*

Gordon Lightfoot, who lives in Toronto, released 16 more original albums between 1968 and 1988 and continues to tour. He divorced Brita in 1973 and has been married to Elizabeth Moon since 1989. Lightfoot has won 17 Juno Awards and received the Governor General's Performing Arts Award in 1997.

Marjorie Harris was a staff writer and senior editor at Maclean's *from 1966 to 1970. Now editor-in-chief of* Gardening Life, *she has written 13 books on gardening.*

Donald Sutherland:
The Funniest Film Actor
Canada Has Ever Produced

Donald Sutherland, 1970

By Douglas Marshall

SEPTEMBER, 1970. TITLE OF MOVIE: *Alex in Wonderland.*

LOCATION: Outside the giant Trans World Airlines hangar at Los Angeles International Airport.

SCENE: A surrealist sequence in which Alex, an underground film maker, imagines himself caught in a killer smog. The camera crane glides in over a baggage truck stacked with smog-felled bodies, then swoops up to a plate-glass window MGM has built into the hangar 30 feet above. Alex and his wife are gazing out across the field where, as the window reflection shows, a departing jet emits trails of filth and an absurd donkey munches in the middle distance.

The shot ends. The camera crew huddles. Behind the window, the actor playing Alex begins to clown grotesquely. He is trying to attract attention and succeeds. The cameraman doubles up with laughter, nearly falls off his crane and yells down to the director: "He wants to ask you something."

"Who does?"

"Our star. Donald whatshisname. He's a very funny guy."

Sutherland is the name, Donald Sutherland. He is indeed a very funny guy. Funny peculiar and, as anyone who has savored the dry-martini bite of his performance in the black war comedy *M*A*S*H* can confirm, funny haw-sob-haw. He is the funniest film actor Canada has ever produced. He may also be the best.

His doleful El Greco face and lank six-foot-four frame—Don Quixote Sutherland—are the distinctive outward features of a highly charged individual. Like, say, Steve McQueen, he could never be mistaken for anybody else. Yet unlike McQueen, Sutherland vanishes into a variety of roles with a fluid magic that reminds one of the early Peter Sellers. Sutherland can portray a slobbering moronic mute one day, a powdered French aristocrat the next, and be utterly convincing as both. Critics sometimes assume Sutherland's talents are a freakish gift of nature. His professional peers know better. He is a superb player because he spent half his 35 years learning how the hard way.

"Donald is one of the five or six best actors around," says Paul Mazursky, director of *Alex in Wonderland*. "He's one of the few guys who can play roles other than himself and still keep his essential personality."

And what is his essential personality? In a word, odd. (In one of his recent films, *Kelly's Heroes*, he appropriately plays a character called Oddball.) Sutherland's reputation for eccentricity goes back to his days as a student actor at the University of Toronto in the mid-1950s. Among the grey, Ivy League undergraduates of that square decade, he stood out like a neurotic flamingo. Living in a splendidly squalid pad, affecting a beard and long, sometimes bleached hair before such things were fashionable and enveloping himself in theatrical capes over faded jeans and sandals, he was a one-man advanced guard for the hippie movement.

"People dismissed him as a weird nut," remembers one of his many girl friends. "That just shows how provincial we were. In fact, he's a sweet, thoughtful, sentimental and tender person. Sure, he was proud of his figure—he's got a great body—and liked dressing up in costume. But who doesn't these days?"

Another former girl friend is less charitable: "I remember him as a brooding, self-conscious man poring over volumes of Stanislavsky and given to melodramatic outbursts. He turned up at a formal dance once in tails and top hat and insisted on ordering champagne. Unfortunately, the rented tails were a bad fit. During a wild dance the pants split, zap, right up the behind. That's my picture of Sutherland."

Later, as a down-and-out actor trying to make it in London, he was still regarded as a bit strange even in an expatriate society that took oddness for granted. Friends recall him loping around Notting Hill Gate in a knee-length leather security jacket, clutching a huge box of pills to soothe his hypochondria and obsessed with the topic of capital punishment.

Success, Hollywood and a happy second marriage have been healthy for Sutherland. He has plenty of money now (typically, he refuses to confirm a report that he commands $100,000 a picture) and the west-coast atmosphere of permanent excess allows him to indulge his nonconformist lifestyle while appearing only mildly exotic. Until moving to New York recently, he leased a 20-room Spanish-style house in Beverly Hills that he hated ("There was hardly a thing in it we could call our own"). Jack Lemmon, a comedian with whom Sutherland is often compared, and James Coburn were neighbors. He delights in throbbing about in a battered red Ferrari ("Some stupid woman who didn't realize Ferraris are bumperless deliberately backed into it after a party") but keeps a Lotus and a station-wagon in reserve. He can afford to rent a $2,500-a-month beach house at Malibu when the mood strikes him. He can also afford to dress as he pleases, usually in the costume he was last wearing on the set, and to carry a webbed khaki pouch as a handbag with nonchalant grace.

Sutherland clearly adores his wife, Shirley, the 36-year-old daughter of NDP leader Tommy Douglas. (His first marriage, to a girl he met at university, broke up during the early years in London.) Shirley, an actress with a warm Drambuie voice, won a Dominion Drama Festival Award in 1952 and went on to study at London's Royal Academy of Dramatic Art. After graduating, she landed top roles in several West End stage productions, including a lead in *Wonderful Town*, and was a regular star of BBC-TV dramas. Her career was briefly interrupted by her marriage to Timothy Sicks, heir to Calgary's Sicks Beer fortune. They were divorced in 1961. She encountered Sutherland in 1964—"I tripped over a dog at a cast party in Rome and Shirley picked me up off the floor"—married him a year later and retired. They have three-year-old twins, Rachel and Kiefer. Shirley also has a 10-year-old son, Thomas, by her first marriage.

If the clown in Sutherland is more under control these days, it is not only because he takes his family responsibilities seriously. He is also suffering from the after-effects of two far-from-funny crises. The first happened a year ago when he collapsed with spinal meningitis while making *Kelly's Heroes* in Yugoslavia. Doctors gave him 24 hours to live. Shirley flew to his bedside—pausing in London to make funeral arrangements. "I was being carried down the corridor of the hospital," says Sutherland, "when I realized I was dying. It really makes you angry." The anger helped pull him through.

He was still flat on his back when Shirley, now back in Hollywood, fell victim to a sordid and frightening entrapment by the Los Angeles Police Department—a force somewhat less dedicated to social justice than the *Dragnet* television series suggested. Police interest in Shirley began when, together with UCLA history professor and dramatist Donald Freed, she was involved in setting up an organization called the Friends of the Black Panthers. The aim of the all-white group is to assist the Panthers' free-breakfast and medical programs. For Shirley, it was a continuation of the welfare work she has been doing most of her adult life. The Sutherland home soon became a meeting ground for blacks and whites.

At some point, the Friends were infiltrated by a hapless young *agent provocateur* named James Jarrett, who claimed to be a cat burglar but was actually a member of the police department's Special Weapons and Tactics (SWAT) squad. Jarrett, wildly overdressed for his spy role in black beret and camouflage jacket, kept urging the group to rob gun stores and kill anti-Castro Cubans. Nobody paid much attention. Eventually, however, he convinced the Friends that they needed aerosol cans of mace gas for protection. (One young woman, a member of the group, had just been raped.) Freed and Shirley both gave Jarrett money to buy the mace. He then turned up at Freed's home in the middle of the night with a cardboard box. Ten minutes later he was back with the police. The box was opened and found to contain 10 hand grenades Jarrett had somehow obtained from a naval arsenal.

A few hours later, in a Gestapo-like dawn raid, police crashed through a window of the Sutherland home and arrested a bewildered Shirley at gunpoint: "Most of them had automatic weapons and were waving them at us. My son Tom came upstairs and one shouted at him, 'Up against the wall.' Then they all rushed downstairs and tried to knock down the door of the babies' room. We keep it locked. They must have thought there were Panthers in there. Meanwhile the babies were screaming. I kept trying to tell the police where the keys were and in the end they found them. They never did tell me what it was all about or what my rights were."

When the police stopped on the way to the station to transfer Shirley to another car, Jarrett put in an appearance: "He was running around singing in a sort of singsong. 'I've got the two biggies, I've got the two biggies.' Somebody observed that I seemed very calm and Jarrett said, 'Of course. It's her Communist training. Her father's the head of the Communist Party in Canada.' "

Shirley and Freed, both charged with conspiracy to possess illegal weapons, spent three days in jail before being released on bail—$15,000 for Shirley, $25,000 for Freed. When the case was finally heard last February, it was thrown out of court. By failing to register the hand grenades, Jarrett had committed the very crime for which he was trying to frame the Friends.

The two close brushes, first with death and then with prison, have understandably left the Sutherlands subdued and protective about their private life. Shirley is determined her children shall have as normal an upbringing as possible, given the inevitable jet-set rootlessness of Sutherland's career. "Donald deserves his success," she says. "He's the most professional actor I know. My only complaint is that he's working too hard. We never see him any more."

One reason Sutherland works so hard is that film making, in these free and post–*Easy Rider* days, has suddenly become a lot of fun. Under contract to no studio, he can pick and choose from among any number of moderately budgeted, relatively experimental features currently being turned out. Watching him at the airport location last June, it was clear why he had chosen *Alex in Wonderland*. It's a comic fantasy about Hollywood, produced by Larry Tucker. Tucker and director Mazursky wrote the script for *Bob and Carol and Ted and Alice*. They started in show business as gagmen for Danny Kaye.

The prevailing mood was zestful irreverence. Shooting stopped while Sutherland paid mock homage to an Air Canada DC-8 thundering down the runway. ("Toronto Pronto Every Day By Air Canada" reads the big billboard on Sunset Strip.) After a particularly complicated tracking scene, Mazursky whooped with the sort of joy you would expect from a 16-mm tyro: "What a fantastic shot! I defy anybody to do a shot as good as that." Throughout the day Mazursky fired off salvoes of old jokes that kept his star—Donald Duck Sutherland—cackling with laughter.

"Actually this is a highly professional team," confided a worried MGM publicity man, the only visible survivor of Sam Goldwyn's regime. "We're weeks ahead of schedule. The picture could be released by Christmas—in time for the Academy Awards." A TWA mechanic ambled over to observe the action. "Who is that funny long-haired guy in the brown jacket?" he asked after a while. "He seems kinda familiar." The PR man, looking pained, enlightened him.

When shooting ended for the day, Sutherland dropped back to his temporary office on the MGM lot—a depressing acre of abandoned sound stages clustered together like Brobdingnagian outhouses. The desk in his air-conditioned office was screened off by a head-high wall of cardboard boxes. "I put those there because there was no lock on the door when I moved in," he failed to explain.

Ostensibly, Sutherland wanted to make some phone calls. In reality, he was more interested in studying the latest batch of stills. For an actor who is genuinely modest in most respects, he remains incredibly vain about his appearance. He can't pass a mirror without pausing to groom himself. On the way out of the lot he popped into the studio's front office, the Irving Thalberg Building. The lobby contains, among other things, the nine Oscars won by *Ben Hur* and a huge blowup portrait of Donald Sutherland. "I saw *Kelly's Heroes* last night and thought you were just super," gushed the stunning brunette whose movie career had advanced only as far as the reception desk. Sutherland beamed. Ah, fame.

Driving home, he gleefully whipped the Ferrari at 60 through the S-curves of a 25-mile-an-hour residential zone and talked about the future: "When shooting winds up here, there is a final scene I have to do with Fellini in Rome. Then I've got three movies lined up in New York. I hope to produce and direct one of them myself. It will cost about $700,000. There's no problem about raising the money as long as I also appear in the picture." He wasn't boasting. He was merely assuming the mantle of success with perfect confidence. The boy from Bridgewater, N.S., the kid with the "interesting face," had become a superstar.

There were a lot of people who figured Sutherland would never make it, including his father who wanted Donald to join the family engineering business. Sutherland, who had tasted show business as a teen-age disk jockey, was determined to become an actor. Ordered to Toronto to enroll in the university's School of Practical Science, Sutherland promptly switched to Arts and became involved in student drama productions under Hart House Theatre's legendary Robert Gill. The summers before he graduated in English in 1958 were spent with a stock company at Port Carling, Ont.

"There was never any doubt Donald had amazing potential as a comic or personality actor," says a director who worked with him during that period. "I remember him playing Elwood P. Dowd in *Harvey* at Port Carling. Perfect. But he can also be terribly gauche on stage. His movements are awkward and gangling and he has a lisp which almost becomes a speech defect when he tries to project. These things don't show in films or TV, of course."

Because of his flawed stage performances, Sutherland was forced to serve a grueling apprenticeship. He spent a frustrating year at the London Academy of Music and Dramatic Art (his father paid for the tuition), then toured the British provinces with countless repertory companies. Back in London, he was reduced to playing a moose in a Wayne and Shuster special for the BBC. Finally Sutherland got a break by landing the part of Fortinbras in a BBC production of *Hamlet* filmed at Elsinore and starring Christopher Plummer.

"That was the turning point of my life," he says. "The director, Philip Saville, had rejected me for the role because of my Canadian accent. So I spent the weekend swotting up the part in Danish. On Monday I got in to see Saville through a trick. He was about to throw me out when I started spouting out the lines in Danish. Suddenly Saville was framing me with his fingers."

Fortinbras speaks only 27 lines in the play but Sutherland threw everything he had into them. Critics began to discover a new significance in Fortinbras; they also discovered Donald Sutherland. He spent the next two years shambling through a series of atrocious but lucrative horror movies until he was conscripted by Robert Aldrich for the bottom half of *The Dirty Dozen*. From that point on he was riding an up escalator. So much so that 1970 is turning into Sutherland Year at the Movies: *M*A*S*H* took the grand prize at the Cannes Film Festival, and if *Alex* is finished soon enough, he'll feature in four other major movies released this year. One, Paul Almond's *Act of the Heart* with Geneviève Bujold, was filmed in Montreal last year. Sutherland plays an Augustinian monk.

That was one of his few return visits to Canada. The Sutherlands, professionally and politically, are committed to causes in the United States. "I'm staying down here to fight racism," says Shirley, her trim jaw jutting pugnaciously. "The U.S. is more repressive now than it was 10 years ago. It's true, I didn't have to come down here to find discrimination. I first saw racism in a Toronto park in 1944 where there was a sign saying 'No Jews Allowed.' But down here is where the real war is being fought."

Sutherland shares his wife's convictions. He will attend a Panther funeral or fund-raising rally, consciously studying the real-life drama with an actor's eye. ("Old Jane Fonda really gave it to them last night; her timing was beautiful.") But his long working hours, seven in the morning until eight at night, leave him little chance to become involved.

Relaxing one night after a candlelit dinner at the tiny Aware Inn on Sunset Boulevard (one of his favourite eating places), Sutherland sipped white wine and reflected on things in general. Canada, it was clear, is fast becoming a sentimental memory. What he remembers best is the $75-a-month apartment he shared with artist Rick Gorman over a Yonge Street store:

"There was dog dirt all over the place when we moved in. We redecorated it with egg crates on the ceiling, expensive fabrics from Shelagh's and red and black paint on the walls. We painted the bannister purple and it was still wet when a girl threw her mink coat over it at the housewarming party. I've often wondered how that girl liked wearing a purple-striped mink.

"People thought we were pretty wild. But to us it seemed a perfectly natural way to live. I haven't changed much. An actor can only work with what's inside him. He's not aware of what's outside him. I looked at some rushes today and became conscious of certain mannerisms I didn't know I possessed. It's embarrassing to see yourself from the outside. I'm still not used to it. I wonder if I ever will be."

As Sutherland got up to leave, a Canadian entertaining a party at another table clutched his sleeve: "Hi, Don. How's things with you and Shirley?" Sutherland, to whom the man was obviously a complete stranger, made charming and courteous small talk before passing on. "Who was that?" hissed another guest.

"That," said the grateful Canadian complacently, "was Donald Sutherland. He's a very funny guy."

Donald Sutherland has since appeared in more than 75 movies, from Klute *(1971) to* Bethune *(1990) and* Space Cowboys *(2000). He and Shirley divorced in 1970 and he married French-Canadian actress Francine Racette in 1997, his companion for more than two decades. They have homes in Paris, Santa Monica, Calif., and in the Eastern Townships of Quebec.*

Douglas Marshall was a staff writer at Maclean's *from 1965 to 1971. He then co-founded* Books in Canada *and served as its editor until 1981 when he joined the* Toronto Star *as its entertainment editor. Marshall now is the* Star's *science editor.*

Mary Walsh: High Shticking

Mary Walsh, cover girl, Feb. 26, 1996

FEBRUARY 26, 1996. It is a slow news week. While politicians bicker over the divisibility of Quebec, the big story is the weather, a cold snap that has the country frozen in a grimace of national unity from sea to shivering sea. And on the first night of February, during the most frigid week of the winter, Mary Walsh is preparing to turn the weather into hard news—while swimming. It is close to midnight in Halifax. The CBC crew from *This Hour Has 22 Minutes* is running into overtime. Clad in a purple swimsuit, Walsh sits on the ladder of a hotel's indoor pool, her legs dangling in the water. She is in character, as the flagrantly outspoken Marg Delahunty, and she looks like a Zellers nightmare: violet eyeshadow, orange lipstick, big glasses, gold-plate jewelry and a bathing cap barnacled with flowers. The director calls for quiet. Walsh asks for a moment to wipe the fog off her glasses, using the skirt of her old-fashioned swimsuit. Finally, the camera rolls.

"It's February in the frozen north," she says, lunging into the water, "and everybody and their dog's got faces on them the length of a wet Sunday in Red Deer." While the camera follows her on a dolly, Walsh performs a talking breaststroke, her voice booming around the pool. By the time she reaches the shallow end, her winter-of-discontent rant has segued from February depression to financial hysteria. "We've got all our credit cards maxed out on bust—60.5-

billion spondoolicks on MasterCard and Visa alone," she brays, now staring into the camera, inches from the lens. "Whoo! How much is that each? Or is 60.5 billion so high a number that, like Quebec, it is not divisible?" Spitting out the figures, she shifts into high rant mode—"Nineteen-per-cent interest on every one of those 60.5-billion bucks. The banksters are delirious! They're dancing a mad merengue down at the Royal Bank all the way back to the vault with their 1.25-billion-dollar profit!"

Mary Walsh means business. As the woman who dreamed up *This Hour Has 22 Minutes* and its most visible star, the 43-year-old performer from St. John's, Nfld., is the bitch goddess of Canadian political satire. And in a country running out of serious alternatives, political satire has become Canada's unofficial opposition. People cannot seem to get enough of it. On Monday nights at 9 p.m., an average of 1.2 million viewers tune in to *22 Minutes*—a mock newscast that often scores higher ratings than the CBC's real news, *The National*, an hour later.

Comedy, of course, is a national sport, with a list of all-star players that includes Jim Carrey, Mike Myers, Dan Aykroyd, Leslie Nielsen, the SCTV gang and the Kids in the Hall. What seems to give Canadians the edge is that they are on the edge—a nation of observers who watch America through the one-way mirror of the 49th parallel. Comedy requires a passion for detached observation. And no part of the country is more detached than the island of Newfoundland—which the entire cast of *22 Minutes* calls home.

All four are gifted writer-performers. Greg Thomey, 33, a versatile physical comedian, has also done dramatic acting and written several plays. Rick Mercer, 26, and Cathy Jones, 40, have toured nationally with popular solo stage shows that they wrote and produced. Jones, a superb character comedian, also spent 20 years performing with Walsh in Newfoundland's Codco troupe, including its seven-year run on CBC-TV. Together, the *22 Minutes* cast achieves a remarkable four-part comic harmony. But it is Walsh who makes the most formidable impression, both on and off the show.

With a courage unrivalled on prime-time TV, Walsh flaunts her un-svelte body and speaks her untamed mind through a gallery of outrageous characters—personalities so strong it seems they could bust through the screen at any moment. The best known is Marg Delahunty, the maverick aunt with no shame who dares to say what everyone is thinking. Others include sniggering Connie Bloor, the doughnut-shop hick who snorts about "the Yanks" from behind her copy of *USA Today*; the swaggering Dakey Dunn, a macho blowhard whose chest hair has gone to his head; and the hectoring Genoa Hellerstein, a butch lesbian who trashes neo-feminist Camille Paglia as a "lipstick lezzie" parvenu.

But Walsh is not just a satirist. She is an exceptional writer, director and dramatic actor. She has directed more than a dozen plays, often co-writing them with the actors. In 1988, Toronto's Factory Theatre produced *Hockey Wives*, her play based on interviews with NHL players' wives. In 1993, at the Grand Theatre in London, Ont., she won glowing reviews for her passionate performance as Josie, the tragic lead of Eugene O'Neill's *A Moon for the Misbegotten*. And she is dying to play Lady Macbeth. "Mary's unique," says *22 Minutes* creative producer Gerald Lunz. "When you watch her live, she literally transforms. You feel anything is possible. And as with all great comedians, there is a brilliant tragedian there."

In Walsh's past, the comedy and tragedy have been inextricably mixed. Her life is a story of strong women and strong drinks, and a series of rough roads that all lead back to the Rock. Walsh still spends summers in her birthplace of St. John's, where she owns a 162-year-old house. But during the TV season, she lives on a tree-lined street in Halifax, in a modest pink frame house rented for her by the show's local producer, Salter Street Films. After recently ending a 13-year relationship with a pewtersmith named Ray Cox, Walsh lives alone with their adopted six-year-old boy, Jesse, and a blue merle collie named Train.

Sitting with a mug of coffee in her living-room, Walsh is dressed in fuzzy slippers and a long sweater-dress over a white nightgown—an outfit that would not look out of place on Marg Delahunty. But unlike Marg, she wears no makeup. Walsh does not really look like any of her characters. She has a handsome face with intelligent eyes and a vivacious warmth. The actor was once turned down for a movie role because she looked too "patrician," she recalls. "I kind of liked that. All my features are squat in the middle of my face. That's what I see when I look in the mirror. I look like years and years of longshoremen and ironworkers."

Walsh is the seventh of eight children (three sisters and four brothers) born to Leo and Mary Walsh. Her father spent most of his life at sea, working in ships' boiler rooms. "Then he retired and went to bed for 13 years," says Walsh. "Dad read a lot and drank a lot, as everybody in the family did." Her mother, who "controlled the house so totally she should have been running IBM," came from a family of ironworkers—Walsh's maternal grandfather helped build the Empire State Building. "There was a huge tension in the family," recalls Walsh, "about what was the more manly pursuit, to go to sea or be an ironworker."

Walsh did not grow up with her parents. At eight months, she was sent to live with relatives next door and never moved back—apparently because she had pneumonia and her parents' house was too damp. "That's what they always said," she laughs. "Some pathetic explanation. It was odd, because my mom and dad lived next door until I was 11 and then they moved to the country." Her parents are now deceased, and Walsh never did get to the bottom of why they gave her away. "Now, I feel it was really funny," she says, "but it didn't feel anything but tragic until a few years ago." Then she adds with a guffaw: "Of course, that is the piece of sand that has made me the, uh, pearl that I am today."

The product of a matriarchy, Walsh was raised by her father's sister, Aunt Mae, who lived with her stroke-afflicted brother, Jack, and their stepsister, Josephine. "Uncle Jack used to drink until he fell asleep, then he'd wake up and drink again," she recalls. "Dad would just drink and never go to sleep, which was heartbreaking for everyone." Having a sense of humour was essential. "It was worth a lot to be funny in the family, and being funny in a mean way was worth even more. You could do anything as far as Mom was concerned if you were funny. And all Aunt Mae's friends were funny."

Fearlessness is another family trait that seems to have rubbed off on Walsh. Aunt Mae (Mary Ellen Waddleton), who worked as a civil servant, lost a leg as a child. "She was truly heroic," says Walsh. "She got her first wooden leg when she was 7 and jumped off a building into the snow and smashed it to smithereens. She was always doing things like that, constantly proving that nothing could stop her."

By the time she reached high school, Walsh herself was becoming an unstoppable force. Schooled by nuns, she rebelled against strict Roman Catholic discipline by becoming a hell-raiser. She smoked and kept a bottle of liquor in her locker. "I was in a constant rage," she recalls. "I spent my entire youth smashing things. At 12 or 13, I lost my religion because I was shoplifting so much I couldn't pay it back—I couldn't get complete absolution."

But there were already signs of the emerging actor. "We thought she was quite the character," says Cathy Jones, who knew her when they were teens. "She had this total British accent. It was so fake. We thought she was kinda weird, but we hung out with her." Walsh even affected a Brooklyn accent at one point. Now, she says, her voice is an amalgam—"it's a completely made-up accent from all the people I tried to be over the years. Actually, I'm fram dawntawn St. Jahn's and I prabably should sound a lot flatter like that."

Like many Newfoundlanders, Walsh felt she had no future. At 17, she got engaged to an American serviceman and followed him to Colorado. She was homesick and had a miserable time. She remembers staging a sobbing tantrum when his family tried to convince her the Americans had won the War of 1812. They broke up and she returned home, getting a job at a five-and-dime arcade. "It was the most embarrassing store in St. John's," she says. "It was better to be a Woolworth's girl—you would look up to the crowd at Woolworth's."

Walsh's first foray into show business, when she was 18, was inauspicious. Casually responding to a TV advertisement, she landed a job as a summer replacement host on the local CBC radio station. "I was horrible," she recalls—but a local stage director liked her voice and cast her in an amateur play. Soon she was touring the province for $30 a week with the Newfoundland Travelling Theatre Company, a troupe of young actors who included Tommy Sexton, Greg Malone, Robert Joy, Dyan Olsen, Cathy Jones and her brother Andy—the future Codco.

At 20, Walsh went to Toronto to take acting classes, but dropped out to join her Newfoundland comrades in a play at the city's

Theatre Passe Muraille. *Cod on a Stick*, Codco's first production, was an act of satirical revenge against generations of Newfie jokes. It was a hit. And Walsh went on to create a vivid repertoire of women—such as the landlady Mrs. Budgell, one in a long line of dear old bats who have been reincarnated under various guises on *22 Minutes.*

Codco was a cauldron of creative activity. But over the years, the collective turned into a dysfunctional family, with an incestuous tangle of personal relations. "Codco wasn't a company, it was a life," says Walsh. "Only a young person would ever decide to create a horrible mess like that—'Oh yeah, this will be good. I'll sleep with this person.'"

They were wild times. At the end of a party one night, Walsh tackled a friend, writer Ray Guy, who was trying to leave at 3 a.m., and broke his leg. "We picked him up and he just fell down again," she recalls. "We thought he was just really, really drunk. But when he came to in the morning, he had five fractures." Andy Jones, who was Walsh's live-in companion for eight years, says that "we were all drinking constantly. When I look back on those days, it seems our lives were bracketed by alcohol."

After its acclaimed seven-year run on CBC-TV, Codco broke up in 1992. Then, Walsh hatched her idea for a news parody show and found support from executive producer Michael Donovan of Salter Street Films in Halifax. She assembled the cast, inviting Andy Jones to be a part of it, but he declined, somewhat perversely. "I was into my personal freedom at the time," says Jones, now acting and writing in Toronto. "Do I regret it? Sometimes. But I regret everything—that's the way I am." Cathy Jones, meanwhile, was shocked when she was invited to join the show, because she has so little interest in politics. "But since I'm uniquely unfamiliar with these things," she suggests, "I always get a fresh take on them." As for Mercer and Thomey, Walsh had followed their work for several years. Mercer remembers their first encounter, at a St. John's community hall where she was directing a show. "I put a cigarette down a pipe in one of the bleachers. And that's how I met Mary. She tore my head off for almost burning the building down."

After coming up with the idea for *22 Minutes*, Walsh had to watch it take shape from the sidelines—she required back surgery when it debuted in 1993. And the show did not turn out quite as she had imagined. "The basic problem," she says, "is that my original conception didn't have five hairy-assed producers making all the decisions. I'm happy with the show, but it's a boys' club." Jones, however, is relieved that the cast is not in charge. "It's healthy," she says. "That's what killed Codco—all the power we had."

As Codco's female alumni, Walsh and Jones are like sisters. Although they perform together with seamless timing, the relationship has frayed over the years. According to Walsh, "we feel differently about everything." Now at least, they have sobriety in common. Walsh quit drinking three years ago. Jones, who quit last year, is a practising Buddhist, a vegetarian and the mother of a four-month-old girl—whose breast-feeding is the only addiction that plays havoc with the show's schedule.

Each Monday, the cast members come in with ideas and divvy up the news. "Rick and Greg will show up with 25 or 30 ideas," sighs Jones. "And I'll come in with two or three." Editorial producer Geoff D'Eon, a 13-year veteran of CBC-TV news, digs up clips for them. "It's highly competitive," says Walsh. "There's only so much news." As stories unfold, people put their dibs on the footage. "Sometimes it's just a question of getting into work early," says Mercer. "The biggest nightmare is that nothing's happening. Some weeks, it's all suicide bombings and tainted blood, things you don't want to joke about."

There is a natural balance in the cast. Walsh and Mercer do the hard-edged political satire; Jones and Thomey do a softer, warmer style of comedy. As the hands-on producer, Gerald Lunz referees the players. Calling himself "the snake handler," he tries to achieve symmetry among the performers and pre-censor anything that would not fly with the "suits" at Salter Street and the CBC. Says Lunz, 42, who has worked with Walsh and Jones for a decade: "Mary comes in with all guns blazing. When she's up for a fight, she goes full bore. Every time Mary is not involved with a decision, she feels she's losing."

It is Thursday afternoon—the day before *22 Minutes* is taped before a studio audience. On a residential sidewalk, the crew tapes Jones and Walsh as Enid and Eulilia, two old ladies gabbing about the French from France—their cream sauces and nuclear tests and bandy-legged furniture. It is bitterly cold. Under their stockings, the women wear thermals. Their blue-rinse banter clicks beautifully, but then they have being doing it in various forms for two decades. They are natural-born biddies. "We've been playing old bags from the beginning," says Walsh, warming up in a car between shots. Jones concurs: "We were old bags when we were 19."

Thursday night. Walsh prepares to do Marg Delahunty in the pool. For Marg, she insists on doing her own makeup and using cheap drugstore cosmetics. It helps her get into character. She slathers on the foundation, scrubbing it into her face with a vengeance. "This is how my mother put on her makeup," she explains. Then with scary efficiency, she paints on the eyeliner, the rouge and the orange lipstick. Walsh nails her swimming mono-logue on the second take. But the director wants another one. Ten takes later, she finally gets out of the pool—at 1:15 a.m.

Friday night, 7 p.m. The cast sits down at the *22 Minutes* news-desk and runs through the show. At 9 p.m., they do it again for an audience, 100 fans packed into bleachers ringed around the cramped studio. The show starts late. The audience has been kept waiting too long in the foyer and scarcely touched the free wine. Always a bad sign. The crowd appears enthusiastic, but in relative terms the cast considers it an off night. There are more flubs than usual. While Jones and Mercer do their bits, Walsh and Thomey pass notes back and forth, like kids in class. The show ends with the whole cast playing the Quinlan Quints—four idiot Newfoundland scam artists in identical tuques and plaid shirts. As usual, the Quints bring down the house.

Saturday morning. At home, Walsh is mulling over the previous night. "I don't want to do the f——g Quints again," she says. "I wrote the first Quints sketch. I know they're enjoyable. But four stu-pid guys from Newfoundland with one of them picking their nose, I feel I'm selling my birthright for a mess of pottage."

As blasphemous as it sounds, she says she is also sick of Marg Delahunty. "I wouldn't mind being at Marg's funeral. And I'm sick of Dakey and I'm sick of Connie. I'm sick of all my characters really." A rant is brewing. Not a Marg rant, or a Dakey rant. Pure

Walsh. "I just don't have much more to say," she insists. "There is nothing new about the news. It's the same news this February as last February. And I feel the same way about it. I'm angered that a rich country like Canada is punishing the poor for fiscal problems we may or may not have." As the rant picks up steam, it is easy to see why Walsh gets hired to give speeches—at such events as the 1994 United Nations Global Conference on Development in New York City. The next day, when told of Walsh's despair, Lunz shrugs it off with a laugh: "It sounds like you had a classic postpartum show conversation."

One week later, Walsh has found a new character, fashion editor Marietta Sanders. Dressed in a frumpy outfit she calls the latest thing, she announces "the era of the emerging Woman Nerd." Interrogated by Thomey, she tries to defend her wardrobe until finally, in exasperation, she rips off her clothes. Suddenly she is standing there in a cutoff lime-green lycra top with no bra, her doughy midriff spilling over blue hotpants.

"What are my fashion options?" she pleads, as the audience shrieks hysterically. "You've got to be a prepubescent with a chronic eating disorder. You've got to have the body fat of a car antenna. I am a 43-year-old working mother and there is not anything out there for to me to wear!" Then, declaring that "there's only one road left open to me—don't try and stop me," she covers up with a house-dress, an apron and hairnet and mutates into, well, an old bag.

A week ago, Walsh had nowhere to go. In one sketch, she has gone further than ever before. Flaunting her flab, she has delivered a rhetorical thesis on the tyranny of fashion. She has zoomed through three characters—and a lifetime of conformism, rebellion and self-acceptance—in three minutes flat.

You can't do that on television?

Mary Walsh just did.

Mary Walsh was named to the Order of Canada in 2000.

Brian D. Johnson, the magazine's film critic, has been a senior writer at Maclean's *since 1986.*

Shania Twain Revealed

Shania Twain rehearsing in Nashville, 1998

MARCH 23, 1998. They are lining up to meet her in the flesh. Hundreds of broadcasters, delegates to a country radio conference, have gathered for a party at the new Planet Hollywood in Nashville. In a room ringed with buffet tables, some queue up for Cajun shrimp, but the major feeding frenzy is around Canadian country star Shania Twain. She is not singing; she is signing autographs and posing for snapshots while a video of her song "Don't Be Stupid" plays on the wall behind her. The broadcasters so eager to meet her are professional fans, fans with influence. And Twain greets them with professional warmth. A hundred handshakes. A hundred autographs. A hundred point-and-shoot smiles. And, with each click of the shutter, a hundred strange hands clasped around her famous midriff. Every so often, like a boxer rehydrating between rounds, Twain turns to her makeup artist, Daisy, who holds up a bottle of water for her to sip through a straw. Finally, after more than an hour, Twain's handlers whisk her upstairs. In the elevator, the star holds out her hands. Daisy, who knows the drill, produces some wet wipes and scrubs them clean.

Later, in a roped-off VIP area upstairs, Twain sits for a moment before resuming the "meet and greet" ritual with another echelon of fandom—employees of her own record company. Does it not all start to seem absurd after a while? Twain fields the question with a puzzled look. "Not really," she says. "It's just part of it now. And people who want to meet you usually get some pleasure out of it. It's nice. It's a nice exchange."

Nice. For the reigning queen of country music, playing the girl next door to throngs of strangers has become second nature. Country singers, like TV soap stars and politicians, are still expected to service the fan base in person. Up close, Shania Twain loses none of her radiance; she has the sort of star power that people expect from royalty. And part of the magic is a life story that reads like a fairy tale—Cinderella meets Bambi in the Canadian bush. A country girl from Timmins, Ont., is raised dirt poor, starts performing in bars as a child, loses her parents at 22 when their car collides with a logging truck, sings to support her three teenage siblings, then finds her prince—reclusive rock producer Robert John (Mutt) Lange—who gives her a studio kiss of stardom and a 2.5-carat diamond.

It is a story that occasionally threatens to veer into melodrama. Twain has had to fend off media controversy over her adoptive native heritage, and early rumors of trouble in her marriage to Lange. But although their careers often keep them apart, producer and star now appear to be living happily ever after. They call home a 1,200-hectare retreat with a private lake in upstate New York. And last week, Twain told *Maclean's* that they are seriously thinking of moving to Europe. They have begun looking for a house in the Swiss countryside.

Eileen Regina Twain—who rechristened herself Shania seven years ago—has certainly fulfilled the promise of her name, which means "I'm on my way" in Ojibwa. Now 32, she has sold more albums than any female country singer in history. Breaking a record that it took Patsy Cline 40 years to set, her 1995 CD *The Woman in Me* has attained sales of 12 million copies worldwide—two million of them in Canada alone. Twain's new album, *Come on Over*, has sold 4.2 million after just five months of release. With her music, Twain has goosed the tired country format with a well-aimed kick of sexy common sense. Her songs, which she co-writes with Lange, range from domestic-bliss ballads to sassy rockers that taunt and tease. "Shania Twain has carved out her own place in country," says Chet Flippo, Nashville correspondent for *Billboard*. "Until she came along, there was no job description for what she is—a pop femme fatale in country. She's playing by her own rules. And she's changing the audience."

Twain, meanwhile, is spearheading a country music invasion from Canada that is rejuvenating an industry rooted in the American South. "She's only the tip of the iceberg," says Nashville music journalist Robert K. Oermann. "A lot of the freshest sounds in country music are coming from Canada. The industry is looking north, because that's where the authenticity is."

Along with Celine Dion, Alanis Morissette and Sarah McLachlan, Twain also belongs to a brave new wave of Canadian women who have taken the U.S. music industry by storm. If Dion is the pop diva, Morissette the angry young rocker and McLachlan the sensitive folkie, Twain is the no-nonsense sex symbol—a take-charge woman line-dancing down the middle of the road, splitting the difference between feminine compliance and feminist effrontery.

Twain's voice has a melting twang, enough to conjure up country, yet more suggestive of the boudoir than the barn. Her songs are flavored with fiddle and steel guitar, but Lange—who has put his studio stamp on Def Leppard, AC/DC and Bryan Adams—upholsters the music with lush arrangements typical of rock. While there is no denying her talent as a singer and songwriter, image is an integral part of Twain's appeal. She is a country singer who looks like a supermodel. Hollywood has, predictably, taken notice—the singer has turned down a stream of movie offers, including a role opposite Al Pacino. On camera, Twain projects a playful sexuality, an allure that is part come-on, part come-off-it. Like a PG version of Madonna, Twain promotes the flirtatious co-existence of glamor and self-empowerment. She is country's Cosmo-girl, a fantasy that works for both men and women. The video for her latest single, the ballad "You're Still the One," unfolds like a Harlequin romance, with Twain on a moonlit beach in a silky robe, dreaming of a Calvin Klein hunk, who steps from the bath dripping wet and lets his towel fall to the floor as he slides into her bed.

No country singer has used video to promote herself with as much audacity as Twain. In fact, it was her very first video—a sexy, midriff-baring number from her first album—that hooked her most important fan. Lange saw it in 1993 and phoned her out of the blue. The same footage caught the eye of actor Sean Penn, who directed a video for her. John and Bo Derek (*10*) also took notice, and together they shot the first video from the second album, with Twain dancing on a diner countertop in a hot red dress.

Twain's style has drawn some flack from traditional quarters of country music. Guitarist Steve Earle once dismissed her as "the world's highest paid lap dancer." And some critics dwell on the fact that, since her breakthrough, she has never proven herself as a performer, except through a camera lens. Others suggest she is a studio Barbie created by a Svengali husband and a high-powered rock management "A lot of people are accusing her of being packaged," concedes Luke Lewis, Nashville president of her Mercury label. "But I don't think this is a marketing-driven artist. It's been her vision from the beginning—all the clothes, all the looks, all the concepts."

In person, Twain certainly seems self-possessed. Sitting down for an interview in a Nashville hotel suite, she extends a firm handshake. In black pants, a black leather vest and a white T-shirt showing a sliver of midriff, she looks perennially ready for her close-up. She does not drink or smoke. She keeps her five-foot, four-inch, 110-lb. frame fit with regular workouts. Her skin has the glow of a woman who rides horses to relax. But Twain's clear-eyed charisma also works as a mask. She never lets down her guard, which can be frustrating for a photographer or interviewer hoping to catch her in a candid moment. Still, for a woman who is so poised and put together, it is a relief to know that she finds fault with her body. "I don't like my legs," she says flatly when asked why she sings about short skirts but never wears them.

It is late afternoon, and Twain has spent the day doing nonstop interviews with country radio broadcasters, ending each one with a snapshot and an autograph. Over and over, she answered questions about the new ripple in her hair, explaining that it comes from a curling iron, not a perm. One unctuous radio host had an unusual request.

"If you wouldn't mind calling me Sweet Cheeks, maybe once," he said.

As the tape rolled, he introduced his guest. "Here we are in Shania Twain's hotel room . . ."

"And I'm with Sweet Cheeks," she said.

"See, Shania Twain does call me Sweet Cheeks . . . I'll pay you later."

"Just leave it on the dresser."

No wonder she is eager to start touring. Is she not nervous about performing live? "I'm going to be overwhelmed at first," Twain admits. "But it's going to be fun, not scary." Although she has not toured since she became a star, Twain points out that she has 20 years of stage experience under her belt—beginning at the age of eight, when her parents first started dragging her out of bed so that she could sing (legally) at the Mattagami Hotel bar in Timmins after it had stopped serving liquor. Talk about paying your dues.

"I love being in front of a live audience where I can control things," says Twain. "What I'm least comfortable with is the studio or anything contrived. I'm never at my best on television. There's a row of cameras between you and the audience, and it's very weird, very confusing."

Shania Twain is onstage, rehearsing with her band for a taping of TNN's *Prime Time Country.* As the nine-piece band runs through "Don't Be Stupid," its young black drummer, wearing headphones in a Plexiglas booth, plays to a pre-recorded cue track. And although Twain is singing live, her vocals are perfectly synched to the song's video, which is projected behind her.

The band plays with unerring precision, fiddles cutting in and out with the galvanized attack of a horn section. Twain, meanwhile, delivers her songs with polished moves that barely change from one take to the next. The toss of the hair, the hand-slap on the hip, each gesture seems built into the song. And as cameras swoop around the stage, she seems in firm command, knowing exactly where to look and how to act. Twain lays to rest any doubts that she can deliver onstage. Her voice may lack power, but she sings with melodic ease. Even when she is just testing the microphone with some a cappella phrases, there is a seductive luxury to her unadorned vocals. And as she searches for an elusive intimacy, the one thing she fusses over is the sound—"too nasal . . . too much bottom . . . too much bite . . . can you take a bit of the hard edge off? . . ."

Between songs, Twain puts in time on the talk-show couch. She tells a story about taking the train to the big city to appear on a TV show when she was 12. After a while, she realized she was going in the wrong direction. The conductor told her she could transfer at another station in six hours. "I said, 'You've got to stop the train right now because I'm going to be on TV.' So they let me off in the middle of the bush with my guitar, like a little hobo. I caught a train going the other way in half an hour, but I did think, 'What if the train never comes?'"

Twain's childhood reminiscences often have an apocryphal ring, but perhaps they have just become buffed by constant repetition. This much is known. She was born in Windsor, Ont., on Aug. 28, 1965, the second of three daughters of an Irish-Canadian mother, Sharon, and her husband, Clarence Edwards, who is of Irish and French descent. By the time Twain was two, her parents' marriage collapsed, and Sharon moved with the children to Timmins, where—four years later—she married Jerry Twain, an Ojibwa forester and prospector. He adopted the children, who automatically gained First Nations status.

Throughout her childhood, Twain was aware of her biological father, and he occasionally visited her family. But she kept his existence a secret until 1996, when *The Daily Press* in Timmins broke the story about the facts of her birth. There was a storm of controversy as Twain was accused of lying, and of enhancing her native heritage for the sake of her career. "It was very hard on my native family," she says. "I'm a registered band member. I've been part of their community since I was a little child. It's very hurtful to know there are people who want to unravel all that."

When asked why she didn't tell the truth from the beginning, Twain's consistently perky composure gives way to a burst of anger. "Half the people in my life didn't know I was adopted," she says. "Why should I have told the press? It frustrates me no end, I can't tell you. I have never referred to Jerry as my stepfather. I never even referred to Clarence as my father, and I didn't care if I was ever in contact with that family again." Then, she adds: "It's never been an issue for me, but it's an issue for everyone else all of a sudden. It's like a big black hole."

In his recent book about country music, *Three Chords and The Truth*, U.S. author Laurence Leamer went so far as to call Twain's life story "a brilliant reconstruction," claiming that she has exaggerated the poverty of her childhood. Twain says that in fact the reverse is true: "Let's put it this way. I'm not sugarcoating, but I've revealed very little of the true hardship and intensity of my life, and that's the way I'm going to keep it."

As a child, the singer recalls, she sometimes went for days with nothing to eat but bread, milk and sugar heated up in a pot. "I hardly ever took a lunch to school. I'd say I'm not hungry. Or I'd bring, like, mustard sandwiches." But Twain has fond memories of learning to hunt and trap in the bush with her father—although she is now vegetarian. And alone in nature, she would create her own world. "I'd take my guitar for a walk and go to a field or the river and write songs," she says. "As a kid I had three dreams: to live in a brick house and eat roast beef, to be kidnapped by Frank Sinatra, and to be Stevie Wonder's backup singer. It was never my dream to be a star. That was my parents' dream. I guess they prayed real hard."

Twain was a reluctant performer, but her parents were persistent. By her early teens, she was popping up on programs such as *The Tommy Hunter Show*. But only when she discovered rock 'n' roll did she begin to enjoy the stage. "I couldn't hide behind my guitar," she says. "I sensed a freedom that I'd never sensed before." Twain completed high school while working at McDonald's and playing bars. Meanwhile, her parents started a reforestation business, and from age 16 she spent summers in the bush, learning about chainsaws and seedlings, until she was supervising her own native crew.

In 1987, the death of her parents changed everything. Twain, then 22, was suddenly forced to become a mother to her younger sister and two teenage brothers. Her manager at the time, Mary Bailey, came to the rescue with a steady gig at the Deerhurst Resort in Huntsville—as a lounge act and as a singer in glitzy cabaret revues such as *Viva Vegas*. Twain paid her dues for three years at

Deerhurst. And Bailey lured a Nashville producer up there to see her perform—which led to her first record deal in 1991.

The first album, *Shania Twain*, had modest sales of about 100,000 copies. But it led to the romance with Lange, which started as a songwriting relationship over the phone. They finally met face-to-face in Nashville, and married at the Deerhurst six months later. Lange, meanwhile, helped finance *The Woman in Me*, a $700,000 work of studio wizardry touted as the most expensive country album ever recorded.

Since then, reports of ruin have swirled around Twain's marriage. "People in the industry were calling my management all the time asking, 'Are they really divorcing?'" she recalls. "Most people thought we were unlikely to succeed. My family were like, 'You just met this guy, you can't get married.'" Twain adds that "You're Still the One" is about Mutt—and "the nice feeling that we've made it against all odds."

They do seem an odd couple. She spends much of her life in a professional romance with the camera; he is so obsessively media-shy that it is impossible to find a published Mutt Lange picture or interview. The South African–born producer never shows up with his wife at industry functions where he might be photographed. At the TNN show in Nashville, however, a backstage sighting—of a blue-denimed figure in his 40s, tall and handsome with a shag of blond hair—confirmed that he does, in fact, exist.

How can such a reclusive husband get along with such a public wife? "I make my living partly by being a celebrity," says Twain. "But I would love to have his life, to do the music and not have to be famous. I'm more private than people realize. I'm not that easy to get to know. My husband's the only one who really knows me. To get through the kind of life I've been through, you have to be strong, and it's wonderful when you find the right person who can share everything about you."

Whatever pain lies behind Twain's nearly seamless public persona, there is little evidence of it in her music. "It's not pure emotion. I mould it so it can be applied to people's lives. But I write a lot of music I don't share, for the same reason people have diaries. I just express myself. It's not a creative thing. It's therapeutic."

Twain's celebrity has brought its own pain to her family, and not just the native heritage controversy. Over the years, her younger brothers, Mark and Darryl, now 25 and 24, have been in and out of trouble with the law. In 1996, after they were caught trying to steal cars from a Toyota dealership in Huntsville, everyone from the CBC to *The National Enquirer* chased the story. "It's difficult for them to be exposed if they do anything wrong," says their sister, "but at the same time it helps keep them straight." Her brothers, she adds, are now working in the bush cutting timber.

Back in the Grand Ole Opry studio in Nashville, the host of TNN's *Prime Time Country* regales his audience with tales of Twain's days as a forestry worker in an exotic place called Timmins. Getting her to put on a yellow hard hat, he challenges the singer to a log-cutting contest. Picking up one of two small electric chainsaws, she says: "This is kind of dinky. It's what men would call a woman's chain-saw." They start their engines. And as the crowd roars, Twain cuts through her log in seconds, leaving her host in the sawdust—and her legend intact.

Shania Twain won two Grammys in 1999 and two more in 2000 for best country song and best female country performer. She has also won nine Junos.

ARTS AND LETTERS

Stephen Leacock:
My Memories and Miseries

Stephen Leacock

By Stephen Leacock

NOVEMBER, 1919. For 10 years I was a schoolmaster. Just 30 years ago I was appointed on to the staff of a great Canadian school. It took me 10 years to get off it. Being appointed to the position of a teacher is just as if Fate passed a hook through one's braces and hung one up against the wall. It is hard to get down again.

From those 10 years I carried away nothing in money and little in experience; indeed, no other asset whatever, unless it be, here and there, a pleasant memory or two and the gratitude of my former pupils. There was nothing really in my case for them to be grateful about. They got nothing from me in the way of intellectual food, but a lean and perfunctory banquet; and anything that I gave them in the way of sound moral benefit I gave gladly and never missed.

But schoolboys have a way of being grateful. It is the decent thing about them. A schoolboy, while he is at school, regards his masters as a mixed assortment of tyrants and freaks. He plans vaguely that at some future time in life he will "get even" with them. I remember well, for instance, at the school where I used to teach, a little Chilean boy who kept a stiletto in his trunk with which he intended to kill the second mathematical master.

But somehow a schoolboy is not sooner done with his school and out in the business of life, than a soft haze of retrospect suffuses a new colour over all that he has left behind. There is a mellow sound in the tones of the school bell that he never heard in his six years of attendance. There is a warmth in the colour of the old red bricks that he never saw before; and such a charm and such a sadness in the brook or in the elm trees beside the school playground that he will stand beside them with a bowed and reverent head as in the silence of a cathedral. I have seen an "Old Boy" gaze into the open door of an empty class room and ask, "And those are the same old benches?" with a depth of meaning in his voice. He has been out of school perhaps five years and the benches already seem to him infinitely old. This, by the way, is the moment and this the mood in which the "Old Boy" may be touched for a subscription to the funds of the school. This *is* the way in fact, in which the sagacious headmaster does it.

The foolish headmaster, who has not yet learned his business, takes the "Old Boy" round and shows him all the *new* things, the fine new swimming pool built since his day and the new gymnasium with up-to-date patent apparatus. But this is all wrong. There is nothing in it for the "Old Boy" but boredom. The wise headmaster takes him by the sleeve and says, "Come." He leads him out to a deserted corner of the playground and shows him an old tree behind an ash house and the old boy no sooner sees it than he says:

"Why, Great Caesar! that's the same old tree that Jack McEwen and I used to climb to hook out of bounds on Saturday night! Old Jimmy caught us at it one night and licked us both. And look here, here's my name cut on the boarding at the back of the ash house. See? They used to fine us five cents a letter if they found it. Well, well!"

The "Old Boy" is deep in his reminiscences examining the board fence, the tree and the ash house. The wise headmaster does not interrupt him. He does not say that he knew all along that the "Old Boy's" name was cut there and that that's why he brought him to the spot. Least of all does he tell him that the boys still "hook out of bounds" by this means and that he licked two of them for it last Saturday night. No, no, retrospect is too sacred for that. Let the "Old Boy" have his fill of it and when he is quite down and out with the burden of it, then as they walk back to the school building, the headmaster may pick a donation from him that falls like a ripe thimbleberry.

And most of all, by the queer contrariety of things, does this kindly retrospect envelop the person of the teachers. They are transported in the alchemy of time into a group of profound scholars, noble benefactors through whose teaching, had it been listened to, one might have been lifted into higher things. Boys who never listened to a Latin lesson in their lives look back to the memory of their Latin teacher as the one great man that they have known. In the days when he taught them they had no other idea than to put mud in his ink or to place a bent pin upon his chair. Yet they say now that he was the greatest scholar in the world and that if they'd only listened to him they would have got more out of his lessons than from any man that ever taught. He wasn't and they wouldn't—but it is some small consolation to those who have been schoolmasters to know that after it is too late this reward at least is coming to them.

Hence it comes about that even so indifferent a vessel as I should reap my share of schoolboy gratitude. Again and again it happens to me that some unknown man, well on in middle life, accosts me with a beaming face and says: "You don't remember me. You licked me at Upper Canada College," and we shake hands with a warmth and heartiness as if I had been his earliest benefactor. Very often if I am at an evening reception or anything of the sort, my hostess says, "Oh, there is a man here so anxious to meet you," and I know at once why. Forward he comes, eagerly pushing his way among the people to seize my hand. "Do you remember me?" he says. "You licked me at Upper Canada College." Sometimes I anticipate the greeting. As soon as the stranger grasps my hand and says, "Do you remember me?" I break in and say, "Why, let me see, surely I licked you at Upper Canada College." In such a case the man's delight is beyond all bounds. Can I lunch with him at his club? Can I dine at his home? He wants his wife to see me. He has so often told her about having been licked by me that she too will be delighted.

I do not like to think that I was in any way brutal or harsh, beyond the practice of my time, in beating the boys I taught. Looking back on it, the whole practice of licking and being licked, seems to me medieval and out of date. Yet I do know that there are, apparently, boys that I have licked in all quarters of the globe. I get messages from them. A man says to me, "By the way, when I was out in Sumatra there was a man there that said he knew you. He said you licked him at Upper Canada College. He said he often thought of you." I have licked, I believe, two generals of the Canadian Army, three cabinet ministers, and more colonels and mayors than I care to count. Indeed all the boys that I have licked seem to be doing well.

I am stating here what is only simple fact, not exaggerated a bit. Any schoolmaster and every "Old Boy" will recognize it at once; and indeed I can vouch for the truth of this feeling on the part of the "Old Boys" all the better in that I have felt it myself. I always read Ralph Connor's books with great interest for their own sake, but still more because, 32 years ago, the author "licked me at Upper Canada College." I have never seen him since, but I often say to people from Winnipeg, "If you ever meet Ralph Connor—he's Major Charles Gordon, you know—tell him that I was asking about him and would like to meet him. He licked me at Upper Canada College."

But enough of "licking." It is, I repeat, to me nowadays a painful and a disagreeable subject. I can hardly understand how we could have done it. I am glad to believe that at the present time it has passed or is passing out of use. I understand that it is being largely replaced by "moral suasion." This, I am sure, is a great deal better. But when I was a teacher moral suasion was just beginning at Upper Canada College. In fact I saw it tried only once. The man who tried it was a tall, gloomy-looking person, a university graduate in psychology. He is now a well-known Toronto lawyer, so I must not name him. He came to the school only as a temporary substitute for an absent teacher. He was offered a cane by the College janitor whose business it was to hand them round. But he refused it. He said that a moral appeal was better: he said that psychologically it set up an inhibition stronger than the physical. The first day that he taught—it was away up in a little room at the top of the old college building on King Street—the boys merely threw paper wads at him and put bent pins on his seat. The next day they put hot beeswax on his clothes and the day after that they brought screw drivers and unscrewed the little round seats of the class room and rolled them down the stairs. After that day the philosopher did not come back, but he has since written, I believe, a book called *Psychic Factors in Education*, which is very highly thought of.

But the opinion of the "Old Boy" about his teachers is only part of his illusionment. The same peculiar haze of retrospect hangs about the size and shape and kind of boys who went to school when he was young as compared with the boys of today.

"How small they are!" is always the exclamation of the "Old Boy" when he looks over the rows and rows of boys sitting in the assembly hall. "Why, when I went to school the boys were ever so much bigger."

After which he goes on to relate that when he first entered the school as a youngster (the period apparently of maximum size and growth), the boys in the sixth form had whiskers! These whiskers of the sixth form are a persistent and perennial school tradition that never dies. I have traced them, on personal record from eyewitnesses, all the way from 1829 when the college was founded until today. I remember well, during my time as a schoolmaster, receiving one day a parent, an "Old Boy" who came accompanied by a bright little son of 12 whom he was to enter at the school. The boy was sent to play about with some new acquaintances while I talked with his father.

"The old school," he said in the course of our talk, "is greatly changed, very much altered. For one thing the boys are very much younger than they were in my time. Why, when I entered the school—though you will hardly believe it—the boys in the sixth form had whiskers."

I had hardly finished expressing my astonishment and appreciation when the little son came back and went up to his father's side and started whispering to him. "Say, Dad," he said, "there are some awfully big boys in this school. I saw out there in the hall some boys in the sixth form with whiskers."

From which I deduced that what is whiskers to the eye of youth fades into fluff before the disillusioned eye of age. Nor is there need to widen the application or to draw the moral.

The parents of the boys at school naturally fill a broad page in the schoolmaster's life and are responsible for many of his sorrows.

There are all kinds and classes of them. Most acceptable to the schoolmaster is the old-fashioned type of British father who enters his boy at the school and says:

"Now I want this boy well thrashed if he doesn't behave himself. If you have any trouble with him let me know and I'll come and thrash him myself. He's to have a shilling a week pocket money and if he spends more than that let me know and I'll stop his money altogether." Brutal though this speech sounds, the real effect of it is to create a strong prejudice in the little boy's favor and when his father curtly says, "Good-bye, Jack," and he answers "Good-bye, Father," in a trembling voice, the schoolmaster would be a hound indeed who could be unkind to him.

But very different is the case of the up-to-date parent. "Now I've just given Jimmy $50," he says to the schoolmaster with the same tone as he would to an inferior clerk in his office, "and I've explained to him that when he wants more he's to tell you to go to the bank and draw for him what he needs." After which he goes on to explain that Jimmy is a boy of very peculiar disposition, requiring the greatest nicety of treatment; that they find if he gets in tempers the best way is to humour him and presently he'll come round. Jimmy, it appears can be led, if led gently, but never driven. During all of which time the schoolmaster, insulted by being treated as an underling (for the iron bites deep into the soul of every one of them) has already fixed his eye on the undisciplined young pup called Jimmy with a view to trying out the problem of seeing whether he can't be driven after all.

But the greatest nuisance of all to the schoolmaster is the parent who does his boy's home exercises and works his boy's sums. I suppose they mean well by it. But it is a disastrous thing to do for any child. Whenever I found myself correcting exercises that had obviously been done for the boys in their homes I used to say to them quite grandly:

"Paul, tell your father that he *must* use the ablative after pro."

"Yes, sir," says the boy.

I remember one case in particular of a parent who did not do the boy's exercise but, after letting the boy do it himself, wrote across the face of it a withering comment addressed to me and reading,

"From this exercise you can see that my boy, after six months of your teaching, is completely ignorant. How do you account for it?"

I sent the exercise back to him with the added note: "I think it must be hereditary."

In the whole round of the school year, there was, as I remember it, but one bright spot—the arrival of the summer holidays. Somehow as the day draws near for the school to break up for holidays, a certain touch of something human pervades the place. The masters lounge round in cricket flannels smoking cigarettes almost in the corridors of the school itself. The boys shout at the play in the long June evenings. At the hour when, on the murky winter nights, the bell rang for night study, the sun is still shining upon the playground and the cricket match between House and House is being played out between daylight and dark. The masters—good fellows that they are—have cancelled evening study to watch the game. The headmaster is there himself. He is smoking a briar-wood pipe and wearing his mortar-board sideways. There is wonderful greenness in the new grass of the playground and a wonderful fragrance in the evening air. It is the last day of school but one. Life is sweet indeed in the anticipation of this summer evening.

If every day in the life of a school could be the last day but one, there would be little fault to find with it.

Stephen Leacock, himself a graduate of Toronto's Upper Canada College, taught economics and political science at McGill University in Montreal until his retirement in 1936. Despite his success as a humourist, his best-selling book was the university textbook Elements of Political Science. *He died at 74 in 1944, and the annual Leacock Medal for Humour was established in 1946.*

The Second Coming
of Morley Callaghan

Morley Callaghan at home in Toronto, 1958

DECEMBER 3, 1960. Three years ago, passing through Toronto on his way to Stratford, Ont., Edmund Wilson—the elder statesman of literary criticism in the United States—lunched with an old acquaintance, Morley Callaghan. As they parted Callaghan presented him with a copy of his eighth novel, *The Loved and the Lost.*

Wilson went home, read it and wrote Callaghan that it was "extraordinary." He said it was "one of the high points of contemporary American literature." He said, "It ought to be read wherever the English language is spoken." He wanted to know when the book would be out: "It'll cause a big stir," he said.

Callaghan had to tell him the book had been out for six years and had been a flop.

For the last 23 of his 35 years as a practising author, Callaghan has been dogged by a maddening combination of indifference from the public at large, absent-mindedness amounting at times to amnesia on the part of the literary world, and occasional critical transports that, like Wilson's, were too intramural to do him much good.

Then, 12 weeks ago, Callaghan's ninth novel was published. Called *The Many Colored Coat*, it is the story of a Montreal public-relations man who insists that society pause to acknowledge his innocence of a crime it has mentally chalked up to him.

This time Edmund Wilson read the book as soon as it appeared, and phoned Callaghan long distance when he'd finished to say it, too, was "extraordinary," and he couldn't make up his mind which he liked better, the new one or *The Loved and the Lost*. He also said he was embarking on a major appreciation of all Callaghan's work for a late fall issue of *The New Yorker*. A similar essay by Wilson in the early Forties was enough to revive the fashion for Evelyn Waugh, a neglected English novelist. "The Wilson piece might do the trick," says Callaghan with superstitious caution.

But even beforehand there are advertisements of a vogue-in-the-making for Callaghan. It has something to do, of course, with the instant warm reception of the book by serious literary figures. For example, Albert Kazin, the most widely respected of the regular New York critics, called it "a remarkable performance." Erskine Caldwell wrote the publishers, Coward-McCann, to say, "This is perhaps (Callaghan's) finest achievement."

It also has something to do with a kind of glamour that mysteriously begins to attach itself to a man, so that people in the smart circles start talking about him. In Callaghan's case, memories are stirring of a fame he won in the Twenties and early Thirties as "the most discussed writer in America." So Budd Schulberg, writing about William Saroyan's career, suddenly remembers that Callaghan, along with Ernest Hemingway, was a style-setter in the short-story field in the Thirties. The intimations of a new *chic* are catching. So Ingrid Bergman's recent biographer finds it worthwhile to mention that the Swedish star had met and been admired by Callaghan in Toronto. And in New York City a firm of hardboiled fame brokers, Celebrity Service Incorporated (supplier of glamour gossip to columnists, indexer of stars who will do cold-cream endorsements, purveyor of guests for interview shows), bets that Callaghan is getting hot, the week his book is launched, and names him Celebrity of the Day. The only other Canadians the outfit has ever found worthy were Wayne and Shuster.

When Callaghan first heard about his selection, all he said, warily, was, "What'll it cost me?"

All it cost him was enough time out from a New York trip for a couple of radio interviews. But Callaghan's search for the hidden catch in any turn of fortune is, by now, chronic. "I have lived a life of humiliation," he explains blandly.

At 57, Callaghan is a lonely, stubborn, outspoken, cranky, charming, wistful, pot-bellied boyo. He is some of these things by nature, for he is second-generation Irish, and some by circumstance, for he has chosen to be that cultural freak, a serious, practising Canadian author trying to make a living in Toronto, where he was born, by writing books and stories about Canadians.

It has, he insists, rarely been a precarious life. Callaghan claims he has done "better than anyone suspects" from his writing. There was, indeed, one period of three years, at the beginning of the Second World War, when he wrote nothing at all and had to borrow on his insurance.

Many Callaghan admirers consider, though, that an even more melancholy stretch came later in the Forties when he turned out sports pieces for *New World*, a short-lived Canadian imitation of *Life*. Characteristically, Callaghan doesn't agree. "At least, I was allowed to write what I wanted without interference," he says. At about this time, too, the CBC began hiring him regularly as a panel chairman, panelist and a commentator on such shows as *Citizens' Forum*, *Fighting Words* and *Audio*. (The suggestion that Canadians know him best as a TV personality infuriates him: "It would be a sad reflection on the intelligence of this country if those stories of mine were allowed to fade away and be lost in a little yacking from a TV screen," he says.)

On the other hand he has fanatically refused any offers of jobs that he considered corrupting. *When Going My Way*—a lovable film about a lovable Irish priest played by Bing Crosby—was about to be released, someone in Hollywood was inspired to suggest that a matching novel would be good promotion. Since Callaghan was Irish and a Roman Catholic he was obviously, it was decided, the man for the job. He laughed savagely in their faces.

Indeed Callaghan has always fought any commitment that might corrupt his talent or his viewpoint. In *The Varsity Story*, a nostalgic fictional appreciation of the University of Toronto, published in

1948, Callaghan wrote of an undergraduate, Tom Lane, who wanted to be a writer. One of his mentors proposed that he try for a Rhodes Scholarship but Lane refused, saying, "All a writer has, if he is any good, is his own eyes and his own ears. Maybe I'm afraid of being seduced by the grandeurs and beauties of Oxford. . . . I see things the way I do because I grew up around here. . . . If I keep it I'll at least be trying to look at the world in my own way."

Callaghan himself, as an undergraduate, vetoed a similar proposal that he try for a Rhodes Scholarship; he has since turned down the offer of a staff job with *The New Yorker*, the editorship of *Saturday Night*, and an honourary LLD. He belongs to no clubs and espouses no political party. He claims to be an "unorthodox" Roman Catholic: "I can name dozens of saints I could dislike."

In fact he is so determined to be uninfluenced that when he moderated a radio discussion about Canadian writing, a couple of years ago, and the panelists insisted on planning the discussion ahead of time, Callaghan waited till they were on the air and then deliberately tore up their outline.

He is therefore unfailingly disgusted at the suggestion that his work is reminiscent of Hemingway's. Early in his career his publishers—at that time Scribner's—described him in their promotion as a second Ernest Hemingway. Critics can't seem to stop making the comparison, and he bitterly resents the label: "Anybody ought to see that my view of life is not Hemingway's view of life." Though both writers pioneered a version of a stripped, laconic style, Callaghan's subjects are metaphysical while Hemingway has simply written all his life about bloodshed and courage.

Living in Canada has undoubtedly made it easier for Callaghan to remain an original, to keep seeing life in his own way. But the penalty has been isolation. "The artist in Canada is kind of a pathetic figure," Callaghan said not long ago, pulling earnestly on his pipe. "I have very few writer friends. And everybody else works." Callaghan and his wife, Loretto, live in the Rosedale district of Toronto in an old 12-roomed house that used to be a boarding-house. Their elder son, Michael, a newspaperman, has his own apartment in the city, though Callaghan says he seems to spend half his time at home; their younger son, Barry, a postgraduate student at the University of Toronto, still lives with his parents. Callaghan's work is often done late at night, on an old portable at a narrow desk in his study. In the daytime he walks a lot, trudging the downtown streets by himself, with his head down and his hands clasped behind him. "You can never go out of an afternoon in Toronto and sit anywhere," he says. "Everyone's busy."

There used to be places to sit in Paris, where he spent a short, fine season in the Twenties, drinking and debating in Left Bank cafés with his friends and equals, men like Hemingway and Fitzgerald. Then, with the 1929 crash, everybody went home. "You'd see people moving off, and you'd still be sitting there," Callaghan recalls. "It was time to go home." For a while, more recently, there were places to sit in Montreal and Callaghan would go down and drink with the newspapermen and admire the pretty girls and see hockey games. "Then," he says sorrowfully, "people sort of weren't there any more. It's like an eddy of wind in the streets, whirling people together for a while and then blowing them somewhere else."

And for all his pains, the Canadian public has administered a notable series of snubs. His first short story, "A Girl with Ambition," was published while he was still an undergraduate at St. Michael's College in Toronto. A Toronto critic said, "It has no plot. It has no climax. It's no good."

His first novel, *Strange Fugitive*, written while he was still studying law at Osgoode Hall, was a flop in Canada. He had used the chronicle of a Toronto bootlegger to examine the itch to be a conqueror; he was promptly accused of "libeling a whole city." One dealer simply returned his quota to the publisher saying the style was not for him.

His fourth novel, *Such Is My Beloved*, considered the consequences, in a mundane Toronto parish, of cleaving to the principle of Christian love. His hero was a priest who tried to redeem two prostitutes, so the book was called "offensive to Roman Catholics." Callaghan had actually hammered out the theme in discussions with Jacques Maritain, the leading lay theologian of the Roman Catholic church. In fact he dedicated the book, "To those times with M. in the winter of 1933." The *Montreal Star*'s critic, Samuel Morgan-Powell, therefore devoted part of his review to suggesting that M's identity was obvious, since one of the prostitutes was named Midge.

Callaghan's fifth novel, *They Shall Inherit the Earth*, was banned by the Toronto Public Libraries. When *The Loved and the Lost* was published, the *Ottawa Citizen* said, "The mountain has brought forth a mouse." To fill out the record, the *Montreal Gazette* has decided that the *Many Colored Coat* "should never have been written."

In defence, Callaghan has become his own propagandist. He's apt to say his first published work was "a very fine story." He has written two plays that he describes as "brilliant." He remarks, "In my candid opinion I was the best writer in America in the Thirties."

Callaghan also defends himself by scorning Canadian critics ("What critics?"), Toronto ("bourgeois"), Canadian culture ("What culture?") and Canadian provincialism ("All our opinions have to be imported from outside.").

Actually, Canada never really imported the outside opinions of Callaghan. At home he was never so unstintingly admired as he was in international literary circles, in the beginning, nor was he later so thoroughly forgotten.

For, during a long fine season, Callaghan was bracketed with writers like Hemingway and Fitzgerald as "the coming man" in serious fiction. At 22, he was selling short stories to the esoteric little magazines published by expatriate Americans in Europe. When he was 25, Scribner's called him "the new fiction star" and published *Strange Fugitive*, which made him $10,000 though it flopped in Canada. As a mustachioed bridegroom of 26 (he had married a petite, smooth-browed art student from Toronto) he was in Paris and hearing himself described as "the fashionable hardboiled novelist of 1929." When he and a promising young U.S. writer, Robert McAlmon, crowded into an ancient *pension* lift with James Joyce, Joyce said, "Think of it. If the three of us should fall and be killed, what a loss to English literature!"

In the early Thirties, he commuted between Toronto and Greenwich Village, where he drank with Thomas Wolfe and sold short stories to every high-class magazine in the United States. When he brought out his second collection of short stories (and eighth book) in 1936, the *New York Times* said, "If there's a better short-story writer in the world, we don't know where he is."

Then, from 1937 to 1960, the world outside Canada virtually forgot him.

A Broadway producer, considering a Callaghan play, said, "But you're an unknown writer."

William Saroyan, encountering a Canadian war correspondent in wartime London, asked, "What ever became of Morley Callaghan?"

Callaghan's agent, Don Congdon, trying to find a publisher for *The Loved and the Lost*, in 1951, was turned down by eight houses: "The younger editors had never heard of Callaghan," he recalled recently.

The period of obscurity began with Callaghan's flirtation with the theatre. A New York producer had suggested he convert one of his novels into a play. He got enthusiastic and wrote two more plays. Two of the three actually came very close to Broadway production before collapsing under casting and financial difficulties. Both were later produced in Toronto by the New Play Society.

In the meantime Callaghan had written eight stories in a row that didn't sell. Then he stopped writing completely for three years. Beyond commenting that he was depressed by the war, he talks very little of this period. During it he made his debut on CBC radio, traveling across Canada as chairman of the program later known as *Citizens' Forum*. He also went to sea in an RCN corvette, on assignment for the National Film Board, and when he began writing again, his first book was one with a naval background. His agent couldn't interest a publisher, however, and Callaghan recalled it for more work. It is still not completed.

Aside from *The Varsity Story*, and a boys' book, both published in 1948, Callaghan produced no major work from 1937 till 1951, when *The Loved and the Lost* was published. "It was a great book," he says firmly. He was genuinely bewildered when it sold a scant 1,650 copies in the United States. After a year his New York publishers got their money out by unloading the book to Signet, a paperback series.

But an astonishing thing has happened in the eight years since then. In a 35-cent edition the book has quietly sold half a million copies. Others besides critic Edmund Wilson have belatedly discovered it. Recently a young New York intellectual picked up a second-hand copy in Greenwich Village and was so enchanted that, though he'd never heard of the author before, he tracked Callaghan down during a New York visit to get the book autographed. Another New

Yorker, an advertising-agency employee at Young & Rubicam, fell in love with it and turned it into a musical, though he hasn't as yet found a producer. It is this quiet kindling of awareness that has undoubtedly prepared the way for the new excitement about *The Many Colored Coat*—and Callaghan.

It is interesting to speculate about the effect of a best-seller on Callaghan, if it should come to pass, after the years of belittlement and isolation.

In the meantime he says wistfully that he would like to go to Rome for a while. He already has a following there: at least one of his books, in translation, has sold 45,000 copies in Italy, and there have been fine critical tributes in the press. Furthermore his next novel, which is almost completed, is to be called *A Passion in Rome.*

Callaghan went to Rome on a journalistic assignment two years ago, at the time of Pope Pius XII's death. He was supposed to stay four days, but he stayed three weeks and got enthusiastic about the decorative Roman women and the intellectual ferment in the cafés along the Via Veneto. "It's like the Montparnasse of the Twenties," he told a friend excitedly when he got home.

But his life as a writer in Canada has apparently left some bruises. "I can't afford Rome," he added sadly. "If I went I'd have to live in back alleys. And if you go to live in Rome you should be able to live in a palazzo."

Morley Callaghan's A Passion in Rome *was a critical success but, like his other works, never became a best seller. In total, he wrote 20 novels and dozens of short stories before he died in 1990 at age 87.*

Barbara Moon was an assistant editor and staff writer at Maclean's *from 1948 to 1953 and again from 1956 to 1964. Later senior editor and editor at large at* Saturday Night, *she now lives in Prince Edward county, Ontario.*

The Apprenticeship of Mordecai Richler

Mordecai Richler in Montreal, 1958

By Mordecai Richler

MAY 20, 1961. I had, like any other young novelist, started out by believing the difficult thing was to get published and that, once you managed that, well, your financial problems were over. I discovered, like any other serious novelist, that actually they had only just begun. A novel may take anywhere from two to five years to write and, in the end, you might manage a couple of thousand dollars on it, no more. In London, where I met many established novelists, I found that almost all of them, even the most celebrated, had something going for them on the side. Some were at the universities, others were reviewers or worked as advisers to publishing houses, and still more functioned as radio, television, or film script writers.

I can say, truthfully, that I started out at the bottom in the film business. Several times, when I was broke in the south of France, I worked as an extra. Broke again, this time in London, I got work as a reader for a studio script department.

For £2—about $5.50—a reader is expected to write a 10-page synopsis of a book followed by a shrewd evaluation of the book as a film. It's hard work. Underpaid, too. But in every reader's mind there is the legendary tale of the man who recommended a book that was actually purchased by the studio for £5,000. The grateful author, the story goes, sought out the reader and tipped him £10. So, even in this lowly job, there was hope. And experts, I discovered, could manage to skim through and report on as many as four books a day. I never got to be an expert. My career was too short-lived. One day a script editor handed me a book for which, she said, I would be paid a double fee. It was Bertolt Brecht's play *Mother Courage*. "The play's only 60 pages," I said. "Why can't the producer read it himself?"

I did not yet know that it was no more expected of most producers to read a book than it was, say, of Ted Williams to dust off home plate. And so, embarrassed but needy, I took the play home, wrote a synopsis, and mailed it off. The next morning the script editor phoned me, horrified. "But you haven't said whether or not it would make a good film," she said.

The late Bertolt Brecht, as you know, is considered to be one of the outstanding playwrights of our time. I felt foolish, but, all the same, I wrote a report on the play's film possibilities. "Very visual stuff," I said. "Goodish battle scenes. Strong suspense-wise. Calls for a big budget, I think, but potentially boffo." And that, I'm afraid, ended my career as a reader. I was, at the time, living in a room in Hampstead. Rent was a problem. Once a week my landlord, an elderly Austrian, would knock on the door and say, "Sorry to derange you, but today is Friday."

The Acrobats, my first novel, came out in German, and the publisher thoughtfully sent me six free copies. I tried to sell them to a German bookstore, but the lady wouldn't have them. "This book has already appeared in English," she said. "It isn't very good."

I began to review books for the literary magazines. The pay was slight. But, like all reviewers, I sold my free review copies for half price to a bookstore on Fleet Street. The most envied of reviewers was the man who got to do the art, that is, the most expensively priced books, but I never rose that high in the game.

Meanwhile, the Canadians had started to come over. Writers, directors, and actors. These writers, unlike any I had known before, actually made money. I was dazzled. I also got to write my first television script. I worked with a Canadian who had written many scripts and knew the medium well. The script, our collaboration, was to be what he called a piece of cheese, that is, a commercial job. We were writing it under a pseudonym. I sat at the typewriter and he paced up and down, dictating, gesticulating, thinking aloud, and acting out all the parts. Finally, after many hours of work, he turned to me, exhausted, and said, "Help me. Give me a line."

So I gave him a line of dialogue.

"Are you crazy?" he said. "That's real. This is television."

The next job I got was to write a pilot script for a half-hour television series. I was introduced to the producer as a vastly experienced script writer—a hotshot. He gave me a two-page character analysis of the lead character for the series—tough, fearless, handsome—and I went to work. The script I wrote was about smuggling in Spain. A few days after I had handed it in I was summoned to the producer's office. "You call this a *script?*" he said. "What's this here? Two guys talking. Talking! Yak-yak-yak for two whole pages. And look here, *three* pages. Two guys talking. Where's the action? They told me you were a good action writer."

I took the script back, bought a book with three screenplays in it, and set to work again. I made absolutely no plot or dialogue changes, but, whereas a piece of my first draft script was likely to read,

CARLOS: Things are very quiet out here tonight. I do not like it, Nick.

NICK: I was just wondering ...

CARLOS: Si, she is very beautiful. Like a Grecian statue. But she is dangerous, Nick.

NICK: I like 'em dangerous.

I copied a number of film terms out of the book I had bought, and the "new" script read,

CARLOS: Things are very quiet here tonight.
    SOUND: IT IS VERY QUIET.

CARLOS: I do not like it, Nick.
    CARLOS SCRATCHES HIS NECK.

NICK: (WITH A FAR-OFF, WONDERING LOOK) I was just wondering ...

CARLOS: Si, she is very beautiful. Like a Grecian statue. (A MEANINGFUL LOOK) But she is dangerous, Nick. CUT TO A CLOSE-SHOT OF NICK. HE LIGHTS A CIGARETTE. HE INHALES. HE SMILES ONE OF HIS CHARACTERISTICALLY SLOW, TOUGH SMILES.

NICK: I like 'em dangerous.

"Now that's what I call a script," the producer said.

I had arrived.

I began to go to the sort of parties where show-business people met and, at one of them, a script writer came up to me, and said, "How would you like to collaborate on a musical? I've got a producer and an advance. We have an absolutely free hand—except for one thing. Vesuvius has to blow up twice."

"The volcano, you mean?"

"It's set in Italy, see. A big production."

I told him no, but a couple of friends of mine took him up on it. They wrote a script, the producer was delighted, and he told the writers that he had booked one of the biggest theatres in London for the production. Opening night was only five weeks off.

"But what about the music?" one of the writers asked. "There's still no music."

"Not to worry. I own 14 songs," the producer said. "*Lovely* songs." They were left over from other musicals. "You boys will fit them in nicely." Then, seeing that the writers looked a little disheartened, he pulled a telegram out of his pocket. "From Magnani," he said, his voice brimming with assurance.

Actually, the telegram was from Anna Magnani's agent. It said something like, IMPOSSIBLE STOP NO INTEREST LONDON PRODUCTION STOP.

"But she doesn't want to do it," one of the writers said.

"Yes, that's possible. But look who I'm dealing with!"

The musical was never produced, but I did get to collaborate with the original author on another project. We were hired to write two half-hour comedies, pilots for a projected series again, but this time for Peter Sellers. Sellers, at the time, had made only one feature-length film, *The Ladykillers*.

My first collaborator had taken me on as an act of kindness. He knew I needed the money. This one, an Englishman, wanted company. He was a would-be actor. He executed all the routines meant for Sellers. I learned to say, "Why, that's swell. A great gag," or, helping him off the floor, "Yes, I can see what you're getting at, but it really doesn't cut any mustard, does it?" I did the typing and brewed the tea. I also whistled with amazement when I was told inside stories about the private lives of the stars. But I never really satisfied my partner. The truth is he had wanted Reuben Ship to work with him. Ship, author of *The Investigator*, was an experienced Hollywood comedy writer. I wasn't. But at least I knew Ship. After a week's work my partner—nervous, upset—said to me, "Why don't you get your friend Reuben to read this script? See what he thinks."

I already knew what Ship thought. "He's very busy these days," I said.

My partner, not usually very quick with his liquor, poured me a drink. "Well, you know, he just might have a couple of ideas. He *is* your friend, isn't he?"

Finally, we were called to a script conference. Present were Sellers, the director, the producer, two assistants, and my partner and I. We sat solemnly round an enormous table in a boardroom overlooking Hyde Park. Before each of us there was a pad, a pencil, and a glass of water. The producer, a shrunken little man with extremely thick glasses, told us, "Gentlemen, we are here to exchange ideas. To my right is our director. Need I say, a *great* talent."

Ten years ago, the director had made a costume film that showed more bosom than any other had before. This, in the trade, is known as a trendmaker. Anyway, the film earned lots of money, but the director had not made another one since.

"A talent that I have engaged, I might say, for a pretty penny."

"I consider this series a challenge," the director said. "A very great challenge." His hands were shaking badly. He twitched.

The rest of us were fulsomely introduced. "Now, about the script." The producer, squinting, held the script no more than two inches from his face. "Page 29, boys. I think we've slowed down here. We need a gimmick. Well, if you saw *Love Happy* with the Marx Brothers you will recall there was a great scene in that picture. Harpo is leaning against a wall. Groucho comes by and says, 'What are you doing, holding up the building?' Harpo nods. He moves away and the building collapses."

Sellers was silent.

"Now, boys, ours is a small-budget film. What I think we could do on page 29 is this. Instead of a building, Mr. Sellers could be leaning against a lamp-post. When he moves away," the producer said, already beginning to break up with laughter, "the lamp-post falls down."

Sellers lit one cigarette off another.

"Page 32, boys. Have you ever had the good fortune to see Mr. Danny Kaye, a great comedian, in *Up in Arms?*"

To my astonishment, the two films were made and distributed. I never went to see them. I did, however, continue to attend show-business parties, and gradually I picked up the jargon peculiar to the trade. I learned, for instance, that a "property" is a script or material for a script, that is, a book or a play. Some properties are hot, others tend to need a little goosing. When a producer asks you to give one of his properties a little goosing it means he is not willing to pay much to have a bad script rewritten. The most desirable properties are those that are in the public domain— scripts that can be based on the works of writers long since dead, and therefore requiring no payment.

One producer once took me aside and said, "Goddam it, I've just been to a library. Have you ever been to a library? What a fantastic place! Hundreds and hundreds of books—thousands! Most of them in the public domain, and I don't know which one to pick up. It's a goddam gold mine, I tell you. Listen, you've got an education. Go to the goddam library and find me a property."

If somebody said, "Say, what about Michael Wilding for the lead in . . . ?", I knew enough, by this time, to reply, "Are you crazy? Why that guy couldn't even sell popcorn." Whenever a leading lady's name was mentioned—any leading lady's name—I came right back with, "But do you know how she got the part? I mean, do you realize what she had to do to get it?" Nobody, I found, ever took you up on it.

I began to get more television work and my standard of living improved accordingly. I did not open an account at Harrods—and still haven't, for that matter—but I no longer ate Walls sausages nightly, and I moved out of a rented room into a flat. My landlord was an abstract painter. One day he stopped me abruptly in the hall and said, "Do you know where yesterday is?"

"No. I'm afraid not."

"Do you know where tomorrow is?"

"Well, no."

"The old masters knew," he said. "Yesterday was over there," he said, turning his head sharply to the right, "and tomorrow is over here," he said, turning leftward. "You shouldn't write for the flicks. It's corrupting."

I began to think I was doing very well, indeed. I was proud of my little flat at Swiss Cottage. By Canadian standards, it was a slum. I wasn't really aware of this until friends from home began to visit me there. One said, "Well, it's a struggle, isn't it?" Another, "Won't it be nice when you can afford carpets?" A third sent me a food parcel shortly after he returned home.

At first, I worked hard on my scripts. I took enormous pains to delineate characters clearly. Once, in fact, I took a full page to describe one major character's physical appearance, gestures, and habits, so that he was, I hoped, made individual beyond confusion. The producer read and reread the description. He chewed on his pencil. "Oh, I get it," he said. "You mean the Bogart type, don't you? Why didn't you just say so?"

Luckily, I put pseudonyms on all these scripts. When I got round to using my own name on television I had already formed a partnership, fortunate for me, with Ted Kotcheff, director, and Tim O'Brien, designer. We did three plays together for Armchair Theatre. Kotcheff and I also shared a flat. He instructed me further in the rules of the game. "Never hand in a script early," he said, "or the director will have you rewriting day and night, even if it's first rate. They're that nervous."

I had just begun to work on my second feature film, a rewrite job, and I soon found out what he meant. It was to be the director's first big film. He wasn't nervous. He was panic-stricken. I was originally hired because, as the director said, "The plot's OK, but everybody in the story is wooden. You've been recommended to us as a very good character man. We want you to put flesh and blood on these lumps." So I began to report every morning at 9:30 with my portable type-writer. The director and I would work a two-page scene over and over again.

"Mm . . . ," he'd say, reading, nibbling on his nails. "Jolly good. Well, not bad . . . but would he say *that?* Is it really in character for him *at that moment?* Do you get my point?"

All the man had said, usually, was, "Thank you, I'll have two lumps."

I'd look pensive. I never answered immediately. "I think you're on to something, you know. It *is* out of character. I think he'd say, 'Thanks,' not 'Thank you.'"

"But isn't that too Americany?"

"Exactly. But that's the point. *He's American-orientated.*"

"Really? How interesting you should say that. Is that how you see him?"

"Indeed I do."

"Mm . . . Maybe. But I think he's the sort who'd only take *one* lump with his tea."

"Well, I'm not sure. Maybe. I'll yield on that."

"No, you mustn't. I don't want you to give in because I'm the director. Fight me. You're the writer. If you see the character differently you must always insist on it."

Finally, after many hours of work, he'd say, "This scene is perfect now. Absolutely first class. Nobody could improve on it."

But the next morning the director would be pale. "My wife's sister-in-law was reading the scene in the bath last night and she hated it." We'd sit down and rewrite it again. "Superb," he'd say. The next day he'd look out of sorts again. "You share a flat with Kotcheff, don't you? Why don't you show it to him and see what he thinks?"

Resentful, but a loyal employee, I gave the script to Kotcheff. He read it. "All I can say," he said, "is I hope you're getting paid plenty for this. Wow!"

I was getting paid plenty, on a week-to-week basis, but the director often kept me a whole day without doing any writing. He'd take out a copy of *Spotlight,* a book with photographs of almost every actor and actress in the country, and ask my opinion on casting. My opinion, when you figured it at a day's pay, was very expensive.

"What would you think of John Mills?"

"He's all right."

"What do you mean 'all right'? Are you holding something back? Do you know something?"

I swore I didn't.

"What about ... Jack Hawkins?"

"Sure."

"If you don't like him, tell me. This is very important."

I had, to begin with, considered the film business to be characterized by lavish spending, but once a star was cast for the film I learned differently. One afternoon, when the director and I should have been putting final touches to the script, the star turned up. It was John Gregson. He was carrying eight, maybe nine, suits over his arm, and he stayed for hours. One of the major problems was that in one scene in the film Gregson flings himself from a speeding car as it passes over a bridge. He gets soaked, naturally, and therefore he would need to ruin one otherwise good suit. He preferred— and so did the director, budget-wise—to ruin an old one. Gregson began to try on suits while the director watched, absorbed, and I, realizing we were not going to get any work done again, reached for the gin.

"Don't you think," Gregson asked, "this one would suit me fine for the scene where she faints?"

"Mm . . . ." The director pulled at his lower lip. "Isn't it a little youngish for the scene?" He turned to me. "What do you think?"

"I think he looks very sweet."

Gregson told me how much he liked the script. "I consider this picture a challenge," he said.

I poured myself another gin and offered to lend Gregson my one prized Jacques Fath tie. The director, I sensed, felt we were a happy unit.

Though I was still without a screen credit, the last time out of choice, I had now worked on rewrites for two feature films, and then one day as, I suppose, it comes to pass in the life of any clean-living relief pitcher, I was offered a starting assignment. Sydney Box phoned my agent and asked if I would read *No Love for Johnnie*. Wilfred Fienburgh, considered to be one of the more promising Labour MPs, had written the novel, his first, and was killed shortly afterward in a car accident. The book was a loosely motivated but realistic piece about an opportunist, a Labour MP, in Parliament. Sydney Box and I met, I was passed on to the producer who would be directly responsible for the picture, David Deutsch, and I was hired to write the screenplay. At the time there was a possibility that Jack Clayton, who had just made *Room at the Top*, would direct this film as well. But, as things turned out, I had been working on the script for only two weeks when everything changed. Sydney Box had a heart attack and went into temporary retirement. David Deutsch moved to another studio, and Jack Clayton signed to direct a different film. The project was taken over by Betty Box, producer, and Ralph Thomas, director.

One of the most enjoyable aspects of working on *No Love for Johnnie* was that it gave me an entrée to British politics. All sorts of things were laid on for me. I was taken to lunch by a man from Rank who was the fixer. A former parliamentary secretary himself, he could, I was told, arrange interviews for me with anybody. Anyway, the fixer got me a pass to the distinguished strangers' gallery and for several days running I attended sessions at the House. At private question time an ancient lady rose anxiously, the hand that held the notes trembling, and asked if a Ministry of Food pamphlet about the uses of bacon could not have been issued with a hard cover rather than a soft as a greater convenience to the hard-working housewives of Great Britain. This, I was told, was the first time she had been heard from in years. And so it went until [Labour firebrand] Nye Bevan walked into the chamber; both front benches filled, and all private conversations stopped. Bevan had only a mild query to put to the minister, but there was no doubt that we were in the presence of political greatness. When he was done, once the threat of eloquence had passed, the benches thinned again.

I turned in my script for *No Love for Johnnie*, bought a small car, and prepared to drive down to Rome for the winter. A week before I left I found out, through another writer, that the first film script I had ever written, the one about smuggling in Spain, had never been produced. On the contrary, it was being used as a model for writers on how not to write for the series. A day before I was to leave a producer phoned me. "I've heard so much about you," he said. "You must come to my office this minute. I have a property here that is a *property*. It only needs a little work."

I explained that I had just completed a film and that I was going away to work on a novel.

"It's an anti-war script," he said. "I'm sure you'd want to see it done."

"There's somebody at the door," I said. "I have to go."

"If you don't want to do it," he said, "it's only because you're a warmonger."

A few days later in Paris I went to some of the four-star restaurants I hadn't been able to afford when I had lived there before. At that time, my problem—the primary concern, in fact, of most of the writers I knew—had been money and a place to sleep. Now I paid income tax, just like a regular citizen. I sought out the cafés where I used to meet my friends, but I did not see a familiar face in any of them. It was good not to be broke, very good, but I also felt a little sad. I could recognize the new arrivals, the young writers and painters I didn't know, by the dufflecoats, the beards, and the blue jeans. They looked at me a little dubiously. Like I was a tourist.

Mordecai Richler continues to live part of the year in London, the rest in Montreal or in Quebec's Eastern Townships. Among his subsequent novels, Cocksure *(1968) and* St. Urbain's Horseman *(1971) won the Governor General's Award and* Barney's Version *(1997) the Giller Prize.*

Irving Layton: The Man Who Copyrighted Passion

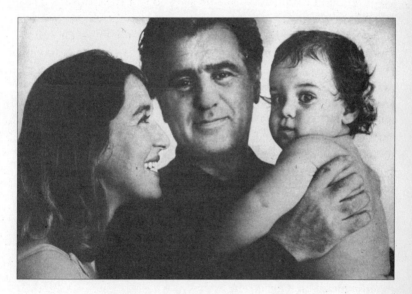

Irving Layton with Aviva and David, 1953

NOVEMBER 15, 1965. Her name was Phyllis, she went to high school in Montreal nearly 40 years ago, and maybe she wasn't all that pretty. But she had this wonderful way of saying "prunes," and that's why Irving Layton, a 14-year-old Jewish kid from St. Elizabeth Street, fell in love with her.

It used to drive him out of his mind, the way Phyllis said "prunes." It wasn't how it sounded, but what happened to her mouth when her lips formed the word. He'd hang around her, he'd try to sit next to her in Math class, he'd keep saying to her, "Look, I want you to say the word 'prunes.' Please say it. I just want to watch you." He was always at her. He'd tell her how he worshipped her like a goddess, how he'd love her forever—14!—and how he loved her eyes and her mouth and so on. One day he even wrote her a poem:

Come my love, since life is short
And stormy as the ocean's breast.
We'll anchor safely at love's port
And loudly laugh at fortune's jest.
Soon will our toiling lives be spent
And dust and ashes be our clay.
So, dearest, to our hearts' content
We'll live and love this very day.

A tender, metaphysical tribute, but Phyllis wasn't impressed. When you're almost 15 you don't get involved with crazy children. Besides, English wasn't one of her strong subjects. So Phyllis went her toiling way and Irving Layton, who'd loved her for all of six weeks with the calf-eyed, sexless reverence of the very young, went on to love other girls and write other poems.

That, broadly speaking, is what he's been doing ever since. And now, 39 years, several thousand poems and an indeterminate number of girls later, Layton has come to occupy a fairly unique position on the Canadian scene.

Today, he is indisputably Important—probably the least dispensable Canadian poet now living. It's a little risky to go around calling him the *best*, but if you took every published poet in the country, locked them up in the ballroom of the Royal York Hotel and refused to feed them until they'd elected a president, Layton would probably emerge as the least objectionable compromise candidate. If this seems like a fairly timid appraisal of his worth, there are several foreign critics who go much further. William Carlos Williams, the late American poet and critic, was an extravagant Layton admirer. "He's a backwoodsman with a tremendous power to do anything he wants with verse," Williams wrote in the introduction to one of Layton's books. "With his vigor and abilities who shall say that Canada will not have produced one of the West's most famous poets?"

Let it be granted, then, that Layton is certifiably Important. What else has he got going for him? Well, for one thing, he is the only Canadian poet to be president of his own real-estate investment corporation. For another—and in the tweed-thicket world of Canadian letters, this is unusual—he has a highly unpoetic flair for attracting personal publicity.

Because he talks so well, he has been a frequent panelist on several packaged-controversy TV shows. Because he has so many opinions and so many detractors attacking him in print, he has become, next to Eugene Forsey, Canada's all-time champion letter-to-the-editor writer. And because he travels a lot, speaks in public a lot and happens to be immensely quotable, he is continually making headlines across the country.

What emerges from these headlines is the fact that Layton, in addition to being a major poet, has set himself up as a sort of press agent for passion. His most persistent conviction is that industrial society is turning us into a race of desiccated, suburban robots. Modern man, he believes, is in danger of forgetting how to feel deeply; and if the situation could be corrected by setting up an Eros Lobby in Ottawa, Layton would be the logical choice for executive secretary.

Like any good propagandist, he delivers his message endlessly: not merely in his poetry, but in classrooms and lecture halls, in restaurants and television studios, in print and at cocktail parties. Last year, for instance, before an audience at a Unitarian church in Toronto, he observed that Canadians "still think sex is a dirty word, something to snicker about. Our Presbyterian- and priest-ridden society seeks to suppress the natural urges of the young. Yet at 15 and 16, children are sexually mature. I hope my 14-year-old daughter has had six lovers before she's 16."

Naturally, this triggered the old outrage syndrome that is one of our more endearing national traits. Fearless Frank Tumpane galloped out with a *Toronto Telegram* column denouncing Layton as, among other things, a "sensation monger." A few people wrote in to regret the existence of premarital sex in general and Layton in particular. And of course Layton wrote a letter to the *Telegram's* editor, too, explaining that he'd been sort of kidding about his daughter's six lovers ("a teacher's gay exaggeration"), but that he still favored premarital sex because "that's the best time to enjoy it."

The whole affair was just another two-day editorial tempest, the kind that city editors find especially helpful in the middle of a dull week. But for all its crashing banality, the incident at least demonstrated that Layton has become uniquely accomplished at provoking controversy.

If Layton stays faithful to his image as the prancing, leering goat of Canadian letters, there should be some more editorial tempests any day now. His publishers, McClelland and Stewart, are sending him on a cross-country speaking tour of Canadian universities this month to publicize his latest book, *Collected Poems*. With nearly 400 poems, all but four of them gathered from previous books or published in the little magazines, it may not be the best book of verse ever published in Canada, but it is surely one of the bulkiest.

Although it doesn't include his Phyllis poem (which is the third verse he ever wrote, and the earliest he can remember), the new collection is still an exhaustive survey of two decades of literary production by an extraordinary man. Since most of Layton's poems lean heavily on incident and anecdote, reading the book from beginning to end is a little like reading an autobiography in code.

Essentially, it is a *happy* story. Layton grew up in the sort of environment that social workers now describe as "multi-disadvantaged," but he enjoyed it. His relations with the world of committees, personnel men, officer selection boards and school trustees have been generally grisly; in this respect, his life has been one long rejection slip. But it's never seemed to bother him. Some people are lucky enough to know their own star and follow it, and Layton is one of them. He was probably destined, as some people apparently are, to be a happy man.

Novelist Mordecai Richler has described how it was to be a Jewish kid growing up in a Montreal slum in the 1940s. Where Layton grew up, 20 years earlier and not far from Richler's neighborhood, it wasn't much different. There were the same gangs of Italian and French punks rumbling with the Jewish punks. There were the same big, squabbling families, the same candy stores run by women with funny accents, with the same back rooms where the old men gathered to argue about the Torah.

Layton's Romanian-born father was another stock figure: the Talmudic scholar, in beard and *kaftan*, who meditated on eternity all day while his wife did the work. In the Laytons' case, there was plenty to do; she bore nine children (one died in infancy) and supported them all by opening a grocery store in the front room of their house on St. Elizabeth Street. To Layton, his father was a silent and austere man "who was on more intimate terms with the angels than with the children he'd helped to bring into the world. He was a holy man who burned with a love of God and God's word." Unsurprisingly, Layton has been an anti-daddy atheist since his early teens; but it is difficult to avoid the impression that he pursues the mysteries of human love with the same sort of Biblical intensity that his father focused on the divine.

There was never enough money. Getting through Baron Byng High School, where the fees started at $2.50 per month, involved pedaling around the neighborhood to dun pennies from neighbors who owed money on their grocery bills. And unlike Richler, Layton never graduated from Baron Byng. Three months before matriculation, he was expelled for refusing to apologize to a teacher who'd bawled him out in front of the class for being late with his monthly tuition fee.

The experience contributed to Layton's aversion to educational bureaucracy. In university—he attended Macdonald College, the agricultural faculty of McGill University, because the government paid the fees—he caused the wildest scandal in that institution's bucolic history. His articles in the student newspaper denouncing Chamberlain's appeasement policy enraged his fellow students, who seized an entire issue of the newspaper and, according to Layton, even prompted the RCMP to send a man down to the campus to investigate.

When war broke out, the army wasn't ready for Layton either. He enlisted in an officers' training course, and spent several months in battleground training at Camp Petawawa. But his fellow trainees were unimpressed when he tried to initiate them into the intricacies of anti-fascist politics. One senior officer was even less impressed when, during a mock battle, he discovered Layton lounging in a foxhole, with live shells screaming overhead, reading Schopenhauer's *The World As Will and Idea*. The end came when Second Lieutenant Layton, in command of several hundred men, fumbled his orders during a battle manœuvre. Somehow he'd managed to line up his troops so they were facing each other instead of the enemy. He was about to give the order to fire when a screaming major raced up in a Jeep, averted what would have been a massacre, and shipped Layton back to Montreal with an honourable discharge. The consensus, Layton feels, was that he just wasn't officer material.

In Montreal he began writing poetry in earnest. He fell in with John Sutherland and Louis Dudek, who were editing a mimeographed poetry sheet called *First Statement*. They were all standard-brand socialists in those days, and their primary target was *Preview*, a little magazine edited by Patrick Anderson, Frank Scott, A. M. Klein and P. K. Page. Twenty years later, the nuances of this dispute are a little hard to grasp; but the idea seemed to be that Layton and company were the roistering, smell-of-the-earth proletarians, while Scott and his well-bred, Oxbridge-oriented *Preview* crowd were guilty of writing effete verse. Despite this vast social gulf, the two groups merged to publish a bi-monthly called *Northern Review*. It was an important magazine while it lasted, certainly the most important poetry magazine ever published in this country. Layton modestly feels it was "the beginning of a renaissance that is still continuing today."

About the same time, in 1946, Layton effected a merger of his own with Sutherland's beautiful sister Betty. He'd been married before—he doesn't talk about it, except to say that the marriage was contracted out of pity and survived three miserable years—but Betty was the first woman that mattered.

Betty was, and is, a painter, and Layton says he fell in love with her the first time he saw her: "She was unkempt, she never combed her hair, she didn't care about clothes. She was a magnificent person with a wonderful embrace for people and the world." They stayed married for 14 years—years in which Layton built a large literary reputation, fathered two children, bought a house and supported his family by teaching at Montreal high schools and moonlighting on the side, sometimes holding down as many as five teaching jobs at once.

The marriage ended in 1959. Why? "I don't know," says Layton. "I still loved her, but it wasn't working anymore." He feels it must have had something to do with the impulse, common in men approaching middle age, to destroy everything they've built, with a view to a new start. But such nuances of feeling are not really the business of journalism. That's what poetry is for—and Layton has written it.

Whatever the causes of its failure, it had been a happy marriage— and in a way, it still is today. Betty lives in California with their 15-year-old daughter, Naomi. Max, their 19-year-old son, now lives in Montreal and has gladdened his father's heart by writing a novel (unpublished) and quitting university in his freshman year because he felt it was a waste of time. They are, as they used to say in Hollywood, still good friends.

But now there is Aviva, a sweetie-pie from Australia who writes children's books and looks to be about 18. She was passing through Montreal 10 years ago when she met Layton through a literary introduction. They were married in 1959.

Layton is 53 now, and thinks he's writing better than ever. He and Aviva live in a book-lined upstairs apartment in Notre Dame de Grâce with their year-old son David, a big kid who may grow up to be a literate football player. Layton feels good about David—as who wouldn't if they'd produced a fine son at an age when many men are producing fine grandsons?

He is also displaying a late-blooming fertility in another field: real-estate investment. Six years ago, after his nonconformist views had got him booted off the faculty of a Jewish high school where he'd taught for 15 years, he began to appreciate the virtues of financial independence. He decided to invest several thousand dollars left over from a government grant in real estate, and picked out a property from the classified ads that looked good to him. The owners, a Montreal couple named Carl and Gertie Katz, were ready to sell until they heard the name of their prospective buyer; then their tune changed. "Mr. Layton," said Mrs. Katz, "I was studying your poetry this week at night school, and we're not going to sell you this dog." The Katzes make their living from property investments, and they took Layton under their wing. Today he is president of a company called Calais Holdings Limited which owns two apartment houses and several other properties. The resultant income, according to Layton, is "enough so I could retire tomorrow."

But he continues to teach at Sir George Williams University [now Concordia], upsetting and enthralling a new crop of students every year. And he still has those sympathetic eyes that compel strange women to come up to him at cocktail parties and ask him what they should do about their floundering marriages. (Layton's advice is always the same: "Since you're asking *me*, it's time you left him." And often they do.)

Of course there are plenty of people who wouldn't ask Layton's advice about *poetry*, let alone domestic relations. Most of the reviews he's been getting lately have been unfavorable. Pop-culture worship is mandatory among intellectuals this year, and Layton's brand of bombast is faintly out of step with all the New Things that are happening in the arts. His views on sterility in the suburbs, the pedantry of anyone (except Irving Layton) who teaches English at a university, the rising tide of conformity, and so on are … well, views like these are awfully easy to outgrow. Besides, there's this endless arrogance in his poetry, this pugnacious assumption that I'm Irving Layton and, dammit, I can outfight and outlove and outcurse you all with one hand tied behind my back.

Robin Skelton, an acute west-coast critic, pinned it down in a review of Layton's last book, *The Laughing Rooster*: "Too often ... he appears to confuse excitement with inspiration, and estimate a poem's worth in terms of the feelings which caused it rather than of the feelings it displays."

But there is no use nit-picking at Layton's opinions and social attitudes. You can get plenty of those on the editorial pages, and they are incidental to the best of his poetry. As a matter of fact, there isn't much point in saying *anything* about Layton's poems. Either they move you or they don't. He is a man who feels things more deeply than most of us, and he has this itch to tell other people about things that can't be expressed in words.

Late in September this itch gave rise to an untitled poem which, in Layton's estimation, is one of his best. It doesn't mean quite what it says—I mean, Aviva isn't about to walk out on him or anything. Instead, it refers to the panicky, desolate feeling that afflicts some lovers when their girl walks out the door—even if it's only to the corner grocery for a pack of cigarettes—and the rush of affirmation they experience when she returns:

> *The air is sultry.*
> *So is my soul.*

> *The coffee is bitter.*
> *So are my thoughts.*

> *The cigarette is stale.*
> *Ditto my emotions.*

> *There's a filthy hole in the wall.*
> *There's one in my heart.*

> *It's going to rain.*
> *The rain can't help me.*

My darling has run off
    with another man.
  Who cares?

I hear her knock at the door.
    She brings me suffering.

She tells me she loves me.
    I tell her I adore her.

The air is sultry.
    So is my soul.

To the unschooled critic, this might indicate that Layton has covered very little psychic distance between Phyllis and Aviva. In fact, it seems *more* adolescent than the poem Layton wrote 38 years ago to the girl who had the wondrous way of saying "prunes."

But any 53-year-old property owner who can boast about writing pubescent poetry should be cherished, not derided. This country is getting richer all the time, but it is not getting noticeably happier, and it has never been noted for its devotion to sensuality. We may need people like Layton more than we think.

Irving Layton, who published 35 books of poetry, divorced Aviva in 1978 and married three more times, the last time to Annette Pottier whom he met in 1981—when she was 28 and he was 69—and from whom he separated in 1995. Layton now lives in Montreal, where he is under care for Alzheimer's.

Alexander "Sandy" Ross worked for Maclean's *twice, as a staff writer from 1964 to 1965 and as managing editor from 1966 to 1968. In an award-winning career, cut short in 1993 by his death at 58 from a stroke, Ross also worked for* Saturday Night, *was founding editor of* Toronto Life *and co-owner and editor-in-chief of* Canadian Business. *He also wrote several books. The National Magazine Awards Foundation's annual Alexander Ross Award is given in his name to the best new magazine writer of the year.*

The World of Alex Colville

Alex Colville in his Wolfville, N.S., studio, 1983

By Gillian MacKay

AUGUST 1, 1983. In August, 1945, young Canadian war artist
Alex Colville spent a day's leave at the Louvre in Paris. The war
had ended and so had what he jokingly called his "Guggenheim fel-
lowship in art": the daily pen and watercolor sketching of battlefields, blackened villages and, finally, the mass graves at the Belsen
death camp that haunted his nights for years afterward. Colville
wandered in delight through the palatial halls of the Louvre, mar-
velling that while Europe lay in ruins those masterpieces of civilization had survived. Although he had never visited a great
museum before, the confident 25-year-old was encouraged rather
than overwhelmed by the experience. "What I wanted to know was,
is it possible to make great art?" Colville recalls. "So I went to the
Louvre and saw that, yes, it was."

Since then Colville has aimed to create the kind of art that could
hang on those hallowed walls. And last week a major retrospective
of his work opened at the Art Gallery of Ontario, proving conclu-
sively that in Canada, at least, his artistic immortality is now
assured. During the 38 years since the war, he has spent his time
enriching a national culture which he found empty and primitive.
His haunting, razor-sharp images of family life—from the tow-
headed child skipping rope in a bleak schoolyard in 1958 to the

middle-aged couple getting a night snack from the refrigerator in 1977—have become emblems of existence for a young nation growing up. Not since the heyday of the Group of Seven has an artist's vision permeated so deeply the lives of Canadians: his elegant designs for the Centennial coins have jingled in the pockets of the nation, and his famous image of a dark horse heading on a collision course with a train graced the cover of a best-selling record album by Bruce Cockburn. Says Toronto gallery owner Mira Godard, who represents some of the most celebrated names in contemporary art: "He is Canada's most important artist." But since 1967, when the prestigious Marlborough Fine Art Gallery in London became the exclusive dealer for Colville's minutely detailed acrylic paintings, Canadian art lovers have had little opportunity to see his work except in reproduction. Now, the retrospective of 57 paintings, seven prints and 96 preparatory drawings will put Colville squarely back in the public domain as it travels throughout Canada and to Germany during the next 13 months.

In the world of art, a retrospective is often seen as the kiss of death, a clear indication that a painter's best years are over. But neither age nor the weight of his own legend sit heavily on Alex Colville. At 62, he is in his prime, a trim, vigorous man who leads a charmed existence with his wife, Rhoda, in Wolfville, N.S. That, too, is the world of his art, although Colville's essentially tragic view takes his paintings far beyond the realm of sentimental snapshots from the family album. Through a range of now familiar techniques—frozen motion, heightened realism, eerie lighting, cropped heads and dramatic compositions—he can instil an ordinary event, such as his family getting into their car in *Family and Rainstorm* (1955), with the menacing air of a Hitchcock film. Even a gentler work like *Refrigerator* (1977) is charged with an ambivalent mood of celebration and lament for a precious moment that must pass.

Colville's sources of inspiration have remained close to home, but they have not lost their power. His recent paintings, such as the 1980 self-portrait *Target Pistol and Man*, are among his best and reflect a subtle transition from the cool, depersonalized classicism of the early work to a more sensuous and specific romanticism. In the self-portrait, the artist, who for years appeared in his own paintings hidden behind his wife, his dog or sunglasses, finally shows his face. In the foreground is the pistol, a symbol of his preoccupation with evil and with the existential view that man must confront his own mortality in order to appreciate the fullness of life. The gun, Colville feels, is the most striking icon of our era. As Toronto art critic Michael Greenwood put it, "He has an obsession, and it has remained fresh."

Like visual poems, Colville's paintings tease the mind with questions to which there is no final answer. But in Godard's view, it is precisely that "element of mystery" that makes the works so compelling. Others have found his drawing "graceless" and devoid of warmth, an assessment that Colville himself shares. But his detractors are easily outnumbered by his admirers, led by British critic Terence Mullaly, who has called Colville "the most important realist in the Western world." His enthusiasm is shared by Canadian, German and U.S. collectors who pay as much as $100,000 for one of the three works he produces each year. Colville enjoys telling a story about the owner of *Seven Crows* (1980), who said, "I have three priorities in life: my family, my wife and this painting." The artist's annual limited edition of 70 silkscreen prints, priced this year at $2,500 a piece, invariably sells out within several months, and there are waiting lists for favorites such as *Cat and Artist* (1979). When such a print comes out, Godard says, "people will scratch your eyes out to get it."

But Colville has only achieved substantial financial success in the past decade. During the 1950s and early 1960s, when realism was out of vogue, he sold few works and supported his family by teaching art at Mount Allison University in Sackville, N.B., where he himself had studied. Through his work at the university, Colville became a major influence on a number of students who went on to become prominent realists in their own right—among them Christopher and Mary Pratt, D. P. Brown, Tom Forrestall and Hugh MacKenzie. But the *example* of Colville's artistic integrity has perhaps been more inspiring to young painters than his actual *style*. Said Greenwood: "Here is a man who has resolutely gone his own way, regardless of fashion, and has come out on top."

From the beginning of his career Colville had no doubt about the way he wanted to paint. During the postwar period, when modern artists were rejecting representationism, Colville stuck stubbornly to the then unfashionable notion that art must carry a message. In a brilliant 1951 speech outlining his philosophy of art, he compared the new design-oriented and abstract art to "some brilliantly played but pointless mathematical game." Instead of turning its back on the world, he proposed that art should address such fundamental questions as "Who are we? What are we like? What do we do?" While the abstract expressionists hurled buckets of paint at the canvas to express their visions of personal and public chaos, Colville believed that the artist had to do more than express his anguish. Fresh from the horrors of war and lacking the comfort of a religious faith, he felt that his responsibility was to stare into the void and find meaning. Says Colville quietly: "I have an enormous desire to make sense out of things."

Like Dorothy in *The Wizard of Oz*, he eventually found that sense in his own backyard. It flows from his attachment to a small community, from his devotion to Rhoda, their children—Graham, John, Charles and Ann—and to domestic animals, which he regards as morally superior to most people. Colville dislikes the anonymity of cities and is clearly happiest on his home turf in Wolfville, a quiet, traditional town of 3,200 in the lush Annapolis Valley, where Rhoda's ancestors settled 223 years ago. Since 1973 they have lived in the handsome stucco house which her father, a prosperous contractor, built in 1920—the same house in which she was born and where she and Alex married in 1942. Rhoda's strong sense of tradition and belonging enfolds her husband like a warm cloak. "I am, in a sense, rootless," he said, settling contentedly into a chair in the library, which, like every other room in the house, is filled with fine antiques, comfortable furniture and his own prints. "It is a somewhat unpleasant thought, but in a way an artist does live off other people and environments and is also, in a certain sense, nobody."

Colville is deeply aware of the contrasts between his and Rhoda's backgrounds. Born in a tiny row house in Toronto in 1920, Colville moved with his family to St. Catharines, Ont., when he was seven and to Amherst, N.S., when he was nine. There, his Scottish-born father advanced to a low-level management job at a steel company owned by Dominion Bridge, exchanging his former worker's uniform for a suit and tie. But David Colville's gentle, romantic nature was basically unsuited to the industrial world. His recurrent bouts of drinking put further strain on an already unhappy marriage to Alex's mother, Florence, a stylish, businesslike woman who started a clothing store in Amherst during the Depression and ran it successfully until her death in 1963. Raised as a Roman Catholic, Colville says that he was never sent to church schools, "probably because my mother sensed it would be a social disadvantage."

As the younger of two sons, Alex was somewhat spoiled, always beautifully dressed and never forced to work in the summer, despite the family's modest income. At the age of nine he almost died of pneumonia, and during his long convalescence he began to draw, an interest that persisted throughout high school. Out of the traumatic brush with death Colville developed a deeply introspective nature. There were few books at home, so he raided friends' libraries for anything he could find—first boys' adventure stories and later T. E. Lawrence's *Seven Pillars of Wisdom* and H. G. Wells's *Experiment in Autobiography. Experiment,* an account of a boy from a modest background who becomes a scientist and writer, inspired Colville with a sense of the possibilities beyond Amherst. When he graduated from high school, the clever, self-confident young man was able to choose between a scholarship to Dalhousie University in Halifax, where he would have studied law, and one at Mount Allison. His parents were fully prepared to let him study painting, a fact that he attributed to their social naïveté. Colville, on the other hand, was hard-nosed about his career. He asked Stanley Royle, an art teacher from Mount Allison who had taught him during the summers, "Will I be poor?" Only after hearing the answer—"No"—did he choose art.

Colville's central commitment, both in his life and art, has been to Rhoda. "I remember thinking," he said, "that if, for some bizarre reason, I had to choose between my wife and my art, I would choose my wife." During the two years between 1944 and 1946, when he was in Europe, he wrote every day to Rhoda, who gave birth to their first son, Graham, while he was away. His paintings from the early 1950s, such as *Soldier and Girl at Station,* are filled with images of loneliness and longing. Since then he has celebrated Rhoda in an endless series of poses: bringing in laundry, putting on her brassiere, carrying a canoe, riding her bicycle and standing on her head. Because of his devotion to Rhoda, predictably Colville's first successful work, *Nude and Dummy* (1950), featured her in an attic staring over her shoulder at a dressmaker's dummy. In the almost surrealistic piece, Colville first employed the kind of composition that became a standard feature of his mature style. His careful method of constructing a painting along clear lines of perspective within a tight geometric framework derives from such early Italian Renaissance painters. Colville's overwhelming need to make sense of the world required this lucid, rational approach to organization.

Although Sackville in the 1950s was an unlikely place to experiment with Renaissance geometry, it suited Colville. His lack of sympathy with the progress of modern art meant he had little interest in being close to any contemporary art scene. He has an aversion to meeting other artists, whom he considers "just boring as hell." He is no fan of the Group of Seven, preferring instead such American painters as Edward Hopper, Ben Shahn and Grant Wood. The empty, desolate work world of Sackville and of Canadian culture as a whole provided an ideal breeding ground for his art. "One of the great things about living in a primitive culture," he says, "is that, in a sense, nothing is done, so everything is yet to be done."

From the start, Colville was recognized by a few collectors such as New York ballet impresario Lincoln Kirstein and Robert Hubbard, whose far-sighted purchases during the 1950s, including *Hound in Field,* have given the National Gallery a splendid Colville collection. Still, it was not until 1963, when he had a successful show in New York, that Colville could afford to leave his teaching job. The next three years were so perilous financially that he even sold life insurance to make ends meet. In 1966, he represented Canada at the prestigious Venice Biennale and after Colville's critically acclaimed shows in Hanover and London in 1969–70, his international reputation was secure.

As his fame has spread in the past decade, so has the image of

Colville as a sinister figure pathologically fixated with guns. Of 122 paintings, in fact, only three feature weapons: *Pacific* (1967), *In the Woods* (1976) and the self-portrait. For Colville, who belongs to his local target-pistol club, the guns symbolize the need to be armed and aware in a world he regards as increasingly "fragile." During a 10-month teaching stint at the University of California in Santa Cruz in 1967–68, he became alarmed by student violence and the disintegration of society. There, he painted the powerful *Pacific*, which portrays the back of a man looking out on the ocean with a gun sitting on a table in the foreground. It raises disturbing, unanswerable questions. Colville says that he only paints people and situations he considers "wholly good." But, for the viewer, the artist's assertion does not banish the sense of dread.

Nothing could be farther from that threatening world than the idyllic frame cottage near Wolfville, where the Colvilles can sit on a clear summer night and watch the setting sun flooding Minas Basin with rosy, transcendental light. Rhoda has been visiting the cottage since she was a child, and the neighbors are old friends, one of them a witness at the Colvilles' wedding. Several years ago, on a visit from Toronto, Godard suggested that they buy the adjacent cottages and tear them down for more privacy—a proposal that highly amused the community-spirited artist and his wife. As the artist tells his big-city friends who ask why he hates to travel: "I am a provincial; I am like an Israeli. There is something I have to get back to."

Whether cycling to the cottage on his Italian touring bicycle or zipping down Main Street in his $38,000 Mercedes-Benz convertible, jauntily dressed in a blue-and-white striped T-shirt, shorts and boating shoes, Colville cuts a distinctive and popular figure. Invariably cordial and unpretentious, he takes care to wave or talk to certain prickly local characters who would be affronted if he did not. He serves on the local parks and trees committee, and since 1981 he has been chancellor of Acadia University, whose small Ivy Leagueish campus dominates the town. Outside Wolfville, Colville is in great demand as a speaker on the university circuit and he has served on both the Canada Council and on the visiting committee of the National Gallery.

But the flip side of that civic-minded persona is an intensely private man who has little interest in playing the role of a celebrity. His idea of a wonderful evening is a long dinner over wine with his wife at home, followed by some Tchaikovsky on the stereo or Wordsworth read aloud. His newfound wealth has allowed him to indulge his boyish enthusiasm for beautiful machines and what he describes as his narcissistic love of clothes: custom-made British suits, cashmere sweaters and dapper hats. But friends and family say financial security has changed him little. He spends his days much as he always has, rising at 7 a.m. to walk his beloved dog, Dinah. Most mornings are spent in his spare, white-walled studio, where the sun floods in through the skylight over the high table at which he works.

Maintaining what Colville calls the "state of grace" necessary for him to work involves saying no to many of the demands on his time—social invitations, such as the recent lieutenant governor's garden party in Halifax, or such burdensome tasks as serving on the Applebaum-Hébert cultural committee, a job from which he resigned after one year. Above all, it means saving part of his soul from the prying eyes of the public. Even his friend of 30 years George Thomson, with whom he enjoys long, rambling discussions about art, literature and philosophy, knows that it is futile to probe too deeply into areas such as the dark side of Colville's paintings. Typically, the artist avoids such questions with a kind of Oriental politeness, diverting the topic with one of his eloquent and entertaining free-form monologues. Says Thomson: "Even now I feel I do not know him well. There is something there, something firmly under control, that he does not show."

Colville's burning desire to keep on painting grows out of that unfathomable core. He notes that the Renaissance painter Titian was thought to have painted his masterpiece *Death of Acteon* in his 90s, and Colville himself hopes to have 30 years of work ahead of him. Although he claims not to believe in an afterlife, he clearly has faith in the immortality of his art. Even if he never enters the pantheon of artists hanging in the Louvre, in his own mind he has reached the goal he set for himself long ago. Sitting serenely in the Art Gallery of Ontario as his paintings were being assembled around him, Colville expressed supreme confidence in history's verdict. "I was never trying to be an A.Y. Jackson, but rather a Vermeer, a Manet or a Piero della Francesca," he said. "I always thought I was in that league." As Canadians come face to face with Colville's lifetime achievement, it will be clear that they have a master in their midst.

Alex Colville continues to paint in Wolfville, N.S., where he still lives with his wife. His works are held in galleries around the world including the Museum of Modern Art in New York City, the National Gallery of Canada and the Art Gallery of Ontario.

Gillian MacKay was a section editor and senior writer at Maclean's *from 1980 to 1984. Later, she wrote a visual arts column for* The Globe and Mail *and now is a contributing editor at* Canadian Art.

Margaret Atwood's Triumph

Margaret Atwood at her Toronto home, 1999

By Judith Timson

OCTOBER 3, 1988. In Margaret Atwood's personally revealing new novel, *Cat's Eye*, the protagonist is Elaine Risley, a middle-aged artist who has become a minor celebrity, especially revered by feminists. Early on in the book, she struggles to come to terms with her fame in a way that Margaret Atwood herself no longer needs to. On a downtown Toronto street, Elaine encounters a poster advertising a retrospective of her work. On the poster is a picture of her face. On her face, someone has drawn a moustache. The artist considers the moustache, first with mild alarm ("Is it just doodling or is it political commentary, an act of aggression?"); next with humour ("That looks sort of good"). Finally, she feels a sense of wonder that she has achieved "a public face. A face worth defacing. This is an accomplishment. I have made something of myself, something or other, after all." In Margaret Atwood's own life, that ironic something or other is called literary stardom.

Now middle-aged herself, the 48-year-old Atwood is orbiting in a galaxy all her own. As a poet, novelist and critic, she has long been a major cultural force in Canada, turning out volumes of wounding, intimate poetry, best-selling novels that offer a laconic, hard-edged framing of contemporary life, and hard-hitting literary and social criticism. But with the publication three years ago of her sixth novel, *The Handmaid's Tale*, a compelling fable about the lives of women in a futuristic, Christian fundamentalist society, she also became an international literary celebrity, the most prominent in a growing number of Canadian writers whose work is now recognized—and sold in ever-increasing volumes—abroad.

Her work has been translated into more than 20 languages and has been published in more than 25 countries. There is even a five-year-old Margaret Atwood Society in the United States that keeps academics busy analysing her writing. In Britain, "she is by far the best-known of Canadian writers," said eminent British novelist and critic Margaret Drabble, editor of *The Oxford Companion to English Literature*. "She has a very bold intellect—she's a strong writer with a strong voice."

In a country hungry for stars, Atwood—since the 1969 publication of her first novel, *The Edible Woman*—has always been more than just a writer. Like a ventriloquist with his dummy, the private "Peggy" Atwood has carried around a public persona named Margaret, characterized in small literary journals as Medusa with snakes in her hair and metamorphosed into an unnaturally glossy cover girl for women's magazines. Along with the extraordinary attention, there has been criticism of both her high media profile and, more importantly, her work. "There was a lot of 'prove it to me' stuff, 'prove you're a good writer,'" she said in a recent interview. On the eve of the publication of her seventh novel, it is criticism that she feels she no longer has to worry about or counter. "There's no longer any answering chord in me," she said. Her confidence and her serenity, says her British publisher, Liz Calder, even her "courage" in putting out a new novel that is deeply personal and that may well surprise her own feminist fans, are attributable to the publication of *The Handmaid's Tale*.

Until then, a common criticism of Atwood was that she was a finer poet than she was a novelist. Some critics said that her novels, from *The Edible Woman* to *Bodily Harm*, had a flatness of tone and smallness of scale that somehow trivialized her powerful voice. It was a voice that seemed to leap out of her poetry, whether it was about love ("you fit into me/like a hook into an eye/a fish hook/an open eye") or global inhumanity ("The facts of this world seen clearly/are seen through tears;/why tell me then/there is something wrong with my eyes?").

But there has been little dispute about the fact that Atwood came of literary age with *The Handmaid's Tale* and found a way to blend her lyrical talents as a poet with the art of storytelling. The book became an instant best-seller in Canada and won the 1986 Governor General's Award, which Atwood had last received 20 years earlier for her book of poetry *The Circle Game*. In the United States, *The Handmaid's Tale* sold a million copies in paperback and remained on the best-seller list for 23 weeks, widely praised by major American writers. In Britain, it was short-listed for the prestigious Booker Prize; in France, it was nominated for the Ritz-Paris Hemingway Prize. In Canada, any new Atwood novel is a major literary event. However, her publisher, Douglas Gibson, the newly appointed head of McClelland and Stewart, says that he was astonished last month by the 30,000 advance orders placed by booksellers for a text they had not seen. "These are extraordinary figures," he said. "She is clearly in a class by herself."

Even Atwood, in recounting that the Book-of-the-Month Club had chosen *Cat's Eye* as its main selection in Canada and the United States, seemed a little surprised. "I had thought of it as a more personal, unpretentious book but it's already very big," she said.

Sitting in the solarium of her large, century-old Victorian home in downtown Toronto, Atwood was recently beginning a series of promotional interviews for *Cat's Eye*—"stepping into the media Mixmaster," as she put it. While her latest heroine is obsessed with the physical ravages of middle age, Atwood seems to be holding up well: she is physically striking, with luminous skin and penetrating blue eyes. Dressed in watercolour pales, with a scarf wrapped around her neck, she was nursing a sore throat. And she seemed more concerned about the possibility of bad germs floating in the air than with what the critical reception would be to a book that is as radical a departure from *Handmaid's Tale* as *Handmaid's Tale* was from her previous works. "Come what may, I'm past caring," she said. "It was important for me to write this book."

In *Cat's Eye*, Elaine Risley returns to Toronto, a city she loathes, from Vancouver, where she is happily ensconced in her second marriage. The occasion is a retrospective of her work. At the same time, she conducts her own personal retrospective of her childhood. Atwood's vision of girlhood is anything but sugar and spice. The book is filled with examples of the treacherousness and duplicity of little girls, the emotional cruelty and betrayals that best friends practise on one-another.

The book is grim, at times funny and, while offering none of the lyricism found in *The Handmaid's Tale*, does leave some memorable if grisly images. Beset by anxiety, the young heroine sits in bed every night and secretly peels the skin off her feet. "I would begin with the big toes," Elaine says. "I would pull the skin off in narrow strips . . . down as far as the blood."

The image has a graphic air of reality to it. There once was a time when Atwood would visibly bristle at the suggestion of a strong autobiographical streak in her work, as if that insulted her talent as a fiction writer. Even now she says people who assume that what a writer writes results from some pivotal childhood experience are going to have trouble with her. "I'm more Dickensian," she maintained. "I go out and view slums and I then write about slums." There is a streak of the journalist in her. "I like to get the facts right," she said, "which in this case meant spending days determining whether there was tinfoil in the 1940s. There was, but it isn't the kind they use today."

But now she readily admits that there are many similarities between what happens in *Cat's Eye* and the way she grew up—although she draws the line at the foot-peeling. Like Elaine, she too had an entomologist father, Carl Atwood, who was given to quirky dinner-table monologues about the future of the human species. She too grew up in Toronto after spending her early childhood in the bush. She too had a mother, Margaret, who was more interested in being a free spirit—who ice-skated and wore men's shirts—than in being a 1940s-style housewife. And while she retains the disclaimer that the book, while reading like an autobiography, is fiction—even adding at the front of the novel that the opinions expressed are those of the characters and not the author—she is clearly more forgiving of people who blur the distinction, even people who should know better. Her paperback publisher, Anna Porter, called her after reading the book. Said Atwood: "She told me it had left her in tears. She said to me, 'But I always thought you were happy!'"

Because of her heroines, because of her themes, because of her ironic detachment when she looks at the foibles of men and women, Atwood has always enjoyed the feminist seal of approval. In an often-quoted phrase, Germaine Greer once referred to her as one of the most important voices writing in English. Yet *Cat's Eye* is very explicit about the potential women and girls have for cruelty, especially to each other. At least one of her publishers says that it is a little "nerve-racking" to contemplate how the feminist writing community will react to the book. Not Atwood. "I wanted to deal with the idea that women somehow are more morally wonderful than men," she said. "There is no gene for moral wonderfulness. To buy into that is to be back in the 19th century."

Atwood credits her newfound sense of serenity—or perhaps the word is immunity—in the face of criticism to the tremendous success of *The Handmaid's Tale*. "It was a hard, hard book to write," Atwood recalled, "and by that I don't mean it caused me pain, but that it was tricky." She succeeded—and now, she said: "I don't even feel a twinge of having to prove myself. If somebody thinks I have to, they are instantly dismissed. They're just jerks."

Most of the "jerks," in her estimation, are from her own country. But, after promoting *The Handmaid's Tale* in the United States in 1985 and 1986, she admitted that she has come to find the Canadian skepticism toward the success of one of their own "rather bracing." She said, "Instant fame in the United States can ruin you." Being well-known interests her in a practical sense—"It means I have more clout"—and also places her in more intellectually challenging situations. "Fame is when it's you who gets asked to write the introduction to one of the *Paris Review* series of interviews with famous writers," she observed. The volume that she will introduce is one dealing exclusively with women writers. Atwood will herself be interviewed in it, by American writer Mary Morris.

Fame is also the Margaret Atwood Society, a group of about 100 academics and Atwoodophiles who exchange information about her work and report on her whereabouts. Kathryn VanSpanckeren, an

English professor at Florida's University of Tampa and president of the society, first became aware of Atwood in the 1960s, when they were both young poets studying English at Harvard. "I read her poetry and I loved it," VanSpanckeren said. "I thought, who is this woman?" By the mid-1970s, VanSpanckeren was urging her own students and colleagues to pay attention to the name Margaret Atwood. Said VanSpanckeren: "I told them she would be the most important woman writer of the next 20 years."

Although her new novel digs deeply into her own life, Atwood is still a writer who maintains that the traditional function of the novelist is to "bear witness and not to bare one's soul." Sometimes, Atwood admits, she tires of the significance, real or imagined, that people attach to her work. "I can't wait until I'm old and gaga and they wheel me into parties just to give them a little tone," she said. But she instantly contradicted herself: "I take that back. If you're not annoying somebody, you're not really alive."

American writer John Irving has said that he appreciates Atwood's "anger as a writer." He added: "She has an interest in who gets hurt, who gets abused. She seems motivated to call attention to people who are in some kind of jeopardy." It has been a compulsion in her writing and it is even more of a compulsion in her life. Indeed, Atwood's causes and concerns are of so broad a nature, says her former publisher and longtime friend Adrienne Clarkson, that "whenever I get a call from her, I never know what it's going to be about."

She has always received high marks as a hardworking member of both the feminist and the writing communities. In the 1970s and early 1980s, she was very active in the Writers Union of Canada and was also a high-profile member of Amnesty International, a London-based organization fighting to free political prisoners around the world. Recently, she has channelled a lot of her energy into PEN International, the global organization committed to the civil and human rights of writers and to freeing those who are imprisoned. Closer to home, she has lobbied against free trade. At first, she declared that there was not enough information available about the deal. Then, she came to the conclusion that it threatened Canadian culture. Last summer, she went to Ottawa along with

Karen Kain and Timothy Findley to press the Mulroney government to increase funding for the Canada Council. Young artists
especially were suffering because of cutbacks, she said. She has also
gone to the provincial legislature to try to convince the Liberal
government to save the Temagami wilderness area in Northern
Ontario. Now, she says, the cause that she feels most strongly about
is the environment: "I think the decisions that are made in the next
10 years are going to determine whether we survive as a species.
The cockroaches are all right. They'll do fine, but human life I'm
not sure about."

Unafraid to use her influence, she recently picked up the phone
and convinced an editor at one of the country's major newspapers to
do a series on the environment, enticing the editor on two levels.
"First I said, 'Let's have lunch,'" Atwood recalled. "Then, I offered
to write something for them about the issue."

There is, on her part, grudging acceptance of the demands that
that kind of activism imposes on her time. "It's a pain in the bum,"
she said. Yet her friends and colleagues say that they are in awe of
her perseverance. "I don't know where she finds the strength to do
all this, to go on," said Clarkson, who has known Atwood since they
were both at the University of Toronto. "She is not a strong woman,
physically. So where does it come from?"

Atwood's close friends say that her family life sustains her. A few
years ago, she wrote an article confessing that when she graduated
from the University of Toronto in the early 1960s, intent on becoming a writer, she assumed that she would have to live in a garret and
forgo the dream of having a family or the kind of close relationship
that her parents had—which included raking up leaves together in
the backyard. A washing machine was also ruled out: "Sartre,
Samuel Beckett, Kafka and Ionesco, I was sure, did not have major
appliances," she wrote, "and these were the writers I most admired."

But she seems to have acquired exactly that. After an unhappy
marriage that ended in divorce, she has lived with novelist Graeme
Gibson for 18 years. They have a 12-year-old daughter, Jess, whom
Atwood proudly describes as "very glam." Their spacious, beautifully furnished house offers them privacy and at least one office

apiece. It is the home of someone who has done very well financially. The standard Atwood answer to any and all questions about her financial affairs is a curt "NOYB—that means none of your business."

Atwood is very much an involved mother. She curtailed touring to promote her books when her daughter reached school age. Instead, she flies back to Toronto between visits to other cities. The coming and going is exhausting, Atwood said. But that style of travel fits in with her priorities—family, writing and the environment. Her days consist primarily of writing, attending to the business of being a writer and dealing with her daughter's needs. "There are endless conversations on the phone with other mothers," she said. "They never had sleep-overs in my day." Atwood wrote that she now lives a life "that is pretty close to the leaves-in-the-backyard model I thought would be out-of-bounds forever. I bake (dare I admit it) chocolate-chip cookies and I find that doing the laundry with the aid of my washer-dryer is one of the more relaxing parts of my week."

While she and Gibson work very separately as writers, they operate very much as a team where their social interests are concerned. This year, Gibson assumed chairmanship of the Canadian English-speaking PEN chapter. And they have both been active in inviting international experts on the environment to visit Canada. Recently, she was trying to line up a dinner party for a person she described as "the bat man from Cuba"—a scientist who she said is the world's leading expert on bat ecology. And it was not just a dinner—"He's staying with us for two weeks."

In a little more than a year, Margaret Atwood will be 50 and, like the character she created in *Cat's Eye*, she has been thinking a lot about being middle-aged. The deaths of three of her writing colleagues—Marian Engel, Margaret Laurence and Gwendolyn MacEwen—over the past few years have left her with a feeling of "being all alone," she said. "None of them should have died when they did. They should have been with me."

The loss of those friends has cast a shadow on what otherwise has been, for Atwood, a time of strength and affirmation. "When I think of how tensed up and fraught one is at 30," she said, "or even in your

20s—you know what you want to be but you don't know whether you can do it or not. Now the question is, can you do it again?" As Margaret Atwood herself says, "That's not quite so horrible."

Margaret Atwood continues to accumulate international acclaim while living and writing in Toronto. The Blind Assassin, *her 10th novel, won the 2000 Booker Prize, while* Alias Grace *won the Giller Prize in 1996.*

Judith Timson worked for Maclean's *from 1975 to 1979 as Vancouver bureau chief and as a senior writer. Now a Toronto-based freelance writer and critic, she has written a regular column for* Chatelaine *since 1991.*

Peter Gzowski's Last Stand

Peter Gzowski in his Toronto studio, 1996

NOVEMBER 18, 1996. On a wet, grey Saturday morning, the host of CBC Radio's *Morningside* is leaning over the kitchen counter of his home north of Toronto, near Lake Simcoe. His feet are bare. He is wearing a green sweatshirt from Fogo Island, Nfld., and pants of an approximate match. This pyjama-like ensemble would give the impression that he just got out of bed, were it not for the fact that Peter Gzowski—with his disarray of grey hair and castaway beard—almost always looks like he just got out of bed.

His voice has been described a hundred ways: warm, honey-dipped, smoke-roughened, friendly, rumpled, natural. It is as familiar in its unravelling hesitations and as Canadian in its unfashionably courteous curiosity as an old hand-knit sweater. But on this rainy Saturday morning it is muffled by the same trace of sadness that attends his famously hangdog expression and the oddly modest, oddly egocentric shuffle with which he passes through the corridors of the Canadian Broadcasting Centre in downtown Toronto.

At the nearby dining table, Gillian Howard, his companion of 15 years, sits reading the newspaper. Timothy Findley's new book, *You Went Away*, is open in front of Gzowski. The coffee is there. So are the Rothmans Lights—a presence that angers him as much as it concerns his family and friends. Gzowski, at 62, is still living in the shadow of the aortic embolism that stopped him in his lumbering tracks for 12 weeks of recovery from vascular surgery last winter.

The interview—which Gzowski is tolerating with the patient grace of an experienced doctor undergoing a medical examination—is heading towards awkward terrain. It is the "you realize that for many people you represent Canada" line. And he makes it clear that he does not care for it. Whatever other people may say about what he stands for—and almost all conversations about Gzowski these days veer quickly towards what he and *Morningside* symbolize—his own self-assessment is a little more down to earth. He is a journalist. He is a broadcaster. He is a writer. He is a professional—"the hardest-working person I know," says his assistant, Shelley Ambrose. If he is a national institution, if he is a Canadian icon, if he is a symbol of unity—that is not his concern. He is—as he once said to Ian Brown, the host of *Sunday Morning*—someone who simply knows how to "think fast and speak slowly."

Gzowski often seems uncomfortable under the freight with which *Morningside* is burdened by its most ardent fans. One sometimes gets the impression that he inclines towards the view of one of its sharpest critics, author Geoff Pevere. In *Mondo Canuck: A Canadian Pop Culture Odyssey*, Pevere writes, "If *Morningside*, which is listened to by less than 15 per cent of the entire nation each day, is all the glue we've got, we might as well be trying to bind the *Titanic* with Bondfast."

Fifteen per cent of the Canadian population every day is, as dismissals go, not very dismissive. In fact, according to the program's executive producer, Gloria Bishop, *Morningside* reaches one and a half million listeners a week.

Still, Gzowski would probably not argue very strenuously with Pevere. Under normal circumstances, Gzowski would never claim that *Morningside* is the glue. He would say, perhaps, that its three hours of nationally broadcast interviews, panel discussions, music and drama every weekday morning (with a one-hour repeat of highlights every evening) manage to show Canadians something of the glue that is already there.

But these are not normal circumstances. Gzowski describes the 28-per-cent cut to CBC Radio's programming budget as announced two months ago by CBC president Perrin Beatty as "heart-wrenching." In this anxious environment, Gzowski can almost—almost—be drawn into the kind of discussion that he prefers to avoid. "This might be a time for renewal and rebirth," he says. "It might be a time for a shake-up. But nobody's thinking that way. There's nobody—nobody—up there with that kind of vision. We are adrift. Management's reaction to the financial crunch is simply to cut everywhere, and I'm afraid they're going to end up with 60 per cent of everything, instead of 100 per cent of something."

The parallels are too obvious not to point out. "You could be talking about Canada," I say. Gzowski looks at me with the quizzical squint with which he sometimes peers through the glass of the *Morningside* studio. "That's not a question," he grumbles—quite a criticism, coming from someone who sometimes formulates his discursive interrogatives the way a beaver patches together a lodge. But then, turning it into a question, he addresses it anyway. "I could be talking about Canada?" He shrugs the sad, resigned shrug he uses when people tell him he should stop smoking. He says: "I know."

Gzowski's family history usually begins with a flourish. "A swash-buckling engineer-nobleman-lawyer," wrote Peter Gzowski of his great-great-grandfather, Sir Casimir Gzowski, in one of the many articles he wrote for *Maclean's* in the late 1950s and early 1960s, "exiled from his native Poland for his part in a revolution in which he fought against his father. He was knighted by Queen Victoria and was appointed her colonial aide-de-camp; Sir John A. Macdonald was among his closest personal friends."

So top-drawer a heritage often surprises listeners who take the Polish name and the Prairie-sounding unfussiness of the voice as evidence of a more contentedly ordinary, rural background. But Gzowski's upbringing was not particularly rural. And it certainly was not contented. He was born in Toronto in 1934—the only child of a brief and unhappy marriage. His surname notwithstanding, he was, and more or less remains, a de facto WASP. His knowledge of Polish is even less than his famously minimal knowledge of French.

He became Peter Brown when his young, divorced mother moved to the Ontario town of Galt and remarried. But Peter Brown—shy, acne-pocked and even more miserable than a teenage boy is supposed to be—became Peter Gzowski again when his grandfather, Lt.-Col. H. N. Gzowski, footed the bill for Grade 12 and 13 at one of Canada's most prestigiously blue-blooded boarding schools, Ridley College in St. Catharines.

Listeners who enjoy Gzowski's common touch might imagine that the young Peter would have floundered in so highly disciplined and traditional an environment. In fact, he flourished. He graduated with scholarships to the University of Toronto. And if the spit shines and grey flannels were jettisoned almost immediately, the confidence that he developed on the windswept playing fields and in the drafty study halls of Ridley College has never left him. At university, Gzowski set his sights on a career in journalism. The *Timmins Daily Press*, the *Toronto Telegram*, *The Toronto Star*, the University of Toronto *Varsity*—all would bear Gzowski's frequently misspelled byline by 1957, the year he moved to Moose Jaw to become the city editor of the *Times-Herald*.

In Moose Jaw he married Jenny Lissaman—five-foot-two, a redhead, an interior designer. The marriage produced five children (all of whom Gzowski claims now as "friends" as well as offspring), but ended in divorce in 1978. Peter Gzowski, seated at the dining room table of the tranquil, somewhat anonymous downtown Toronto condominium where he and Gill Howard share what weekday hours he is not in a radio studio and she is not at work as head of public affairs for the Ontario Cancer Institute/Princess Margaret Hospital, squirms a little uncomfortably at questions of a personal nature. "Jenny gave up her career as an interior designer," he says, "to be a stay-at-home mother. I was focused on my work."

The internal fault lines of the marriage had begun to show as Peter Gzowski passed from the rank of well-known journalist into the realm of media star. The laid-back congeniality that listeners know is, in many ways, the creation of a driven personality. The easiest person to listen to, clearly, is not the easiest person to live with. The separation coincided with the nosedive of Gzowski's two-season foray into television as the host of *90 Minutes Live*. "So who's the villain?" asked Gzowski, as he looked out from his condominium to the bleak prospect of a wind-blown Lake Ontario and reflected on a marriage that failed long ago. "I was the one who was always downtown. I was the one working late." (The one, as more than a few of his friends and former colleagues have pointed out, who was putting in the smoky last-calls with fellow writers at the roof bar of Toronto's Park Plaza.) "So, the villain? Me. But to some extent it was the times."

In a cloud of Buckingham cigarette smoke, Gzowski passed through those times—from *The Chatham Daily News* to *Maclean's* to the editor's desk of *The Star Weekly* magazine. In the magazine business, it was clear he was a rising star. It was also clear he was a writer—a writer in the weighty sense used by the magazine that Gzowski then most admired, *The New Yorker*. Gzowski wrote about everything—from a profile of an intellectual Montrealer named Pierre Trudeau (1962), to an essay about why a young singer named Bob Dylan was important (1966). Says John Macfarlane, editor of *Toronto Life*: "I remember the awe in which I held him, even then. He had turned *The Star Weekly* into the most exciting magazine the country had ever seen, and he surrounded himself with wonderful writers—people like Sylvia Fraser, Jack Batten, David Lewis Stein. And Gzowski himself had this conversational way of writing—a style that was new and fresh and intimate. A lot of traditional magazine writers kept their distance from their readers in those days. But Gzowski was there."

He was there, in the tightly structured stories that are, to this day, the basis for the way he likes to construct interviews—interviews that, revealingly, he calls "pieces," the magazine writer's term for stories. "A typical Gzowski question," says Alex Frame, "is 'I want to ask you about this, but first I want to ask you . . .' And that always reveals to me how carefully he has thought things through. Gzowski knows in the first five minutes of an interview where he wants to be in the last five minutes."

The transition from print to radio is often a difficult one. But remarkably, the rhythms, ellipses, repetitions, the direct informality and the ironic points of emphasis that are so familiar to listeners of his *Morningside* bulletins today were there, years before he first approached a microphone. This style did not come easily; it still doesn't. He does not toss his pieces off—a fact to which thousands of overflowing, desk-top ashtrays and a million half-drunk cups of coffee have eloquently attested. But he has moved from print to radio and—by way of several books, his long-running column in *Canadian Living* magazine and the occasional "piece" elsewhere— back again to print without much altering his essential, immediately recognizable voice. "The key to Gzowski's success on radio," says Macfarlane, "was that he wasn't a radio guy. He was a magazine guy without a magazine."

The Star Weekly was killed in 1968. In 1969, he returned to *Maclean's*—this time as editor. It was, in his words, "a forlorn and futile attempt to go home again." He resigned nine months later. And Gzowski might have languished, a dimming star in the low-ceilinged freelance firmament, were it not for Frame, then a long-haired, bespectacled CBC radio producer with an eccentric idea for a radio program that became, in 1971, *This Country in the Morning*. The freewheeling program enjoyed not only the youthful vigor of its creators (Gzowski, at 38, was the oldest member of the program's 14-person staff; Frame was 29), it also had the eager support of a management desperate to revive a moribund radio network. And it managed to catch, within its very Canadian context, the zeitgeist of the times. Journalist Robert Fulford remembers that it was a hit "right away. There was nothing like it on air. It was the best radio there was in the country. It may even have been the best Canadian radio ever."

This Country in the Morning made the assumption—an assumption that *Morningside* continues—that Canadian subjects are inherently interesting to Canadians. Remarkably enough, this quirky programming directive reverberated successfully throughout the culture at large. The program hit its stride at the same time that Canadian nationalism was emerging as a real force. John Diefenbaker, Lester Pearson, Pierre Trudeau, Margaret Atwood, Robertson Davies, Irving Layton—these were people Canadians wanted to learn more about. And they did not want to be lectured to about them, or sermonized by them. They wanted to chat with them. *This Country in the Morning* became the perfect place to hear what they had to say.

This Country in the Morning travelled frequently—a portability that was extremely costly but that greatly enhanced its reputation as a national glue. This, along with the national book tours that have attended the publication of Gzowski's books (*Spring Tonic, The Sacrament, The Game of Our Lives, An Unbroken Line* and *The Morningside Papers*), helped turn him into the rarest of creatures: a genuine Canadian celebrity. This pan-Canadian stature—not exactly welcomed by a man who cherishes his privacy—has been put to good use. In 1986, he founded the Peter Gzowski Invitational Golf Tournaments for Literacy—now called the PGI—and has in the past decade raised almost $5 million for literacy across the country.

This Country in the Morning went off the air—to use a favourite Gzowski simile—like Ted Williams, not like Willie Mays. The legendary Williams hit a homer in his last at-bat; Mays, who made the most famous catch in baseball history, lumbered around in the outfield long past his prime. After only three seasons, *This Country* hung up its cleats, still at the peak of its game.

The youthful adventure of the program depended on a spirit of optimism that, in the corridors of the new broadcast centre, is in very short supply. Gzowski's frequent criticism of the new CBC building in Toronto, for instance, is far more bitter than the good-natured grumbles that always attended the decrepit old Jarvis Street headquarters. His comments are made within the context of a very anxious present. Tears are by no means uncommon these days in the CBC building. Anxiety is as high as morale is low—a disastrously counterproductive mind-set that comes at the very moment in its history when the CBC should be looking to what creative resources it has left for its future. Says one *Morningside* producer: "There is no leadership. No vision. There isn't even the courtesy of the greeting of the troops."

On his way to the smoking room, Gzowski grimaces at his gleaming, soulless surroundings. He says: "The thing about this building . . ." Then, as if overwhelmed by what the building represents, he stops in mid-sentence. He casts a baleful eye over the vaulted atrium—a vast emptiness that, had things worked out differently, might have been something more modest, something more ingenious, something more meaningful, something more full of promise, something more inclusive. A better vision might have prevailed. But it didn't. A big mistake was made, and now there is nothing anyone can do about it. The parallels between the building and the CBC itself seem too clear to leave unstated.

Morningside makes the assumption that listeners in Newfoundland want to know something about issues in Saskatchewan. But beyond that, *Morningside* approaches its subjects in what is often described as a particularly Canadian way. "*Morningside* gives you a community," says broadcaster and writer Stuart McLean. "It's inclusive. And what it does, in a very Canadian way, is assume a neighbourliness. We're here, all around the table, talking, and it would only be polite to ask and to listen."

And *Morningside* covers ground that commercial radio rarely goes near. Its impact is particularly strong in the literary community. Says Paul Wilson, a *Morningside* producer: "When American publicists book writers for interviews, they're astonished at the kind of national exposure they get on the program." Sharon Budnarchuk, co-owner of Audreys Books in Edmonton, says that while *Morningside*'s children's book panel is always influential, it was Gzowski's interview with Donna Williams, the autistic author of *Nobody Nowhere*, that demonstrated to her what impact the program has: "The phones just rang off the hook."

Still, many more Canadians do not listen to *Morningside* than do. The show's critics do not mince their words. Hell, Pevere once said—on CBC Radio, as a matter of fact—would be having to listen to the best of *Morningside* over and over. But 10 days after my last meeting with Gzowski, I find myself driving the Trans-Canada, in Newfoundland, listening to the program. He is interviewing Elly Danica, the author of *Don't: A Women's Word*, and now *Beyond Don't*. Danica was sexually abused by her father as a child, and when *Don't* came to Gzowski's attention in 1988, he travelled to Saskatchewan to interview her. Danica's courageous and emotional appearance on *Morningside* brought the book to national attention, and the interview remains one of the best he has ever done.

Gzowski has interviewed every prime minister since John Diefenbaker. He has had encounters with everyone from Margaret Thatcher to Robbie Robertson. And yet, when I ask people about memorable Gzowski "pieces," no one mentions the high-profile interviews. They remember the items that could not have appeared anywhere else. One of Alex Frame's fondest memories of *This Country in the Morning* was the letter from Vic Daradick from High Level, Alta., describing an encounter with a wild horse. Listeners recall the free trade debate, the Camp, Kierans and Lewis political panels, or the time that Stuart McLean's "live" cricket turned out to be decidedly dead: for the better part of five on-air minutes, Gzowski and McLean were unable to stop laughing. And when I asked Gzowski about his best interview, he did not—uncharacteristically enough—hesitate. "Elly Danica."

The sweep of Newfoundland forest disappears into the mist on either side of the Trans-Canada. Eight years after his first interview with her, Gzowski forms his questions to Elly Danica gently but persistently. I realize that this—the vast landscape, the familiar voice, the unhurried curiosity—is a quintessentially Canadian experience. This is the kind of observation—the sort of non-question—that infuriates *Morningside*'s critics as much as it makes Gzowski uncomfortable. Still, as I drive, I recall something Ian Brown said to me: "You know, for some reason in this country we try to resist the notion of things being momentous. But when Gzowski leaves *Morningside* it will be momentous. It's hard not to think it will represent the end of something. An end of a particular phase at the CBC. The end of a certain conception of nationalism. The end of something in Canada. The instinct to connect the departure of Peter Gzowski to these kinds of momentous conclusions is very, very strong."

Morningside went off the air in 1997, but Peter Gzowski continues to write and broadcast. In 1997, he became the only Canadian singled out in New York City for a Peabody Award for his outstanding contribution to broadcasting.

Freelance writer and novelist David Macfarlane has won 11 National Magazine Awards and has a weekly arts column in The Globe and Mail.

ROGUES, ROYALS, HEROES AND HEROINES

Mrs. Nellie McClung

Nellie McClung, 1929

By May L. Armitage

JULY, 1915. When *Sowing Seeds in Danny* appeared in 1908, Mrs. Nellie McClung, 42, made her first inroads into the affections of the Canadian people. *The Second "Chance"* appeared two years later, and was an even greater success than the first book judging by the number of editions it went into. *The Black Creek Stopping House*, a book of short stories came next in 1912, and by this time Mrs. McClung had made her *début*, not only as a writer, but also as a public speaker, and the West was beginning to keep a jealous eye on the movements of this talented woman; for to the West she belongs.

She has kept the name Nellie, "because," she says, "I have always been called that, and why should I change it? My old friends would not know me!" which is exactly typical of Mrs. McClung. Little Nellie, born at Chatsworth, Ont., 1873, was a fearless, whole-souled, genuine child and the woman has kept all these characteristics which so often fly with childhood.

In 1880, the family moved West going by train part of the way, and crossing the Red River to their home in Manitoba in a rowboat, one dark rainy night in May. The Indians were everywhere, so Nellie, then about seven years old, had a real taste of pioneering. She liked it though; hear what she says, in some reminiscences.

"I played with a nice, fat, greasy, little fellow called Indian Tommy, whose mother fought intermittently with a lady friend of hers for three days on the river bank. I attended all the sessions, and all would have been well only, in the excess of my delight over Indian Tommy's mother's victory, I came home hilarious. After that I stayed in my own yard. Indian Tommy looked in through the gate, and brought me beads and gum—almost as good as new—and we were very miserable."

For three long happy years the little girl ran wild on the prairie, accompanied by her faithful dog. There were no schools in that district, and Nellie had no desire for "book-learning." Her mother and sisters were in despair of ever teaching her anything, but she was having too good a time to care.

"One day," she says, "a neighbor arrived bringing her little boy, also 10 years old. He had been at school in England, could read, tell the capitals of England, Ireland and Scotland, and other wonderful things. His mother had him recite: then everybody proceeded to rub it into little Nellie. I bore it all with sullen indifference, but my heart was hot for battle. Pretty soon he and I were sent out to play. When he came in again—which was soon and hurriedly—his nose was bleeding."

A school opened near them shortly after this, though, and Nellie attended in fear and trembling; she was afraid the teacher would dub her a dunce. On the contrary, he understood her at once, and so kindled her ambition and industry that in five years she had taken her second-class certificate. It is like Mrs. McClung to treasure a great debt of gratitude to this teacher, Mr. Frank Schultz, of Baldur. She has never forgotten the inspiration he was to her—a little ignorant child. And whatever she has accomplished, she lays tribute at his door.

Mrs. McClung attended Normal and collegiate in Winnipeg, was a successful teacher in two or three schools, and married in 1896, living first in Manitou, Man., and then in Winnipeg. This prairie-bred girl had dreams of writing. Her first attempts—at a very tender age—by her own confession were epitaphs for dead dogs and kittens. She says, too, that fiction was her line; she never spoiled a good story for facts, for Silvie Moggie was shaken to death by the dog Phillip rather than killed in the tragic manner outlined. But she had to make it rhyme, so—

Here lies dear little Silvie Moggie,
Silvie died—oh, far too young,
From a bite from Phillip Sutcliffe,
Phillip bit her on the tongue.

It was about two years ago that Mrs. McClung first entered the field as a public speaker. She went on the platform in Manitoba in opposition to the Sir Rodmond Roblin's Conservative government and for prohibition and equal franchise. During the election campaign she spoke as often as 60 times in two months, sometimes as often as three times a day. The campaign was a whirlwind. Mrs. McClung's name was on every lip; the papers even featured her as Manitoba's prospective woman premier. When the Roblin government was returned, its majority was reduced from an overwhelming one to a mere skin-of-the-teeth affair. Aside from *Sowing Seeds in Danny*, this woman had sowed enough seed in the province of Manitoba to make suffrage and the liquor traffic real and vital issues, which will be fought to a finish in the near future.

Mrs. McClung has the courage of her convictions; you know that the moment she mounts the platform and begins speaking. She speaks to *you*. This is her charm. Time, place, audience and conventionalities all fade away; and there is no one but you and Nellie McClung speaking of things you should have known long ago, but did not. She does not talk at you, through you, around you or above you, but to you, and the "sweet reasonableness" of it all sinks into your very soul.

As she reveals her tenderness towards mankind between the lines of her wonderful stories, as she makes her readers laugh and cry with "Pearlie" and "Danny," so she sways her listeners when she speaks, not by any flights of rhetoric or fancy, but by giving herself to them frankly and freely. "Studied" is the one word you can never connect with Mrs. McClung; her talks are as natural as her movements and, when she flings wide her arms and assails you with some sweeping argument, there is only one answer—the one she wants.

The family lately moved from Winnipeg to Edmonton to live, and naturally Mrs. McClung was at once made welcome by the Alberta Equal Franchise League, of which she is vice-president.

The Woman's Christian Temperance Union also claimed her support, and the invitations she had to speak last winter would have swamped a cabinet minister; she has a drawer full of them which she could not accept. She is indefatigable though and has filled as many engagements as possible, both in Edmonton and through the province.

On February 26 she headed the largest delegation that was ever assembled on the floor of the Alberta Legislature to lay before the members of the House the Equal Suffrage petition. Halls, galleries, antechambers were all packed, and surely the stately building never rang with such applause as when Mrs. McClung arose to address the House. Even the Premier had to smile when she began with a characteristic straight-to-the-point-attack.

"You will not tell me politics are too corrupt for women," were her first words and, when the members of the Legislature had regained their gravity, for they saw where her argument led, she continued:

"And men tell us too, with a fine air of chivalry, that women should not be given the vote, because women don't want it, the inference being that women get nothing unless they want it: Women get a lot of things they don't want—the war, the liquor traffic, the lower pay for equal work. Surely you would not want the irresponsible women to set the pace for the rest of us? Surely no irresponsible woman has any right to force her votelessness on us!"

In her concluding remarks, Mrs. McClung spoke of the pioneer women, some of whom had paid the price of colonization with their lives. "On behalf," she said, "of these noble women whose daughters we are, and whose heroic blood throbs in our hearts, recognize us as citizens, and say by your actions that your confidence in us is as great as your confidence in the least intelligent lad of 21!"

The Franchise League was pleased with the reception the petition had in the House. They had a courteous and attentive hearing, for, as Mrs. McClung remarked afterwards, women suffrage had ceased to be a joke. "If the women of England had been allowed to speak as we were on this occasion," she said, "if they had been given a hearing there probably would never have been windows smashed. Our men, I believe, try to be fair, but prejudice is hard to uproot. We are out to win. Women suffrage is inevitable, and it is a wise man who cheerfully accepts the inevitable."

Mrs. McClung never misses the funny side either. "I wish you could see the proportion of my mail," she laughed, "that tells me to go home and darn my husband's socks. I never would have believed that one man's hosiery could excite the amount of interest those socks do—and yet, do you know, they are always darned!"

Of course they are; the McClung home is the happiest place in the world, and the four sons and one daughter who are proud to call Mrs. McClung "Mother," are the apple of her eye. Her home-made bread has made more converts to suffrage than all the speeches she ever made, she thinks, for men seem to regard it as wonderful that she can give them a good square meal as well as do so many other things.

It was not, in fact, till her children were growing up that Mrs. McClung began to take a vital interest in public affairs. She had four sons, and not one of them to spare to the liquor traffic; she had a daughter, and wished that she might have woman's widest privileges. And so she was able to find time from her home duties to become a keen advocate of reform.

She finds time too, to write a thousand words a day as a rule, and a new book is now nearly ready for the publishers.

Eight months after this article appeared, Manitoba became the first province in Canada, on January 29, 1916, to give women the right to vote and run for public office. Alberta followed suit a year later. Nellie McClung helped win another milestone for women's rights as one of the Famous Five who, in the Persons Case, secured a 1929 judicial decision that declared the word "persons" in the British North America Act, 1867, included women.

Nellie McClung, who wrote 16 books before dying at age 77 in 1951, served one term as a Liberal opposition member in the Alberta legislature during the 1920s and was the first woman member of the CBC *Board of Broadcast Governors.*

Billy Bishop:
The Allies' Greatest Ace

Billy Bishop in France, 1917

By Major George A. Drew

JANUARY 15, 1929. On August 4, 1914, there were 272 aeroplanes available to the British army and of these less than 100 were fit for military service: at the time of the Armistice, after thousands had been destroyed, worn out or become obsolete, there were 22,171, all of them infinitely more powerful, faster and reliable than the best of those in use at the beginning of the war. In August, 1914, there were less than 250 officers in this new service; in November, 1918, there were more than 30,000. During the period of this phenomenal expansion the British air forces accounted for more than 8,000 enemy machines; destroyed nearly 300 enemy balloons; fought more than 50,000 fights in the air; fired more than 12 million rounds of machine-gun ammunition at enemy targets on the ground; took more than half a million aerial photographs; and in doing all this suffered nearly 18,000 casualties.

In this almost incredible story of British achievement, Canadians played a tremendous part. It is true that it was some time before they joined the Flying Corps in any numbers, due to the apathy of our military authorities toward this new arm of the service, but once their interest was aroused they rushed to the air service in ever-increasing numbers, until by the end of the war one-third of the officers in the Royal Air Force were Canadians. Nor do numbers alone begin to tell the story of Canada's astonishing share in the war in the air. It must also be measured in terms of the accomplishments of the men who served, for strangely enough the service which Canadians were so slow to adopt was the one in which individually they were destined to play their most conspicuous part.

Canada's share, individually and collectively, was out of all proportion to her population. Not long after Canadians really took up flying in earnest, it became apparent that they were at least the equals of any of the airmen in the war. It is interesting to speculate as to why they displayed such an undoubted superiority in this new service. There must be some explanation for the fact that Canada with about one-tenth of the white population of the Empire should have supplied one-third of the pilots in action with the Royal Air Force at the end of the war, and there must also be some explanation for the individual dominance of Canadians among the British fighting pilots. Perhaps the wide horizons of life in Canada, the atmosphere of optimism, the confidence of individual opportunity, and general adaptability to unexpected tastes, born of life in a still undeveloped country, all contributed to the qualities which so peculiarly fitted Canadians for success in this new and incalculably hazardous adventure. Whatever the reasons may have been, the simple fact remains that without any qualification as to population or otherwise Canadians proved the greatest air fighters in the world.

It is unfortunate that so little is known of their remarkable story. Their exploits should be an inspiration to young Canadians for all time because at the height of their glory these men were mere boys, and what Canadian boys did then forever renders unnecessary the need of seeking beyond the borders of Canada for examples of the highest bravery, devotion to duty and self-sacrifice. The reason why so little is known is not hard to find. John Buchan, the British historian, tells us why in a few words: "The Germans and the French made no secret of their heroes, but rather encouraged the advertisement of their names; but the Royal Flying Corps true to its traditions contented itself with a bare recital of the deed, till an occasional Victoria Cross lifted the veil of anonymity." The press reports of British air successes never named the individual engaged.

Opinions differ as to the wisdom of this course, but there is no question about the result. It was not until the *London Gazette* announced in terse official sentences that Captain Albert Ball had destroyed nearly 50 enemy machines that the British public throughout the Empire awoke to the fact that British airmen were the peers of any in the world. Canadians, throughout the war, had no separate unit in the Royal Air Force and Canadians were, therefore, equally ignorant of what their flying men were doing. It was the award of a V.C. which lifted the veil of anonymity from the greatest Canadian pilot.

Canadians read with pride that Captain William Avery Bishop, of Owen Sound, Ont., had been awarded the most coveted decoration for valour in the world, the Victoria Cross, "for most conspicuous bravery, determination and skill." Unknown to most Canadians at home, he had already won the Military Cross and Distinguished Service Order for deeds of great bravery. When he attended at Buckingham Palace late in the summer of 1917 to be invested with these decorations, the King in congratulating him upon his successes said that it was the first time he had been able to give all three to one person. It was only then Canadians realized that in the air their men were gaining the same high reputation for courage and determination which they had already earned at Ypres, the Somme and Vimy.

In the course of time Bishop's record stood beside those of the great British aviators, Ball, McCudden and Mannoch, and finally well above them. As the months of 1918 passed, other Canadians rose to claim a place in this select company. Collishaw, Barker and McLaren were not far behind, and there were many others whose exploits ranked them among the greatest pilots in the war. In spite of such a record there are many who will be surprised to know that the four greatest living war aces in the world are Canadians, and that the combined record of these four Canadians surpasses that of the leading four war pilots, living or dead, of either Germany, or the United States, as well as that of any other four British pilots.

This may be a somewhat startling declaration to many who have absorbed the fabulous tales of aviators of all nations but our own. The correctness of the statement may, however, be readily demonstrated by a comparative illustration showing the four leading aviators and the number of enemy aeroplanes destroyed in each case. British, American and German military authorities all required satisfactory proof of reported victories before official credit was given.

CANADIAN

Bishop	72
Collishaw	60
Barker	50
McLaren	48
	230

GERMAN

Richthofen, Manfred	80
Richthofen, Lothar	40
Boelcke	40
Immelman	18
	178

AMERICAN

Rickenbacker	21
Lufberry	17
Vaughn	12
Springs	12
	62

It must not be forgotten that there were other British pilots such as Ball, McCudden, Mannoch and Rhys-Davies who had a few more or a few less than 50 machines to their credit. With these figures it is not difficult to understand British air supremacy in the closing days of the war.

Among the fighting airmen of the Allied armies Bishop stands supreme. There is no reason for false modesty about it. His official record demonstrates this fact to all the world. It is something to be shouted from the housetops; not whispered quietly among ourselves. Perhaps the reason for our silence has been that Bishop is, fortunately, still very much alive. But surely death is not a condition of our honouring bravery. While Canadians of the post-war generation have been reading of the legendary air heroes of France and Germany—to say nothing of the United States—they know little or nothing of our own.

Bishop's record of 72 victories stands well above that of any other Allied airman. Who is there to question it? Ball, the greatest English pilot was killed by Lothar von Richthofen just after his record had passed the 50 mark. Guynemeyer, the French ace of aces, whose name is engraved on the walls of the Pantheon and in the hearts of most living Frenchmen, met his death when his victories had reached 53. Rickenbacker, the leading American, had 21.

Nor was it in total victories alone that Bishop was their superior. On May 25, 1917, the French ace Guynemeyer destroyed four machines. In the course of a valedictory delivered after the airman's death, Paul Deschanel, afterwards President of France, said: "He surpassed himself and achieved the most memorable of his many victories. He destroyed four of the enemy battle-planes in a single day. This exploit, unique in the annals of military aviation, won for him the officers' cross of the Legion of Honor." Henri Bordeaux in *Guynemeyer, King of the Air*, referring to the same event said: "Could it be possible? Had Guynemeyer really succeeded four times? Four machines brought down in one day by one pilot was what no infantryman, gunner, pioneer, territorial, Annamite or Senegalese had ever seen." Thus did the French regard Guynemeyer's achievement, and yet within a few months Bishop had not only equalled but surpassed this exploit by bringing down five German machines in a single day.

Bishop was far ahead of any American aviator, although his first fight as a pilot came just a few days before the United States declared war. In fact, his individual total of 72 is 10 more than the combined total of the four leading Americans.

Only one man challenged Bishop's record and that was Baron Manfred von Richthofen, the Red Knight of Germany, with 80 victories officially recognized. He was the flower of the German flying corps, the idol of the whole nation and by long odds their greatest ace. Yet without in any way detracting from his record as a great fighter, a sportsman and a gentleman, it is necessary, if the facts are to be understood, to point out the vast difference in the circumstances under which he and Bishop fought. Whereas Richthofen scarcely ever fought alone, Bishop's greatest successes were achieved in solitary flights. Then, too, nearly all of the fighting during the time of Richthofen's and Bishop's activities was carried on well behind the German lines.

This had two important effects. In the first place, there could not fail to be uncertainty at times as to which pilot had fired the fatal shots when a whole squadron attacked a single machine, pouring thousands of bullets from their twin Spandau guns. Where such doubt existed, it was only natural that the leader of the squadron should receive the credit, particularly when he was as famous as Richthofen had become. In the second place, the fact that nearly all the fighting took place behind the German lines had a very important bearing on the results. If a British machine was forced down for any reason during a fight, it had little chance of reaching its own lines. If it landed in German territory it would be counted as a victory for the German officer engaged. A German machine might be forced to land under precisely similar circumstances, but when the fight had been over its own territory it would land well within its own lines. An examination of Richthofen's record shows several machines forced to land but not destroyed which were counted as victories. On the other hand, Bishop forced many German machines to land on their own side. These were not counted as victories.

This situation was not because of caution on Richthofen's part or superior bravery on Bishop's. Each adopted the role best suited to the policy dictated by their respective air forces. The air force had replaced the cavalry as the eyes of the army, and it was the definite policy of the British to keep their eyes over the enemy by maintaining the offensive in the air regardless of losses. The situation in 1917 was well described by Gibbons in *The Red Knight of Germany*.

"The German flyers had all the advantage. Their machines were the latest word in aviation. In speed, they could literally fly circles around their adversaries.

"But in spite of this mechanical superiority, the British with characteristic tenacity, refused to change their offensive policy and continued to carry the war in the air to the enemy's side of the line. Whereas, during the British superiority in the air in 1916 the German air force had been completely swept from the skies, the turning of the tables did not bring the same results in 1917.

"The severity of the British losses broke all existing records; but they were not allowed to interfere with the orders to 'carry on' as usual."

That was the difference. Richthofen fought practically all of his fights over his own territory; Bishop over that of the enemy. Richthofen had decided that close formations were best in fighting off the continuous British air offensive. Bishop was simply "carrying on" his share, and more than his share, in the offensive scheme. There is, perhaps, good reason for suggesting that Bishop was not only the greatest Allied pilot, but also the greatest individual fighting pilot in the war, but there is no occasion to press the point further. Each performed prodigious feats and each deserves full honour. It is sufficient to say that among the millions of fighting men ranged in two great armies each was the leading aviator on the side with which he fought. Surely that is honour enough for any man.

Richthofen was killed on April 21, 1918, by a Canadian, Roy Brown, but Bishop lived. He took fearful chances, never hesitated to accept battle against the greatest odds and yet he was never even wounded. His was, indeed, a charmed life. Day by day Death hovered over him, stretched out its hand with barking Spandaus and crashing high explosives, and then withdrew. Time and time again he found himself in the midst of a whirling maelstrom of enemy machines, in which a greater danger than the flaming bullets was the chance of a collision such as had cost the life of Richthofen's teacher, the great Boelcke. Yet when the "dog fight" cleared away, Bishop's machine, riddled with bullets, would wing its way safely home while a smoking heap of wreckage behind the German lines told the watching armies that the master marksman had won again.

There were several interesting similarities in the stories of Bishop and Richthofen. Both were young men when the war began. Bishop was 20 and Richthofen 22. Both served first in the cavalry, Richthofen as an officer with a Uhlan Regiment, Bishop as an officer with the Mississauga Horse, of Toronto. Both joined the air service as observers before becoming pilots.

Bishop was a cadet of the Royal Military College at Kingston in 1914. Born at Owen Sound on February 8, 1894, he had passed through the ordinary educational routine of a Canadian boy until he entered the Royal Military College. There was nothing in his early life to suggest that he was soon to become one of the world's outstanding airmen. He enlisted and proceeded to England with the Mississauga Horse, where fate, in the form of the British War Office, directed his unit to a particularly muddy training-camp. Mud caused the death of many men during the war. Indirectly, it brought death to more than 100 German airmen because it was mud that persuaded Bishop to join the Flying Corps. Bishop himself has told us the story in *Winged Warfare*:

"We were in England. It had rained for days in torrents, and there was still a drizzle coming down as I set out for a tour of the horse lines.

"Ordinary mud is bad enough, when you have to make your home in it, but the particular brand of mud that infests a cavalry camp has a meaning all its own. Everything was dank, and slimy, and boggy. I had succeeded in getting myself mired to the knees when suddenly from somewhere out of the storm, appeared a trim little aeroplane.

"It landed hesitatingly in a nearby field as if scorning to brush its wings against so sordid a landscape; then away again up into the clean gray mists.

"How long I stood there gazing into the distance I do not know, but when I turned to slog my way back through the mud, my mind was made up. I knew there was only one place to be on such a day—up above the clouds and in the summer sunshine. I was going into battle that way. I was going to meet the enemy in the air."

This was in July, 1915. Less than two months before this, Richthofen had transferred to the flying service and was then in training at Cologne. What decided him to change was the dull prospect ahead of the cavalry. Static warfare had limited its use and he and his Uhlans were sent back for duty in the supply service. The motive in each case had a decided similarity.

Bishop applied immediately for his transfer and got it. A few months later he had qualified as an observer and was in France.

He spent four months in action as an observer. During this period he carried out the customary routine of observation, photography and bombing. This four months was in marked contrast with his later experiences, for although he was almost daily over the German lines he did not have a single fight. He was forced to return to England because of an injury to his knee when his pilot made a bad landing. He was laid up for several months on account of this—his only injury during the war and not a serious one—and then, his sick leave over, was given his chance to become a pilot.

He spent the winter of 1916–17 in training, going through the usual steps from a ground school up to night flying, during which he served on the Zeppelin patrols. Early in March, 1917, he received instructions to report for a course at a special school where he learned to fly one of the small and extremely fast single-seater fighting machines which had just been developed by the British aircraft designers. A few days later he reported to the headquarters of the Royal Flying Corps for his orders to proceed to France as a pilot. At last he was ready for the great adventure in which he was destined to make so proud a name.

After the war, Billy Bishop and fellow Victoria Cross winner Billy Barker ran a charter air company that soon went bankrupt. Bishop then went to England, but returned to Canada after suffering financial losses during the stock market crash of 1929. During the Second World War, he was air marshal in charge of recruitment. He died of a heart attack in his sleep at age 60 in 1956.

George Drew, a future premier of Ontario and national leader of the Progressive Conservatives, served in the artillery during the First World War. Later, while a lawyer, he wrote several major pieces for Maclean's in the 1920s and 1930s, including dramatic exposés on international arms merchants. Drew served as Ontario premier from 1943 to 1948, when he took over the federal Tories as leader of the opposition, but he lost both the 1949 and 1953 federal elections. He was high commissioner to Great Britain from 1957 to 1964, and died 10 years later at age 79.

Edward VIII: He Will Be King

Edward VIII as the Prince of Wales in Hyde Park, London

By Richard Dent

JANUARY 1, 1930. The scene is the terrace at Windsor Castle. King Edward VII is talking to one of his ministers when a small boy in a sailor suit rushes across the lawn below them, chasing a barking spaniel. Watching them, the "Peacemaker" turns to the statesman at his elbow and says quietly, "There goes the last King of England!" The child was Prince Edward, now H.R.H. the Prince of Wales.

Will King Edward VII's prophecy come true? And will the Prince ever ascend the British Throne? The answer to the query is, Yes, most emphatically he will.

I suppose that if you were to take any 10 men in any part of the British Empire, North and South America, or Western Europe, and were to ask them who were the dozen most popular men in the world, nine out of every 10 would include in their list H.R.H. Edward David, Prince of Wales. "Prince Charming," "Our Smiling Prince," "The Most Popular Young Man in the World," "A Regular Feller"—these are but a few of the names that have been applied to him in the past and show every sign of still being applied in the future. And the most typical feature of them all is that they consider the Prince of Wales always as a "young man." For the last 15 years, the Prince of Wales has been referred to in the newspapers as a young man, and there is no evidence that this description will be altered within the next 15 years.

Yet already the Prince of Wales is 35 years of age, and in actual years he is far from being a young man now; he is already mature. In another 15 years he will be 50, yet I do not mind making a small wager that he will still be the most popular "young" man in the world then as now.

It is about time we removed the scales from our eyes and looked at the matter in a sensible light. This "young man" stunt, though it is supported by the tradition of 15 years, and exists, as I have good reason to know, with the consent and almost with the connivance of the Prince's staff at St. James, is one of the most harmful influences toward the throne today. The press has decided that the Prince of Wales is the "world's most democratic young man," just as it has decided that Rudolph Valentino was the world's most perfect lover, and Charlie Chaplin the world's best wearer of ridiculous boots. It has ranked the Prince of Wales as it ranks film stars, and it will only allow him to play one part, and that is the part of a democratic young man, with all the venial sins of ordinary young men, all the uninteresting virtues of ordinary young men, and absolutely none of the dignity of a prince.

Now 15 years' close personal knowledge of the Prince of Wales has shown me that he is as much like the newspaper idea of himself as he is like a performing clown. Certainly he has most of the characteristics of an ordinary likeable man, rather young for his 35 years, but in addition to that he has a fund of dignity that is quite sufficient to carry him through any of those duties that would fall to him as King of Great Britain, and already he exercises that dignity on state occasions. The tragedy of the whole matter is that not only does the Prince of Wales enjoy being dignified—he told me personally that he was looking forward to the State ceremonial of his brother's wedding—but also he refused to recognize the amount of harm that this press "democratic young man" publicity is doing him.

At one time of the Prince's life, one of his private amusements was to read through at breakfast the newspaper reports of what he had been doing the night before; or sometimes he would defer the process until some of his most intimate friends were present. "Oh," I remember him saying on one occasion, "so that's what I was doing yesterday, was it? Telling a housewife in the Midlands the kind of cakes my mother makes. To the best of my knowledge my mother has never made a cake since I was born, and so far as I know she couldn't if she tried. Oh, well, I suppose these newspaper fellows know their own business best."

If only the Prince of Wales were described as being the sort of man he really is, instead of a democratic puppet, his popularity would be nearly as high as it is at present, and there would be no more of this "open secret" that he does not want to come to the throne. But though half the blame for this lies with the British press in reporting only the dignified things that he does, or more often does not do, the Prince of Wales is not entirely blameless himself.

He has the normal desire of every man to have a good time as long as he can, and he realizes that after he is King his dancing at night clubs, week-ends at golfing house parties, and long hunting trips will no longer be possible. He, therefore, decides to make the most of his opportunities while they are here. So have most other princes, though not to the same extent as the Prince of Wales. The trouble is, of course, that the press has invented a character for the Prince of Wales, and he feels that it is his duty to live up to it to a certain extent, particularly when his own inclinations happen to run in the same direction. There is another question that the public asks itself. "If the Prince of Wales wishes to be King, why does he not marry at once and get it over?"

That is not quite such a stupid question as it sounds; for although there are a great many husbands in this country who have not married until they were on the other side of 40, there have been very few princes in the history of any royal family who have not been husbands and fathers before they were out of their 20s. It therefore strikes the public as strange that the Prince of Wales should be so striking an exception to this regal rule.

The answer to the public's question is stated in terms of the greatest admiration by the daily press: "The Prince of Wales has not yet fallen in love!" That answer is substantially true, though it might perhaps be more accurate if it were framed instead that the Prince of Wales has not yet fallen in love with a suitable wife. With his opportunities for meeting the most beautiful and the most interesting women of four continents, it would only be natural for him to have been attracted quite strongly by some of his acquaintances. But though we are prepared to welcome a democratic prince, we are not willing equally to welcome a democratic future Queen. The Duke of York has certainly married outside the royal families of Europe, and a similar match on the part of the Prince of Wales would probably be enthusiastically received. But there are very few young women today who are as eligible as the Duchess of York to be the future Queen of England, and to none of them has the Prince of Wales been tempted to plight his troth.

Now it is all very well saying that the marriage of the Prince is a private matter that affects himself alone, but actually it is nothing of the kind. The public has a perfect right to say to the Prince of Wales, "It is time that you married. There is England's future Queen to be thought of, and there is the succession to the throne to be provided for. Therefore you must marry at once." But the public, though it may whisper these very words to its next door neighbor, will not for a moment dare to speak out, and the old sycophantic story in the press of the "democratic young man who has not yet fallen in love" goes on. Certainly there is something romantic and attractive in the idea for a prince, but there is nothing to commend it in a future king.

But the Prince of Wales, brought up on this same theory that runs through newspaperdom, and through his own staff and publicity managers, is quite unable to appreciate these whispers that go on in the corners of the drawing-rooms and the smoking rooms of the country. He feels that he has the right to please himself about his marriage, and no one attempts to disillusion him. If once he realized the true state of affairs behind this veneer of sentimentality, I guarantee that he would be wed within a year.

"Will the Prince of Wales come to the Throne?" The answer is Yes—most emphatically Yes. He wishes to, himself; he has all the dignity required to make him suitable to do so. He is not trying to throw up the sponge and hand over the job to the Duke of York.

All things considered, when one realizes how excruciatingly boring a great deal of his official life must be, he has been remarkably successful in avoiding the least breath of scandal. Naturally there are always malicious tongues ready to wag to his discredit. But though the Prince of Wales at present has the right to take ordinary legal action against slanderers through the law courts, and later, when he has succeeded his father, he will in theory be able to take any sort of arbitrary action that he pleases, yet in point of fact he can do nothing of the sort. It would be quite incompatible with the dignity of the throne to take any notice of malicious slanders that were printed against his name; and that is why not only do enterprising journalists invent stories to his discredit, but also why the Prince of Wales has to be more careful than any other man in the world to avoid the least suggestion of scandal.

Most people think, because they have heard in the newspapers that the Prince of Wales enjoys more liberty than any other prince in the history of his country, that he is able to follow his own inclinations in those hours that he can call his own. Nothing could be further from the truth. Actually the Prince is under greater surveillance than a certified lunatic. Only because he has been brought up to it, does he not rebel every other day, and kick over the traces to do something that would ruin his reputation forever.

If you would look in *Whitaker's Almanac* under the heading of "The Household of H.R.H. the Prince of Wales," you will find a list of half-a-dozen names of his staff; private secretaries, comptrollers, equerries and other officers. You probably think that these men are employed only to look after the vast amount of clerical and official business that the Prince of Wales is obliged to undertake. Actually perhaps the greatest part of their job is to see that the Prince of Wales does not get into mischief! Mischief, from the point of view of the Prince of Wales's staff, consists in their charge enjoying himself as an ordinary young man of his station.

I remember one occasion at a charity ball in London. There happened to be a famous musical comedy star there whom the Prince of Wales had met several times. She was a woman who had delighted the whole of London with the grace of her dancing feet. The Prince of Wales, who has been to thousands of charity balls, entered at the appropriate time, smiling, but under the smile looking phenomenally bored, an expression which, if you observe him very carefully, you will often find under his tactful smile. His eyes just do not smile as well.

After he had shaken hands with all the proper people and expressed his delight at being present, he glanced round the ballroom with a look that said, "Now who on earth can I find here who can dance decently?" His glance lighted on the musical comedy star, and his face lit up. He went over to her and asked her for a dance. They started dancing, and until the music stopped the Prince looked as if he were enjoying himself at last. He stayed by her and talked to her during the interval, and when the band started again he was just escorting her to the floor for another dance when an equerry made his appearance. A few whispered words passed between them, and the Prince begged his partner to excuse him, while he hurried over to another portion of the room. He danced with several other partners before he left, but not again with the musical comedy star, and I noticed that though his lips were parted in a smile, there was no trace of enjoyment in his eyes.

That is precisely what is happening wherever the Prince goes. He plays a round of golf at Le Touquet [in northern France] with Mrs. So-and-so, who is there without her husband. She is one of the most attractive women of the younger set, and anyone would be delighted to have a chance of playing with her. But unfortunately her reputation has just a suspicion of blemish about it. When, after the round, the Prince meets his equerry again, the equerry conveys to him tactfully that he had better find another partner next time, and in nine cases out of 10 the Prince obeys. On the 10th occasion he rebels.

I was present at Le Touquet on one occasion when this happened. The Prince insisted on playing on three successive days with the same woman. On the evening of the third day, there was only one topic discussed in Le Touquet, and that was the Prince's "love affair" with Lady This-and-that. Now, as it happened, I knew the lady in question, and met her the same evening. As we were old friends we talked together; but the Prince was not mentioned. For the whole evening we talked about her own problems, which was nothing less than the fact that she was in love with a penniless young officer who could not afford to marry her.

If this sort of thing goes on while he is still Prince of Wales, to whom, after all, a certain amount of license is permitted, it will be very much worse when he has ascended the throne. That is why the Prince of Wales tries to make the most of what small opportunities that he has of enjoying himself; because he knows that even those will pass away when he is King Edward. And that is why when he returns from his brief excursions to France and elsewhere you will find him looking a bit groggy about the eyes from too many late nights, too much dancing and too little sleep. He is trying to make the most of what liberty he has while he still has a chance of doing so.

The Prince of Wales has two main pleasures. One is hunting, and the other is dancing; and just as he likes a good horse in the hunting field, so he likes a good partner on the dance floor, and as far as is possible to him he sees that he gets both. When he is King he will have to give up both. Already, because of his father's illness, he has had to give up the former, and he gave that up with a good grace. When the time comes to give up the latter, he will do so even more reluctantly but with an even better grace. The night clubs of London will suffer by his accession, for the knowledge that the Prince may be present brings quite a lot of visitors to the fashionable night clubs who otherwise might not go at all. Americans particularly hope to have a chance of seeing the Prince shake his feet on the dance floor.

I remember one case in particular. I shall not name the night club but you may be sure it was not 100 miles from Piccadilly Circus. It was one of the most crowded evenings that they had ever experienced, and though the Prince was there, there were not a few visitors at other tables who had looked upon the wine when it was red. One party of Americans in the corner was particularly happy, and the waiters bringing new bottles of champagne and removing the old ones made almost a procession. It looked like a large family party with father, daughter and several young friends of both sexes. The father in particular had been celebrating his holiday from prohibition, and it was with unsteady steps that at length he ventured on to the dance floor with his daughter as partner. In about the middle of the dance he found himself wedged up against the Prince of Wales. "Say, Prince," he muttered thickly, "my gal here would certainly be pleased if you would take the floor with her. She's said to be a pretty fine dancer back in Ohio." The Prince laughed easily. "I am afraid I am booked up for this dance," he said, "but I should certainly like to later on."

By the time "later on" occurred, tactful waiters had led the father out of the room, but the daughter remained behind. The Prince lived up to his word, and asked her for a dance. The American girl was abjectly apologetic about her father, but the Prince laughed it off. As he took her on the floor, he said: "Please don't mention it. You don't know how pleased I am to see a man enjoying himself too much, for once in a while."

That is the atmosphere in which the future King of England lives. He must not speak to the same woman twice, unless she is over 60 and as ugly as sin, or else wagging tongues will start again. He must not go to night clubs as every other young man of his income and taste does, because they are haunts of gilded vice.

For, once the Prince of Wales has ascended the throne as King Edward VIII, you will find that he is much like his grandfather and namesake. He will be a popular King. The habits of democracy that he has so carefully acquired will not be shaken off, and in a pleasant respectable way he will probably be unconventional; but the scandal-mongers who hope to find some traces of dissipation in him are going to be disappointed. He exercises 90 per cent of caution now: he will exercise 100 per cent then.

Edward was King Edward VIII for 11 months until he abdicated in December 10, 1936, in order to marry American divorcée Wallis Warfield Simpson. When his brother received the crown as George VI, Edward became the Duke of Windsor and later served as governor of the Bahamas during the Second World War, from 1940 to 1945. The Windsors then moved to Paris, where he died in 1972, aged 78. The duchess outlived him by 14 years and died at age 89.

The Dionnes: The Quint Question

The Dionne Quints and their nurses
in North Bay, Ont., 1941

By Frederick Edwards

JULY 15, 1941. On the afternoon of Saturday, May 10, a little six-year-old girl living in an Ontario hamlet had a fit of tantrums. She set her rosy lips in an obstinate pout, stamped her tiny slippered foot and cried, *"Non, non, NON!"* in a shrill piercing treble. From this seemingly insignificant incident many unexpected happenings eventuated, including this article. The revolt of Yvonne Dionne may not have possessed the international importance of the Riel rebellion, but it got a lot more immediate publicity.

The circumstances surrounding and leading up to the outbreak of temperament among the Dionne quintuplets were these: It had been planned to feature the Quints on a Sunday-afternoon radio show sponsored by the Ontario government, designed to promote tourist business within the province and addressed chiefly to residents of the United States. The May 11 broadcast was the third of a series of 13 half-hour programs transmitted over the Columbia Broadcasting System through 52 radio stations covering 18 states.

Personal appearance of the Quints on the May 11 show had been pledged at the close of the May 4 program. At that time listeners were told that the famous Dionne sisters would have a special message for them. Everybody seems to have taken it for granted that the message would be delivered in English. The program was planned and the original script written with that idea in mind, and no other.

Two simple English sentences, each of nine words, had been prepared. Yvonne was to have said: "Won't you come up and see us this summer?" And, because the broadcast date fell on Mother's Day, the message given to Marie was: "We hope that all mothers are very happy today."

There was no reason to anticipate trouble. The Callander babies had made previous radio appearances on behalf of the Red Cross and other war efforts. Each time they had spoken a few words of English. They had even sung a verse or two of "There'll Always Be an England." They were by no means mike shy.

At first everything went fine. Assisted by the nursing staff at Dafoe Hospital—Head Nurse Chaput and Nurses Provencher and Vezina; all of them bilingual—producer Purdy quickly taught Yvonne and Marie to repeat the short phrases assigned to them. After two or three repetitions both children were letter perfect. This was on Saturday morning before the broadcast date. Between that first rehearsal and Saturday afternoon something happened to change Yvonne's precocious and stubborn mind. She told the nurses, in French, "I don't want to speak English." She would give no reason for her refusal, but she couldn't be budged from the position she had taken, either by coaxing, command or threats of an early bedtime for a whole week. Yvonne said: *"Non!"* and stuck to it.

There was no time to waste arguing with a wilful little girl. Rai Purdy eliminated Yvonne from his plans and concentrated on teaching her lines to Cecile. By noon on Sunday Marie and Cecile were thoroughly rehearsed and apparently willing to go through with the assignment. Then, in mid-afternoon, and with zero hour approaching, Marie and Cecile joined Yvonne's insurrection. They didn't want to speak English. They wouldn't speak English. *"Non!"*

Nobody spoke English. Producer Purdy made last minute revisions in his script. All five Quints chorused the invitation and the Mother's Day greeting in French, Purdy supplied a rough English translation—and that was that.

Repercussions of this sudden exposure of the angelic quintuplets in the horrible disguise of problem children were immediate and numerous. In three days, 4,000 communications were dumped from mail bags into Provincial Tourist and Travel Bureau headquarters.

In the office of Douglas R. Oliver, the bureau director, telephone service was swamped with calls, local and long distance. The purport of correspondence and phone messages was the same: "Don't the Quints speak English? And if not, why not?" The only difference was that some enquirers were angrier than others.

By Wednesday the newspapers had it. Interviews and editorials burgeoned all over the province. It was reported that the Quints had been forbidden to speak English by their parents, a statement instantly denied—in excellent English—by Oliva Dionne, the father of the five. Premier Hepburn was asked to guarantee that on future programs broadcast in the United States the Quints would speak English. Mitch promised to do his best. For the most part the editorials deplored the incident as damaging to cordial relations between Canada and the United States. Some of the more sombre disquisitions hinted strongly that the Quints were attempting to sabotage the national war effort.

Until this summer the Quints have received no instruction whatever in the English language. Critics who detect some sinister significance in this are reminded that these French-Canadian children, now only just turned seven years old, are not in the same position as children attending public school, or a separate school supported by the taxpayers. Their status is exactly the same as that of any other young child receiving instruction from a private tutor. The cost of the Quints' schooling is met from the Quints' income, and they are being privately taught in their own home. Arrangements have been made during the past few weeks for the Quints to receive regular lessons in English reading, writing and conversation. So far as money is concerned the Quints owe the province of Ontario nothing. They pay their own way. They have never been a public charge. Rather, the shoe is on the other foot. Citizens of Ontario owe the Dionne sisters a debt that cannot accurately be measured in currency. Their presence in the province, their good looks, their amiability, their gay reaction to public showings, have brought many thousands of visitors into Ontario during the past seven years, and many thousands of dollars into Ontario cash registers. The marvel of their birth and the even greater wonder of their survival and normal development have advertised the province as no other single idiosyncrasy identified with Ontario could have done.

Immediately after word of the Callander miracle got around, a large number of perfect strangers suddenly developed an intense interest in the Dionne family. One enterprising Barnum wanted to exhibit them in incubators at the Chicago Century of Progress. There were others with equally fantastic schemes. Dr. Allan Roy Dafoe, a brusque individual, vigorously opposed all attempts to exploit the tiny infants. Dr. Dafoe and the nurses he engaged brought the five prematurely born babies through their first perilous year, up to the time in 1935 when the Ontario parliament passed the Quintuplet Guardianship Act, making the five wards of the Crown. This act set up a board of trustees to protect the Quints' interests and supervise their upbringing until their 18th birthday, with the reservation that the legislation might be cancelled before that time by proclamation of the Lieutenant-Governor.

The Quints are big business. Their income is derived from the sale of various advertising privileges and movie and pictorial rights. They now have a combined estate of $1 million. Their earnings in one year have run as high as $200,000. They must have a business manager to represent them in dealings with industrial executives, motion-picture producers, advertising agencies, radio sponsors, newspaper reporters, feature writers and all the rest of the motley crew who have business, or think they have business, or would like to have business at Dafoe Hospital. Four years ago, Keith Munro, a Toronto newspaper man, was appointed business manager for the Quints.

Keith Munro was a reporter on the *Toronto Daily Star* when the Dionne story broke. He was one of the first news hawks to reach Callander from the outside and he stayed with the story all through its exciting early stages. Afterward he was frequently in the village keeping in touch with developments. He came to know Dr. Dafoe intimately, and his appointment was made largely on the physician's recommendation.

The village of Callander is nine miles south of North Bay. Dafoe Hospital, the home of the quintuplets, is two miles east of Callander, about halfway between that village and Corbeil. A broad paved highway connects Callander with Corbeil, running past the hospital.

Before the Quints arrived, this road was hardly more than a cow path, deeply rutted in summer, hub deep in mud when it rained and a snow-covered trail in winter.

Dafoe Hospital proved a disappointment. The house itself is attractive enough, designed as an outsize in log cabins, neat and painted; but its surroundings are bleak and starkly exposed. No attempt has been made at landscaping the grounds. There is a wide expanse of well-kept lawn, but no trees and no garden save for a narrow strip along one side. The entire property is enclosed by a seven-foot-high naked wire fence, with strands of inward-sloping barbed wire at the top. The rooms are all on one floor, and all are air-conditioned. Miss Chaput, the head nurse, turned out to be a smartly modern young lady, good looking and alert. When we arrived she was hanging pictures; or rather trying to figure out where would be the best locations for the pictures she intended to hang. Yvonne, Emilie, Cecile, Annette and Marie were having an afternoon lesson in their classroom. Nurse Vezina was teaching them. On the wall blackboard were several drawings of simple objects and a number of four- and five-letter French nouns. There was a chatter of shrill voices as Nurse Chaput opened the door and whatever discipline had existed until then vanished at the sight of a stranger. The quintuplets scrambled around their small desks and clustered about Nurse Chaput. Nurse Vezina lined them up for formal introductions.

It was *"Bo' jou' M'sieu"*; then, from Yvonne, Cecile, Marie, Emilie and Annette, a tiny soft handshake accompanied by a neat small bow. Except from Marie, who, for some reason of her own accorded us the great honour of a deep curtsy. Introductions were not yet complete. Two other children were in the room; Daniel, a brother of the famous five, and Pauline, an older sister. Daniel and Pauline are the nearest of the other Dionne children to the quintuplets' age. They share the Dafoe Hospital schoolroom and playground every day with the babies. All members of the Dionne family have free access to the Quints, but Daniel and Pauline are their regular playmates.

Annette, Cecile, Emilie, Marie and Yvonne were dressed alike in long dresses reaching their insteps, cut along the lines of a house coat or a hostess gown, made of a printed material gaily patterned. The Quints have two playgrounds. In the public one they slide down chutes, build castles in a sand pile and keep house in a doll's mansion as tall as they are, while their unseen visitors watch from behind glass screens in a raised gallery surrounding three sides of the space. The private playground is a pleasantly sloping grass plot inaccessible from the street. Here string hammocks have been slung, the gift of an American admirer, each bearing the name of one of the children on a brass plate. They bring their own toys to this secluded nook and play games of their own devising.

Whenever the weather is reasonably good the Quints are on exhibition twice daily, from 9 to 9:30 in the morning and from 3 to 3:30 in the afternoon. Large signs demand "SILENCE," one of them adding a plea for public co-operation. The glass-gallery screens permit visitors to see the children plainly, but the Quints cannot see their admirers. At first the babies did not know they were being observed. They know now. They have learned during the past year that they are the Quints, and that people are watching them as they play. They speak of themselves as *"Les Quints,"* and study audience reaction like motion-picture stars. On days in the slack season, or when visitors are few, the girls have been heard feeling sorry for themselves. "People did not come to see the Quints today." "It was not good today. It will be better tomorrow."

On rising ground west of the hospital, but outside the fence is the duplex dwelling used as a staff house. The nurses live in one half, the guards in the other. All costs of maintaining Dafoe Hospital; the fences, the grounds, the furniture, the air-conditioning, the heating, the salaries of the nurses and the guards, the bills for food and clothing; everything is paid for out of the income earned by the children.

The Ontario government does not contribute toward the Quints' support. It is not necessary that it should. But the Ontario government has laid itself open to criticism in that, although it is spending large sums in advertising the Quints and urging people to visit Dafoe Hospital, it has done nothing to make them comfortable when they get there.

On the south side of the highway, directly opposite the hospital is the "souvenir and refreshment booth" operated by Oliva Dionne, where the Quints progenitor will sell you anything from a hot dog to a set of genuine Wedgwood china. A big sign above the counter advertises that this is the only Dionne concession not owned by the Quints. Behind the Dionne refreshment booth is a large open parking space. A couple of hundred yards away there are wooded areas but there is no shade at the road's edge or along the hospital fence, and nothing for tourists to do while they are waiting to see the Quints but sit in their cars, walk around the dusty uninteresting countryside, or just wait. At midsummer, when the tide of visitors to the Quints is at its height, thousands of men and women and children stand patiently in line outside the wire fence, with the hot sun beating down on them as the long queue moves slowly around the gallery.

Oliva Dionne and his family live in the house where the Quints were born, on the side of the highway opposite the hospital, about a quarter of a mile away in the direction of Callander. The house is a neat cottage. Dionne, whose income is said to be in the neighborhood of $16,000 a year, has made some improvements during the past year or so. He has covered the wooden side walls with asbestos shingles and put on a new roof of the same material; but he hasn't yet got round to installing inside toilets. The cottage has a grass plot around it, an acre of tilled land beside it and a barn. There are a couple of trees in the front yard. A sign has been nailed to one of the trees. It reads: "No admittance."

Mr. and Mrs. Oliva Dionne are much more youthful in appearance than most people imagine them to be. They are only in their 30s. Mrs. Dionne has retained her good looks and published pictures of her have done her an injustice. She is plump, but not fat. As for Oliva, he is a slender dark chap, a bit under average height, shy and suspicious of strangers, carrying around with him—whether with justification or not—an angry feeling that he has been badly done by. This seething resentment colours all his behaviour. He avoids personal contacts save with a few long-standing intimates, dodges interviews, despises and fears reporters.

Oliva Dionne's response when we told him we were going to write an article about his family, and had already visited the quintuplets was indicative of his usual mood. He said: "If you are going to write anything about my family, then you should come and see me first."

Fair enough. We asked him about this business of teaching the Quints to speak English. "I want them to learn English. It is important to them that they should learn English. I have never had any other idea; but I want them to learn English only at the proper time."

And when did he think the proper time would be? At some certain age?

"No, it is not that. The age does not matter. The proper time for them to learn to speak English is after they have learned to speak French fluently.

"If you are going to write about my family, you should write the whole story. Both sides of it," he went on. "My side has never been told. The reporters write things that are not true. They make me look like a fool. They are not fair. They do not want the truth."

One of Oliva Dionne's most frequently voiced complaints is that he is not consulted about plans made for his daughters. Oliva is a trustee. Yet, he is not always made aware of projects concerning the Quints. He was not asked to consent to the May broadcast. There is a sort of bilateral reason for this situation, a diamond-cut-diamond feud compounded of Oliva's resentment at other people's interference in what he regards as strictly his own private affair, and the impatience of men familiar with modern business methods at Oliva's deliberate and sometimes obtuse reasoning.

From statements often publicly made by Oliva Dionne it may be concluded that his solution of the problem would be for the trustees to build a new country home for the Quints large enough to house the parents and their 12 children all under one roof, continue their instruction by nuns as planned, but turn full control of their affairs over to Oliva and his wife. There is sure to be a lot of argument about the feasibility of such a plan, if only from sordid causes. Something very similar has been discussed before, as far back as the summer of 1938, when it became obvious that the Quints' seven-acre estate was getting too small for them and the rest of the Dionnes. Two sites were considered then, beside Trout Lake a few miles farther from Callander than the present location.

The proposals fell through. Vigorous, even angry protests were made to Queen's Park by Callander merchants, hotel keepers, cabin-camp owners and others who had invested their money in commercial enterprises that they saw ruined by the removal of the Quints, even a short distance away.

The Callander controversy, brought to a head by Yvonne's revolt last May, will continue. Turning the Quints' education over to trained nuns will provide the answer to only a part of the complex situation, involving as it does racial prejudices, personal differences, and considerable money interests.

But the Quints will go on smiling.

The Dionne smiles, however, were not to last. Emilie died at 20 during an epileptic seizure. Marie died at 35 in 1970 from a blood clot in her brain after suffering from depression and alcoholism. In 1998, the remaining three sisters—at the time, living outside Montreal on a combined pension of $746 per month—demanded compensation from the Ontario government for their early exploitation. They got $4 million and an apology from Premier Mike Harris.

Frederick Edwards wrote more than 100 freelance articles for Maclean's *between 1927 and 1942, before moving to New York City where he died in 1944.*

The Inside Story of Gordon Sinclair

Gordon Sinclair on assignment

DECEMBER 1, 1949. *No one knows Sinclair better than egotist Sinclair (excepting Mrs. Sinclair). And when* Maclean's *told him to interview himself, he said he had a great story there. A scoop, in fact.*

At the height of this year's Channel swimming season a much bally-hooed American schoolgirl, Shirley May France, went to England to splash the gap and quickly fell afoul of the newspapers. The chunky mermaid (who didn't make it) spent her 17th birthday sob-bing that she was homesick and didn't like England. Reading this as a news item over Toronto's CFRB, trouble-loving Gordon Sinclair couldn't help but blurt: "Okay, Shirley, if it makes you feel happier, I don't like England either."

A moment later the switchboard spluttered. Over the next several hours it stayed red while bored operators drew abuse and insult in dialects ranging from Cockney to Cornish to Chester. For several days sponsors put smoothies to work with honeyed words. To demands for apology Sinclair yawned something about liberty of opinion and to requests for further dope said there was none. He'd been to England at least a dozen times, he said, and didn't like the place. "Shucks," he added "why should I like England? Plenty of people don't like Canada; thousands don't like me. Do Canadians get heated up? Do I worry?"

Sinclair is a Canadian who is used to being in the middle of a rhubarb. He likes it. He has been in more arguments than an umpire, called a liar more often than Ripley and suffered a broken nose three separate times at the hands of vexed readers. He's been on the carpet in such faraway places as Bangkok and Mandalay, Rangoon and Mexico. He's been sued for $120,000 and lost every action by out-of-court settlement. In each case the money has been paid by the *Toronto Star* without so much as a reprimand although the same paper once fired him for speaking over the air against orders.

This Sinclair was born, raised, educated and married in Toronto where his four children were born. The only daughter, first female of the clan in 56 years, died there at Christmas, 1942, after an illness of only 17 hours. From Toronto, Sinclair has spied out the world and from the world come home to what he thinks is the best city on earth. He is Canada's most traveled reporter and one of the least popular. As a reporter who never was, never can and never wants to be either editor or publisher, he's probably Canada's richest, but he seldom lends or gives money to anybody. In many ways he's a man without sympathy, feelings or religious belief, but he's a good reporter.

He cheerfully admits that he wears loud sports jackets because "I'm in show business." Many people consider him vain but the only qualifying sentence in his one-paragraph will insists that no stone shall mark his grave.

For six years he's been broadcasting news over CFRB where President Harry Sedgwick says, "Sinclair gets us into more brawls than all other newscasters combined because he's always tossing salty opinions. Gordon's built up the biggest daytime audience of them all."

Sinclair's jobs have included banking, bookkeeping, perfume, calendars, tires, reporting and radio in that order and he's been fired from every job he ever held. It's possible he holds the *Toronto Star* record for firings, having been given the heave-ho 10 times. The last time was in 1943 when the *Star* gave him $5,000 in cash to get out and stay out. Six years later they handed him an air ticket and an assignment to fly around the world by any route he liked. During that trip he was one of the last out of Shanghai before the Communists came and one of the few Canadians in Berlin when the Russians lifted their blockade.

He has seen men die by shooting, drowning, burning, hanging and earthquake. He's covered wars, revivals, strikes, sinkings and art shows. He's visited a dozen nudist camps, interviewed such celebrities as Hitler, Gandhi, Roosevelt, Queen Elizabeth and the Pope.

He swam in the Ganges, drifted down the Nile, crossed the Jordan, and posed beside the Suwanee, the Rhine and the Wabash faraway. He's visited nearly every country on earth and traveled by all kinds of transport from rickshaw to railway, from dog team to cable car and from bum boat to luxury liner.

Sinclair has twice fallen from boats in the middle of big lakes, twice been forced down in planes and once hit by a train going a mile a minute. He has three times found dead bodies.

A free lance in the cut-throat fields of writing and radio, Sinclair is considered arrogant by many, and cocky by most. Gerald Brown, the city editor under whom Sinclair served longer than any other, puts it this way: "As one who on occasion suspiciously challenged and cross-checked the accuracy of some hair-raising Sinclair article, I should like to vouch for his conscientious accuracy. Sinclair sees events through a special pair of eyes. And he has a rare nose for adventure. Things happen when Sinclair is around."

Among the challenged stories Brown mentions is Sinclair's scoop on the scuttling of the German pocket battleship *Graf Spee*. You remember that ship, chased into Montevideo, had to sail out of the harbour toward the guns of three much smaller British warships on December 17, 1939. On the chance that officials of the British Consulate would be watching the action Sinclair telephoned the South American city, got the consul personally on the wire and as he stood at the window watching the ship scuttle, the British official gave a firsthand account to Sinclair in Toronto.

When the story was turned in to the desk a subeditor was assigned to call Montevideo again to see if Sinclair had in truth been talking to the consul. The whole result had seemed a bit too good to be true. The surprised consul said, "Certainly he was talking to me. Why did you ask?"

Sinclair was the first reporter sent around the world by a Canadian paper and he made the circuit four times, each by a different route. He hopes to go again with a tape recorder.

He stands five-foot-seven, weighs 160 lb., and has blue-grey eyes which his three sons say are hard as steel. He has more hair on his chest than on his oval-shaped head and pays lip service to such sports as hunting, fishing and golf though his only serious hobby is home movies. Financially, Sinclair is an oddity among reporters because he could lay hands on $100,000 without borrowing a nickel, within a month. He has a mortgage-free home and summer place, two cars, a boat, part of an island and good stocks. He has followed an investment policy since 1932 and it's pretty simple: "Never buy unless they pay a dividend, sell the instant the dividend is passed."

But being a financial success sometimes divides homes. At radio station CFNB in Fredericton is Gordon Sinclair, Jr., who has this to say, "Dad kept hammering at us at home that a man had to do his own job, make his own decisions and live his own life. So here I am doing just that and he objected right down the line. Didn't want me to go into radio, didn't want me to leave Ontario, didn't want me to marry at 21. Well I did ... and I'm not sorry."

The trigger-tempered Gordon Sinclair was born on Toronto's Carlton Street. Bolton School was followed by Riverdale Collegiate. It was 1915. When a former classmate, Melbourne Passmore, then a junior in the Bank of Nova Scotia, enlisted he was asked to suggest a youth to take his place. Sinclair got the nod. Ten months later Sinclair was fired for accidentally hitting the manager with a wet counting sponge. He went to Eaton's as a punk in the bookkeeping end and promptly got the heave-ho for sassing a customer.

Next he tried to sell outrageous perfume. Few sales; no job. Soon afterward the perfume boss blew his brains out, but that's mere coincidence. Calendars followed and Sinclair was fired for criticizing such higher art. Rubber came next. One of the reasons why the Sinclair books failed to jell in the rubber emporium was a blond and buxom switchboard girl named Gladys Elizabeth Prewett. In 18 months Gladys will celebrate her silver anniversary as Mrs. You Know Who.

At the time of this bookkeeping courtship, Sinclair was playing hockey in a church league of little consequence. He was indignant when the team's games never drew publicity. The rickety old *Toronto Star* building was a block from the rubber office so Sinclair went there to try and learn the why of this neglect.

Sports editor W. A. Hewitt explained that he had no reporters to send to such small games but if Sinclair chose to write the stuff it would be printed. What's more he'd be paid. Thereafter the Hope Church team was never overlooked and a spindly kid named Sinclair began to taste the thrill of seeing *his* deathless prose in print.

In March, 1923, when the outdoor hockey season ended, Sinclair decided that this writing dodge was built to measure for his free-wheeling style so he asked the *Star* for a job as a reporter. In response came a letter from H. C. Hindmarsh, then city editor and now president, to name an interview date for Thursday. The letter was dated Monday but was not received until Thursday noon. The budding reporter did a headlong race for the *Star* building and asked the elevator man where to find this guy Hindmarsh.

"Why," came the reply, "that's Mr. Hindmarsh there."

A giant looking like a sergeant of the Prussian Guards stood puffing a cigar the general size and outline of a prize cucumber. Sinclair asked if he was Hindmarsh and was ignored. He asked again and the cigar walked away with Sinclair in pursuit. The pursuit resulted in a job that carried him to the world's far places, and frequent tenancy in the *Star*'s doghouse. Hindmarsh has since fired and hired Sinclair as many times as either have fingers but there's no hard feeling either way.

At that time the *Star* had no sob sisters or feminine editors. After two years, to his great surprise, Sinclair became woman's editor. He was the worst in Canada, but it was several years afterward—when he tried his hand at sports writing—that he discovered how it felt to be *really* bad. Happily he was fired from both jobs and put to general reporting.

He helped cover a story about the Japanese earthquake of 1923 with Ernest Hemingway, who was already becoming known as a writer of short stories. Soon afterward the *Star* decided to buy whatever animal the children of Toronto would vote upon—through coupons in the paper—as a gift to the zoo. A baby elephant was the popular choice and a task force of reporters and photographers was assigned to glorify Stella the pachyderm. Then, hating to drop such a profitable stunt, the *Star* decided to buy a white peacock too because this bird had been second choice in the voting.

Hemingway was ordered to beat the drums for this peacock and indignantly resigned with what was probably the longest, wordiest and most brilliant resignation in the history of journalism. This resignation, about 18 feet long, was pasted to the staff notice board, in relays, by admiring juniors of whom one was Sinclair. None realized that had the paper been kept it could now have been sold for the price of a new car.

The turning point of his rough-and-tumble career came in 1929 when a hobo jungle on Toronto's outskirts was raided by police who scooped up more than 100 vagrants. Editor Hindmarsh decided no city would detain so many drifters so assigned a reporter to go with these bums when they were ordered out of town. Sinclair accidentally drew the assignment. That night he linked up with a small group headed by a noisy sailor and they crossed the U. S. border in the empty ice compartment of a refrigerator car. But on the third day Sinclair got into an argument with the sailor over whether the Himalayas were in India or Australia. The sailor attacked Sinclair with a stick, opened a gash over his eye, and by evening time the *Star*'s hobo reporter was on a rattler headed for home.

Satisfied that he had no story he wrote nothing, took a day off then reported to his desk. But Dave B. Rogers, editor of that day, took one look at the mouse over Sinclair's eye and persuaded him to write something. So the story of the journey with bums was put down and left in the editor's mailbox. Sinclair went home and dug in his garden. The story was not printed and nobody was surprised.

But a day or so afterward Fred Davis, later to become famed as the original photographer of Papa Dionne's five daughters, came and said, "Hey, Sinclair, what have you been up to? I'm to take your picture." Sinclair looked in his own assignment box and there was the hobo story returned: "H. C. H. likes this. Please break it up into six installments and hand them back soonest. D. B. R."

The story was broken into four parts (one for each day of the journey) and printed on page one. But it ended abruptly just as the bums were planning to head for England.

"How come?" asked various readers. "Why didn't this man continue? It was interesting."

Sinclair was paraded, shown the letters, told: "Start out again tonight. Catch up with those boys. Sail to England."

Sinclair never did see his boxcar companions again but he wangled a job as assistant boots aboard the *Laurentic*, brushed aside certain union difficulties, and found the job the softest possible because nobody can get their boots dirty at sea. He landed in Liverpool on a rainy midsummer day, was soon coughing and spluttering in one of the countless tunnels which make rod riding impossible in Britain.

To wind up that trip he went to Germany which was just beginning to emerge from a postwar stupor. Then the plot repeated itself. Returning unheralded from Germany he found letters from old pal Pro Bono Publico demanding why he hadn't stayed on to tour Germany.

So back to Germany he went, and the news career which was soon to become the most far-flung in Canadian records was well launched. It was no longer hobo stuff but first-class, and by 1932 visits with such personalities as the exotic Maharanee of Cooch Behar were part of the glamour.

During spells between the exotic spice gardens of the Orient, the prison stockades of Devil's Island or the gold camps of Yellowknife, Sinclair spent much time, cooling off, in the *Star's* spacious doghouse. The technique seemed to be that the man was getting swelled-headed and the way to whittle him down to size was have him write meetings of the ladies' aid, obituaries of pious but obscure citizens and promotion about photogenic terriers or trained seals.

Of the 23 foreign journeys undertaken during an unbroken spell of 11 years, Sinclair lists five weeks on Devil's Island as the most profitable because it gave him a syndication of about 300 papers. His most successful book, *Footloose in India*, was written in 19 days and Sinclair hasn't read it to this minute. Oddly enough the Devil's Island articles, as a book, were a disappointing flop.

His most frustrating journey was the one to Ethiopia. When the *Star* threw him out that time he wrote advertising, helped Foster Hewitt by doing the 'tween-periods chatter on the coast-to-coast hockey games and made the horrifying discovery that he was expected to keep regular hours. Then Lou Marsh, colourful sports editor of the *Star*, died and Sinclair rejoined the paper as sports reporter. He was one of the lamest sports writers in the history of ink and eventually pleaded for a chance to regain the carefree spirit by going with hobos again. The *Star* cut his pay 40 per cent and turned him loose. Sinclair headed for Florida, spent two idle weeks there then heard of a gold rush at Yellowknife and went north. He talked to the pioneers of that camp from Paine to Ingraham, to Thompson to Lundmark, and eventually crossed the Pacific to visit such Manchurian cities as Harbin, Mukden and Manchouli. There he crossed a wooden bridge into Siberia but after eight hours the Russians sent him south again.

He spent the spring of 1939 in Pekin [Beijing] and there he got instructions to come back to Canada and help cover the cross-country tour of the King and Queen.

Sinclair's blond and chunky wife sometimes carries a picket against him, charging egotism, laziness and extravagance—qualities seldom found in the same personality. "He's been lucky," she scoffs. "Sinclair was sent to Europe 20 years ago and he's been cashing in on that trip ever since. The many subsequent journeys to such weird spots as Borneo, Arabia, Togoland and heaven knows where else were just afterthoughts. He became a big shot in his own mind when he got off the *Laurentic*, in England, in 1929.

"Another thing that irritates me is all that talk about being Scottish. He's no more Scottish than Stalin is. He was born in Toronto of a Canadian father and an American mother, but he's always buying up tartans, cairngorms and heather. This year at the Exhibition some woman showed him a kilt in the Sinclair tartan so he bought the thing. It will make a nice feed for the moths.

"And that stuff he spouts about hard work and always thinking of the main chance. Man and boy, that Sinclair never worked regular hours in his life. At first he'd start working at seven in the morning and sometimes he'd work at night, too, but he was free every afternoon. Then he got interested in shows and started writing for that slap-dash show paper called *Variety*.

"He had passes to everything and thought it smart to bring showgirls home. Had a Cadillac, too, and clothes that shone up like forest fires. He still wears clown clothes and has at least 20 jackets. One day he landed in here with a big redheaded woman. We had a little car then besides this green Cadillac with all the chrome. This day I was driving the green car so he comes in and says he wants it because this redhead is Aimee Semple Macpherson the big evangelist and he's driving her to Ingersoll where she was born, or something.

"Well, I say he's plumb mad and if this is Aimee Macpherson I'm Cleopatra. The big redhead laughs like crazy and they go out in the kitchen where she whips up a few martinis and I'm blowed if she didn't turn out to be Mrs. Macpherson after all.

"But I was talking about the few years when he used to go downtown at seven. For the past 10 years he's never been out of bed before nine unless he had a fishing date or maybe golf, and he's off doing the town by two in the afternoon.

"What writing Gordon does comes so easy to him that you can't believe it. I remember a day last July when we were up at the cottage and it started to rain so there wasn't much to do. He sat down at a typewriter and put three articles together before suppertime. Sold them all.

"I know he didn't get that gift for fast writing out of a Christmas stocking. He got it from reading. That's probably the feature about my husband that most people overlook, especially the many who don't like him. He reads for hours. He reads in bed, at meals, in moving cars or trains or planes. He looks things up, too, and has big dictionaries, books of synonyms, year books and an encyclopedia.

"Another thing he reads a lot is the Bible, but he doesn't believe all of it and sometimes says so in the wrong places. That leads to arguments too, but when that kind of hullabaloo gets going I leave. Life's too short."

Gordon Sinclair became a national figure in 1957 when he began a 27-year run as a panelist on the CBC*'s* Front Page Challenge. *A radio commentary he delivered in 1973 defending American involvement in Vietnam was transformed into a best-selling record in the United States. He died at 83 in 1984.*

My Friend Joseph
Albert Guay, the Murderer

Albert Guay, murderer, 1951

MAY 1, 1951. On the afternoon of Sept. 9, 1949, a Canadian Pacific Airlines DC-3 left Quebec City with 23 people aboard, heading for Baie Comeau, Que., a lumber town of 220 miles to the northeast. Above Sault-au-Cochon, 41 miles out of Quebec City, the plane exploded like an electric light bulb. All the passengers were killed.

Ten days later a Quebec woman, Marguerite Pitre, who was recovering in hospital after having tried to commit suicide, told police she had put a package aboard the plane on behalf of a young Quebec jeweler, Joseph Albert Guay, whose wife, Rita Morel, was among the victims. Guay was arrested for the most horrible mass murder in the history of crime in North America.

Since then the details of the murder and the trials have filled the front pages of the nation's newspapers. Albert Guay has been hanged. Marguerite Pitre, who delivered the time-bomb which destroyed the plane, and her crippled brother, Généreux Ruest, who manufactured it, have been condemned to die for complicity in the murder. Both have appealed the death sentence.

One question has been asked time and again since the incredible news first became known: How could a man, no different from any that you might meet on the streets of any town at any time, conceive and carry out such a murder—as useless as it was diabolical?

Of all the journalists who had dealings with him, I am the only one who knew Joseph Albert Guay well before the catastrophe. I believe that I can lift one corner of the veil which hides the mystery by revealing certain aspects of his character which did set him apart from his fellows.

About five o'clock on the afternoon of Sept. 9, I turned on the radio in my car and heard the first news of the crash. When the announcer read the name of Rita Morel, wife of Joseph Albert Guay, jeweler, among the victims of the accident, I experienced such a shock that I had to pull my car into the curb. The plane, according to the broadcast, had simply disintegrated in mid-air, as though it had been blown up by dynamite.

The first thought that came to mind was: "Why, that's Albert's wife!" And, incredible as it may seem looking back, my second reaction was "Albert had something to do with that explosion."

The fact that I had instantly and almost instinctively suspected Albert scared me. I started my car but instead of turning in the direction of the Sillery, where I have lived since my marriage, I drove to Lower Town and the St. Sauveur district, where I had lived for the great part of my life and where Albert Guay had lived for eight years.

During these years, Guay and his wife had been neighbours of mine on the opposite side of the street. We had dealt with the same grocer, Pat Allen, patronized the same printer, Victor Tardif, and Guay was a member of the little club where I played poker. I was curious to know what the grocer, the printer and the poker players thought of the accident.

I went into Pat Allen's store. Pat came running toward me. His manner was distracted: he pulled me behind some sacks of potatoes and whispered to me, "I think Albert might have blown up that plane." Some of the poker players came in and joined us at the back of the store. The same idea had occurred to all of them—that Albert was responsible for the crash.

How was it that these people could without hesitation believe Guay guilty of so fiendish a murder? These were sensible people; they knew Guay well, knew his charming character, his generosity, his good manners, his childish boasting. Ignorant as they were of even the slightest knowledge of psychology, they were well enough acquainted with this highly strung jeweler, who on the surface appeared not a bad fellow, to believe him quite capable of anything at all. Here then is what all of us, and I in particular, knew of him.

Joseph Albert Guay was the youngest of a family of five. His father died when the boy was still very young. His mother's favourite, he was a thoroughly spoiled child. By the time he was 16, Albert was spoiled beyond redemption. He began to hang out in pool halls and to lead the life of the gay young man-about-town. To keep himself supplied with cash he sold watches and other jewelry on commission. When the war broke out he was taken on at the Canadian Arsenals Limited at St. Malo, where his job consisted of watching a grinding machine. Here he earned $40 a week.

In spite of his youthful extravagances, Albert was always neatly dressed, had good manners, and his thin face was that of the successful adolescent. His self-important manner, his air of assurance and the Mercury sedan he drove to work made him popular with the girls who worked in the arsenal. Of all these girls, Rita Morel was by far the prettiest. With her great dark eyes of Andalusian beauty, a sensual mouth, fine teeth and magnificent black hair, she was far and away the most attractive girl in the factory. Passionately in love with her, Albert decided she was for no one but him. In Quebec that means marriage. As irresponsible then as he was to show himself all his life, Albert married Rita.

I shall always remember that spring morning when the happy couple, followed by a crowd of singing, laughing wedding guests, appeared suddenly in the Rue Colomb where I then lived to inspect their apartment opposite my house. Joseph Albert was wearing evening dress complete with top hat, a garb rarely seen at a working-class wedding. I was struck by that fact. "There's a bluffer," I thought.

My acquaintance with Guay and his wife dated from that day. One other thing that impressed me from the beginning was the great show of affection he put on. Each noon Rita would come down to the sidewalk with Albert where, in full view of all the neighbourhood gossips, he would embrace her passionately and at great length in seeming emulation of a Hollywood actor. His way of embracing his wife before the eyes of the whole parish astonished and shocked the neighbours, who believed that kisses and demonstrations of affection were better indulged in private.

At the same time that he was demonstrating every symptom of a passionate attachment for his wife, he continued to go out on occasion with girls from the arsenal. Spoiled child as he was and would remain, he could not accept the idea that the possession of one woman robbed him of his right to have affairs with others. Yet Albert was jealous of Rita, who nevertheless was faithful to him.

One evening about five o'clock, when I was driving from work, I met Rita Morel in the Rue St. Joseph and, since we were bound in the same direction, offered to drive her home. In front of her door I stopped to let her out. Albert, in short sleeves, was leaning against the house, watching us in a sombre manner. He came up to me. His eyes were cast down; he always looked at the ground and his hands, never still, rattled the coins in his pockets. Guay said, "Roger, I'll give you a word of friendly advice. No more of that. That sort of thing can only end in tragedy."

A few months after his marriage every householder in the parish received a business card signed "Joseph Albert Guay, Jeweler." That was the first time any of us had ever heard that he was a jeweler.

He appeared as sure of his ability to repair watches as he had once appeared certain of his skill as a mechanic. Naturally he kept his job in the war factory and he repaired the watches in the evenings at home. At least that is what he said. Actually, he was not at all interested in repairing watches and would send them out to jewelers to be fixed, marking the price up to his advantage. He liked to have his customers believe that a watch in trouble was a mysterious and important thing and that the price could be determined only after the watch had been thoroughly examined and repairs had been completed.

It was in this way that he was later to engage the services of Généreux Ruest. I knew Ruest too. I remember one night, a few months before the crash, when I went to play poker with some old friends. During the game I noticed my wrist watch was broken and later I crossed the street to where Albert Guay had opened a small jewelry store in 1945 and asked him to look at it for me. "Let's take it and show it to Généreux," he said and took me into the back shop where he introduced me to the hawk-faced cripple. It was a familiar face to me, and I said, "Do you remember me, Généreux?" Ruest nodded and his lips parted in a thin smile.

Fifteen years before, when I was recovering from pleurisy in a public ward in hospital, there was a patient in the bed next to me whom I shall never forget. In the first place he had an odd name—Généreux Ruest. Then, not only did he repair the watches of other patients with remarkable skill, but he displayed an extraordinary aptitude for anything mechanical. He spent the long days constructing various small and ingenious machines of his own invention. For example, wires connected his alarm clock to his radio in such a way that the alarm clock, instead of ringing, turned on the radio at exactly eight o'clock.

Finally, Généreux Ruest suffered from an incurable malady. He had tuberculosis in both hips, and he would never walk again.

Guay's speciality was the sale of watches on credit to his fellow workers in the arsenal and his neighbours in the parish. In 1943 I left him with a Roamer watch with the spring broken. Two months later he had not returned it to me. I asked him about it and he told me laughingly, "Your watch had such a complicated movement that I had to send it to New York." Finally he told me the New York experts had telephoned him to say that the watch was useless. In telling me this he had such a serious manner that I could not get annoyed with him. But from that moment on I realized that he was not honest.

One Saturday evening in July, 1944, about midnight, Guay returned home with his wife. A few moments later he came rushing downstairs, waving his arms in the air and yelling, "I've been robbed. Somebody has stolen $1,000 worth of watches from me." The lock of his door had been forced. The thief was never discovered and the insurance company had to pay up. Guay had great faith in insurance companies. In the next two years he was robbed four or five times. People began to look on him with suspicion, but Albert continued to hold his head high.

On Sunday mornings, arm in arm with his wife, a great prayer book under his left arm, he would make his pious way to high mass. He neither drank nor swore and was on good terms with the parish priest. Moreover, he often spoke sadly to us of the thefts of which he had been a victim. "I was born under an unlucky star," he would say. "Fortunately, I was insured."

In 1945, the arsenal closed. Albert Guay opened his jewelry store just opposite the parish church. His business went well enough in 1946 and 1947. It should be noted that on two occasions his store was damaged by fire. Again the insurance companies paid up. Then quarrels broke out between Guay and his wife. Rita had learned of her husband's little adventures and to make him jealous had engaged in a few mild flirtations. Neighbours have told me that in their quarrels the Guays would throw bottles and yell insults at one another. The day after an argument of this kind, Albert frequently bought his wife a present.

Life was not bestowing its rich gifts on the spoiled child. He had not become rich; on the contrary, he was running into debt. Yet for eight years he had been telling everybody that one of these days he was going to be a rich man. What would people think of him? It was at this time that he met Marie-Ange Robitaille.

There dwelt two men in Albert Guay: the ambitious man and the sensualist. Now his ambitions were bankrupt. He threw himself passionately into a love affair to forget. As his sentimental life too was to founder, these two failures, coming in contact with one another, closed the fatal circuit.

He met Marie-Ange in the restaurant Chez Gerard, where she was a waitress. She was still almost a child, only 17 years of age, and looked like a timid girl fresh from a convent. Under an assumed name he began to call on her three nights a week like a young suitor with serious intentions. Marie-Ange's parents saw a good match for their daughter in this distinguished young man who occupied the big armchair in their living room and paid conventional suit to their daughter.

When he visited Marie-Ange at her home he took the name of Roger Angers. He was no longer the 30-year-old man who had failed to become rich; he was the ambitious youngster. The little game lasted several months. He even bought an engagement ring for Marie-Ange. Then one night Rita Morel burst into the Robitaille living room and the game was up.

Guay took Marie-Ange to Sept-Iles, where they lived together for some time as husband and wife. She left him, then returned to him. Finally Marie-Ange realized there was no future in this affair and that she was wasting her time. She left Albert, telling him that since he was married there was little object in continuing the liaison. In despair the spoiled child took stock of his situation. His home life was destroyed, his ambitions ruined; and now his mistress was abandoning him.

Guay had probably been giving thought to the problem of getting rid of his wife ever since she had made her sensational entrance into the Robitaille living room. For was she not the great obstacle between him and Marie-Ange, between him and the moon? But how was it to be done, he must have asked himself. He was afraid of blood. He might shoot her, of course, but he lacked the courage for that. It would be best, he apparently decided, if his wife were to disappear in some sort of an accident.

It is possible that the idea of a bomb dwelt in his subconscious as a result of his experience in the arsenal. It probably swam into his conscious thoughts during an air journey from Sept-Iles to Quebec. The idea of a plane crash attracted him for several reasons. First, there was the pleasure of designing and constructing the bomb, with the aid of Généreux Ruest. This appealed to his taste for ingenious mechanical devices which he had loved ever since his boyhood. Further, since the bomb was to have a time device, the plane would fall apart over water. There would be only bits of unrecognizable bodies, if indeed anything was recovered; so there would be no corpse to identify.

Perhaps, too, the great explosion would succeed in shattering the ill fortune that had dogged his steps and he could begin life all over again with Marie-Ange, a life full of hope and love. This time he would not fail. He would become rich, for with the insurance money he would receive on his wife's death he would pay off his debts. Guay had $5,000 on his wife's life, to which he added another $10,000 at the airport before she took off on the fatal flight.

And what of the other passengers in the plane? His mind refused to dwell on that problem. He was capable of conceiving this grandiose scheme of murder down to the last detail; and yet with a curious lack of caution he shared his secret with Ruest, who made the bomb for him.

By the time of the crash Guay had succeeded completely, it seems, in convincing himself that it was all an accident. On receipt of the news he burst into tears of unfeigned grief. Astonishing as it may seem, there were signs that Guay loved his wife dearly. Two weeks before the crash, he bought his wife flowers, as he had so often done since their marriage. Before they hanged him for his crime he requested that he should be buried beside her.

For the funeral of his dead wife he ordered a magnificently bedecked mortuary chamber. He had a floral cross made, five feet high, bearing the inscription, "From your beloved Albert." He had mourning cards printed by his friend Victor Tardif, urging him to take special pains to see that Rita's photograph came out well on the cards. In spite of his grief, his drawn features and his weariness, he remained at the funeral parlour from morning till night.

Dressed in black, thin and pale, he shook hands with those who called to pay their respects. When I offered him my condolences, he said: "You know how much I loved her. But the important thing is that she didn't suffer. You don't think she suffered, do you." Then he stifled a sob which was not feigned. While I was at the funeral parlour a priest entered. Guay asked him to recite the rosary. Everyone kneeled. As other priests came in he would ask each to recite the rosary. After one such occasion I heard a man sobbing in the room above us. It was the husband of Madame Romeo Chapados who, with her three children, had died in the crash. Guay made his excuses, quickly went upstairs and began to console Chapados. He said, "Be brave, M. Chapados. Do as I do: put your trust in God. I have lost my young wife."

He came back to me and I told him that some of the newspapers were talking of an explosion of dynamite as the cause of the crash. He shrugged his shoulders. "I can't believe it," he said. "In my opinion it was a faulty feed line. There's nobody monstrous enough to blow up a plane."

At the funeral he was proud of the great crowd which followed the hearse and he said to Victor Tardif, "See how well known I am and how much everyone loved Rita." At the cemetery, as the coffin was lowered into the grave, he said to his little daughter, "Look, dear! Mama is leaving us forever." Then he burst into real sobs. He cried so hard and he was so weak that he had to be helped into the taxi.

After his arrest, indeed up to the time that Marie-Ange Robitaille began her evidence, Guay conducted himself with all the offhandedness of a man who has been arrested by mistake. In prison he hummed little French songs. He played endless games of rummy with his guards, whom he consistently beat to his great satisfaction. Shortly before his trial he said to one of the guards, "I've been held here for three months now. Think of all the money this nonsense is making me lose. When I get out of here I am going to sue the government."

I covered the trial and I saw Guay remain impassive as witness after witness gave evidence. Then Marie-Ange was called, the woman for whom he had killed his wife and 22 other people. I shall never forget the brief glance between them. It cannot be described. The 18-year-old girl was well dressed and her auburn hair hung down to her shoulders. She spoke in a weak but clear voice, her eyes full of tears, of her liaison with Albert Guay. She wove a rope for her lover's neck without once looking at him and, when she concluded with the words "I don't love him anymore," Guay's face turned ashen grey, his lips took on a bluish tinge. He looked like a man whose body was beginning to decay while he still lived. Then he closed his eyes. He made no motion, said nothing.

The sentence of death he received almost absent-mindedly, his eyes on his polished shoes. He was asked if he wanted to enter an appeal. "Why? For whom?" he said to his lawyer. "I've no more interest in living."

In the condemned man's cell another interesting aspect of his personality revealed itself. He wanted to sell the story of his life to a magazine to earn a little money for his daughter, to obtain the possible publicity and to teach a moral lesson to his readers. To the Crown attorneys he made a confession that filled 100 pages. It ended with words something like this: "And now I hope that this story will serve as a terrible lesson to those who, like me, have been blinded by passion and ambition."

The newspapers reported that he faced his death with arrogance, saying, "I die famous." That is not true. For a week before his execution he was unable to eat. During all the last day he kept asking the prison doctor, "Will it hurt? Will I still be conscious when my neck breaks? You do die instantaneously, don't you?" He was a pitiful remnant of a human being as he walked to the scaffold. Two guards had to support him.

Joseph Albert Guay died true to himself. He was the spoiled child who had killed 23 people in his effort to get to the moon.

Accomplices Généreux Ruest and Marguerite Pitre lost their appeals and were hanged.

Roger Lemelin, a novelist and journalist, is best known as the author of Les Plouffes, *which was the basis for a widely popular 1950s French language television series in Quebec. From 1972 to 1981, he was publisher of Montreal's* La Presse. *Lemelin died at age 72 in 1992.*

Queen Elizabeth II:
The Girl Behind the Mask

Queen Elizabeth II inspecting the guards, London, 1953

By Pierre Berton

JUNE 1, 1953. Elizabeth II, as all the world knows, is a petite serious-faced girl with a 25-inch waist and golden eyebrows, who can't stand oysters but likes champagne, doesn't smoke in public but keeps cigarettes on her desk, prefers canasta to bridge and horse racing to boxing, likes her drapery cherry-red and her note paper bottle-green, enjoys Jane Austen but thinks Dickens rather a bore, is madly in love with her husband and knows how to shake hands at the rate of 12 a minute.

She is also, as these crumbs of personal trivia indicate, the most widely publicized young woman of modern times. Her orbit is as carefully charted as that of the planet Jupiter, and she lives so much within a goldfish bowl that it is difficult to disassociate her private life from her public existence. Yet the two are, in many ways, quite dissimilar.

So much is known about her that is superficial: that she enjoys Li'l Abner, keeps a faithful daily diary, likes to suck on barley sugar, doesn't like the sea. So much less is known about her that strikes deeper. Long after the ink has dried on the acres of newsprint devoted to her person, the question still remains: what is the girl in the palace really like?

What would she be like if she were subject instead of sovereign? A man who has observed her since childhood recently indulged in this game of make-believe. She would, he said, have been a country girl, the kind usually described as "horsy." She would have ridden a lot, always astride, and most of the time she would wear tweedy things. She wouldn't come into the city a great deal and when she did it would be to see a musical comedy or a vaudeville show or a movie. She would be a lively girl, laughing a good deal, not too interested in style or the arts, surrounded by her own kind of unsophisticated, unintellectual, upper-middle-class country folk. She would have a large family and be great fun at a party where she would dance all the lively dances with bounce and enthusiasm. She would be matronly and she would be wholesome.

This is not the picture of Elizabeth Windsor that the public sees. The serious, almost prim figure in the modish suits and frocks reading her careful speeches, the austere military form in the sidesaddle at the Trooping ceremony, the dazzling fairy queen at the ballet do not seem to bear much relation to a bouncy country matron in tweeds. It is hard to remember sometimes that this is the same girl who likes to lead a conga line through the palace, dance eight-some reels all night and hum Cole Porter's "Night and Day" in her husband's ear; who loves to stalk deer through Scottish forests, angle for trout in mountain streams or put five pounds on a horse's nose at Goodwood; who has learned how to tap dance well, enjoys cowboy movies, especially those starring Gary Cooper, and likes to lean over a piano of a winter evening singing "Greensleeves" with the gang.

It is almost as if there were two Elizabeths, one public and one private, and this curious double existence was quite apparent to those who traveled with her on the royal train across Canada in 1951 when she was still Princess Elizabeth. In the privacy of her quarters she was a lively animated girl who rocked with laughter at small talk and cradled a cocktail glass between her hands. But the train would stop and the laughter would die; the talk would cease, the cocktail would vanish, the smile would fade, the shoulders would stiffen and Elizabeth would move resolutely toward the rear platform, exactly, in one observer's words, "like a soldier coming to attention." Then, the anthem sung, the greeting accepted, the cheers acknowledged and the speech delivered, she would return again to her private world, sink into a couch and double up with mirth at a remark or an incident or a scene that had tickled her.

"I have been trained since childhood never to show emotion in public," Elizabeth once remarked to a dinner companion, and this is one key to her outward reserve. Infused in the hard metal of her character are those qualities of stoicism and constraint which the British prize so highly. They have always been with her. As a child she was particularly enchanted one day by the quick action of a group of marching sailors, one of whose members fainted. The others simply closed in on either side of him and, without missing a beat, marched the insensible man along with them. At the age of 10, she added to her reputation for being able to maintain a poker face when, during a church sermon, a bee settled on the minister's nose. Those around her stuffed handkerchiefs in their mouths to stifle their laughter. But Elizabeth's face retained its composure and only the flowers jiggling on her hat revealed her inner mirth. Years later she was inspecting an honour guard of servicewomen when one girl collapsed, almost at her feet. Elizabeth walked on without changing expression.

When she smiles she seems to be a different person, but she has not yet got that facility for smiling before crowds which distinguished her mother as Queen. On her Canadian tour as princess, Elizabeth phoned her mother from Vancouver. "Are you smiling enough, dear?" the elder Elizabeth asked. "Oh, Mother!" came the reply, "I seem to be smiling all the time." But it is not in her nature to smile all the time in public. When she does the photograph flashes around the world.

Indeed, she sometimes seems to be wearing a mask, and so of necessity she is. It is the iron mask of royalty which those who came before her have worn on public occasions: the peculiarly blank expressionless stare that can be seen in the official portraits, effigies, bas-reliefs, stamps of the nation and coins of the realm. All the members of this emotional Windsor dynasty have worn this emotionless mask. Only occasionally has the frozen guise slipped momentarily to reveal a swift fascinating glimpse of the face behind it.

So with her ancestors, so with the new Queen. She wears the family face. It is not that she lacks a woman's emotions. But her whole background has made her chary of revealing them. "I am not a Hollywood movie star," she told her staff at the outset of her 1951 Canadian tour, "and I do not propose to act like one." Nor did she.

To some Canadians this was a puzzling side to Elizabeth's personality. There was an incident in Calgary when the Dosiettes, a group of little orphanage children skilled in square dancing, put on an exhibition that delighted the royal couple. The plan was that toward the end of the dance two of the smallest children would lead the visitors onto the floor and dance with them. But Elizabeth, when approached about the idea in advance, flatly refused to dance before a crowd. Dancing in public to her was rather like undressing; it belonged to the secret world behind the mask.

There was the time in Toronto in the Sick Children's Hospital when she was to walk past a row of tiny patients laid out for her to see. The photographers reached this vantage point well in advance for here, surely, was an opportunity for a great photograph. The Princess was the mother of two and it was in the cards that she would pick up one of the tiny bodies and cuddle it. The cameras were trained and the crowd waited, but Elizabeth walked down the line as if she were inspecting a rank of guardsmen. For sentiment too is a luxury which must only be indulged in private.

Beyond the gaze of the public eye her grave look melts away. She laughs and cries easily. She rocks when she laughs, throwing her head back and swinging her clasped hands high above her head and down between her knees. She literally dances when she is excited or interested, balancing on her heels and executing two little steps to the left then two to the right. If things don't go well she can look daggers and tap her foot in fury. Like her forebears she has two swear words which she isn't afraid to use, "damn" and "bloody."

There was one moving moment at Government House in Ottawa at the end of the private square-dance party that Governor General Lord Alexander held for his royal guests. Elizabeth had been dancing gaily all evening when suddenly, at 11:30, she prepared to go and the band struck up "God Save the King." The chatter and the laughter ceased and, in the words of one observer, "a sort of emotional wave swept over the guests." One man began to sing the words of the anthem and the others took it up. Somebody stole a look at Elizabeth. The mask had slipped and she was starting to cry.

The serious mien which Elizabeth presents to the world is a direct reflection of her attitude to her job. Not long ago she commented tartly on the fact that, after she succeeded to the throne, everybody went around saying that she looked 20 years older. But in her moments of seriousness she has always looked older than her years. She is still, in every sense, the good little girl who used to jump out of bed every night to get her shoes exactly straight and her clothes arranged just so, who insisted on wearing her gas mask for the prescribed period every day during the war as the regulations required and cleaning the eyepiece methodically every evening, and who warned her sister that it wasn't polite to rush for the tea table at a royal garden party.

On the battleship that took them to Africa she and Margaret entertained a group of sailors. A few days later they had occasion to pass the same group again. Elizabeth looked straight ahead of her but Margaret could not resist a smile. "Behave yourself," Elizabeth whispered sternly. Whereupon Margaret made her famous retort: "You look after your Empire, and I'll look after my life."

She is a woman who leaves little to chance. In Winnipeg, Canada's windiest city, a *Toronto Star* photographer was assigned to get a photograph of her with her hat blowing off. He tried in vain. She had taken the precaution of securing it firmly with a pin. Her handbag, which she carries into banquets, is fitted with a special clip so it can be secured to the table within easy reach and never drop onto the floor. Her lady in waiting is equipped with extra shoes and stockings in case of a run or a loose heel. Elizabeth is a woman who keeps a firm eye on the clock, a royal trait that goes back to the days of Edward VII. In Calgary she suddenly stopped short in the midst of a reception and said firmly: "*Now!* ... we must go back to the carriage." She set off immediately, leaving her husband chatting with the crowd. "Good heavens!" he cried, "where's my wife got to?" and off he ran to catch her.

One of the most famous pictures of Elizabeth shows her riding erect in the sidesaddle on the occasion of Trooping the Colour. She practiced for a month in order to do it properly, riding each morning in the Royal Mews and on weekends at Windsor to build up the muscles in the right thigh which are needed to hold the horse. For though it would have been easier, and certainly more pleasant to ride astride, it would not have been the right thing to do.

Elizabeth is not a brilliant woman, nor is she required to be, but she can be stubborn and this quality, which is also an ancient family trait, will stand her in better stead as Queen. Sir Henry Marten, the bald savant from Eton who taught her constitutional history, once told her that some of the bright boys over at the school could rattle off the names of all the kings of England together with the dates in so many seconds. Elizabeth determined to better this record, and she did. In her early days as Queen she brought the same stubborn concentration to the state papers set before her. She insisted on reading all of them and asking questions about most of them. The questions were often more searching than her late father's and there were some ministers of the crown who felt she was taking the whole thing just a little too seriously. But it is not in her nature to treat such matters sloppily or lightly.

In this context it is intriguing to examine her relations with her husband. In private the strong-willed Philip is master. It is he who decides on vacations at Sandringham or Balmoral, what the family will do. It is he who gives the orders to the servants and looks after domestic details. But on all public matters Elizabeth takes charge and sometimes, when occasion demands it, she overrules him. During the royal tour she was told in Victoria that an Indian princess had come several hundred miles to see her but couldn't be fitted into the ceremonies. "The Indian princess stuff is out!" snapped Philip. But Elizabeth told him quite firmly that she intended to see her. Later, in Montreal, the mayor approached the couple to explain that a lot of people wanted to shake hands. Philip said there wasn't any time. Elizabeth turned to him and said, "Philip, I *want* to shake hands." And she did. In Greece, in December, 1950, she asked a photographer to come along and record her visit to the Acropolis. Philip, who is not fond of photographers, tried to wave him away, but again Elizabeth intervened. Later she could be heard saying to her husband, a little heatedly, "That may be so, Philip, but it is not *my* way." When the couple's marriage portrait was being painted the artist had trouble getting Philip to pose. He simply didn't see why he should. Finally Elizabeth put her foot down and told him the portrait had to be done. "You just stand there!" she said to Philip. And he did.

She is just as stubbornly determined never to be a party to any diminution of the ancient dignity of the monarchy. "How is your father, ma'am?" someone in Canada asked her in the 1951 tour. Elizabeth replied with an icy look. "Are you referring to His Majesty the King?" she asked, and turned away. There is an even more telling story recounted of her first weeks as Queen. During this period a veteran courtier, leaning casually against a mantelpiece, had engaged the new sovereign in conversation. Suddenly the Queen interrupted him. "Are you tired?" she asked. The courtier, puzzled, said he wasn't. "Are you perhaps ill then?" No, ma'am, certainly not ill. "Then," said the Queen in a good-humoured voice which showed only a suggestion of mettle, "don't you think you should stand erect when talking to the sovereign?"

Last summer Elizabeth grew furious at press reports that hinted she was pregnant. Several members of the cabinet, including Churchill, were meeting at the palace one day and the Queen in a blazing voice discussed the matter and ended with the command: "I expect these rumours to stop!" It was after this incident that the Prime Minister was credited with the much quoted remark: "She may not be pregnant but she is certainly regnant." She was equally unmovable a few months ago when she discovered to her annoyance that a silver trophy she was to present in Edinburgh had been inscribed simply "Queen Elizabeth"—a reminder that the Scots do not recognize her earlier namesake. Elizabeth had the trophy shipped back and ordered that the numeral "II" be appended.

And yet she is in no sense an arrogant or a domineering woman. When waiting at the airport to leave for Malta she was quite capable of purchasing a pack of cards and dealing out hands to her staff in a Canasta game. And the personality behind the mask is still that of the shy nervous little girl who had to suck barley sugar to keep her spirits up on her first official inspection. One man, who knows her well, remembers seeing her and Philip driving by carriage to some of their first functions together and, as the carriage drew closer, holding on to one another's hands so tightly that the knuckles went white. "Elizabeth is not only shy," says an acquaintance, "but she's also shy of making other people shy."

For the first 15 years of her life she led a confined existence. She was not known to the public and she did not get to know them. As a result until she married she had only a hazy idea of the world beyond the palace and she still has not got the happy facility for official small talk that her husband has. In the receiving line she often seems to be trying to think of something to say next and she has a habit of looking away after a gap in the conversation and then turning back and starting in again when a new thought has occurred to her. Once, in Malta, during one of these interludes she said naïvely, "Well ... I can't think of anything more to say about that," and drifted off.

As the years go by these shortcomings will vanish. In her year on the throne, she has already acquired a sureness of manner that is a surprise to some of her ministers. "We thought she'd be pretty stuffy," one of them remarked not long ago. "She's anything but."

Elizabeth cannot yet make extemporaneous speeches and this was again particularly evident during her tour of Canada. In the Sunnybrook Hospital for war veterans in Toronto she suddenly realized that she was expected to speak. She did not know what to say until her private secretary, Lieut.-Col. Martin Charteris, scribbled a few notes on the back of a cigarette package and handed it to her. In Calgary a microphone was set up for her and the citizens had the impression she would say a few words. But there had been a mix-up and no prepared address was ready. Elizabeth declined to say as much as "hello." Similarly in Montreal she was supposed to make a few remarks to a group of children announcing a half holiday. Somehow the speech was missing from her purse. Somebody suggested she just tell the children anyway, in French. But Elizabeth found she simply could not do it. On the other hand she reads a prepared speech clearly, if in a rather stilted fashion. She braces herself, looks at her husband, swallows, moistens her lips and plunges ahead.

Her speeches are written for her and she does not make many changes in them for she is not a woman who initiates ideas. Once she and Philip visited the London Palladium to watch Danny Kaye, then the idol of England. After the show Philip suggested they go backstage and congratulate Kaye. Elizabeth was quite startled at the suggestion, which she was happy to comply with. It simply had not occurred to her. In her personal tastes she has shown a similar passivity. As a princess she had no strong ideas about furnishing or decorating her room as her sister had. She was quite happy to settle down in surroundings arranged by someone else. Nor, until her marriage, was she in any sense clothes conscious. She has never had any desire to be a fashion leader and although her general attire has become much smarter than it used to be some stylists still shudder at her accessories. Recently Elizabeth attended a fashion show at Claridge's, looked at the new dresses and commented that "they frighten me!"

For she is not a woman whose nature is marked by the extremes of taste and inclination, nor is it proper that she should be. She does not pluck her eyebrows or wear bright varnish on her nails. She would rather foxtrot than rhumba. She knows her Kipling but has no affinity for Gertrude Stein. She can understand horses but she does not pretend to understand Picasso. Exotic foods leave her unmoved: she would rather have roast lamb and green peas. Her disposition is generally pliable and undogmatic. She has few fanaticisms, always excepting the crowning fanaticism with which she approaches her job. In this she is resolute and unswerving. She might prefer the infinitely simpler role of a horsy young woman in country tweeds, but she knows that this is not to be.

Pierre Berton began writing for Maclean's *in 1947 and was managing editor of the magazine from 1953 to 1959. He is the author of nearly 50 books and continues to write from his Kleinburg, Ont., home.*

Prince Charles: Born to Reign—But Groomed to Fail?

Prince Charles, 1978

By Alan Edmonds

MARCH, 1967. The tragedy of the boy born to be King of the United Kingdom, Canada and His Other Realms and Territories, Head of the Commonwealth and Defender of the Faith, is that he's not the son his father would have liked him to be. And so H.R.H. Charles Philip Arthur George, Prince of Wales and heir to the throne, has thus far been groomed for the crown in a manner that many consider absurdly unsuitable for the age in which he must reign—a manner demonstrably not the kind of grooming a boy of his temperament is likely to enjoy.

Philip, the father, is an extrovert, a man of action, a man's man, often arrogant, prideful and demanding. In many ways his is the kind of new blood the British royal House of Windsor needed. His eldest son Charles is—as far as one can determine on available evidence—an introvert, a dreamer, a boy of tenderness and self-effacing humility who will probably grow to be like his shy but dedicated grandfather, George VI. Prince Philip, for instance, once deliberately doused press photographers with a garden hose, then guffawed with laughter. But when, during a school fire-fighting demonstration, Prince Charles accidentally splashed the feet—the *feet* only, mind you—of a photographer, he flushed and apologized: "Oops—I *am* sorry."

Through chinks in the armor of protocol that surrounds royalty,

390

Prince Charles emerges as a boy growing to manhood—he's 18 now—suffering from conflicts set up by an upbringing constantly at war with his inclinations. It would seem that Philip is harder on his son than are most fathers; that Charles may face the danger of even becoming slightly neurotic by constantly trying to meet a set of standards arbitrarily set by a parent to whom the child is an extension of self, of ego. All this would be serious enough at any time, in any boy. But in this age of rampant innovation and change, the fact that Charles is not his father's son (in the sense that they are totally unlike each other) could change the structure of Britain, of Canada, of the rest of the Commonwealth.

Britain is now convulsed with a social revolution the main aim of which seems to be to free the country from the deadening effects of tradition maintained for its own sake. In this climate the very need for any sort of monarchy is being openly questioned, often on the alarmingly fallacious grounds that the system is traditional and, therefore, valueless. Even so, it needs no clairvoyance to predict that, if the world survives long enough, the monarchy will last out Queen Elizabeth's lifetime, and that thereafter the survival of the monarchy will depend on King Charles III. If, by the standards of his contemporaries, he is a good and useful monarch, then the system will likely survive because he will have shown that it works. And if it works, its antiquity will be irrelevant.

But a monarch can only be useful, dynamic, if he is in tune with his age and with the needs of the states that comprise his realm. Despite the fact that a constitutional monarch is without power as such, his influence is immeasurable, incalculable. To be a beneficial influence on the Britain he will inherit, Charles must display a knowledgeable interest in, and acute concern for, those areas of endeavor that will be important to the progress of the country. For instance, a stuffy, reactionary monarch in the Britain of Charles III would not only be unpopular, he would be a national disaster. Charles will reign in an age of technology so complex it is, even now, little understood and often feared by those whose lives it changes daily. Yet thus far Charles's education has apparently been willfully unscientific, so that one Labour MP claims it has been more suitable for training an embryo lumberjack than a future king.

The focal point of the criticism is in the choice of austere Gordonstoun school in the Scottish Highlands as the place where Charles has gained most of his education so far. Prince Philip is the school's most famous old boy, but the school itself has an almost Prussian atmosphere which is, apparently, designed to produce an elite in whom the qualities of leadership, character and self-reliance have been developed and refined. And yet Gordonstoun's academic record is poor, and in general examinations its standard is well below Britain's national average.

"In the name of heaven, what are they doing to the boy?" wailed British Labour MP Woodrow Wyatt when Charles was first sent to Gordonstoun. "If everyone went to Gordonstoun, we would soon cease to keep up with other nations. Climbing trees and cliffs, horrible physical contortions, jumping into cold water and walking aimlessly for miles apparently comes under the heading of 'self-reliance.' I call it lunacy."

Perhaps it is. The Queen is known to have been apprehensive about the effect of spartan Gordonstoun on her shy, nervous heir. Charles himself burst into tears at the prospect. But Prince Philip told friends, "It'll make a man of him." But will it—has it—made Charles the kind of man Britain and the Commonwealth need?

There are many in Britain and the Commonwealth who echo Wyatt's sentiments when he says, "If we were a peasant society there might be some point in this back-to-nature stuff. But we are not. We are a technological, highly civilized and even partly cultured society." Charles, he says, should be provided with a common-sense education more suited to the world he will inherit.

Paul Nash, a onetime assistant professor of education at McGill University in Montreal, has suggested that a co-educational school would suit Charles better. "A cold shower and a 400-yard run every morning," he observed, "is a poor substitute for a sensitive, imaginative insight into the needs and strivings of all sorts and conditions of men and women."

The amount of advice gratuitously directed at the royal family on how they should raise the future king has been a measure of the more frankly critical approach taken toward the monarchy ever since Malcolm Muggeridge first vented his then-radical views on the subject back in the mid-1950s. A Labour MP has said that Charles should go to a state school, and thus help end forever the stultifying class system based on education that still bedevils England. A trade union leader wants Charles to be given at least some scientific and technical education as an example to the rest of the nation.

The Conservative *Daily Mail* agrees, and in an editorial has said: "If he [Charles] could go the Institute of Technology in Massachusetts, or learn the French way of life at the Sorbonne, or go to a mixed college at one of the new universities, he might forget how to put a tourniquet on a snake bite or light a fire in the rain without a match. But he would meet modern problems and contemporary people and acquire the self-confidence which so many princes have so tragically lacked." Other suggestions for Charles's education include a proposal he be sent to a Canadian university: a move that might make him more truly the King of Canada.

All of which more precisely defines what the realm needs, not what Charles the human being either wants or needs. At Gordonstoun, Charles appears to have been something of a misfit among his more aggressive schoolfellows. He doesn't seem to have mixed well either during his year at Geelong Grammar School in Australia. When his year there ended, T. R. Garnett, the headmaster, said with immense tact, "He has had long periods where he has been left alone, and he has appreciated them because I think he realizes there are not many such periods ahead of him."

Charles has amply demonstrated that he is unlike his father. He loves Shakespeare, and played Macbeth when Gordonstoun staged the play. He emerges from the chinks in royal protocol as a pensive boy, neither a leader nor a follower of others. And yet he hero-worships his active, aggressive, gregarious father. It was to win Prince Philip's approval that Charles worked hard to become a good polo player, though at one polo meeting in Windsor Great Park he was overheard saying to Anne, "I hope it rains today—we won't be able to play polo."

On other occasions, Charles has behaved aggressively to either ape, or impress, his father, and has subsequently regretted the impulse. In Athens for the wedding of King Constantine, he tried to show off by overturning a boatload of prying French photographers.

The publicity that earned also earned Charles a rebuke from his mother. That famous cherry-brandy incident in 1963 was almost certainly an attempt to show off in front of Harry McKenzie, a close friend of Prince Philip's. At a pub Charles ordered and drank a cherry brandy. It was a well-publicized incident, and forced Charles's beloved bodyguard, Donald Green, to resign. When he did so, Charles gave him a crude bowl, his first attempt at pottery, and said, "I'm sorry. I hope we'll stay friends." It seems that his education to date has done little to alter his basically amiable, warm personality.

When, in 1965, Charles was 17, the critics of that education began arguing publicly about the kind of university they believed he should attend. A strong case was made by those who thought he should attend one of the new colleges recently built in England. This, they said, would help provide impetus to the university building program and status to the new institutions, which are still somewhat scathingly called "redbrick" universities. Egalitarians agreed, arguing that the new universities were untainted by any apparent connection with the Establishment, and that if Charles were to attend one it would help change the social structure under attack in Britain today. Both factions were encouraged by reports that Charles himself favored the University of Sussex, which is barely 15 years old and said to be one of the most exciting, and liberal, institutions of advanced education in Britain.

But, while Charles will be the first monarch to have been educated publicly, as opposed to privately, by tutors, Sussex University and others like it proved too radical a suggestion for the royal family: in December, soon after his 18th birthday, Buckingham Palace announced that Charles had been accepted by Trinity College, Cambridge, one of Britain's most respected and venerable university colleges. While he will still be surrounded by the panoply of tradition, Charles will at Cambridge meet many kinds and conditions of people: even Cambridge and Oxford—traditionally the nurseries of the Establishment—have long since opened their doors to students of merit, as well as those of wealth and influence.

Charles will, almost inevitably, graduate as a member of the new young Establishment produced by today's Oxbridge environment. But that young Establishment is in many cases leading the present social revolution in Britain. So Charles may yet blossom as a rounded, self-assured human being: a man equipped for his age—for his prescribed role of King of the United Kingdom, Canada and His Other Realms and Territories, Head of the Commonwealth and Defender of the Faith.

Alan Edmonds was a staff writer at Maclean's *from 1967 to 1971. Subsequently a best-selling author and television host, Edmonds now lives and works in Toronto.*

Margaret Trudeau's First Hurrah

Margaret Trudeau during the 1974 election campaign

By June Callwood

AUGUST, 1974. In the years of Trudeau reign that lie ahead it may well develop that the Prime Minister is the second most interesting resident of 24 Sussex Drive.

What the crisp and collected Liberal campaign of '74 accomplished this summer, in addition to the considerable feat of electing a majority government, was the coming out of Margaret Sinclair Trudeau, who was révealed as a first lady whose personal flair has not been equaled in Canadian history since John A. Macdonald's spouse rode through the Rocky Mountains on the cowcatcher of a CPR engine because she wanted an unobstructed view.

Only 25 years old, the youngest-ever wife of a Canadian prime minister, the youngest woman at present married to any world leader, cloistered in rigid privacy throughout the three years since her marriage, Margaret Trudeau went into the campaign a figure of mystery to Canadians and hoped to keep it that way. She was gambling that she could electioneer for two months to help Pierre Elliott Trudeau to victory and, when the election was over, escape back to seclusion without having been turned into a pillar of plastic in the meantime.

She accomplished it and in the process turned your average federal election campaign into the nearest thing to a love-in that has been seen since young people in bare feet used to give flowers to policemen. About half way through the election campaign, it became apparent that the Prime Minister of Canada is married to a perfectly preserved flower child. "She's so genuine you can't stand it," observed Dan Turner, whose lengthy and revealing interview with her a year ago was both a scoop and a sensation. Doug Small, a Canadian Press reporter with such enthusiasm for his craft that even younger associates feel old, shared a car with Margaret Trudeau toward the end of the campaign when she had made a circuit without Trudeau of some small towns in Quebec's Eastern Townships. They talked for about an hour on the way back to Montreal and he later confessed he was almost relieved when she said it was off the record.

She produces that effect on people who talk to her for any length of time: they worry she's going to get hurt. Her truthfulness and trust are like the artistry of a high-wire act, all guts and beauty—but what is she *doing* up there? What's the matter with sidewalks?

None of this was immediately apparent when the campaign began because Margaret Trudeau was giving a performance of what she thought was expected of a prime minister's wife appearing in public. Since she had almost no experience in that line of work she had to keep concentrating: smile, shake hands, be reserved, say *nothing*!

It proved a strain. "I was just sitting there, hiding in a role," she later explained. "I had this crazy idea that I had to have everyone's approval. I think it has something to do with being one of five daughters."

Nevertheless, she was well received. The only criticism, in fact, was directed at Trudeau and the Liberal strategists who were seen as exploiting her appeal to gain votes, out of cynicism and desperation. It had a contrived look: the rareness of her exposure to the public and Trudeau's 1972 statement that she would never be used in a campaign ("The whole idea is repugnant to me") seem to bear that out. Her qualities of dewy beauty and nervous ways, the curiosity generated by the 29-year age difference between the Trudeaus and the almost total information blackout on her, all combined to bring out the crowds and assure media alertness. She also helped improve the image of her husband as the haughty Trudeau of the flared nostrils. With her by his side it was easier to believe him changed, a roseate family man.

However slick it looked, and it happened to coincide with what the Grit strategists had in mind, Margaret Trudeau's participation was her own idea, arrived at independently on the night of the '72 election while her husband was bleakly counting his losses. The problem as she saw it was that the voters just didn't know Trudeau. If they thought he was aloof and cold, as the commentators said, they were wrong. She reasoned that if she went with him during the next campaign, people who saw them together would see his gentler side.

So late in May, as the rented nine-car train dubbed the Trudeau Express whistle-stopped for four days through the Maritimes and Quebec, Margaret Trudeau was along to be introduced everywhere as "wife and mother" and to listen with an ethereal smile and rapt eyes full on her husband while he delivered his speeches. Their two-year-old Justin remained at home, but the campaign train carried Sacha, five months old and still being breast-fed. After the first jolt it began to seem commonplace that a baby was traveling on a federal election campaign, his wail of indignation when he was hungry rising over the clatter of typewriters as reporters met deadlines and speech writers prepared drafts. People on the Prime Minister's tour even grew accustomed to the high comedy of the Trudeau arrivals at airports or train stations. Their bullet-proof limousine would draw up behind the pulsating red lights of a motorcycle escort to be unloaded by burly security men of bassinets, diaper bags, folding strollers and teddy bears, while Sacha in his mother's arms watched the scene with round blue eyes.

The presence of Sacha, a flourish no fiction writer would have dared to include in a script about a prime minister fighting for political survival, was too much for some critics, who were already portraying the campaign as a long ride on Margaret's coattails. There was also a mild complaint from Margaret herself. What she minded, she told one reporter, was being made into a platform object labeled WIFEANDMOTHER.

It was rare for her to talk to reporters, even briefly. Ever since her obsessively secret wedding on March 4, 1971, the former Margaret Sinclair had simply disappeared into 24 Sussex Drive, emerging only to greet the Queen or, on alternate Christmas Days, give birth to sons. "Trudeau kept saying that she was none of our business," reflected Charles Lynch, Southam News Services' paterfamilias in the Ottawa Press Gallery. "There was a lot of pressure on us from our editors to get stories about her, but eventually we did as he wished and left her alone. I think we were wrong. He was asking for more privacy than any other public figure in Canada."

During the closing days of the '72 campaign Margaret Trudeau made a few appearances with her husband but spoke to no one outside the Prime Minister's party. Reporters therefore were thunderstruck when she jumped into the press bus one day and said cheerily, "Hi! I hear you have more fun back here."

Her poise and offhandedness simply didn't fit with the media's vision of Margaret the Unsure. She found an empty seat next to a young reporter, Dan Turner, and chatted with a candor that startled him. When he asked for an interview she put him off, but after eight months of patient negotiation finally agreed to it. The result was Turner's famous story syndicated across the country by the *Toronto Star*. In it Margaret Trudeau talked of the deep influence on her of the British poet William Blake and J. Krishnamurti, both of whom believe in an infinite cosmos beyond space and time.

She spoke of "being innocent, being giving, being spontaneous, loving and living now," of passing from Child-Innocence through the sulphurous hell of Experience and breaking through into High Innocence, a weightless state of total self-realization transcending ego. Many readers could make neither head nor tail of it and took comfort in Turner's homey aside that she served him cakes and cider. But a number of young Canadians of approximately her age suddenly knew exactly who was living at 24 Sussex Drive and couldn't believe it.

Bob Hunter of the *Vancouver Sun*, that paper's link with the counter-culture, expressed his unbridled delight. Turner's interview, he said, "broke the bubble of illusion." The story placed Margaret Trudeau "squarely in the mainstream of nonviolent hippie thought." With that the princess returned to the castle and the drawbridge was declared permanently up once more.

There was a curious absence of public interest in some of the disclosures in Turner's article or in the earlier cover-girl story in

Chatelaine magazine (*Margaret Trudeau—The Girl Who Caught the PM*) done by two able Vancouver reporters, Simma Holt (now a Liberal MP) and Kay Alsop. They had circumvented the refusal of her family to be interviewed by tracking down former schoolteachers, neighbors and childhood friends. The two accounts agreed that Margaret Joan Sinclair, fourth born of five daughters of a former federal cabinet minister, James Sinclair, and his 12-years-younger wife Kathleen, was well-to-do, brainy, beautiful and adored by all. The ideal childhood brought her, at 18, to exactly the right time, place, age and background to take part in the 1967 summer that began the youth revolution variously blamed on Spock, the Vietnam war, Bob Dylan, marijuana, permissiveness, affluence, the Beatles and the U.S. Supreme Court decision on school desegregation.

She got involved in the student radical movement at Simon Fraser University, though never in the riots (fanaticism of any kind always turns her off—she even hated Trudeaumania); she camped out on Long Beach on Vancouver Island's west coast; and after a precociously early college graduation at 20 she spent seven months in Morocco living as close to the Moroccans as she could get, which in a 60-cents-a-day hotel room was close enough to keep her parents in a state of panic known only to other middle-class parents with similarly inquisitive children.

It says a good deal about the equanimity of Canadians that these revelations about the activities of their Prime Minister's wife seemed to have no significance. The judgment of her elders, based on the evidence of Margaret Trudeau as a bride trembling and clinging to her husband during their state visit to Russia, Margaret Trudeau as a broody mother full of tenderness, and Margaret Trudeau on a political platform with easy blushes flooding her porcelain complexion, was that she was simply a nice, sweet young thing with good manners.

Nothing plunges Margaret Trudeau into quicker despair than being categorized, which is why in the middle of the election campaign early in June she was feeling depressed. The tour had reached her home town, Vancouver, where she would be leaving Justin and the newly weaned Sacha with her parents for a few weeks. It was a sunny evening, June 4, and the agenda required the Trudeaus to attend a Liberal rally being staged in a high school. She was moving slowly through the press of people outside the school, smiling steadily, making a few conventional greetings, shaking hands and reflecting unhappily on the easy intimacy crowds assume toward public figures. Just inside the door of the building were two women and a child. Margaret Trudeau stuck out her hand automatically, then realized they were her sisters, Heather and Betsy, with Heather's daughter Katie. Moved to tears by the unexpectedness of it, she embraced them.

Something in that small encounter dissolved her anxiety of being in public, gave her confidence enough to stop feeling the need to be formal. She took her sisters' appearance as a gesture of love and approval: it was just what she needed. She turned over a new leaf: she would be herself on all future occasions, private or public.

That was the evening she gave her first speech on her own, introducing her husband to the crowd as "a very loving human being," "shy and modest and very, very kind" and "quite a beautiful guy." It's the open, unguarded style of her generation but it had never before graced any political rally in the western world.

It was only the beginning. She got rid of the demure blue patent pumps she had been wearing and substituted earth shoes, supremely comfortable but odd-looking with their lowered heel. "I hadn't worn them before because I thought people would think them ugly," she explained, "but after that night I decided *why not?*" She put away the matching blue patent purse and began to tote a burlap bag labeled BON WEEK END, a nice bilingual touch.

In her new emancipation, she would tolerate nothing trite. Her conversations with strangers had the flavor of genuine interest. A woman in Vancouver spoke of an 18-year-old child and Margaret said reflectively, "Eighteen is wonderful—they've got their dreams." She said to Keith Mitchell, a Liberal Party worker in Vancouver, "You've got to risk losing in order to win big. I put my skepticism in my back pocket four years ago and I'll tell you it's the only way to be, a total believer ...". When someone in Summerside asked about her children, she stopped cold and told the woman about Sacha stuffing himself on ice cream now that she wasn't around to enforce his routine, how Justin marked off the days of her absence on his own calendar.

In the middle of June, when the chartered DC-9 was bringing the Prime Minister's tour back to Ottawa after a swing through the Maritimes, Margaret Trudeau gave *Maclean's* an interview. It was nearing midnight and she had changed to jeans and was curled up in the corner of the aircraft's first row of seats, her knees drawn up. "It took five years off my life when I started to be real on this campaign," she said. "It's like Margaret Atwood's *Surfacing*. I feel as though I've been underground for a long time." She considered. "My contribution is that I'm the real stuff," she said sturdily. "I'm not going to play games. I've got nothing to hide, no one can do me harm. I'm sure I can improve, but right now I'm being the very best person I can."

Ottawa has noticed that she walks a good deal by herself, deep in thought. What she thinks about, frequently, is how to avoid being packaged. "I've fought hard for freedom, and I'm not going to be taken over as property."

The few years after 1967 when, she says, the social revolution that started in her generation offered "a chance to prolong innocence, to wonder at life, the right to be children," she and her parents struggled with the consequences this had on their expectations for her. "I've never known one moment's hunger or anxiety," she told them, pleading for a chance to explore. Her father wondered if she was becoming dangerously radical.

She was just back from Morocco, growing vegetables and watching the sea coming in and out at her grandmother's, when her mother called to say that the Prime Minister wanted to have dinner with her. She'd met him before during a family vacation, and liked him, but she didn't want to go. She felt too confused and unready. Her mother coaxed her. Margaret stalled by saying she had nothing to wear, nothing but ragged skirts. Her mother said she would pick out some suitable clothes and did. She went to dinner feeling like someone in disguise. "But he spotted me through it," she said. She loved him at once. And over months spent walking in woods and on mountains talking about their lives, he became convinced that marriage would work.

When she arrived in Ottawa in 1971 as the wife of Canada's Prime Minister, 22 years old and fresh from being barefoot in her grandmother's garden by the sea, transported with no transition period to the receiving line of a diplomatic reception, she was offered much advice. "Lots of people were ready to package and use me," she said bluntly, "which made me react strongly against getting involved with them." Matter of factly, without self-pity, she added, "I was cut off from my friends, and I get nourishment from friendships. It's not easy for me to make new friends, and the women of Ottawa aren't of my generation, haven't been through the experiences I have."

After her Vancouver speech, her defence of her right to be herself moved to a new battlefield. The Liberal Party's strategy team, hearing the sounds of retching from many colleagues, descended on her and said her thoughts on loving were marvelous but in the future they would be happy to write her speeches for her. She said no. She said she would campaign in her own way and give her own speeches. When she was scheduled to talk about women in politics at a Liberal rally in Saint-Hyacinthe, Que., a woman in her husband's office thoughtfully provided "some basic points." Margaret Trudeau replied that she didn't want them.

"But that's political dynamite," she recalls the woman saying. "You might say something wrong."

"No, I won't."

Usually a silent spectator at campaign conferences, she found herself thinking that she was an intelligent woman, an honors graduate, a mother of two children who had a stake in the country, and that she had a contribution to make. "My mouth just opened and I said I've got something to offer," she relates.

What comes out, usually, is advice that the politicians find outrageous: that they should be simple, real and, well, loving. They tell her that isn't practical; she says, try it. She has been undermining the boys in the backroom for years. In the past it has been a confined war. When her husband comes home tired after a long day at the office and tells her that *they* think he needs a haircut, she says hotly, "Don't let them package you!" It's a matter of principle with her: she's anti-plastic.

Her family's close friend, Senator Ray Perrault of Vancouver, once commented, "Anyone who says that Margaret Trudeau can be ordered around doesn't know Jimmy Sinclair or the Sinclair girls. They have a stubborn Scotch streak in them and they can really dig in." On the campaign, she was urging the Prime Minister to throw away his prepared speeches and talk to people "from inside," advice he seemed to take, at least in part. His vocabulary seemed to be shifting: such words as "gentle" and "compassionate" kept cropping up.

Through it all, from the first moment when she began to campaign with him in Newfoundland to the final afternoon on Toronto's Centre Island, she watched him adoringly whenever he was speaking and smiled without ceasing, her posture tranquil and undistracted. She said during the interview that she erred on the night she said he had taught her about loving (and when her comment provoked a ribald laughter from the audience, she was shocked: love is a sacred word with her). *She* taught *him* about love; he taught her about living.

Her comment affords some insight into the relationship between them. The Prime Minister, 54 and an aesthetic intellectual, conditioned to be frugal with feelings, must marvel at how free she is. For her part she was feeling adrift when they began dating, and he provided the strength she needed at that time. "He took me by the hand and helped me face life," she explains. "Pierre helped me find the strongest answers."

Both seem to be changed in the three years they have been married and almost isolated socially, since she had little in common with his old friends or he with hers. During the campaign both kept meeting people they had known a long time who marveled at the differences. His changes were said to be in the direction of easiness, while the young people who slipped out of crowds to hug her would say, "She's really settled down. She's found her love and she's happy. You can tell by looking at her."

On the final day of the campaign, 36 hours from the Liberal victory, the Trudeaus were paying a call on an international picnic on Centre Island in the Toronto bay. The PM made a brief speech, extolling the "beautiful day, beautiful people," and then gave the last word to her. She stepped to a microphone dressed in a floor-length gingham dress and her earth shoes, with a SAVE OUR ISLAND button a protester had thrown to her and she promptly had pinned on.

She said, in her light little-girl voice, "I started this campaign by getting into a lot of trouble because I tried to tell people about love and many of them took it the wrong way. But that's about all I can talk about because I really believe in love ..."

She made it all the way through the campaign, as she hoped she would. Nobody programmed her, nobody packaged her, nobody pushed her around. Anyone who thinks he can doesn't know the Sinclair girls.

Margaret and Pierre Trudeau separated in 1977, after numerous well-publicized incidents showed the strains in their marriage. They divorced in 1984 with Pierre retaining custody of their three sons. That year Margaret married Ottawa businessman Fried Kemper, with whom she later had two more children, before divorcing him in 1999. She remains in Ottawa, promoting avalanche awareness in memory of her youngest son, Michel, 23, who died in a B.C. avalanche.

Princess Di: Our Next Queen

Lady Diana Spencer with Prince Charles after
announcing their engagement, Feb. 24, 1981

By Carol Kennedy

MARCH 9, 1981. When Prince Charles, on a tour of India last November, returned to base from an expedition in the solitude of the Himalayas, a perceptive reporter with the royal entourage noted a change in his demeanor. The worried and strained look had disappeared, and for the first time in months he seemed completely at peace. That transformation, the reporter later opined to friends in England, signified that Charles had made up his mind on a prospective bride.

Whether or not that was the moment when 32-year-old Charles, heir to the oldest surviving throne in Europe and for years the world's most eligible bachelor, decided on his Queen-to-be, the clincher was an intimate dinner for two in his private quarters at Buckingham Palace in early February which culminated in a proposal. Last week, the increasingly leaky secret was out after months of mounting rumor: the future King of England had indeed chosen his bride, and 19-year-old Lady Diana Spencer, blonde, pretty and in his own words "full of life," was sporting a huge sapphire and diamond engagement ring for the world's cameras.

Charles's first reaction seemed one of relief. No longer, he joked with photographers, would he have to worry about headlines speculating on a royal wedding; this time, it would be true, "thank heaven." Facing the TV cameras for their first interview together, the couple talked of things they had in common—a sense of humor, love of sports and the outdoor life, of how they met "in a plowed field" at a shooting party and of the relentless exposure to public eyes that anyone marrying the future King must endure. Said Charles, smiling fondly at his blue-eyed bride-to-be: "Frankly, I'm amazed that she's been brave enough to take me on." Replied Diana, "With Prince Charles beside me I can't go wrong. It's what I wanted, what I want." Were they in love, the TV interviewers ponderously inquired? "Of course," pouted Lady Di, eyes cast down demurely. "Whatever 'in love' means," shot back Charles in a typically teasing riposte.

It had been a courtship of secrecy and subterfuge with meetings planned, Charles admitted last week, "like a military operation." One of Diana's most relentless pursuers, reporter James Whitaker of the *Daily Star*, said she "treated it all like a game"—even the occasion when, he recalled, she was smuggled dramatically off the royal estate lying facedown in the back of a Land Rover.

The couple first met in 1977, when Diana was a giggling 16-year-old and Charles, 28, was at the Spencer family's 463-year-old Northamptonshire mansion as a guest of Diana's elder sister Sarah. It seemed likely then that Sarah, who later spent a 10-day skiing holiday with Charles, might win his affections, but she dropped out of the running after a tabloid reported a remark that she wouldn't marry Charles if he asked her. Sarah now recalls that she unwittingly "played Cupid" to her kid sister, introducing her to the prince in the middle of a field on the Spencer estate. Charles remembers Diana then as "very jolly and amusing, an attractive 16-year-old, great fun, bouncy and full of life." Diana, asked what she first thought of Charles, said laughingly, "pretty amazing."

The first sign Diana might be the girl Charles once said would have to be "pretty special" came when she was invited to Balmoral Castle during the Royal Family's annual Scottish holiday last August. By November, the mass-circulation *Sun* claimed the Queen had given her blessings to the romance and had allegedly told close friends: "She is a delightful girl. Charles could not find a more perfect partner."

The hunt by the press now became frenzied. Questions were asked in Parliament and letters written to *The Times* about the "hounding" of Lady Diana. Meanwhile, it was learned that the prince managed to conduct his courtship in a house he bought last year in London's expensive Kensington district, conveniently close to Kensington Palace where Diana's other sister, Jane, has an apartment. Diana, then sharing an apartment with three other girls in the southern part of Kensington, told friends she was going out with "Charles Renfrew"—Baron Renfrew is one of Charles's many titles. Her apartment mates never met the prince, but at the beginning of February, said Virginia Pitman, 21: "Di just sat on the bed beside me one night and said she was going to marry Prince Charles. There was a big smile on her face. We started to squeal with excitement and then we started to cry."

Charles told interviewers last week he made his proposal just before Diana left for Australia on Feb. 6 for a three-week holiday. "I wanted to give her a chance to think about it—to think if it was all going to be too awful." In fact, she accepted right away.

It was an admitted strain keeping the secret, and a few leaks did seep out. Gossip writer Nigel Dempster reported that Crown jewellers were working on an engagement ring, and last Tuesday *The Times* scooped Fleet Street with a statement that this would be the day. The guessing game finally ended at 11 a.m. as the announcement by the Queen and Prince Philip was flashed around the world. It could not have come at a better time to cheer a Britain deep in economic gloom and political wrangling. Diana is a genuinely popular choice as the first Princess of Wales in 70 years: for one thing, she is the first English girl to marry an heir to the throne since James II's wife, Anne Hyde, 321 years ago (the Queen Mother comes from the Scottish peerage). She will also be the first Queen consort to have worked for her living, as a children's nanny, part-time cook and, most recently, kindergarten teacher. "It's good news—the country needs it," said a TV repairman as the screen came to life showing the smiling couple. In Parliament, amid news of the worst unemployment since the 1930s, Prime Minister Margaret Thatcher broke the announcement to cheers from both sides of the Commons. The only dissenting voice came from Labour's Willie Hamilton, a veteran Scottish anti-monarchist, who growled at the prospect of "six months of mush."

On a day that saw more millions of the taxpayers' money vanish into bankrupt British Steel Corporation, even the stock market perked up at the news of a royal wedding, especially the shares of companies connected with the souvenir business such as Wedgwood, the china firm, and of hotel chains anticipating an influx of foreign tourists. Drawn by the news spreading on car radios and taxis, hundreds flocked to Buckingham Palace. First confirmation for the watchers came when the band of the Coldstream Guards, their scarlet uniforms muffled in greatcoats against the bitter cold, struck up the 1960s pop song "Congratulations" in the palace forecourt.

Champagne corks popped in palace offices and on the royal estates. A newspaper seller in London's Piccadilly Circus told a customer: "Yes, it's true at last—and about time." And the great machinery of state ceremonial, always ready to roll into action at a moment's notice, began its majestic progress toward the day—probably in late July—when Charles and Diana will be married by the Archbishop of Canterbury, Robert Runcie, in Westminster Abbey or St. Paul's Cathedral.

Perhaps not everyone had cause to rejoice last week. Prince Charles's betrothal puts an end to the great marriage game among society mothers with ambitions for their daughters. So how did Diana gain the coveted prize? Mainly, it is suggested, because, apart from her winning personality, she won palace approval for being a girl with a history but no past. No serious boy-friends entered her life before Charles; she tended to go around in a foursome whose idea of entertainment was a glass of wine or gin-and-tonic in a Chelsea pub. Although Charles once said a girl of royal blood would have an advantage as his bride because she would "know the ropes," Diana Spencer's family history is as impressive as any in Europe. Her father, the eighth Earl Spencer and an equerry to King George VI and the present Queen, has a family tree going back to medieval times. Diana even brings royal Stuart blood back into the monarchy by being descended from King Charles II. As well, Prince Charles and Diana are distantly related—seventh cousins once removed —and the family tree includes links with the Duke of Marlborough (and hence Winston Churchill).

Diana's parents divorced in 1969 and both have remarried: up to a few years ago that fact might well have barred their daughter from consideration as a royal bride. Her mother, Frances Shand-Kydd, is married to a wallpaper heir and her stepmother, the former Lady Dartmouth, is a well-known public figure and the daughter of Britain's best-known romantic novelist, Barbara Cartland.

Diana Frances Spencer, the youngest of four children, was born July 1, 1961, in a house rented from the Queen, Sandringham in Norfolk, literally the girl next door—the house was separated from the Royal Gardens only by a wall, and Diana grew up romping with the younger princes, Andrew and Edward. She is remembered as academically average at school, proficient at tennis and swimming. Like all the Royals, she is a country person at heart. Columnist Lynda Lee-Potter of the *Daily Mail* says that Diana's "idea of heaven is to spend an afternoon fly-fishing, waist-high in freezing water."

Lord Spencer, who last week mingled with the crowds outside Buckingham Palace, "photographing the photographers," said of his daughter: "She's very good-natured, publicity doesn't worry her." She was also, he said, "very practical" and "a good house-keeper." He added, chuckling, that as a baby she was "a superb physical specimen." Today, the long-legged Diana is five-feet, 10-inches tall, just an inch below Prince Charles. It has also been reported that she had a medical checkup to ensure she could bear children.

Diana studied at a private girls' school in Kent and at finishing school in Switzerland, where she became fluent in French and developed an outstanding skill at skiing—a passion of Prince Charles. She does not, however, care for riding since she once fell off a horse. She is said to be a born mimic and will enjoy the charades and party games that the Royals love. Diana has always been fond of young children and was popular with her charges at the

Young England kindergarten in London's Pimlico. Throughout the hectic courtship, she was only once embarrassed by the publicity—when photographers manoeuvred her against the sun in a see-through skirt.

Charles has taken longer to get married than any Prince of Wales since Charles II, except for his unfortunate predecessor, later King Edward VIII, who had a propensity for married ladies. In a rare moment of unguarded frankness on his Indian tour last year, Charles told reporters of his difficult love life. *Sun* reporter Harry Arnold remembers the prince saying: "It's all right for you chaps. You can live with a girl before you marry her, but I can't. I've got to get it right from the word go."

After their July wedding—the first wedding of a Prince of Wales since 1863—Charles and Diana will live mainly at Highgrove House, a Georgian mansion Charles bought last year for $2.7 million from the son of former prime minister Harold Macmillan. But after their honeymoon—at a spot as yet undecided—the couple may not have long to enjoy the quiet country life. It is strongly rumored that Charles will be named governor-general of Australia. Next month, Charles is scheduled to visit that country for four weeks, leaving Diana to get used to her new life: she is already in residence at Clarence House, the Queen Mother's London home.

Whatever his future job, one thing will change from now on for Charles: wherever he goes, the kissing will have to stop. The international sport of embracing the bachelor prince began in Australian surf in March, 1979, with a buss from a bikini-clad swimmer. And when can Diana expect to become Queen? Reports that Queen Elizabeth II is planning to abdicate in favor of Charles have always been repudiated in royal circles. However, the Queen, now 54, was reportedly impressed by the smooth abdication of Queen Juliana of the Netherlands last April in favor of Princess Beatrix, and is known to feel Charles should not endure the tedious apprenticeship of Edward VII, who was 59 when he succeeded Queen Victoria in 1901.

When Diana does become Queen, she would be entitled, the palace says, to adopt a completely different name if she so wished. In the meantime, one enterprising British pop singer rose to the occasion last week by rushing out a new version of a 1950's hit—Canadian Paul Anka's composition "Diana."

Diana, Princess of Wales, and Charles separated in 1992 and divorced in 1996, agreeing to jointly raise their two sons, William and Harry. In 1997, Diana, 36, died in a Paris automobile accident along with her boyfriend, wealthy film producer Dodi Al Fayed, and his driver, who was drunk at the wheel.

Carol Kennedy, who was a Maclean's *London correspondent from 1977 to 1985, has written a number of books on management, business and social history. She lives in London, England.*

Photo Credits

page *photo*

2 Maclean's file photo
14 The Gazette/CP Archive
24 Don Newlands
33 National Archives of Canada PA85792
43 CP Archive
53 CP Archive
62 Crombie McNeil
74 CP Archive
85 Rice and Bell
93 CP Archive
102 Horst Ehricht
109 CP Archive
118 Tom Hanson/CP Archive
128 National Archives of Canada PA 022966
136 R. Notman and Son/National Archives of Canada PA 125775
156 Peter Bregg/Maclean's
168 CP Archive
179 Ken Bell
189 Louis Jacques/National Archives of Canada PA 140565
210 Horst Ehricht
221 Don Newlands
231 Dan Callis

241 Phill Snel/Maclean's
260 Jack Olsen
269 Horst Ehricht
281 John Max
291 Ron Watts
301 Peter Bregg/Maclean's
311 Peter Bregg/Maclean's
322 Jessop/National Archives of Canada PA 030212
328 William Rider-Ride/National Archives of Canada PA001654
339 Keystone
348 King Features
379 Federal News Photos
389 Terry Fincher
396 Blaise Edwards/CP Archive
407 AP